THE PATH TO BLITZKRIEG

The Stackpole Military History Series

THE AMERICAN CIVIL WAR

Cavalry Raids of the Civil War
Ghost, Thunderbolt, and Wizard
Pickett's Charge
Witness to Gettysburg

WORLD WAR II

Armor Battles of the Waffen-SS, 1943–45
Army of the West
Australian Commandos
The B-24 in China
Backwater War
The Battle of Sicily
Beyond the Beachhead
The Brandenburger Commandos
The Brigade
Bringing the Thunder
Coast Watching in World War II
Colossal Cracks
D-Day to Berlin
Dive Bomber!
Eagles of the Third Reich
Exit Rommel
Fist from the Sky
Flying American Combat Aircraft of World War II
Forging the Thunderbolt
Fortress France
The German Defeat in the East, 1944–45
German Order of Battle, Vol. 1
German Order of Battle, Vol. 2
German Order of Battle, Vol. 3
Germany's Panzer Arm in World War II
GI Ingenuity
Grenadiers
Infantry Aces
Iron Arm
Iron Knights
Kampfgruppe Peiper at the Battle of the Bulge
Luftwaffe Aces
Massacre at Tobruk
Messerschmitts over Sicily

Michael Wittmann, Vol. 1
Michael Wittmann, Vol. 2
Mountain Warriors
The Nazi Rocketeers
On the Canal
Packs On!
Panzer Aces
Panzer Aces II
The Panzer Legions
Panzers in Winter
The Path to Blitzkrieg
Retreat to the Reich
Rommel's Desert War
The Savage Sky
A Soldier in the Cockpit
Soviet Blitzkrieg
Stalin's Keys to Victory
Surviving Bataan and Beyond
T-34 in Action
Tigers in the Mud
The 12th SS, Vol. 1
The 12th SS, Vol. 2
The War against Rommel's Supply Lines

THE COLD WAR / VIETNAM

Flying American Combat Aircraft: The Cold War
Here There Are Tigers
Land with No Sun
Street without Joy

WARS OF THE MIDDLE EAST

Never-Ending Conflict

GENERAL MILITARY HISTORY

Carriers in Combat
Desert Battles

THE PATH TO BLITZKRIEG

Doctrine and Training in the German Army,
1920–39

Robert M. Citino

STACKPOLE
BOOKS

Published in paperback in 2008 by
STACKPOLE BOOKS
5067 Ritter Road
Mechanicsburg, PA 17055
www.stackpolebooks.com

Cover design by Tracy Patterson
All photos courtesy of Philip Francis

Printed in the United States of America

ISBN 978-0-8117-3457-8 (Stackpole paperback)

The Library of Congress has cataloged the hardcover edition as follows:

Citino, Robert Michael, 1958–
    The path to blitzkrieg : doctrine and training in the German Army,
      1920–1939 / Robert M. Citino
    Includes bibliographical references.
    ISBN 1-55587-714-1 (alk. paper)
    1. Lightning war. 2. Germany—Military policy. 3. World War,
    1939–1945—Campaigns—Europe. 4. Tactics. 5. Military doctrine—
      Germany—History—20th century. I. Title.
D757.C58   1998
355.00943'09042—dc21   98-5251

*To the
memory
of
Barbara Jelavich*

Contents

Acknowledgments

This work is based largely on unpublished sources, especially the following documentary collections: *United States Military Intelligence Reports: Germany, 1919–1941* (Frederick, MD: University Publications of America, 1983); *Records of the German Army High Command*, or OKH, currently available on microfilm from the U.S. National Archives, Washington, D.C., Microcopy T-78; the papers of Generals Seeckt and Groener (National Archives, Microcopies M-132 and M-137, respectively); and the *Records of the German Foreign Office* (National Archives, Microcopy T-120).

As always, this book is in part a tribute to Barbara and Charles Jelavich, my mentors and friends during my graduate years at Indiana University. Barbara's recent passing has only made me realize anew how truly special she was. Thanks must also be offered to Rebecca Dunkel at the Hatcher Library, who allowed me such free and complete access to many of the pertinent documents; to my graduate students at Eastern Michigan University, especially Ray Schepansky and Randy Talbot, who have been so hardworking and helpful; to Collin Boyd, Eastern Michigan undergraduate and tank expert; and above all, to my wonderful family—my wife, Roberta, and my daughters, Allison, Laura, and Emily—thanks for bringing me back to the present every now and then!

CHAPTER 1

Introduction: The German Army from Collapse to Rebirth

[handwritten note:] Fall Weiss- mechanized warfare.
supplied the german army with
tanks and the Stuka dive bombers.

remember:
Wehrmacht - German Army
Lotwaffe - Air force

Three Campaigns: 1939–1941

On 1 September 1939, lead units of the invading German army (the *Wehrmacht*) crashed over the border into Poland. The operation, code-named Case White (*Fall Weiss*), was the world's first look at a devastating new type of mechanized warfare. Highly mobile German formations, spearheaded by massed columns of tanks and working in close cooperation with the German air force (*Luftwaffe*), attacked on a very narrow front, making deep penetrations of the Polish defenses within hours. The speed and violence of the attack paralyzed enemy response. German tanks scattered enemy reserves as they were coming up, overrunning headquarters, supply dumps, and railheads, preventing the Poles from reforming their line or bringing up their reserves. The climax of these armored drives came far behind the front lines, as the spearheads linked up, trapping the bewildered Polish formations in a series of isolated pockets. Despite the speed of their advance, in a recent innovation for mobile columns, the armored units stayed in communication with their own headquarters and with each other through radio. Air power also played a crucial role, helping the tanks blast through the line, with the German dive bomber (*Sturzkampfflugzeug*, or *Stuka*) serving as a sort of mobile artillery on call to the armor. Finally, once the tanks had cleared a path, mechanized infantry and artillery followed up, occupying the terrain the tanks had seized, defending it against enemy counterattack, and tightening the ring around the trapped enemy forces. Despite their bravery, the infantry and cavalry of the Polish army were no match. Cut off from supply and from communications with the rear, they had no choice but to surrender. The main fighting was over in two weeks, although Warsaw would hold out for another two. In those initial two weeks, the first mechanized campaign in military history, the Germans essentially destroyed the Polish army, inflicting about 200,000 casualties and taking almost 600,000 prisoners. Their own losses were negligible.

1

The events in Poland began a two-year period that would rewrite the book on modern warfare. While many Western observers were ready to chalk up the German success in Case White to Polish incompetence or backwardness, the events of the following spring should have changed their minds. In May 1940, the German army launched its great offensive in the West, Case Yellow (*Fall Gelb*). With a rapidity that shocked both the military experts and the world at large, Germany's tank and mechanized formations shredded the French, British, Belgian, and Dutch armies. The British did manage to retreat from the Continent at Dunkirk, although their equipment losses were nearly total. In Case Yellow, the mechanized German army showed what it could do when wedded to expert staff work and commanded by generals in the field who truly understood the strategic possibilities offered by its mobility. It was as impressive and complete a victory as the annals of military history have to offer, and still stands as proof of the genius of German generals Erich von Manstein and Heinz Guderian.

The results were in many ways even more impressive in the Soviet Union in 1941. When Adolf Hitler unleashed Operation Barbarossa in June, it seemed that the tanks had reached their full maturity, breaking through and encircling huge concentrations of enemy troops, with some 900,000 Soviet prisoners of war taken in the pockets around Uman and Kiev alone. As the armored spearheads of *Panzergruppe* Guderian approached Moscow in November, it seemed that the war was over. Even more important, it seemed that the age of the long, drawn-out war, the sort of bloody stalemate that had characterized World War I, was gone forever. The age of "lightning war," or *Blitzkrieg*, was upon us.

From the Ashes

How different the situation had been just twenty years before. On 8 August 1918, after four long years of brutal trench warfare, a combined attack by Allied troops—British, French, Australians—did what had previously been thought impossible: it broke through the German defensive positions on the western front. Allied assault troops, supported by the slow-moving tanks and flimsy aircraft of the period, tore a great hole through the German lines in front of Amiens and drove through into the open country, those elusive "green fields beyond" that had tantalized military planners on both sides of the conflict for so long. The Germans, physically and morally spent, could offer little resistance. There were signs of panic, and the first and only mass surrenders of German troops in the entire war. Gen. Erich Ludendorff, whose ill-considered spring offensives (the pretentiously named *Kaiserschlacht*) had spent Germany's last reserves, called it "the black day for the German army in this war" and began muttering distractedly about the need to bring the fighting to an end.

Although the Germans finally regained their good order, and the rout turned into an ordinary retreat, Amiens was the end of an era. It marked the death of the old Prussian army that had done so much to shape European politics since the days of Roon and the elder von Moltke. The army that had united Germany by defeating the Austrians at Sadowa (Königgrätz) and the French at Sedan, the army that had come within an eyelash of victory at the Marne in September 1914, the army whose myth of invincibility had probably led to the war in the first place—that army was no more. Marking the path to its defeat were signposts bearing names like Langemarck and Ypres and Verdun, but it was at Amiens that imperial Germany's military might may be said to have expired. On that August day, the Allies seized the initiative in the war, and did not let it go. Spearheaded by vigorous attacks of newly arrived U.S. troops, the Allied armies proceeded to chase the Germans back to the borders of the *Reich*. By October, with Germany's allies falling away one by one, a thoroughly panicked Ludendorff decided that there had to be an immediate armistice. U.S. President Wilson had made it plain, however, that he had no intention of negotiating with the "military masters and monarchical autocrats" who had been running Germany. Ludendorff now made a pathetic, last-second attempt to create a parliamentary regime in Germany by appointing liberal Prince Max of Baden to the post of chancellor of the *Reich* in October. Prince Max did his best, and sent notes to Wilson asking for an end to the fighting.

But it was all too little, too late: Germany was in the throes of internal collapse, four years of total war and blockade having taken their effect. Mutiny in the fleet at Kiel in late October spread to the army; Kaiser Wilhelm II fled to Supreme Army Headquarters at Spa, Belgium, there to be surrounded by his generals, and he was there when the Allies agreed to grant Germany an armistice. The announcement that the fighting was over and that Germany had lost the war struck most Germans like a thunderbolt, for the Germans had committed a grave error—perhaps the gravest—in believing their government's claims about the outcome of the war. "Victory is in sight," the regime had promised, right up until October of 1918.

The shock of unexpected defeat in this, the greatest war of all time, plunged Germany into revolution. Angry mobs poured into the streets of Berlin and other major cities, calling for the heads of those who had led Germany into this disaster. They accosted officers on the street and tore the epaulets from their shoulders; they trampled on the black, white, and red imperial flag. Workers' and soldiers' councils (*Räte* like the *sovieti* in Russia) sprang up, claiming to be the legitimate government of Germany. The kaiser, blamed by most Germans for the war and for the disastrous defeat, abdicated and fled to Holland.

Mirroring the internal unrest were threats aplenty on Germany's borders. In the east, remnants of the German army and irregulars of the new

Polish state were already engaged in what today would be recognized as a "low-intensity" conflict; East Prussia and Upper Silesia also appeared to be in danger. Polish statesman Roman Dmowski made it clear he intended to press for the "borders of 1772" for Poland at the upcoming peace conference, an idea that appears only slightly less mad today than it did at the time. In the West, of course, stood the behemoth—the huge Allied military force that had finally ground down the Imperial Army (*Kaiserheer*). Although the Armistice had stopped the advance of the Allies, it was clear that they would push into the *Reich* itself if Germany stepped out of line during the peace talks. Meanwhile the Allied naval blockade, which more than any single factor had led to Germany's defeat, continued in full force. Malnutrition and even outright starvation were everywhere.

All told, the seven months after the end of the war were perhaps the most uncertain period in the history of the German nation. Not since 1807, when Friedrich Wilhelm III rode his horse nervously on the banks of the Niemen while the tsar of Russia and Napoleon met at Tilsit to decide Prussia's fate, had the situation been this grave. Germany was almost completely defenseless. Four years of total war had broken the German army—despite later claims of a *Dolchstoss* (a "stab in the back" by Socialists and traitors on the home front)—and it seemed possible that it might have broken Germany as well. The Treaty of Versailles, imposed on Germany in June 1919, merely set an official, international seal on the situation created by the collapse of the Imperial Army in late 1918.

What was left of the army and its once mighty General Staff was now under the leadership of Gen. Wilhelm Groener, the first quartermaster-general (Ludendorff's old position), who was an atypical staff officer, one of the most unusual in the old army. Originally from Württemberg, it was he who had uttered the fateful words to his Supreme Warlord Wilhelm II, when the latter had bemoaned the fact that the officer corps was no longer willing to abide by the oath of loyalty it had sworn to him. The oath was mere words, Groener had told Wilhelm, adding that "the army no longer stands behind Your Majesty." That evening, 9 November 1918, it was Groener who had telephoned the new chancellor, socialist Friedrich Ebert. With Berlin engulfed in chaos, and Karl Liebknecht of the Spartacus League haranguing the crowd about building a new Soviet Germany, Ebert and Groener made an arrangement: Groener promised the new government military support against any attempt to overthrow it; Ebert promised that the government would cooperate with the army to suppress bolshevism in Germany. With that, as J. W. Wheeler-Bennett puts it, "a pact was concluded between a defeated army and a tottering semi-revolutionary regime," a pact that would have fateful consequences and eventually lead to the death of the Weimar Republic.

But that is not a story that needs retelling; historians have done so over and over again. Instead of analyzing the army's political role in the

Weimar Republic, this work will deal with the military activities of the German *Reichswehr* in the interwar period. It will trace the path by which the army not only managed to survive, but laid the groundwork for its rebirth by preparing a veritable military revolution, one that would do more to change the face of warfare than any development since the introduction of gunpowder. It was a dramatic, yet cautious, process of preserving what was salvageable from the past, refining it in the light of wartime experience, and creating a new, modern synthesis.

During the early part of the Weimar era (1921–1926), under the leadership of Gen. Hans von Seeckt, the army underwent a thorough and at times painful reassessment of its methods of making war. The result was a new doctrine stressing the war of movement (*Bewegungskrieg*). For the remainder of the republican years, under the leadership of Defense Minister Groener and a group of younger staff officers like Werner von Blomberg, Joachim von Stülpnagel, Kurt von Schleicher, and Oswald Lutz, the army began not only to work on concrete strategies for national defense (*Landesverteidigung*), but to devise a realistic operational doctrine—based on constant wargames and exercises—for tanks and other mechanized vehicles. Seeckt's theoretical work on the war of movement would combine with the practical work of men like Groener and Lutz to create *Blitzkrieg*, which the German army would show to an astonished world in the early days of World War II.

CHAPTER 2

Seeckt and the Rebirth of Doctrine

Seeckt's Military Thought

General Hans von Seeckt has generated his share of controversy among historians. The principal charge against him over the years has been political: that he obstinately refused to accept the legitimacy of the Weimar Republic in which he served as chief of the Army Command (*Chef der Heeresleitung*) from 1921 to 1926. He had no love for the new republican system; at most, he was a *Vernunftrepublikaner*, one who accepted the republic as a temporary expedient because no other options were currently available. He organized the interwar German army (the *Reichswehr*[1]) as "a state within a state," so the argument runs, and never fully integrated it into the political or social life of the republic. Reflecting his own prejudices, and those of most of the old officer corps, the army's attitude toward Weimar ranged from an angry denial of its legitimacy at worst to lukewarm support at best, a tragic state of affairs that contributed in no small way to the downfall of the republic and the rise of Adolf Hitler.[2]

Such is the political indictment. About his military abilities, however, there have been very few complaints. Facing the herculean task of restoring the German army after its collapse in 1918, he went about his work with wisdom and professionalism, blending the best of the old Prussian-German military tradition with the lessons that had been learned in the crucible of four years of total war. He was not an original military thinker, but his achievement laid the groundwork for the return of Germany to the ranks of the great military powers, a process that was under way well before Hitler came to power in 1933.

As he surveyed the postwar scene, Seeckt might have been forgiven a sense of utter hopelessness. The disarmament provisions of the Treaty of Versailles left very little room for maneuver in the military sphere. The treaty left Germany with an army of only 100,000 men (of whom no more than 4,000 could be officers). It dictated the organization and armament of

7

the force: seven infantry and three cavalry divisions, without any "offensive weapons" such as tanks, aircraft, or heavy artillery. It prohibited conscription, so that the force was to consist solely of long-term volunteers (twelve years for the men, twenty-five years for the officers), stipulations that made it impossible for the Germans to accumulate a trained reserve. Finally, it abolished the Great General Staff, as well as the *Kriegsakademie* that had produced its members.[3]

Unfortunately, Germany's security needs had never been greater. Along with France's victorious million-man army in the West, the thirty infantry divisions and ten cavalry brigades of reborn Poland threatened from the East.[4] The treaty's territorial provisions contributed to Germany's predicament. In the east, the creation of the "Polish Corridor" had separated East Prussia from the *Reich* proper, while the German loss of Posen meant that the Polish border stood just 150 miles from Berlin. In the west, the Rhineland (German territory on the left, or west, bank of the Rhine river, along with a 50-kilometer strip on the right bank) was to be occupied by the Allies for fifteen years and permanently demilitarized, allowed no garrisons, fortifications, or military installations of any kind. And at three places, the bridgeheads at Mainz, Koblenz, and Cologne, the Allied armies were already over the Rhine, Germany's principal strategic barrier in the west. Add to that a domestic situation bordering on chaos, threats to public order from both the left and the right, and Seeckt's situation was as difficult as any German general had ever faced, with the possible exception of the Prussian military reformers after the Peace of Tilsit in 1807.[5] Given all of this, Seeckt's choices were necessarily limited: on the strategic level, defending the borders would have to take precedence; any aggressive strategy was out of the question. Nevertheless, with an eye to the day when the German army would be reborn, he did imbue his tiny force with an offensive spirit in the realm of tactics.

For Seeckt, leadership of the *Reichswehr* marked "the last and most brilliant phase of an illustrious career."[6] Born in 1868 in Schleswig, the son of a general in the Prussian army, his military career was characterized by rapid promotion. He received his commission in 1887 with the Emperor Alexander Guards Grenadier Regiment: in 1888 he commanded the death watch at the bedside of Emperor Wilhelm I, during which he exchanged a few words with the great Bismarck[7]; in 1899, while still a lieutenant, he earned a post with the Great General Staff in Berlin. By 1902, he was a captain, by 1909 a major. He became chief of staff of the III Army Corps in 1913, a post he still held when war broke out in 1914. Perhaps the most unusual note in his past was his education. Rather than the traditional cadet school, he attended secondary school at Strasbourg, an experience that broadened his vision beyond that of the typical Junker, allowing him to see the world without the traditional blinkers of the Prussian-German officer corps.[8] He also did an incredible amount of traveling across Europe and the world, a habit that he would carry with him into adult life, as well.

Although he saw action on all the wartime fronts, including service on the crucial right wing of the Schlieffen Plan in 1914, his wartime laurels were won in the east. As chief of staff to the armies under the command of Gen. August von Mackensen, he directed the decisive breakthrough of the Russian front between Gorlice and Tarnów in 1915, which established his reputation both inside and outside Germany. In 1916, still assisting Mackensen, he led the German armies in their lightning conquest of Romania. These campaigns would indelibly stamp Seeckt's vision of war. Although he saw a great deal of hard fighting, the vastness of the Eastern Front and the absence of covering terrain in that theater prevented the development of the *Stellungskrieg,* or war of position, that had occurred in northern France. For the rest of his career, Seeckt would be unimpressed with the so-called lessons of World War I, at least those which he saw as nothing more than the lessons of the Western Front (the invulnerability of entrenched infantry, the futility of infantry assault, the omnipotence of the machine gun).

He was aware of the impact of new technologies, but he did not see machines necessarily dominating men on the future battlefield, leading to an inevitable stalemate. He continued to think in terms of a war of movement (*Bewegungskrieg*). During the 1915 Gorlice campaign, Seeckt had personally observed the 2nd Guards Division take no fewer than fifty-three fortified Russian positions through skillful use of fire and movement. With proper direction, he thought, the army of the future could still fight decisive battles of maneuver and annihilation rather than sterile and indecisive contests of position and attrition.

But certain changes were necessary. The new army would, first of all, have to be a great deal smaller than the World War I mass armies which Seeckt saw as anachronistic. During the war, all European armies had increased in size and decreased in effectiveness; their huge mobs of half-trained soldiers had been incapable of forcing a decision.[9] He felt their immobility was the root cause. New military technology like armor, airpower, and rapid-fire artillery simply chewed up such immovable blocks of men, making them "cannon fodder for a small number of technicians on the opposite side."[10] The army of the future needed only to be large enough to fight off an enemy surprise attack. Its strength would lie in its mobility, aided by a large contingent of cavalry, well-conditioned infantry, a full complement of motorized and/or mechanized units, light machine guns, and mobile artillery. He wrote that, by contrast, "The mass cannot maneuver, therefore it cannot win."

In order to ensure adequate time for training, Seeckt envisioned a professional force of long-term volunteers. Seeckt was no fan of conscription, preferring "a professional army, if you will, a type of mercenary army," as he wrote to General Groener in February 1919, even before Germany had received the terms of the Versailles treaty.[11] Universal conscription meant nothing more than poorly trained recruits, increased casualties, and discipline problems. The limitations imposed by these forces had, in his view, led to the war of position in the west. The army of the future, he wrote, would be small, elite, and highly mobile, "rendered distinctly more effective by the support of aircraft."[12]

Superior mobility would enable the army to wage offensive warfare, culminating in the traditional aim of Prussian-German military strategy, the decisive battle of annihilation (*Vernichtungsschlacht*). At a time when the French army was thinking of a future war in terms of static positions, overwhelming firepower, and stalemate, Seeckt still talked, in the manner of the elder Moltke or Schlieffen, of surrounding and destroying the enemy.[13] In his 1928 article "Moderne Heere," he wrote that "destruction of the opposing army . . . is still the highest goal of war."[14] Total victory, he wrote in a later article, was still possible through exploitation of superior mobility: "The goal of modern strategy will be to achieve a decision with highly mobile, highly capable forces, before the masses have begun to move."[15]

The composition of his ideal force deserves special mention, however. Tanks and mobile artillery had an important role to play, but he was not one of those, like J. F. C. Fuller in Great Britain, calling for the abolition of the traditional arms. In his 1927 article "Modern Cavalry" ("Neuzeitliche Kavallerie"), Seeckt argued that the "obsolescence of cavalry" was nothing more than one of the day's popular catch-phrases (*Schlagworte*), which stemmed from a basic misreading of wartime events.[16] Clearly, cavalry was limited in what it could do in the face of heavy firepower. But his study of the U.S. Civil War, the Russian Civil War, and the recent Greco-Turkish War (1921–1922) had convinced him that cavalry was still capable of effective battlefield maneuver, even though the "age of the use of cavalry in large, close order formations is over, due to the development of fire weapons; the age of the battle-deciding cavalry charge is over."[17] That was not, in fact, one of the lessons of the recent world war; it had been obvious to "every thinking soldier" years ago.[18] The German cavalry's lack of achievement in the war was due to poor and unrealistic training, nothing more. How different the early weeks of the war might have been, he speculated, if rather than parceling out the cavalry to units at the front and using it in senseless attacks on fortifications and mountains, the German High Command had deployed it *en masse* on the open right wing as it passed through Belgium and France.[19] Horse cavalry's wartime transformation into rifle divisions and its employment as infantry was a natural consequence of its uselessness in a war of position. The present development of air and armor, far from replacing cavalry, would make it more effective. Air units could help the cavalry with long-range reconnaissance; motorized and mechanized forces would be able to accompany and support the cavalry in pursuit of a broken enemy.[20]

Other operational tasks envisioned for the new cavalry included taking a foe in the flank or rear, protection of the national borders while the main force mobilized, disruption of an enemy's mobilization, and protecting the flank of friendly armies on the march. Tactically, cavalry could use its mobility to seize favorable terrain, engage the enemy in short firefights using light machine guns and carbines, break off the engagement, then reappear elsewhere, all with an eye to discomfiting the foe. Although it was axiomatic that cavalry must engage the enemy dismounted, Seeckt urged it to remain in the saddle as long as possible to exploit its advantage in maneuver. Where the enemy was weak or disrupted, however, even mounted attack was still possible. In short, Seeckt viewed the future of cavalry as an extension of its past, once the conduct of war had been freed from the shackles of positional warfare. In 1927, he wrote that "he never regretted" the decision of the Allies to include so much cavalry in the *Reichswehr*.[21]

Despite the conservative, even reactionary note struck by "Modern Cavalry," Seeckt realized that motor vehicles had won a place for themselves on the modern battlefield. In October 1921, less than three years after the Armistice, the *Reichswehr* conducted maneuvers of motorized units in the Harz Mountains. In the winter of 1923–1924, the army used maneuvers to investigate the possibility of cooperation between motorized ground forces and air forces.[22] And, course, there was no lack of exercises involving dummy tanks made of cardboard or papier maché, mounted on automobile chassis.

German unit organization was subject to the Versailles Treaty, however, which laid down specific limits on the seven infantry and three cavalry divisions—and forbade tanks altogether. Seeckt could therefore do little in terms of implementing the actual motorization or mechanization of the German army. His stress on high mobility and rapid maneuver was an important contribution to the later rise of *Blitzkrieg*, or lightning war, but it is tempting to overemphasize his contribution in this regard.[23]

Combined Arms Leadership and Battle (F.u.G.), 1921

The nature of Seeckt's military contribution is clear in the new tactical manuals issued during his tenure. In September 1921, Seeckt issued the *Reichswehr's* new field service regulations, *Combined Arms Leadership and Battle (Führung und Gefecht der verbundenen Waffen*, known as *F.u.G.*).[24] He followed this in rapid, almost dizzying succession over the next two years with a series of other manuals: the *Infantry Training Regulations (Ausbildungsvorschrift für die Infanterie*), *Artillery Training Regulations (Ausbildungsvorschrift für die Artillerie*), *Regulations on Field Fortification (Feldbefestigungsvorschriften*), *The Signal Service in the*

*National Army (Der Nachrichtendienst im Reichsheer), Training of the
Rifle Squad (Ausbildung der Schützengruppe),* and *Individual Training
with the Light Machine Gun: The Training of the L.M.G. Section (Einzelausbildung am L.M.G.: Ausbildung der L.M.G. Gruppe).*

In his introduction to *F.u.G.,* Seeckt declared that the manual assumed
the "strength, armaments, and equipment of a modern military great
power."[25] It was therefore not merely a guide for the 100,000-man army of
the present, but a blueprint for the expanded army of the future. He felt
that the German army had to take into account forbidden arms like aircraft,
heavy artillery, and tanks to be ready to fight a modern, fully equipped
force—but also to be ready for the day when political considerations permitted Germany to rearm. The introduction to *F.u.G.* also expressed concern that lack of these weapons might lead to a loss of offensive spirit on
the part of the *Reichswehr.* But "greater maneuverability, better training,
cleverness in the use of terrain and night conditions" could all help make
up for the absent weapons; for instance, troops on the attack could avoid
enemy air reconnaissance through use of camouflage. Here Seeckt stressed
a concept that was the hallmark of his military thought: the cooperation of
all arms, but especially of infantry and artillery, down to the very smallest
units. Combined arms, not mechanization, was the essential element of
Seeckt's art of war. The manual was intended to give to both officers and
troops a unified course of training, grounded in the experience of World
War I. Its emphasis on combined arms was intended to give each soldier in
the *Reichswehr* some knowledge of all the military arms.

The manual began by discussing leadership, and then worked its way
across the technical spectrum. The table of contents included eleven chapters:

I.   Leadership and Its Means
II.   Aircraft and Army Cavalry
III. Reconnaissance and Security
IV.   The March
V.   The Camp and the Bivouac
VI.   The Meeting Engagement and the Conduct of the Attack
VII. The Pursuit
VIII. Breaking off the Attack; the Retreat
IX.   Positional Attacks
X.   Defense
XI.   Battle Under Special Conditions

Most of the chapters are self-explanatory. The final one (dealing with
"special conditions") provided guidelines for delaying battle (*hinhaltendes
Gefecht*); battles for villages and woods; battle in night and fog, confined
spaces and river crossings, mountains, and the proper use of mines in warfare.[26] In 1923, Seeckt would issue six new chapters:

The first chapter, Leadership and its Means, dealt with the organization and establishment of the troops, leadership, intelligence and reports, orders, and situation maps. Its characteristic sections dealt with Seeckt's definition of military leadership. In many ways, this definition would have been right at home in the old *Kaiserheer*. The leader had to have the "trust and the respect" of his troops. Besides knowledge and ability, "strong will and a forceful character" were prerequisites, as well as a joy in taking responsibility (*Verantwortungsfreudigkeit*).[27] But much had changed. Belying his Prussian upbringing (or perhaps merely our general misconception of the Prussian military tradition), *F.u.G.* omitted for all practical purposes any discussion of discipline. Instead, it emphasized "personal contact" between the leader and his men: "If the troops know that the leader lives for them and shares their joys and sorrows, they will willingly give their all to achieve success, and will bear up under setbacks."[28]

In an even more radical departure from the days of the Imperial Army, *F.u.G.* declared that the leader was not simply a machine carrying out detailed orders for every contingency. Instead, it harkened back to the more flexible Moltkean tradition known as *Auftragstaktik*: the commander was to devise a mission (*Auftrag*), explain it in a short, clear order, then leave the methods and means of achieving it to the officer on the spot. In the light of his mission, the officer had to evaluate a given situation (*Lage*) and then make a decision (*Entschluss*).[29] Seeckt wanted to ensure that his German army not suffer from the same adherence to out-of-date orders that had doomed the Kaiser's army at the Battle of the Marne. Orders were still orders, but they were no longer to be regarded as an end in themselves. "From the mission and the situation arises the decision," he insisted.

> If the mission no longer suffices as a basis for action, or has been superseded by events, then the decision must take account of these conditions. The leader bears full responsibility if he abandons or changes an order. However, he must always act in the framework of the whole.[30]

Decisions must be taken firmly, and display the leader's "unshakable will." They must only be changed for weighty reasons. But *F.u.G.* finished this section with a bow to flexibility. "In the changing situations of war, however, a strict adherence to a decision can lead to error. The art of leadership is recognizing when a new decision is required,"[31] a passage that could have been written by Moltke.

Tactically, *F.u.G.* codified the changes that had occurred in land combat since 1914. World War I is justly known as the tactical nadir of military history. Verdun, the Somme, Passchendaele—all have come to stand for the senseless slaughter of attacking infantry ordered into battle against entrenched defenders. Grandiose prewar plans for battles of encirclement and annihilation foundered on the new tactical realities of barbed wire, the trench and the machine gun. The result was three years of stalemate, punctuated occasionally by large-scale attacks, "big pushes" that gained almost no ground, but did succeed in getting large numbers of the attackers killed.[32] "Idiotic reciprocal mass murder" is how one German officer described it.[33]

The German infantry had marched off to World War I trained in the concepts of the 1906 manual, *Drill Regulations for the Infantry (Exerzierreglement für die Infanterie)*, not much changed from the 1888 version. It laid little stress on combined arms; battalions consisted exclusively of infantry; there was one machine gun company per regiment. Infantry attacks were to proceed with nothing more than supporting rifle fire from the infantry itself.[34] Troops were called upon to form "tactically strong lines of riflemen in close order" as they deployed for the assault,[35] with the goal being to make an "irresistible attack" upon the foe.[36] Close order was the rule; "the abandonment of the closed formation was a bad thing which might often be avoided, especially when the firing line had approached close to the enemy."[37] Often entire battalions were formed into broad or deep columns (*Breitkolonne* or *Tiefkolonne*), phalanxes of four companies abreast or four deep, respectively. Most German officers still viewed shock as the ultimate arbiter on the battlefield; "fire superiority" was recommended, but methods for attaining it were never described in detail.[39] In fact, as units dashed forward in waves, they had to be careful not to hinder the fire of other riflemen lying on the ground. They could, therefore, usually only dash straight forward.[40] And even if they succeeded in reaching the enemy trench, there was the danger of becoming isolated there if friendly troops on both flanks had found themselves held up. "The assault is to be made in as uniform a manner as possible."[41]

The 1906 regulations also laid down rules for the employment of supporting weapons: machine guns and artillery. The use of the machine guns was left up to the regimental commander; he could keep them concentrated in a regimental reserve or parcel them out to his battalions. The regulations laid great stress on avoiding their "premature" use, especially at extreme range, due to their steep ammunition requirements. There was resultant confusion over how to advance the machine guns to practicable range: under cover of the infantry advance, or simultaneously with it. In open terrain, they were, "in case of delayed employment, to join the reserves that were being filled into the line." According to one German officer "systematic cooperation with the infantry from the beginning was, in this way, not required and not intended."[42]

As for artillery, its formation for combat was to be as linear as the infantry's. The infantry was to clear a path for artillery to be inserted into the battle, "which was then to be carried on by both arms together; the work of one was to merge with the other."[43] Infantry was to deploy far in advance of artillery, both to protect the guns from enemy fire and to avoid being directly involved in the artillery combat. Infantry advancing from the reserve had to take great pains to proceed around the artillery, though in the case of "great artillery lines" infantry could proceed through "the gaps which it found most convenient." If the penetration of the firing line could not be avoided, portions of the artillery would have to cease firing. The artillery's chief duty was to bombard those objectives most dangerous to the infantry: "In assaulting an enemy position, the infantry will be thankful to its sister arm, if the latter, until immediately before the penetration, directs its fire against those points where the penetration is to take place."[44] There was no direct subordination of artillery to specific infantry units, however.

Regarding defense, the 1906 regulations recommended a strong, rigid line provided with a wide field of fire, with infantry at about 600 meters in front of the artillery. Only one defensive line was selected, and it was then strengthened with all means at the army's disposal. Once again, machine guns were inserted into the battle at the whim of the regimental commander. Defensive action was left principally to rifle fire. Unlike the French, the Germans did not see the benefit of advanced positions to disrupt the enemy assault; all too often, the only effect was to hinder defensive fire by the main line. Of course, if the defensive line was broken, the action was for all intents and purposes over.[45]

By late 1914, it had become clear to the Germans that such prewar conceptions had no place on the modern battlefield. The destruction of the four reserve corps at the battle of Langemarck, in which recently raised units of enthusiastic young volunteers—the patriotic cream of the German middle class—were shot to pieces by defending British infantry, marked the end of the great close order assaults. However, right after this *Kindermord* ("child murder") as the Germans called it, there was an equally disastrous attempt to crack the British lines with an assault by the Imperial Guard. Even these well-trained and thoroughly drilled troops took sickening casualties in the advance, victims not of machine gun fire for the most part, but of well-aimed British riflery. Now the situation was clear. The failure at Langemarck was not simply a case of poor soldiering on the part of untested volunteers, but the fault of German tactics.[46]

New approaches were needed to get the attacking infantry to the enemy trench in the face of enemy firepower. The first solution was to use

"Boer tactics" (basically an open skirmish line). But skirmish lines were still large targets for enemy fire and took unacceptable casualties in the attack. After much trial and error, the German army developed a new method of fighting. Stormtroop (*Stosstrupp*) or infiltration tactics were the solution to the trench stalemate. Infantry could once more cross "no man's land" and come to grips with the enemy. Movement returned to the battlefield. It was not, by and large, an innovation devised by Germany's military leadership. It was the German infantryman, faced with an impossible situation on the modern battlefield and saddled with old tactics that simply did not work, who instigated this tactical revolution. The General Staff had little to do with it, though it did encourage tactical progress by forming an experimental Assault Detachment (*Sturmabteilung*) in 1915. Neither were these tactics the invention of a single great mind. They were not, as they are still often called, "Hutier tactics," after Gen. Oskar Hutier. He had nothing to do with their development, though he did use stormtroopers in his victory at Riga in 1917. In fact, if any one deserved credit for the evolution of stormtroop tactics, it was a mere captain, Willy Martin Rohr, commander of the Assault Detachment.[47]

The heart of *Stosstrupp* tactics was the use of independent squads or battlegroups (*Kampfgruppen*), each armed with a variety of weapons—machine guns, grenades, flamethrowers, and artillery. Each group advanced on its own; no attempt was made to maintain contact with units on the flanks; and obstacles were simply bypassed, left for the follow-up waves of regular infantry. Infantry and artillery maintained the closest possible mutual support. Thus the engagement broke down into numerous "little battles." What began as a war of armies and corps "dissolved" into a war of squads. Germany honed these new tactics in a number of "battles with limited objectives," then used them on a larger scale at Caporetto and Cambrai.[48] Finally, they were at the heart of Ludendorff's 1918 spring offensive, his grandiose plan to shatter the Allied armies once and for all.[49] Stormtroop tactics necessitated the nearly complete decentralization of command, the surrender of much of an officer's authority to the squads, fire teams, and individual soldiers making the assault. It is a great paradox that this more decentralized, perhaps even "democratic," form of warfare arose not in the armies of the democratic west, but in imperial Germany.

Seeckt enshrined these land warfare developments in the new regulations. *F.u.G.* repeatedly emphasized that troops must be trained in the attack; they must proceed to the attack with flexibility in mind, seizing opportunities and bypassing obstacles. What one analyst has called a "near-classic credo of German military doctrine" may be found there:[50]

> The attack alone dictates the law to the enemy. The superiority of leader and troops comes best into play here. Especially effective is the *Umfassung* [envelopment] of one or both flanks and the attack in the enemy's

rear. In this way the enemy can be destroyed. All orders for the attack must bear the stamp of great decisiveness. The leader's will to victory must be shared down to the last man.[51]

From here, *F.u.G.* moved on to specifics by describing the principal types of attacks: meeting engagements and attacks against positions, both in a war of movement and in a static war. It called particular attention to the meeting engagement, "the freest, most original type of offensive resulting from movement, from the stirrups as it were."[52] It could result from sending a mobile force ahead of the army to seize a river crossing, a defile, or tactically important high ground, and usually involved both sides deploying from the depth of the march column.[53] The role of the leader was essential here.

> He must make his decision without reconnaissance, which would rob him of time. He must give orders in uncertainty and can assume that the enemy is just as unready as he is. A surprising burst of enemy fire into a march column mustn't be allowed to stop the advance; indeed, it must force the troops forward. Jumping in boldly is the rule.[54]

But here, as elsewhere, Seeckt refused to lay down hard-and-fast rules to apply to specific cases. Frontal attacks might be effective in some cases, envelopment and driving in the enemy flank in another—but these all depend on the situation and the terrain. In a war of movement, each case was different. Seeckt's formula with regard to this point was this: *Das Begegnungsgefecht hat kein Schema!* ("the meeting engagement has no diagram!").[55] No *schema,* perhaps, but it still had its laws. "It is no wild storm breaking loose; like every battle, it has its own tempo from which one may not depart; the advance guard scouts, establishes the position and strength of the enemy, and fights according to orders." The objectives of the meeting engagement were above all "to win the main body time and space for deployment and to secure the mass of the artillery good conditions for observation."[56]

Under Seeckt's undogmatic approach, a commander therefore had to study the various tactical situations that might arise in order to develop his sense of tempo and timing. If the context was a war of movement, the commander had to decide whether to attack immediately to preclude the enemy's reinforcing, or whether the enemy was already so strong that more careful preparations, including phase lines and bombardment by artillery were necessary. If the attack was transpiring in a war of position, then there were any number of steps that had to be taken, based on the experience of the previous war: assembly of troops in the jumping-off point; specifying the point of main effort for the attack (*Schwerpunkt*), as well as discrete axes of attack for each unit; identifying primary and secondary objectives; or working out detailed plans for heavy weapons, artillery support, and observers.

This was the role of wargames, as well as planning and tactical exercises. The directors of each game had to make sure that each new situation required a fresh, nonschematic decision by the commanders. Creativity was the highest requirement of these simulations and games, which more often than not featured the attack in a war of movement, usually in the form of meeting engagements. Attacks on prepared defensive positions were hardly ever actually wargamed, being much more often the subject of theoretical studies (*Planstudien*) by the artillery. The use of artillery in the great *Stosstrupp* assaults of World War I, particularly the detailed fire plans of Col. Georg Bruchmüller, the German army's artillery expert, were studied closely.[57]

Occasionally *Stosstrupp* exercises were held in "practice trenches" (*Übungsschützengraben*) that still existed on the various training grounds, but so strong was the prejudice against trench warfare in Seeckt's military thought (one *Reichswehr* officer speaks of trench warfare having been "prohibited" in the 1920s) that most unit commanders shied away from such exercises so as not to appear to be in contravention of the new manual. Certainly the standard World War I grinding attack against a defense in depth, what used to be known as "chewing through" the defenses (*Durchfressen durch die Tiefenzone*) was a thing of the past in terms of German military exercises.[58] Nowhere in the German army's practice grounds was there a deeply echeloned defensive system of several kilometers' extent of the sort that such exercises would have required. However, maneuvers involving individual *Stosstrupp* squads against individual fortified positions took place constantly. Large-scale infantry attacks were therefore envisioned, in best *Stosstrupp* fashion, as a series of individual combats involving squads and platoons. Close cooperation with heavy weapons was always a feature of such practice runs. In particular, the exercises investigated the utility of indirect fire by machine guns over the heads of the forward troops, as well as through the gaps in infantry formations. It might be argued that such training in the various kinds of attacks bore almost no practical relation to the nation's actual strategic requirements. But Seeckt saw the need to train the army for any conceivable future case, even if only for the far future. Training in the attack was the only way to preserve offensive spirit and verve in a force whose current mission was basically defensive.

In another link to tradition, Seeckt's conception of the attack revolved around the question of the *Schwerpunkt*, the decisive point of the battle requiring the insertion of all forces.[59] But just as each battle was unique, a combination of forces, terrain, and the overall military situation, so too was its decisive point. Although *F.u.G.* contained no firm directives on how to identify the *Schwerpunkt*, the commander had to be aware of its existence. Only then was a rational conduct of battle possible. As von Hindenburg had once said during the war, "a battle without a *Schwerpunkt* is like a man without character, who leaves everything to chance."[60]

This emphasis on the *Schwerpunkt* was not meant to put blinders on the commander. Quite the contrary, he had to remain flexible enough to recognize the battle's decisive point, especially as it changed in the course of the fighting. He was required to display a resolute determination to win, side by side with an extreme flexibility in the choice of means. Only a "strategy of improvisation" was suitable to the rapid pace of modern war, and it had to be based on the totality of the situation, taking into account strategy, operations, and tactics.

Like Moltke, Seeckt laid a great deal of emphasis on the possibility of achieving an envelopment of the enemy. In concert with a frontal attack, envelopment offered the highest possibility of a decisive victory. It could be most easily achieved, Seeckt felt, if the approach march of the attacking troops was aimed at the enemy's flank or rear, that is, if it were planned far in advance of the attacker's arrival on the battlefield. But he was clear on the point of what should happen if the envelopment failed: "If an envelopment is not possible, one must not shy away from the frontal attack."[61] Carrying out an envelopment required close cooperation between infantry and artillery. Through appropriate deployment in breadth and depth, he wrote, the commander could achieve unconditional superiority at some favorable position (terrain, a weak spot in the enemy lines), perhaps even a small-scale envelopment. A successful frontal attack would lead to a breach (*Einbruch*), which through further penetration in the direction of attack and through throwing back the enemy reserves might be increased to a breakthrough (*Durchbruch*). Once the enemy line was broken through, neighboring sectors of the front could themselves be enveloped and rolled up deeply.[62] But the victorious troops, he cautioned, had to advance as far forward as possible to engage the enemy reserves, rather than wheeling as soon as the breakthrough had been made. An immediate wheel by the breakthrough force would mean nothing but a tactical success. But a deep penetration that crushed the enemy reserves meant something else: victory.[63]

True to Seeckt's belief in the importance of combined arms, the concept of the interrelationship of infantry and artillery also received a great deal of attention. Artillery was an extremely powerful weapon, charged with the task of "breaking the resistance of the enemy, paving the way for its sister-weapon, the infantry, and with it fighting on to victory."[64] It had to be quick in deployment to be ready to support the infantry at the earliest possible moment. Infantry, for its part, had to recognize the limits of the artillery's ability and not put forward demands that the latter was incapable of meeting. "Infantry which acts without regard to its artillery usually hurts itself."[65]

Despite its emphasis on the attack, the manual also offered a detailed treatment of the defense. Seeckt's stamp is evident in the aggressive and maneuver-oriented manner he brought even to defensive questions. The main principal was this: "Defense is justified only against a vastly superior

enemy, and only if it makes possible the resumption of the offensive at a
later date or another place."[66] Even a weak defender had to strive to end
the battle with an attack and thereby strike a decisive blow against the
enemy.[67] *F.u.G.* was emphatic in liberating the defense from any connection to trench warfare; it was by now obvious that the tremendous development of air reconnaissance had eased the attacker's task of identifying
and destroying a defender's system of trenches. Digging in and camouflage were still essential to protecting the defender from the attacker's fire,
as was deployment in depth.[68] Seeckt's concept of defense, however, was
no trench line, but an aggregate of numerous individual nests of machine
guns and strongpoints of rifle squads, dispersed throughout the terrain, capable of direct fire against an advancing foe—preferably on the enemy's
flanks—yet also invisible to the foe until the last possible moment.[69] The
most forward line of strongpoints and machine gun nests was the main line
of resistance (*Hauptkampflinie*), a term used in the German army through
World War II.[70] The determination of the *Hauptkampflinie* depended above
all on the location of observation posts for the artillery. The guns had two
missions: direct fire against targets immediately in front of the main line
of resistance (*Sperrfeuer*) and the preparation of indirect-fire missions
against suspected enemy concentrations deep in the enemy attacker's rear
zone (*Vernichtungsfeuer*).[71]

Sticking to its rule of providing only general guidelines, *F.u.G.* did not
discuss the dimensions of a defensive battle. The depth of a position depended on the strength of the unit, the width of the front assigned to it, the
circumstances of the battle and the terrain.[72] In addition, numerous battle
outposts (*Gefechtsvorposten*) were to be deployed in front of the main line
to deceive the enemy as to its actual location and to provide some insight
into the state of the attacker's position. Whether these outposts should
draw back or offer resistance in the face of an enemy attack depended on
the overall situation and could not be the subject of any general rule.

The deeper the enemy forces broke into the defenses, the stronger
should be the fire they encountered from resistance nests and strongpoints.
At some point, the commander had to decide whether to launch an infantry
counterblow (*Gegenstoss*) with the locally available troops or a larger
counterattack (*Gegenangriff*) with troops from the tactical reserve (belonging to the battalion, regiment, or division), backed up by artillery.[73]

F.u.G., in sum, offered a completely modern, up-to-date discussion of
defensive tactics as they had been transformed by the previous war, from
a linear defense to a defense in depth. Defense in a war of position, including entrenchments and barbed wire, received about half the discussion
in *F.u.G.* as did defense in a war of movement. According to one observer,
it was only practiced on the exercise square, rather than during maneuvers,
and then only half-heartedly. In open country, trenches were merely indicated rather than dug, to avoid damage to crops and forests. The same

observer makes the point that the German soldier's aversion to digging trenches, which was so obvious in the early years of World War II, dates back to this period. Even on the Eastern Front, where trenches might have been of some use in holding down casualties from Russian bombardment, they appeared rarely. Only in the last years of the war, when a purely passive defense was all that was left in some sectors, did trenches reappear.[74]

The delaying defense (*hinhaltendes Gefecht*) was the one "new" type of battle introduced in *F.u.G.*, a style of battle that actually bore some practical significance for the *Reichswehr*.[75] In a normal defensive posture, the manual provided for counterblows and counterattacks to ensure that the position remained in the defender's hands at battle's end. In a delaying defense, however, the objective was to fool the enemy into thinking he had reached the main line of resistance, pin him in place with vigorous counterattacks, and then retire. The objective was not to hold terrain but to win time. In operational terms, attackers were to be engaged by fire as early as possible after crossing the German border in order to delay their advance and to cause them losses. Then, however, the defender was to retire to another prepared position 8 to 12 kilometers in the rear. Here the process would begin again. Fire and movement were to be echeloned as economically as possible toward the rear to slow down and perhaps even halt the advance of a superior enemy. With the time won by such delaying tactics, strong defensive forces might be raised inside the country, or perhaps the League of Nations might intervene and force negotiations.[76]

Though this type of battle had certainly been seen before (Fabius against Hannibal and the invading Carthaginians comes immediately to mind), it had never received the kind of systematic treatment afforded it in *F.u.G.* It was certainly not the easiest type of battle to fight. *F.u.G.* advised the commander not to tell his men of the intended retreat, so they would carry out their counterthrusts with determination and vigor. He also had to have the prudence to determine the exact moment to order the retreat, which could not occur until effective fire had been brought to bear on the attackers. Finally, it required high morale on the part of the troops, who had above all to avoid an overly hasty retreat from the first line of resistance. Numerous maneuvers and exercises were devoted to teaching the delaying defense, particularly for the cavalry regiments. It became a characteristic of maneuvers in the eastern border regions, the most likely site of an invasion. Here pioneer detachments would be present to create roadblocks and other obstructions. Such hindrances to enemy movement could render great stretches of forest uncrossable and thus channel the attack directly onto the prepared defensive positions.

In fact, it might be said that *hinhaltendes Gefecht* was the *Reichswehr's* characteristic style of fighting, the one that most closely corresponded to the army's actual situation and the one that was most thoroughly practiced in wargames and exercises. It remained an important part of German military doctrine even after the shift to offensive *Blitzkrieg* tactics in the 1930s, and remained so until 1942, when Hitler forbade the German 6th Army to retreat from Stalingrad. A vast gulf separates Seeckt's delaying defense from Hitler's disastrous no-retreat order, which would bring the German army so many catastrophic defeats in the latter years of World War II.

The additional six chapters of *F.u.G.* released in 1923 are important mainly for their discussion of armor and aircraft. Again, the approach was both progressive and cautious, exhibiting what the greatest historian of the *Reichswehr*, Harold J. Gordon Jr., described as "enlightened conservatism."[77] *F.u.G.* saw tanks as a tactical weapon, intended for battlefield use, since the current state of technology limited their range and speed to little more than that of the infantry. They were to fight as platoons of five tanks[78] in direct support of assaulting infantry, using their unique ability to overcome obstacles such as trenches, barricades, and barbed-wire entanglements.[79] But tanks suffered from weaknesses: they offered a large target, their fire was especially unreliable when moving; and visibility was quite limited for the tank crew, making a serious problem of command and control.[80] The best use that could be made of them was in an attack during a war of position (*Stellungskrieg*), rather than in a more mobile environment.[81] None of this may reasonably be seen as the forerunner of *Blitzkrieg*, nor was it even especially progressive for its day, compared with the debate already raging in Great Britain, for example. However, *F.u.G.* also included the idea that tanks were to be inserted only at the *Schwerpunkt* of the battle, and were to be used "with surprise, in mass, on a broad front."[82] In sum, then, Seeckt appears to be much more of a transitional figure—not to mention a more sensible one—than a true "armor prophet" in the style of Colonel Fuller. In fact, *F.u.G.* spends as much time discussing antiair and antitank measures as it does the aggressive use of these modern arms, a perfectly logical approach for the disarmed *Reichswehr*.

One other important component of the second set of chapters was Seeckt's proposal for a "division of a modern army" (*Division eines neuzeitlichen Heeres*)—how an infantry and cavalry division might appear "if unlimited resources were at our disposal."[83] Not only is this clear evidence how transitory the Versailles settlement appeared to the *Reichswehr*, it also demonstrates how Seeckt's inclination toward the battle of maneuver might affect unit organization in the future. Compared with the standard "Versailles" infantry division, the "division of a modern army" was a greatly augmented unit: each of the standard 3 infantry regiments had its own battery of 6 infantry guns; there were 2 field artillery regiments instead of 1(6 batteries of which would be fully motorized); there was an antiaircraft battalion of 4 batteries; 3 signal companies rather than 2; and instead of a single cavalry squadron there was now a large and versatile reconnaissance battalion (2 cavalry squadrons, a bicycle company, a detachment of 4 armored cars, and a mobile signals detachment).[84] The division would also have its own squadron of observation aircraft.

Training Regulations for the Infantry (A.V.I.), 1922

Seeckt followed *F.u.G.* in October 1922 with the *Ausbildungsvorschrift für die Infanterie* (*Training Regulations for the Infantry,* or *A.V.I.*), which would be revised slightly in 1925. It conceived of war as consisting predominantly of infantry battle: "The infantry decides the issue in an engagement; the task that determines the tactical work of all other arms is to make possible and facilitate success for the infantry."[85] German infantry had learned some hard lessons from 1914 to 1918, above all about the tremendous firepower of automatic weapons and rapid-fire artillery. There was no more possibility of a shock attack (*Sturmangriff*) on a broad front such as envisioned by prewar maneuvers.[86] Such attacks had been shot to pieces too often in the war's early months. Furthermore, officers in prewar battle exercises had viewed going to ground or retreating under enemy fire as dishonorable behavior, and that behavior had to be unlearned under the pressure of wartime battle. Stressing firepower above all, in the attack as well as the defense, *A.V.I.* called for battle on a dispersed front, using terrain as protection wherever possible. There was also significant discussion of defense from tanks and air attack, although, unlike *F.u.G.,* the new infantry regulations assumed the German army in its present size and configuration.

A.V.I. consisted of five volumes: *Fundamentals of Infantry Battle; Details of Training for an Infantry Company; Machine Gun Platoons and Companies; Trench Mortar [Minenwerfer] Platoons and Companies; and The Infantry Battalion/The Infantry Regiment.*[87] It also contained tables of organization and equipment for all units up to and including divisions.

The infantry company (*Schützenkompanie*) consisted of three platoons of three groups (*Gruppen*) each. Each group contained a rifle troop as well as a light machine gun troop. Altogether, a rifle company contained nine light machine guns, making it capable of dominating only a limited area. In the *Schwerpunkt* of a battle, therefore, an infantry company would expect to be reinforced by heavy machine guns from the battalion's machine gun company.

The battalion included three rifle and one machine gun company. The latter consisted of four platoons (with two light machine guns each), equipped with horse transport. There was also a signal platoon with telephones and a troop of messenger dogs (*Meldehundtruppe*) for communications from battalion to company. According to *A.V.I.*, "the battalion is the smallest tactical unit with which the middle leadership has to concern itself," that is, the *Reichswehr's* basic unit of battlefield maneuver.[88]

The infantry regiment consisted of three battalions for use in the field as well as a training battalion, made up of three recruit companies. It also included a trench mortar company, consisting of four platoons (each holding two mortars). They would later be combined into an infantry gun company (*Infanteriegeschütz-Kompanie*) of three light and one heavy gun platoons. There was also a regimental staff, a mounted reconnaissance platoon, and a signal platoon equipped with telephone and telegraph. The regimental commander played a key role in battle:

> He exerts his influence over the troops subordinate to him through the imparting of tasks, which are received by the individual units either as comprehensive orders or as single commands. But constant personal contact ("dauernde persönliche Fühlung") is necessary to maintain the spirit and morale of the troops placed under him.[89]

A.V.I.'s description of the various units culminated in the infantry division, now formalized as consisting of three infantry regiments. Prior to the war, divisions had consisted of two brigades of two regiments each. But experience had shown how difficult it was to engage the reserve regiments in a "two up-two back" deployment: by 1917, virtually all German divisions were fighting in a "two up-one back" arrangement. The frontline firepower was exactly the same, and the divisional commander could now move up his reserve much more easily. *A.V.I.* simply made official this wartime improvisation.[90]

The manual also included discussion of realistic battle training, based on the experiences of the war. *A.V.I.* aimed at creating an independent-thinking infantryman, capable of the clever use of terrain, always conscious that he was moving and firing within the context of a group.[91] Training in riflery received heavy emphasis. Marksmanship was generally high in the *Reichswehr*, a result of more or less constant competitions and prize shoots. This was particularly true of the *Jäger* (light infantry) battalions, parceled out one per division and recognizable by their green insignia. They consisted exclusively of soldiers with first-class sharpshooting credentials. The best marksmen in the infantry and *Jäger* companies received the Shooter's Braid (*Schiessschnur*).[92] In the course of the interwar years, such qualified soldiers also received telescopic sights for their rifles. All this aimed at instilling the fundamental principle of battle: in both attack and defense the infantry had to be able to win fire superiority, through individual as well as volley fire.

A.V.I. envisioned the attack as a series of individual encounters on the small-unit scale (platoons, companies, battalions). The practice of identifying objectives and axes of advance, and then allowing the unit to plan its own attack, had proven itself in the war. "A good commander is ingenious in the selection of his means."[93] Operational boundaries to right and left limited the maneuver area for the division and regiment. But within these boundaries, units were free to employ fire and movement in whatever combination seemed most effective, driving forward constantly while limiting their own losses through skillful use of terrain. Units were sometimes even allowed to overstep their operational boundaries if an opportunity for advance arose. *A.V.I.* stressed that the individual soldier was to view the protective quality of terrain predominantly as a means to continue the advance; eyes had to be sharpened for good terrain formations that at first glance might be invisible. Darkness was also valuable in this context, and the *Reichswehr* made a habit of nighttime exercises.[94]

For movement of small units *A.V.I.* described three basic formations: the rifle line (*Schützenkette*), the file (*Schützenreihe*), and a more indefinite formation known as the pack (*Schützenrudel*). These were not valid for larger units like regiments, but for companies, always keeping in mind the terrain and the presence of the enemy. They were to "adapt themselves to the terrain, in the manner of a serpent and avoid places swept by enemy fire or exposed to view."[95] The choice of formation was up to the company commander, but always within the context of his mission.

If the terrain was flat and thus offered little protection, or if the enemy was occupying a prepared defensive position, the advancing infantry would have had to rely on the fire of heavy weapons, artillery above all, for its protection. Individual advancing groups also had light machine guns that could offer protective fire as the rifle troops moved forward. Nothing should be allowed to stop the advance of the infantry.

Heavy infantry weapons (the heavy machine gun platoon of the battalion and the regiment's 13th Trench Mortar Company) were to be inserted so that both before and during the advance they could engage enemy forces, whether they were newly arriving or already identified. Trench mortars fired over the heads of their own units from protected positions; heavy machine guns fired from an elevated position through gaps between the advancing groups or from flanking positions. Indirect (unobserved) fire from heavy machine guns was possible, but *A.V.I.* stressed that it was intended mainly for the defense. The purpose of supporting fire from heavy weapons was offensive, to destroy as quickly as possible all enemy resistance nests and strongpoints that might hinder the infantry advance. Observers for heavy weapons teams therefore had to be schooled in careful inspection of the terrain and the identification of camouflaged objectives.[96]

According to *A.V.I.*, there were three principal characteristics to the infantry battle. First was a stress on combined arms, especially through the formation of mixed *Kampfgruppen* (battle groups).[97] Second was the envelopment of the enemy on one or both flanks, in the manner of Schlieffen: taking an opponent in the flank or rear was the "patented solution" (*Patentlösung*) for a whole host of training exercises and problems. In wargames and troop maneuvers, both sides typically sought the deep flank of the foe; indeed, this was the basic characteristic of German tactics throughout World War II. Finally, *A.V.I.* mandated a *Schwerpunkt* for each battle, characterized by heavy fire support on a narrow sector of the enemy's position. The *Schwerpunkt* gave each battle a distinct character. In exercises on the platoon and company level, units were taught to aim at the weakest spot in the enemy line or where the terrain favored the effectiveness of their own heavy weapons, especially artillery.[98]

Reichswehr officer Adolf Reinicke boiled down all he was taught in this period into three slogans: "Fighting means firing!" (*Kämpfen heiss feuern!*); "Attacking means shooting forward!" (*Angreifen heisst vorwärtsschiessen!*); and "Action before protection!" (*Wirkung geht vor Deckung!*).[99]

A.V.I. also discussed in some detail the effects of armor and air power on infantry operations. In the absence of tanks and planes, it was obvious that any antitank or antiaircraft tactics could never be more than emergency solutions. Machine gun and rifle fire against aircraft could never substitute for an air force. Antitank weapons, though effective one on one against the thin-skinned tanks of the 1920s, could never substitute for an armored force. Like all armies of the day, the Germans experimented with motorization (truck-borne infantry, for instance). But with tanks forbidden by the Treaty of Versailles, Seeckt could do little beyond theoretical studies of mechanization.

Training of the Rifle Squad (A.d.S.), 1921

One of the most important manuals of the Seeckt era was the *Training of the Rifle Squad* (*Ausbildung der Schützengruppe*, or *A.d.S.*) issued in December 1921. It identified the squad as the smallest combat unit and the only formation that during combat may be led "by a single word or command of its leader." It was truly an inseparable whole, characterized by cohesion and cooperation. "Those belonging in it should be united for life and death by loyal comradeship (esprit de corps)."[100]

The squad leader trained the men of his squad; he was their leader and fought at their head. This carried with it grave responsibilities. He had to possess high moral qualities and a thorough knowledge of his duties. He had to be able to recognize and seize favorable opportunities and have the ability to overcome difficult situations with "calm determination." Due to the danger of his position, there must always be a designated successor to lead the squad forward in combat. If both squad leader and acting squad leader were lost, "then a resolute private must take over the command."[101]

A.d.S. specified that the rifle squad consisted of the squad leader and, at most, seven riflemen, though the actual number of men and weapons could vary in the case of special combat duties (an assault detachment, for instance). The training of the squad had to begin with learning the various formations: close order, extended order, and their evolutions. But squad training also had to include specific combat problems as early as possible: the best use of terrain; behavior under enemy infantry and artillery fire; how to conduct an assault; techniques for close combat. Cooperation with neighboring squads and auxiliary weapons was also an important skill, especially cooperation with light machine gun sections. The men had also to learn the importance of aircraft—both friendly and enemy—on the battlefield, as well as the impact of armor.

The manual discussed the various formations of the rifle squad. There was the line (of two ranks); the double column (one file behind the other with the men of the file side by side); and the column (with the men standing behind one another). The distance between ranks was specified at 80 centimeters from the back of the file leader to the breast of the second man (it should be possible to touch elbows easily with the man on either side). When a rank is formed up, the leader should be on the right side of the front rank; in a double column he should be in front of the front rank man on the right; in column at the head of the column. Orders to "dress" or "guide" were presumed to refer to the right, either standing still or moving. Dress was correct "when the man in the front rank, standing perfectly correctly, can, by turning his head towards the guide wing, see with his right eye only the man next to him on his right, and with his other eye makes out the whole line."

In cases where the terrain or the situation prevented such close-order formations, the squad had to pass to extended order: the skirmishing column, the skirmishing file, and the skirmishing chain. In fact, any formation was permissible if required by the situation. In the end, enemy fire was the determining factor in the choice of friendly formation. The squad leader should never bind himself to any one particular course of action.

The skirmishing column was formed behind the advancing squad leader, with intervals of 5 feet or less between the men. The private acting as second in command brought up the rear. This formation was particularly useful for taking advantage of the terrain where coverage was restricted in width, for passing through artillery fire, or for protecting a flank. Since it appeared from the side as a line, however, care was necessary to avoid flanking machine gun fire. When using this formation, the squad leader should not hesitate to go on far ahead of the squad, scouting both the terrain and the enemy.

The skirmishing file was a flexible formation, loose and subject to frequent variation. It too formed up behind the advancing squad leader and was well suited for advancing under enemy fire, for using extended cover, for negotiating broken country, and for assembling the squad under cover during an engagement. Again, a 5-foot interval between the men was specified as ideal.

In the skirmishing chain, the squad deployed one-half on the right, one-half on the left, behind the squad leader, who was to bound forward a few paces in the direction of march. Intervals were left unspecified, depending on the terrain and enemy fire. This formation, obviously, was best suited for fire combat toward the front.[102]

The manual included a great deal of discussion on the evolution from one formation to another, in both close and extended order, as infantry manuals have done for centuries. But a far more interesting section of *A.d.S.* was its discussion of the "combat method of the rifle squad." How was the squad to engage the enemy? A battle would typically open with the squad leader receiving his orders from the platoon commander. At the same time, the manual observed that there were many situations in which the squad leader would have to act on his own initiative. He had to strive, therefore, to keep a clear idea of the overall situation, based both on his personal observation and from the reports of his riflemen.[103]

During battle it would often be necessary to concentrate several squads for the purpose of some important task. *Kampfgruppen* were the result, frequently consisting of one light machine gun section and one or more rifle squads. Any composition was possible, however. A *Kampfgruppe* might even include individual artillery pieces or infantry guns. The squad leader had to be ready to assume command of any such group, without in any way neglecting the command of his original squad. Although the formation of such an ad hoc group usually resulted from the platoon commander's orders, the squad leader was permitted to form one on his own initiative.[104]

In the end, every battle came down to the "vigorous assaulting strength" of the rifle squad. The true ability of the squad leader lay "in leading this force up to the foe, as far as possible undiminished in strength."[105] He could achieve this by careful exploitation of every favorable undulation in the terrain, by skillful use of covering fire from light machine guns, infantry guns, and artillery. Speed was essential. The more rapidly the squad leader brought his men forward, the greater the chance for success. But the squad leader was not to lose sight of the overall situation of the platoon, and he was not to risk casualties foolishly.

To exploit the possibilities of terrain, the squad leader had to do a great deal of personal reconnaissance. He would often have to seek his own patch of high ground for this purpose, and from there direct the evolution of his squad by calling out or signaling the orders. In this case, the private farthest in the front was responsible for leader-squad liaison. Terrain, as always, prescribed the correct formation; that is, given the lay of the land, the squad leader had to determine which formation best protected his squad from enemy fire. The less cover and the heavier the incoming fire, the more extended the order. Often he would have to divide his squad into smaller sections, half-squads for instance. Positions under heavy fire could often be occupied only by a single man. Through it all the squad leader had to endeavor to keep firm control of his men.[106]

The protective nature of terrain was increased by the spade. The squad leader had to keep in mind that even hastily erected cover could be of great value. Even if he expected to occupy a piece of ground for a short time, the squad leader should order his men to dig in. The traditional concern of the officer that digging in tended to sap the offensive spirit of his troops and lessened their forward drive was true, but it could be overcome by the willpower of the squad leader. He must also urge his men to use camouflage: "a branch that he has put on, or a few handfuls of grass, may serve to conceal the rifleman (skirmisher) from the eye of the foe."[107] But there was also care to be taken here. The riflemen must not seek protection behind single trees, for they afforded no real protection from shells or bullets, and in fact tended to attract enemy fire. And the squad leader must never fail to remind each man that even when his position is invisible from the ground, it is still necessary to worry about concealing it from enemy aircraft.

The more open the terrain and the nearer the squad came to enemy fire, the more it depended on the fire of its own guns to act as cover. As the location of the enemy's strongpoints now became clearer, the squad leader directed the fire of the auxiliary weapons, whether light machine guns, heavy machine guns, or trench mortars. The moment success was ensured, or enemy fire slackened, was the time to advance. Sometimes the whole squad could go forward by rushes, as long as the squad leader took care to see that no one broke away from the unit. That would only interfere with the friendly machine guns, which kept up a vigorous fire as the squad worked its way up to the enemy. Nonetheless, occasional targets would present themselves, which "the single rifleman may hit with a well-aimed round."[108] In such a case it was the responsibility of the squad leader to bring into action the snipers armed with telescopic sights, effective out to 1,000 meters.

Fire by the squad generally opened up at the command of the squad leader, though once again if favorable targets did present themselves (likely in a town or woods), then each man could fire without orders. The closer the squad came to the enemy, the more intense the situation became. Here, "every foe who still dares to lift his head must be shot." As each single rifleman approached the enemy line (by rushes or by crawling), he should be covered by the fire of the rest. Once within 150 meters, rifle grenades could supplement the fire of the other arms. When the squad had worked its way to point-blank range (within 100 meters), the squad leader ordered bayonets to be fixed, and the assault began, typically signaled by a hand grenade, whistle, or call. This signal also served to order the heavy weapons to lengthen or shorten the range. After the assault had been launched, "the squad must swing forward relentlessly up to the enemy. With a shout of 'Hurrah,' penetration is made at the point of a bayonet."[109]

Once penetration had taken place, the squad occupied the enemy's former position and pursued the fleeing foe with fire. Now the squad leader's role became even more important. He had to reassert control over his squad, now disorganized by the assault; he had to reconnoiter the ground ahead by field glasses; he had to decide how to continue the fight. Especially important was establishing close liaison with the light machine guns, adjoining squads, and the platoon commander. The crucial decision was whether to press on with the attack or prepare to repel a counterattack. This decision depended upon his mission (*Auftrag*) and the situation (*Lage*).

The moment of weakness immediately following the assault required a high level of caution and energy on the part of the squad leader. He could not allow his troops to loot (a severe problem for German *Stosstruppen* in the Ludendorff offensives of 1918); "severe measures" had to be employed to prevent it. Even more important was security against incoming fire: "He is responsible that his squad shall not at this moment be needlessly shot to pieces by the fire of the enemy directed from his positions far in the rear."[110]

At some point following the penetration, the squad leader would have to continue the attack in order to break into the depth of the enemy's position (*Tiefenzone*). In cooperation with adjoining squads and light machine gun sections, he would assault one enemy resistance nest after another. His ultimate aim was to take in the flank those parts of the enemy force still holding out. If the squad met no resistance it had to press forward. Whenever targets were encountered, they were to be destroyed by fire. The squad had to pursue energetically, following on the heels of the retreating foe, "so that the latter may not be permitted to halt."[111] Throughout, the example of the squad leader had to serve to spur on his riflemen.

Such was the method of attack in open warfare. But *A.d.S.* also dealt with the very different situation when the defender occupied a prepared position. In *Stellungskrieg*, the first penetration was not a spontaneous decision of the squad leader, but a planned result of a definite order. In this case, the squad leader would often have to lead his men into a "jumping-off trench" under cover of darkness (a maneuver discussed thoroughly in the earlier *A.V.I.*) When the moment came for the assault, he led his men forward, being careful not to lose contact with the artillery barrage advancing before him. Only in this way could he avoid the deadly fire of enemy machine guns. If, in spite of friendly artillery support, he encountered resistance, he was to attack and crush it if possible, bypass and leave it for follow-up forces if necessary.

The spirit of *A.d.S.* was aggressive. Even when discussing defense, it was placed in the context of a successful attack and an enemy counterthrust. Riflemen had to "cling persistently" to the ground recently gained. "The ground captured must not again be surrendered."[112] By establishing contact with adjacent light machine guns and infantry guns, the squad leader established "reciprocal support" for his new position. Infantry screened the guns from enemy fire; the guns protected the infantry by suppressing it. Spades now came out; the position might range from a single resistance nest to a series of rifle pits. If the defensive lasted long enough, the squad leader transformed his position into a "miniature fortress" by putting up wire entanglements and enlarging the rifle pits with galleries and dugouts. As a rule, this work could only take place under cover of darkness.

In defense, the squad leader directed the fire of his squad in cooperation with machine guns and trench mortars to break down the attack before it reached the main line of resistance. Once he spied the enemy approaching, or recognized the imminence of an assault by a shift in the range of enemy artillery, he was to hustle his men into the firing line: "It is a matter of honor that the assaulting enemy shall not surprise the squad in its cover." In case the assault included tanks or aircraft, the defenders had to find support in their leader's calm and presence of mind. Nonetheless, if retreat became necessary, the squad leader was to see that it was carried out as quietly and unobtrusively as possible. A recommended method was to withdraw the men one by one. It was up to the squad leader to designate which men were to remain behind to cover the retreat of the rest. The squad leader, however, "must remain with the element which is closest to the enemy."[113] Machine gun fire was always the best cover for a retreat.

Individual Training with the Light Machine Gun: The Training of the L.M.G. Section (A.L.M.G.), 1921

A closely related training manual was issued alongside *A.d.S.* This was *Individual Training with the Light Machine Gun: The Training of the L.M.G. Section* (*Einzelausbildung am L.M.G.: Ausbildung der L.M.G. Gruppe, A.L.M.G.*). It described the light machine gun as "the most important weapon that the infantry possesses for the conduct of fire battle."[114] But the crew had to be familiar with the peculiarities of the weapon, have a thorough knowledge of its working, and have great skill in dealing with its jamming. It was a matter of intense training that extended over many months.

Although a crew of four served the weapon, the gunner (number two man in the crew) was the most important man. He aimed and fired the weapon; numbers one, three, and four carried the ammunition. The gunner was an elite soldier, trained in a number of specialized activities: how to use the weapon in all types of terrain—open ground, shell craters, in houses, behind walls and fences, trees, even on top of roofs; how to improve the terrain to increase the effect of his weapon and how to prepare simple means of protection quickly; how to crawl, glide, and creep from one cover to the next; how to carry the gun for a distance of several kilometers at a time, over difficult ground, in darkness, or when wearing a gas mask; how to overcome jamming; how to mount the gun correctly and without attracting attention; how to open fire quickly, achieve surprise over the enemy, and hit the target, all the while practicing the necessary fire discipline.

Although *A.L.M.G.* discussed technical points like loading procedures (with belt or drum), firing position, and how to avoid jams, most of it dealt in detail with battlefield tactics. Combat orders for the light machine gun were to be carried out in close cooperation both with adjacent squads and heavy machine guns. In making an attack, the section commander led his unit as close to the enemy as possible. The section, in fact, was to advance just behind the scouts. In this way, it could be said that the section was leading the attack. As in the advance of the rifle squad, the machine gun section was to take advantage of every piece of terrain, improving it with the spade where necessary. Often the commander would be ahead of his men, reconnoitering. It was his responsibility to give the "open fire" command, unless the platoon commander had reserved the right beforehand. There were also certain cases where the gunner could open fire on his own (if haste were necessary, for example). Fire should begin within effective range (up to 800 meters for small targets, up to 1,000 meters for sharpshooters aiming at special targets). But fire should only proceed when their own rifle squads required it, or when enemy fire called for a response "and provided the enemy offers good targets."[115]

Taking his mission into account, the section commander was the one who generally had to fix and designate the target of fire. Nevertheless, he should also be prepared to consult with the commander of the platoon or *Kampfgruppe*. Generally, the target had to be the enemy position that most jeopardized the mission, and this often might be fire from an unidentified position. In this case the light machine gun would have to engage in area fire (i.e., at spots where the enemy might be). It could be a thicket, a row of hedges, the edge of a woods, cultivated fields, or areas shrouded in fog. But every burst of fire at an area had to be weighed against its potential effects, or the expenditure of ammunition would be tremendous.

In the advance, the light machine gun might press on quickly or it might linger at one point or another if it found a good firing position. The choice depended, as always, on the terrain and the situation. The section always had to keep one thing in mind, though. Its most important mission was fire protection for its rifle squads, thus enabling them to come to grips with the enemy infantry. Even in the case of friendly infantry advancing close up to the enemy line, the light machine guns had to keep up their fire, aiming through gaps in the friendly formations.[116]

If the light machine gun was spotted by the enemy, it could expect to draw fire; in this situation, a change of position was advisable. If such a change were possible without the enemy noticing it, it could cause considerable confusion in his ranks. But a section's change of position always had to take place in echelon, with the guns offering each other mutual support.

Frequent changes of position lessened the effectiveness of machine gun fire, and were therefore inadvisable.

Shortly before the moment of penetration, all the guns of the light machine gun section were to open fire on the spot where the penetration was to be made. Whenever possible, the section commander led his gun carriers into the assault together with the adjoining rifle squads. During the assault, "the light machine gun fires as long as it is possible without endangering its own unit, and then hastens to rejoin its section."[117] If the gun was unable to offer fire support to the assault, then it was to go forward with its section, "in some cases firing as it moves forward."

After penetrating a portion of the defenses, the section was to be engaged in the front line. Here it stood, ready to oppose counterattacks and offer antiaircraft protection, to open pursuit fire at the retreating foe, or even to support a rapid resumption of the attack.

Breaking into the depth of the enemy's position offered a series of particularly challenging tasks for the section. It had to keep a keen watch on enemy movements, strive to identify key targets whose destruction would open a path for the infantry, protect the flanks of groups coming forward into the assault, and maintain contact with the infantry commanders. The section had to take special care to keep enemy machine gun nests and strongpoints engaged by frontal fire, "while the rifle squads can utilize this fire protection for attacking and assaulting the flanks and rear." Conversely, the section might try to establish a flanking position against the enemy strongpoint, distracting it so that friendly infantry could launch a frontal assault.

As for those sections not engaged in the front line, it was their task to remain ready and perhaps fire through gaps in the front rank groups. It was only possible for light machine guns to fire over the heads of their own troops if their guns were deployed in considerably higher positions (e.g., trees, houses), and only when the infantry was directly in front of the light machine gun. At any other time this practice was forbidden.

On the defensive, both light and heavy machine guns were to work in close cooperation (with the light guns deployed in advance of the heavies) to repel any attacks. The light machine gun had to be protected against both ground and air observation and be dug in so that it could support adjoining light machine guns and rifle pits. By engaging the most dangerous targets, the light machine gun alone could cause the breakdown of an enemy assault, even by a numerically superior foe. Nonetheless, the weapon's limitations could not be ignored. Long-range fire should be left to the heavy machine gun and artillery; attackers advancing singly should be targets for the rifles with telescopic sights. Taking these simple precautions would prevent the foe from spotting and engaging the light machine gun prematurely. At short range, the bunched-up ranks of an assaulting

enemy offered a lucrative target for the light machine gun, particularly if
it had kept silent and unrecognized up to that point.

On the defense, if fire had penetrated the position, the light machine
gun must offer its own rifle squads the opportunity to counterattack. It
must patiently hold its position and take advantage of every favorable target. The enemy would be disorganized to some extent during the assault.
Well-timed machine gun fire would ensure that the enemy stayed that way,
and thus prevent a continuation of the attack. The light machine gun must
continue firing until the last cartridge was gone, even if the section were
threatened in the flank and rear. At this point, the gunners were to defend
themselves with their sidearms, or hand grenades "or by using the rifles
of their fallen comrades."[118]

In the retreat, the light machine gun section was to act like the rifle
squad. It was to be, however, the "last element to give way before the
enemy."[119] In this way its fire would enable the rifle squad to disengage
safely.

Conclusion: Seeckt and the Rebirth of Doctrine

Seeckt's new *Reichswehr* manuals offer an object lesson in how far the
German art of war had come since 1914. In place of the old rigid system
of linear attack and defense, Seeckt had devised a system of mobile tactics
that took into account the changes demanded by the new technology of
firepower. While he encouraged the aggressive spirit at all times, he tempered that aggression with a great deal of flexibility. *Stosstrupp* tactics had
gone from being a radical new alternative in tactical matters to the main-
stream. The attack was to go forward as a blizzard of independent but in-
terconnected squads, crews, and fire teams, relying at all times on firepower and terrain for protection, seeking one or both of the enemy's
flanks, never losing sight of the ultimate objective: a complete breakthrough of the enemy's defenses and a penetration into the depth of his
position.

The well-known irony of the situation is this: as commander of the
army that had lost the war, Seeckt had a great deal of incentive to seek the
new, the novel, and the modern when it came to military doctrine. No
other wartime power—the Americans, the British, and certainly not the
French—had any reason to go through the sort of agonizing reappraisal of
their wartime methods that Germany did.[120] Their current methods of waging war had been good enough for victory, after all. As British Col. J. F. C.
Fuller put it in his inimitable way, describing the postwar "mental
lethargy" of the British army, "the cease fire sounded, and the cavalry was
saved."[121] But what is often neglected is the fact that the temptation was
there for the Germans, too. It would have been the easiest thing in the

world for Seeckt, forced by the Versailles Treaty to maintain a state of military weakness, to ignore the unpleasant experiences of the war, to succumb to the lure of nostalgia, and to look longingly on the past and ape the doctrine of Moltke and Schlieffen in a sterile and uncreative fashion.

There was equal danger in rushing after military novelty. Think of the French army after the Franco-Prussian War; it identified the roots of defeat in its failure to inculcate an offensive, aggressive spirit in its men and commanders. For the next four decades, the French swore that the next war would be different, that next time they would attack, that they would dictate the course of events by imposing their will on the enemy through nonstop, furious infantry assault. In the age of the machine gun and rapid fire artillery, this lesson was wrong, tragically wrong, as the opening days of World War I would demonstrate. Seeckt's great achievement was not so much in overcoming the lure of the past, nor in inventing anything wholly novel, but in fusing past wisdom with present knowledge, and thus readying the German army for its future rebirth.[122]

Notes

1. Technically, the term *Reichswehr* refers to all the German armed forces of the Weimar period, including both the army (officially known as the *Reichsheer*) and the navy (the *Reichsmarine*). I have followed what has become common usage, however, in using the term *Reichswehr* to refer to the army alone.

2. Two seminal works continue to define the poles of *Reichswehr* historiography. Harold J. Gordon, *The Reichswehr and the German Republic 1919–1926* (Princeton, NJ: Princeton University Press, 1957) defends Seeckt and the *Reichswehr* against charges of treason against the republic. He credits Seeckt not only with rebuilding the army, but with weeding out hot-headed officers hostile to the republic and thus helping to consolidate the new order; conversely, he argues, the republic's socialist leaders showed little sympathy to the army's needs or security issues generally. Arguing against that point of view, and still representing the scholarly consensus, is F. L. Carsten, *The Reichswehr and Politics 1918–1933* (London: Oxford University Press, 1966). In its refusal to accept parliamentary democracy, the *Reichswehr* weakened the democratic order and contributed mightily to the downfall of the republic and the rise of Hitler. "If the republic after 1930 had possessed an army entirely loyal to it, the great crisis would have taken a different course," he argues (p. 405). These two works set the tone for virtually all of the *Reichswehr* historiography to follow, especially in the focus on the army's political role. Both Gordon A. Craig, *The Politics of the Prussian Army, 1640–1945* (London: Oxford University Press, 1955) and J. W. Wheeler-Bennett, *The Nemesis of Power: The German Army in Politics, 1918–1945* (London: Macmillan & Co., 1964) set the discussion of the *Reichswehr* in the broader context of Prussian-German history. Both Gaines Post Jr., *The Civil-Military Fabric of Weimar Foreign Policy* (Princeton, NJ: Princeton University Press, 1973) and Michael Geyer, *Aufrüstung oder Sicherheit: Die Reichswehr in der Krise der Machtpolitik, 1924–1936* (Wiesbaden: Franz Steiner Verlag, 1980) focus on the relationship between the *Reichswehr* and the German foreign office. Kurt Schützle, *Reichswehr wider die Nation: Zur Rolle der Reichswehr bei der Vorbereitung und Errichtung*

der faschistischen Diktatur in Deutschland, 1929–1933 (Berlin [Ost]: Deutscher
Militärverlag, 1963) is a useful Marxist interpretation of the army's role in the fall
of the Republic. The most useful synthesis of the entire question of army-state relations is Rainer Wohlfeil, "Heer und Republik," *Handbuch zur deutschen Militärgeschichte 1648–1939*, VI: *Reichswehr und Republik* (Munich: Bernard & Graefe
Verlag, 1979). Otto Ernst Schüddekopf, *Heer und Republik: Quellen zur Politik der
Reichswehrführung, 1918 bis 1933* (Hanover and Frankfurt am Main: Norddeutsche Verlagsanstalt O. Goedel, 1955) and Heinz Hürten, ed., *Die Anfänge der
Ära Seeckt: Militär und Innenpolitik, 1920–1922: Quellen zur Geschichte des Parlamentarismus und der politischen Parteien*, series 2, vol. III (Düsseldorf: Droste,
1979) provide many of the pertinent documents. It is only recently that the ques-
tion of the *Reichswehr's* military doctrine has begun to engage historians. Robert
M. Citino, *The Evolution of Blitzkrieg Tactics: Germany Defends Itself Against
Poland, 1918–1933* (Westport, CT: Greenwood Press, 1987) analyzes *Reichswehr*
planning for war on Germany's eastern frontier with Poland; James S. Corum, *The
Roots of Blitzkrieg: Hans von Seeckt and German Military Reform* (Lawrence, KS:
University Press of Kansas, 1992) looks closely at the Seeckt years.

3. Documents relating to the military settlement of the Treaty of Versailles, including the disarmament talks at Spa, are to be found in *Stücke* (items) 111 and 112
of the Seeckt *Nachlass*, a microfilmed copy of which is on deposit in the U.S. National Archives, microcopy number M132, microfilm reel 21. In shorthand notation, these documents would be listed as Seeckt Papers, M132, 21, 111–112. The
reels, unfortunately, do not include frame numbers. See also Friedrich von
Rabenau, *Seeckt: Aus seinem Leben, 1918–1936* (Leipzig: Von Hase und Koehler
Verlag, 1940), 159–202.

4. Documents relating to the military strengths of Germany's neighbors are to
be found in Seeckt Papers, M132, 22, 131. See especially "Derzeitiges Stärke d.
franz. Armee, 8 November 1920" as well as "Gesamtstärke der Britischen Land-
macht, 12 November 1920."

5. There has been a veritable library of books devoted to the pluses and minuses
of the Versailles Treaty, most of it highly condemnatory. Setting the tone early on,
of course, was John Maynard Keynes, *The Economic Consequences of the Peace*
(New York: Harcourt, Brace and Howe, 1920). Following in his path, historians laid
a weighty indictment at the door of the treaty, blaming it for everything from the
Great Depression to the fall of the Weimar Republic to the rise of Hitler—and many
other crimes besides. It is only fairly recently that a revisionist view has arisen. It
began with Andreas Hillgruber, *Grossmachtpolitik und Militarismus im 20. Jahrhundert: Drei Beiträge zum Kontinuitätsproblem* (Düsseldorf: Droste, 1974), who
pointed out that the treaty had left Germany intact and in a position to once again become a great power. With Austria-Hungary gone, he argued, German industry had a
golden opportunity to penetrate eastern and southeastern European markets. Hillgruber's thesis has become the consensus among German historians. See, for example,
the treatment of the Versailles settlement offered by two recent general texts on the
Weimar Republic: E. J. Feuchtwanger, *From Weimar to Hitler: Germany, 1918–33*
(New York: St. Martin's Press, 1993), pp. 45–54, and Detlev J. K. Peukert, *The
Weimar Republic: The Crisis of Classical Modernity* (New York: Hill and Wang,
1992), pp. 42–46. Both take a hard, sober look at the treaty, with none of the ritual-
istic denunciations of the past. For a useful synthesis and bibliography of the entire
question, see Eberhard Kolb, *The Weimar Republic* (London: Unwin Hyman, 1988),
pp. 23–33 and 166–178. And for a good, short discussion, including numerous extracts from the minutes of the Versailles deliberations themselves, Ferdinand Czernin, *Versailles 1919: The Forces, Events, and Personalities that Shaped the Treaty*
(New York: G. P. Putnam's Sons, 1964) continues to be useful.

6. Gordon A. Craig, *The Politics of the Prussian Army, 1640–1945* (London: Oxford University Press, 1975), pp. 382–383. See also *United States Military Intelligence Reports: Germany, 1919–1941* (Frederick, MD: University Publications of America, 1983), microfilm reel XIII, frames 364–365, for a summary of Seeckt's career. In shorthand notation, the above document would be labeled USMI, XIII, 364–365. The best biography of Seeckt is Hans Meier-Welcker, *Seeckt* (Frankfurt am Main: Bernard & Graefe Verlag für Wehrwesen, 1967). Rabenau, *Seeckt: Aus seinem Leben*, was for nearly thirty years the standard treatment of its subject, but is now generally regarded as superseded. The book certainly has its flaws: it is often difficult to separate the sources from Rabenau's own opinion of them; he rarely gives citations for his sources, and when he does they are often inexact or inaccurate; most seriously, Rabenau was at pains to portray a Seeckt who was acceptable to Nazi military doctrine, especially difficult given the gap betwen Seeckt's own views on the desirability of a professional volunteer army (the *Reichswehr*), as opposed to a national, conscription-based force (the *Wehrmacht*). Rebenau also tried to paint a much more antirepublican portrait of the general than the sources warranted, again in an attempt to harmonize his subject with the spirit of the times.

7. Meier-Welcker, *Seeckt*, p. 22.

8. Carsten, *Reichswehr and Politics*, p. 104.

9. In Seeckt's own words, "Das Sinken der Qualität der Truppe unter gleichzeitiger Steigerung der Zahl und des Materials führte zum Stellungskrieg und damit zum Ende der auf schnelle und entscheidende Erfolge abzielenden Kriegführung." Hans von Seeckt, "Grundsätze moderner Landesverteidigung," reprinted in *Gedanken eines Soldaten* (Leipzig: von Hase und Koehler Verlag, 1935), p. 69.

10. See "Moderne Heere," reprinted in Seeckt, *Gedanken*, pp. 51–61. For the quote on cannon fodder, see p. 56; the quote on the poor maneuverability of mass armies is on p. 54.

11. Seeckt Papers, M132, 21. The letter is quoted in Corum, *Roots of Blitzkrieg*, p. 21.

12. Seeckt, "Moderne Heer,"p. 58.

13. For Moltke's role in strategy and war planning, see the monograph by Arden Bucholz, *Moltke, Schlieffen, and Prussian War Planning* (Providence, RI: Berg, 1991). Larry Addington, Jr., *The Blitzkrieg Era and the German General Staff, 1865–1941* (New Brunswick, NJ: Rutgers University Press, 1971) explores the relationship between Moltke's doctrine and the later development of *Blitzkrieg*. Moltke's own writings are available in an extremely useful recent volume, Daniel J. Hughes, ed., *Moltke on the Art of War: Selected Writings* (Novato, CA: Presidio Press, 1993).

14. "Vernichtung des feindlichen Heeres . . . ist noch immer oberstes Gesetz der Kriegskunst." Seeckt, "Moderne Heere," in *Gedanken*, p. 56.

15. "Das Ziel einer modernen Strategie wird es sein, mit den beweglichen, hochwertigen operationsfähigen Kräften eine Entscheidung herbeizuführen, ohne dass oder bevor Massen in Bewegung gesetzt werden." Seeckt, "Grundsätze moderner Landesverteidigung," in *Gedanken*, p. 77.

16. See the 1928 article "Schlagworte," reprinted in Seeckt, *Gedanken*, pp. 9–18. Seeckt here expresses his contempt toward those for whom slogans and catch-phrases replace independent thought. For example, one could understand the importance of the Cannae-style battle, without demanding that every operational plan aim at the double envelopment of the enemy (pp. 13ff). During the great breakthrough against the Russians at Gorlice, he related how difficult it had been to get men and officers to avoid a premaure envelopment of the retreating Russian

forces "when success lay in going forward" (p. 15). For Seeckt's thoughts on cavalry, see his 1927 article "Neuzeitliche Kavallerie," reprinted in *Gedanken*, pp. 99–116. For the denial of cavalry's obselescence, see p. 99.

17. Seeckt, "Neuzeitliche Kavallerie," p. 100.

18. Ibid.

19. Ibid.

20. For the discussion of armor and airpower's contribution to cavalry, see Ibid., especially pp. 101, 110.

21. Ibid., p. 102, "Ich habe diese Festsetzung nie bedauert. . . . "

22. Craig, *Politics of the Prussian Army*, p. 396.

23. For a contrary view, which places Seeckt very much at the center of the German development of *Blitzkrieg*, see Corum, *Roots of Blitzkrieg*, pp. 122–143.

24. *Führung und Gefecht der verbundenen Waffen* (Berlin: Offene Worte, 1921), usually abbreviated *F.u.G.* For a comprehensive discussion of the manual, see Adolf Reinicke, *Das Reichsheer 1921–1934: Ziele, Methoden der Ausbildung und Erziehung sowie der Dienstgestaltung* (Osnabrück: Biblio Verlag, 1986), pp. 92–100; Corum, *Roots of Blitzkrieg*, pp. 37–43; and Heinz-Ludger Borgert, "Grundzüge der Landkriegführung von Schlieffen bis Guderian," *Handbuch zur deutschen Militärgeschichte 1648–1939*, IX: *Grundzüge der militärischen Kriegführung* (Munich: Bernard & Graefe Verlag, 1979), pp. 542–549.

25. *Führung und Gefecht* (hereafter *F.u.G.*), paragraph 1. In shorthand reference, the citation would be *F.u.G.*, 1.

26. The table of contents to *F.u.G.* may also be found in Reinicke, *Das Reichsheer*, pp. 417–418.

27. *F.u.G.*, 5.

28. Ibid.

29. Ibid., 6.

30. Ibid., 9. See Reinicke's discussion of this point in *Das Reichsheer*, p. 94.

31. Ibid., 9. See the discussion in Borgert, "Grundzüge der Landkriegführung," pp. 542–543.

32. The books dealing with the tactical situation on the Western Front in World War I are too numerous to mention. Two older works are still quite useful: B. H. Liddell Hart, *The Real War, 1914–1918* (Boston: Little, Brown, 1930) and C. R. M. F. Crutwell, *A History of the Great War, 1914–1918* (Chicago: Academy Chicago, 1991). The former, written by one of the great "armor prophets" of the interwar period, is always interesting and often tendentious; the latter, originally published in 1934, is judicious and well written throughout. For the battles of the Somme and the Third Battle of Ypres (also known as Passchendaele), see the works by Martin Middlebrook, *The First Day on the Somme* (New York: Norton, 1971) and Lyn MacDonald, *They Called It Passchendaele: The Story of the Third Battle of Ypres and of the Men Who Fought in It* (London: Michael Joseph, 1978). The actual trench experience is detailed in Denis Winter, *Death's Men: Soldiers of the Great War* (New York: Penguin, 1978). And for gritty realism, no historical work—scholarly or popular—can touch Erich Maria Remarque, *All Quiet on the Western Front* (New York: Fawcett Crest, 1991), which, although a fictional account, is based closely on Remarque's own wartime experiences.

33. The officer is Gerhard Ritter, who served with the German army in France and later became a historian, author of the magisterial history of German militarism, published in English as *The Sword and the Scepter*, 4 volumes (Miami: University of Miami Press, 1969–1973) and *Der Schlieffenplan: Kritik eines Mythos* (Munich: Verlag R. Oldenbourg, 1956). The quote is found in Holger Herwig,

Hammer or Anvil: Modern Germany 1648—Present (Lexington, MA: D. C. Heath, 1994), p. 209.

34. The discussion of wartime German infantry tactics appears in *Die Kampfweise der Infanterie auf Grund der neuen Ausbildungsvorschrift für die Infanterie von 26.10.1922 (A.V.I.)* by Major Hüttmann, which appeared in 1924 as a special supplement to the *Militär Wochenblatt*, the semiofficial military weekly. It appears in English translation as *Tactics of the Infantry, on the Basis of the New Training Regulations for the Infantry of Oct. 26, 1922* in USMI, XI, 277–352. Also quite useful in this context is Bruce I. Gudmundsson, *Stormtroop Tactics: Innovation in the German Army, 1914–1918* (Westport, CT: Praeger, 1989), especially "Prologue: The Massacre of the Innocents" pp. 1–15.

35. Hüttmann, *Tactics of the Infantry*, USMI, XI, 285.

36. Ibid., XI, 280.

37. Ibid., XI, 286.

38. Gudmundsson, *Stormtroop Tactics*, p. 8.

39. Borgert, "Grundzüge der Landkriegführung," pp. 431–432.

40. Hüttmann, *Tactics of the Infantry*, USMI, XI, 286.

41. Ibid., USMI, XI, 286.

42. Ibid., USMI, XI, 286–287.

43. Ibid., USMI, XI, 287.

44. Ibid., USMI, XI, 287–288.

45. Ibid., USMI, XI, 288.

46. Gudmundsson, *Stormtroop Tactics*, 10–13.

47. For the organization and development of the Assault Detachment, see Gudmundsson, *Stormtroop Tactics*, pp. 47–52. Gudmundsson builds on the earlier work done on the topic by Timothy Lupfer, *The Dynamics of Doctrine: The Changes in German Tactical Doctrine During the First World War* (Fort Leavenworth, KS: U.S. Army Command and General Staff College, 1981).

48. For a good short introduction to the battle of Caporetto, see John Keegan, "Blitzkrieg in the Mountains: The Battle of Caporetto," *Military Review*, 50, January 1966, pp. 78–92. The classic primary source on the battle is still Erwin Rommel, *Attacks* (Vienna, VA: Athens Press, 1979. See also Gudmundsson, *Stormtroop Tactics*, pp. 125–138. The battle of Cambrai, which Liddell Hart called "the coronation" of the tank as the new queen of battle, has hardly received the scholarly attention it deserves. The volume of the British official history by Wilfrid Miles, *The Battle of Cambrai* (London: HM Stationery Office, 1948), is a useful starting point. The popular work by Bryan Cooper, *The Battle of Cambrai* (New York: Stein and Day, 1968) describes the battle, but lacks citations. See also Robert Woolcombe's *The First Tank Battle: Cambrai 1917*, with a foreward by Liddell Hart (London: Barker, 1967). William Moore's *A Wood Called Bourlon: The Cover-Up After Cambrai, 1917* (London: Leo Cooper, 1988) describes the battle's aftermath.

49. The best account of the Ludendorff offensives of 1918 remains the chapter in Correlli Barnett, *The Swordbearers: Supreme Command in the First World War* (New York: Morrow, 1963). Rod Paschall, *The Defeat of Imperial Germany, 1917–1918* (Chapel Hill, NC: Algonquin Books of Chapel Hill, 1989) and Gudmundsson, *Stormtroop Tactics*, pp. 155–170, incorporate more recent research.

50. Borgert, "Grundzüge der Landkriegführung," p. 543.

51. *F.u.G.*, 10.

52. Reinicke, *Das Reichsheer*, p. 94.

53. *F.u.G.*, 255; Borgert, "Grundzüge der Landkriegführung," p. 544.

54. Ibid., 246; Borgert, "Grundzüge der Landkriegführung," p. 545.

55. Rabenau, *Seeckt: Aus seinem Leben*, p. 511.

56. *F.u.G.*, 262; Borgert, "Grundzüge der Landkriegführung," p. 545.

57. Bruchmüller's artillery methods are the subject of a recent monograph by David T. Zabecki, *Steel Wind: Colonel Georg Bruchmüller and the Birth of Modern Artillery* (Westport, CT: Praeger, 1994).

58. The phrase "Durchfressen durch die Widerstandzone" is used in *F.u.G.*, 152; Reinicke's testimony about its rarity in German army maneuvers is found in *Das Reichsheer*, p. 106.

59. "An entscheidender Stelle ist stets die Hauptkraft anzusetzen." *F.u.G.*, 10.

60. Borgert, "Grundzüge der Landkriegführung," 543.

61. "Ist eine Umfassung nicht möglich, so darf der frontale Angriff nicht gescheut werden." *F.u.G.*, 275.

62. "Aus dem Durchbruch müssen die seitliche Anschlussfronten umfasst und tief aufgerolt werden." Ibid.

63. Ibid. "Nur so wird der Durchbruch zum Sieg."

64. *F.u.G.*, 265.

65. "Infanterie, die ohne Rücksicht auf die Artillerie handelt, schadet sich selbst am meisten." Ibid.

66. *F.u.G.*, 12.

67. *F.uG.*, 354; Reinicke, *Das Reichsheer*, p. 91; Borgert, "Grundzüge der Landkriegführung," p. 544.

68. *F.u.G.*, 354; Reinicke,. *Das Reichsheer*, p. 97.

69. *F.u.G.*, 355.

70. Ibid., 357.

71. Ibid., 388.

72. Ibid., 355.

73. Ibid., 363, 366.

74. Reinicke, *Das Reichsheer*, p. 99.

75. Ibid., 13, 414–417.

76. Ibid., 417; Reinicke, *Das Reichsheer*, pp. 99–100.

77. Gordon, *Reichswehr and the German Republic*, p. 303. According to Gordon, "There seems good reason to doubt that Seeckt realized the tank was to be the horse of the future. He saw the way that a future was should be waged, but he failed to recognize the only means which could make his tactical concepts practical under modern conditions." Again, for a contrary view, see Corum, *Roots of Blitzkrieg*.

78. *F.u.G*, volume II, which contains the second set of six chapters added in 1923 (hereafter F.u.G. II), 524. The manual gives the regulation speeds for the tanks as follows: on roads and favorable terrain, 8–12 kilometers per hour (kph); in difficult terrain, 1–6 kph; at night, 1–2 kph. Regulation range was 15 to 20 kilometers at the most. The reference to five-tank platoons is found in *F.u.G.* II, 525.

79. *F.u.G.* II, 530.

80. Ibid., 531.

81. Ibid., 534.

82. Ibid., 535.

83. Ibid., "Anhang," pp. 269–273.

84. For details of the proposed organization, see Corum, *Roots of Blitzkrieg*, pp. 44–45, and the appendix, pp. 207–210.

85. *Ausbildungsvorschrift für die Infanterie* (hereafter *A.V.I.*), vol. I, sec. 40. In shorthand notation, the citation would be *A.V.I.* I, 40. This discussion of *A.V.I.* relies heavily on that found in "Tactics of the Infantry" (see note 34), as well as that in Reinicke, *Das Reichsheer*.

86. Reinicke, *Das Reichsheer*, p. 101.

87. *Tactics of the Infantry,* USMI, XI 281–282; Reinicke, *Das Reichsheer*, p. 101.

88. Reinicke, *Das Reichsheer*, p. 102.

89. "Tactics of the Infantry," USMI, XI, 283–284; Reinicke, *Das Reichsheer*, pp. 102–103.

90. Reinicke, *Das Reichsheer*, p. 103.

91. "It is the business of the commander and the troop unit to utilize every favorable element in the circumstances. This flexibility is clearly emphasized everywhere [in the *A.V.I.*]." *Tactics of the Infantry,* USMI, XI, 290. See also Reinicke, *Das Reichsheer*, p. 103.

92. *A.V.I.* II, 145, "Sharpshooting with the Telescopic Sight." Reinicke, Das Reichsheer, p. 103.

93. *A.V.I.* I, 80.

94. Reinicke, *Das Reichsheer*, p. 104.

95. *Tactics of the Infantry,* USMI, XI, 295–296; Reinicke, *Das Reichsheer*, p. 104.

96. *A.V.I.* IV, 8, 225; Reinicke, *Das Reichsheer*, p. 105; "Tactics of the Infantry," USMI, XI, 300–301.

97. *A.V.I.* II, 139.

98. See Reinicke, *Das Reichsheer*, pp. 105–106. For directives on flanking fire, see *Tactics of the Infantry,* USMI, XI, 309–310.

99. Reinicke, *Das Reichsheer*, p. 106.

100. *Ausbildung der Schützengruppe*, translated as *The Training of the Rifle Squad*, USMI, XIII, 625–655. The quote is from section 1 (in shorthand, *A.d.S.,* 1).

101. *A.d.S.,* 2.

102. Ibid., 32–34. The column is discussed in section 32, the file in 33, the chain in 34.

103. Ibid., 54.

104. Ibid., 55.

105. Ibid., 56.

106. Ibid., 57.

107. Ibid., 58.

108. Ibid., 59.

109. Ibid., 66.

110. Ibid., 67.

111. Ibid.

112. Ibid., 72.

113. Ibid., 77.

114. *Einzelausbildung am L.M.G.: Ausbildung der L.M.G. Gruppe* (hererafter *A.L.M.G.*), translated as *Individual Training with the Light Machine Gun: The Training of the L.M.G. Section*, USMI, XIII, 656–683. The quote is from *A.L.M.G.*, 1.

115. *A.L.M.G.,* 33.

116. Ibid., 35.

117. Ibid., 38.

118. Ibid., 45.

119. Ibid., 46.

120. See, to give but one example, the analysis of contemporary French military doctrine in Corum, *Roots of Blitzkrieg*, pp. 48–49.

121. J. F. C. Fuller, *Memoirs of an Unconventional Soldier* (London: Ivor Nicholson and Watson, 1936), p. 363. In the same place, Fuller described his cavalry

foes as "this equine Tammany Hall, which would far rather have lost the war than have seen cavalry replaced by tanks."

122. Seeckt's own words confirm the point: "Heute wollen wir nur so lange den Blick rückwärts wenden, um aus glorreicher Vergangenheit die Kraft zu neuem Tun zu schöpfen. Das Unglück der letzten Zeit soll uns in gleicher Weise eine Quelle neuer Arbeitsfreudigkeit sein." See Seeckt Papers, M132, 21, 119.

CHAPTER 3

Seeckt: Doctrine and Reception

General von Seeckt never led the *Reichswehr* into battle, of course. He would never add another chapter to the impressive battlefield reputation he had acquired during the war. His service in the interwar period was different, the work comprising a number of separate facets. He was the tireless organizer who worked to maintain a disguised German General Staff (*Truppenamt*) in defiance of the terms of the Treaty of Versailles; he was the great military diplomat whose secret arrangements with Soviet Russia allowed the construction of a tank school at Kazan and a flying school at Lipetsk; he was the wise guarantor of the Prussian-German military heritage who preserved the traditions of the old army by having each company and battalion assume the heritage and traditions of a former imperial regiment.[1] But in fact, all of these pale in significance when compared with his principal role in the period as a formulator of doctrine.

The doctrine was not anything wholly new. It combined older Moltkean traditions like the *Schwerpunkt* and *Auftragstaktik* with the new tactical system of infantry assault (*Stosstrupp* tactics) that had evolved during World War I. It was not *Blitzkrieg* (that term would arise later); Seeckt's own term for it was *Bewegungskrieg,* the war of movement, a tactical system combining high maneuverability with the intimate cooperation among all arms.

We have already discussed the new manuals that Seeckt prepared in the early years of his tenure as army chief. They do describe his doctrine, but they also have the disadvantage of being frozen in time—1921, to be precise. We may derive further insight into Seeckt's views from examining the annual reports he issued during his tenure as head of the army. Entitled *Observations of the Chief of the Army Command (Bemerkungen des Chefs der Heeresleitung),* they draw a portrait of the *Reichswehr* that is at once broad and deep, and they deal with virtually every imaginable category from troop training to maneuvers to the use of the various arms, both individually and in combination. Not only do they make for fascinating

43

reading on their own, they move well beyond the theoretical realm of the manuals to respond to the real-life achievements and problems faced by the *Reichswehr*.[2]

Observations of the Chief of the Army Command
Based on His Inspections in 1921

The *Observations* for 1921 are a good example of the comprehensive character of Seeckt's concerns. They include general sections on education and training (including maneuvers and other battle exercises); separate sections on the infantry, cavalry, artillery, pioneers, motor and wagon transport corps, and signal corps; and, as a supplement, an appendix consisting of comments by the inspector of each of the various arms.[3] This is, therefore, as complete a portrait of the early *Reichswehr* as we can possibly find.

After Seeckt had begun by expressing his "satisfaction with the results obtained by officers and men during the year 1921,"[4] he also made three suggestions based on his observation of troop maneuvers:

1. Germany required a more effective program of physical education. Long summer maneuvers had taxed many of the men to the limits of their physical endurance. And although "heavy exertions and occasional privations" were unavoidable, "systematic physical training" would raise the troops "to a more efficient level and keep them there." He recommended in particular that the troops receive more bayonet training and opportunities for sport, not as an end in itself, but to create a fitter soldier.

2. He was pleased with the "great eagerness and enthusiastic interest with which all troop organizations—particularly the younger men—took part in the training," but he exhorted his men to preserve "this fresh mentality." Commanders had to nurture enthusiasm and "interest their men in discussing their ideas prior, during, and after the exercises, to awaken their imagination and cause them to draw their own conclusions and act independently."[5] Machine-like behavior was undesirable, and ultimately unacceptable.

3. Combined arms training was the great imperative. He regretted what he called a certain "weapons particularism" among some instructors that had to be overcome. He ordered mounted troops to be attached to dismounted units the latter to receive training in riding and armored cars. Artillery instructors should be attached to the infantry during their training in indirect firing. Overall, "the various branches of the service must become acquainted with each other."[6] Physical fitness, youthful enthusiasm, skill at combined arms warfare were the three demands that Seeckt placed above all others.

In general, Seeckt felt that maneuvers had been too long and too complicated.[7] Battalions, companies, and smaller units did not need detailed written orders in a maneuver. A short, oral description was all that was required. Every order should be repeated in a few words by its recipient. In small-unit maneuvers maps should be used only when absolutely necessary, but conversely, exercises by larger units (division on up) should confine themselves to maps. Often divisional maneuvers resulted in only a very small part of the troops actually seeing action, so it was easy in such situations for the interest of the troops to wane. Thus "the higher leaders are more expeditiously taught by maps."[8] Divisional maneuvers could still be profitable, though, as long as all the troops saw action.

He also noted that the postmaneuver discussion (*Schlussbesprechung*) tended to go on too long. Short discussions were effective, long ones merely dull: there was no need to go into every detail of the exercise; a simple emphasis on the main points was enough, and speakers should make a special effort to avoid repetition. Very often, a twenty-minute talk should suffice for a three-day exercise. As we will see, this advice was a hallmark of the maneuvers during Seeckt's tenure.[9]

Maneuvers had to stress two things. First was the teaching of combined arms. Infantry must practice as part of all-arms detachments, so that it could come to understand "the indisputable time requirement of the other arms, especially the artillery." Second, both men and leaders had to know how to engage the enemy on their own in a meeting engagement, if necessary. They had to be ready to take advantage of special opportunities, seize the tactical advantage that offered itself and not let, attacks become schematic. "Mental elasticity" was to be the imperative goal of men and officers, which was all the more necessary given the war of movement he had in mind for the future.[10] For example, he pointed out how important it was that troops avoid deploying on hilltops: the "massing of troops on hills" disregarded the actual lessons of the war, and the army had to learn "to keep away from the tops of hills and not locate the observation posts and arms thereon."[11] Machine guns in echelon along the hillside could flank those heights and sweep the dead zone more efficiently than could units on the hilltop itself.

He was also emphatic in repeating his advice, found in the introduction to *F.u.G.*, that at least one side in each maneuver be equipped with modern weapons. Tanks, aircraft, and heavy weapons had all been present, at least symbolically, in the 1921 maneuvers, and Seeckt ordered that to continue. Tanks had some success in simulated attacks, at least in favorable weather, but air defense had left a great deal to be desired. Sirens and flashing lights (the two basic methods used to simulate the approach of enemy aircraft in these maneuvers) were not completely satisfactory, but further experiments were underway.[12] In the meantime, troops formed in columns had to immediately scatter into small bodies when threatened from the air.

In Seeckt's war of maneuver the reserve took on added, in fact crucial, importance. Seeckt called attention to "the principle of utilizing but a small portion of the forces in the front lines and retaining the major forces in the rear reserve." An attack could in some circumstances consist of scout patrols and a few light machine guns. The machine guns (both light and heavy) were the backbone of a unit's firepower. Manpower (in the form of the body of riflemen) was to be saved for the attack (or counterattack). Likewise, it was preferable to hold artillery batteries in reserve until a suitable opportunity arose, rather than having them all deployed and firing at once. A change in the battle situation—and maneuver warfare would experience this constantly—invariably forced some batteries to change position. This changing wasted time, particularly when it also involved advanced observation posts, camouflaged firing positions, signal installations, and gun carriages located far to the rear. It was much more reasonable to have reserve batteries ready to go into position, especially if the commander had already reconnoitered the new position. Artillery had to be ready, at any time, to protect friendly infantry as it advanced. In maneuver warfare this did not necessarily mean a great number of guns firing constantly, as it had in the position warfare on the Western Front; rather, it required rapid concentration of all available guns on the principal targets. Artillery had to cooperate with the small infantry unit. Wartime experience had shown how useless "corps artillery" was; there was no discussion of it in either *F.u.G.* or in the *Observations*.[13]

Seeckt also directed specific comments to each of the various branches of the service.

Infantry

Seeckt conceived of the infantry almost completely in terms of combined arms. No longer were infantrymen merely rifle bearers, they now required in-depth training in use of the light machine gun. On the battlefield, all infantry (as well as machine gun and heavy mortar crews) were to fire at the deep zones of the enemy position. This would be "our daily bread," Seeckt wrote.[14] All infantrymen had to become proficient with the hand grenade, even if they only practiced with dummy models. Likewise, no infantry exercise should proceed without the men digging in: "The spade saves nerves and blood," he wrote, but unfortunately he rarely saw them used during maneuvers.[15]

The supporting arms were crucial to the infantry's success. For instance, there could be no fixed rules for the use of the heavy machine gun. The machine gun company commander was responsible for his own observation and reconnaissance and for making recommendations to the battalion commander about the proper use of the heavy machine guns. There was nothing to stop heavy machine guns from being employed outside their own battle sector, and often this was the only way to achieve the necessary flanking firing within the sector.[16] Trench mortars were not just intended for fire at targets that artillery or machine guns could not hit; in the event of the artillery's absence the mortars were to replace the heavier guns. The commander of the trench mortar company had to be close enough to the front line to make suggestions for the insertion of the weapons. He had to take great care in locating his mortars and never simply divide them mechanically among the battalions, which would lead to their absence from where they were most needed (i.e., where the fighting was most serious). In view of the small amount of ammunition that could accompany the mortars, they were to fire only at important targets and concentrate on those targets that the heavy machine gun could not reach. Indirect fire was their specialty, making it hard for the enemy to locate the trench mortars' position, let alone target them for return fire.[17]

Cavalry

All squadrons had to acquire a greater efficiency and discipline, keeping in mind the axiom of "at the enemy as far as possible on horse."[18] This required dispersal of squadrons into individual horsemen, protected by camouflaged machine guns or artillery. Seeckt felt that, in many cases, the troops did not advance far enough on horseback and therefore failed to use their speed to strike at the enemy's weakest spot. Speed, after all, was their major advantage. Besides actual combat, the cavalry needed to devote special training to marching, protective measures, and reconnaissance, as well as the postbattle resumption of mounted movement, pursuit, and retreat.

Artillery[19]

The war of movement presented special problems here. Batteries had to be ready for surprise and for immediate fire if the enemy carelessly exposed it. They should never consist of guns lined up hub to hub; wartime experience had shown the need for large, irregular intervals. This was all the more important in the age of aerial observation and gas attack. Exercising with these larger intervals was necessary, since the new formations put great responsibility on the shoulders of the commander. Not only were the mathematical problems more difficult (in fact, we can say that they would require a computer to solve adequately), but it was much more difficult to pass verbal commands along the battery. The rule was that the battery leader must always be able to maintain complete fire control. Motorizing the batteries (mounting the guns on truck chassis) was also a method of limiting danger to the gun. But completely exposed as they were, they could not move within an enemy's line of sight for more than a few seconds. After getting off several rounds, it was absolutely essential for a gun to switch position; it could then reappear suddenly to fire again from an unexpected position. Motorized batteries also required liaison with the artillery commander. The use of one motorcycle for each motorized battery (standard in both the German and Allied armies) was completely insufficient for the task.

The *Observations* do not merely encompass the traditional arms. The signal service received its own section, a mark of its increasing importance in the new war of movement. So too did the pioneers, whose work at road improvement and bridging would be crucial in overcoming obstacles and bottlenecks. Finally, both wagon and motor transport received thorough treatment, further evidence of Seeckt's Janus-like gaze at both the past and the future.

In summation, the *Observations* for 1921 enshrined Seeckt's view of war: a mobile and hard-hitting affair carried out by combined-arms teams of tough, well-conditioned soldiers. Like so many cultural achievements of the early Weimar Republic, a spirit of youth permeated this new doctrine. Here, we leave behind the purely military sphere. It is yet another example of the "revolt of the sons against the fathers," which cultural historian Peter Gay held to be typical of the early years of the Weimar era.[20] Rejecting as it did the *Stellungskrieg* of the immediate past, Seeckt's war of movement was a doctrine for the new generation. For a man with such strong ties to tradition, his sensitivity toward the young is one of the most appealing sides to his character, even though it was more than a simple predilection on Seeckt's part. He knew that the brutal pace of maneuver warfare placed enormous burdens on the men and their equipment and demanded youthful spirit and strength.

Observations of the Chief of the Army Command Based on His Inspections in 1922

The *Observations* for 1922 addressed many of the same questions. Seeckt was pleased with the obvious attempt by the officers and men to study the new training regulations and to make them their own. The "theoretical and practical occupation with the new regulations" would be one of the major aims of 1923. Each arm had had to learn not only its own trade but the "principles and methods of combat" of the other arms as well. Even though Seeckt expressed his "full satisfaction" with the achievements of the troops, who were well conditioned and met all the demands placed on them, the officers had to continue to spur on the men in a spirit of cooperation.[21] Rote drill simply would not do for an army of twelve-year volunteers.

Although maneuvers had been quite satisfactory, Seeckt warned against "the beginning of a new formalism." Using "blue" and "red" as the opposing sides, too many manuevers had dealt with stylized, unrealistic situations, such as "Blue shall attack the enemy flank and Red shall seek to prevent this." It was difficult to analyze such an action in a vacuum, independently of the main forces, he cautioned (a bit, one might interject, like gaming the action at the Little Round Top without reference to the larger battle of Gettysburg). To Seeckt, it was "a fortunate accident which seldom arises if a division, after the main action has opened, hastens up from a favorable direction of march to bring about a decision through a flank attack." Despite all the theories that could be devised, "the enveloping movement can only begin after the meeting with the enemy has permitted a front to be formed." Flanking forces had to come out of the reserve units marching to the front. One did not simply draw them from some distant spot into a favorable position aimed at the enemy flank. Likewise, the defender could not simply throw a unit out at an angle to the battle line to prevent envelopment, but should seek security by echeloning its forces deeply on the exposed flank. Seeckt gave examples of more sensible maneuver problems involving envelopment from a stable battle line. For example,

> A Red regiment stands as a divisional reserve behind an exposed right flank. The two other regiments stand in frontal combat. The divisional commander believes that he is able to discern a lengthening of the hostile left flank and consequently a threatened envelopment. He gives the regiment the order to lengthen its own front and by echeloning, prevent envelopment. An artillery battalion is subordinate to it.[22]

The war of movement required more problems in meeting engagements and withdrawals. For the former, a skirmish between two advance guards was a useful exercise: limited to a battalion on each side (supported by one or two guns), this would be a suitable exercise for a regimental commander. For the latter, Seeckt gave another example: a battalion in retreat withdraws with several guns on a broad front. The enemy pursues at a distance. The battalion then encounters hostile cavalry (indicated by flags) that blocks further retreat. The battalion must break through the cavalry quickly or risk encirclement by the pursuing infantry.[23]

Above all, Seeckt worried about "becoming superficial and deceiving ourselves" in these maneuvers. His suggestions were not necessarily models to be followed slavishly, but they did require quick decisions on the part of the commanders and rapid movement by the men. Maneuvers were a difficult and serious business, he felt. Above all else, they must teach responsibility, which was the only way to make soldiers into thinking warriors.[24]

Exercises should neglect no aspect of modern battle. *F.u.G.* had dropped the old distinction between "combat" and "field" services; both were "joint expressions of the same act of war." The change from camp security to combat conditions, for example, would make an excellent exercise. So too would exercises for combat runners (messengers), conducted in dusk or nighttime conditions.[25]

Maneuver warfare placed special demands on the commanders. Seeckt exhorted them to ride forward and carry out their own reconnaissance during maneuvers, "as far forward as hostile fire permits." There was still entirely too much reference to maps in giving orders, he noted, and not enough attention to the terrain. For examples, orders for the artillery were reminiscent of those from World War I, far too long and detailed. Short, clear-cut instructions based on terrain one had reconnoitered personally were to Seeckt's liking.[26]

The commander's chief duty in every attack was to identify the *Schwerpunkt,* which did not need to be mentioned in the orders, since it depended not only on the intentions of his own side but on other such factors as terrain and the attitude of the enemy. The commander had to judge both of these latter factors, and on that basis decide on a *Schwerpunkt.* But this did not end the matter. He now had to create the *Schwerpunkt* by progressively narrowing the sector of attack by more numerous allotment of heavy weapons and orders to the artillery.[27]

A crucial factor here was the liaison between infantry and artillery. Seeckt observed that this, unfortunately, was too often lacking during the exercises of the past year. The infantry had the responsibility—even at the level of the smallest unit—of informing not only the artillery assigned to it, but all artillery that could be reached by any means whatsoever, of the infantry's own needs. The artillery, too, had to maintain contact with any nearby infantry. "Success," Seeckt wrote, "can only be expected if both parties strive for the same object." The previous year's comments regarding the necessity of keeping batteries in reserve had led to withholding batteries in many situations calling for artillery support from the beginning. This was a grave error. "Erroneous withholding of artillery costs the infantry blood."[28] And while on the subject of blood, Seeckt reasserted what he had said in the previous year's remarks (no. 61) on the necessity of digging in, whether on the attack or the defense. The spade saved lives, yet still he had not seen enough of its use in 1922.[29]

Observations of the Chief of the Army Command
Based on His Inspections in 1923

The *Observations* for 1923 bore signs of that terrible year in the life of the Weimar Republic.[30] As Seeckt put it in a classic understatement, "Internal and foreign political events have interrupted the routine training of the troops." In fact, significant elements of the *Reichswehr* in Bavaria—including the 7th Infantry Division's Officer Training School—had supported the Hitler *Putsch* and thus had technically been in a state of mutiny. "Greater effort," he wrote, "must be made than heretofore in the training of the young and non-commissioned officers."[31]

But the *Observations* for 1923 spent far more time discussing maneuvers than politics. The variety of maneuver problems had been greater than in 1922, but too many of them were based on a situation of trench warfare: Seeckt had heard too many arguments for trench warfare in appropriate situations. The *Reichswehr* had to keep in mind its ultimate goal: training for the war of movement.

He noted that there was still a tendency, however, toward stereotypical combat situations. There was no need to issue printed orders for small-unit maneuvers; verbal orders were preferable. There was no need to use the map for minor tactical problems; orders should derive from the terrain. Consideration of superior officers should not influence the arrangement of a problem, this having been the bane of German army maneuvers in the past, with the Kaiser's side always winning.[32] No one should have premature knowledge of the problem. And, reiterating his orders from the previous two years, he wanted to see modern weapons like tanks and aircraft represented more often, based on the view he had expressed in the introduction to *F.u.G.*[33]

Seeckt drew special attention to the problem of command. Orders were still too formalistic and unrealistic: they often he said seemed to be the product of a "war council" between the commander and his officers.[34] Many commanders, therefore, seemed not be taking the exercises seriously. Seeckt demanded adherence to actual war conditions: orders should be "clear, positive, and simple"; there was no need for "long-winded discussions"; and there was certainly no need for what he called "prolix written combat orders," which he had seen issued even in urgent situations. There was no place in the *Bewegungskrieg* for typewriters or mimeograph machines, which were accouterments of trench warfare. Finally, the *Schlussbesprechung* was still too long, with too many speakers, too much detail. As in the case of orders, the final critique should be short and to the point.[35]

Weapons forbidden by the Versailles Treaty were still high on the agenda. There was a special section on protection against aerial observation.[36] There remained much to do in this area; a number of "foolish ideas" had to be stamped out. Although no one must use the presence of enemy aircraft as an excuse for failing to achieve the tactical objective, protection against reconnaissance from the air was a necessity on the modern battlefield. It did not matter, for instance, whether a battery in firing position camouflaged itself nicely if it had already been spotted from the air while going into position. Individual guns (and wagons for the battery) had to cross open terrain at different times and points. The entire process of camouflage also required attention to the surface vegetation of the area—poor camouflage was an easily visible target from the air. The best camouflage, he wrote, involved taking advantage of natural cover, taking position under trees, among shrubs, grain stacks, or groups of houses.

Seeckt also recommended more frequent use of the gas mask in maneuvers.[37] The men needed to get used to the discomfort of wearing it while still serving their weapons efficiently. It was understood, all the same, that a long stretch of time in the mask degraded the efficiency of any soldier or crew; the longer the time, the greater the chance the commander might have to allow some guns or trench mortars to drop temporarily out of the fight.

With regard to the individual arms, Seeckt saw good progress being made.

Infantry

He was pleased with the development of light combat formations and had only spotted unnecessary massing on several occasions. Infantry seemed to be striving for intimate cooperation with the light and heavy machine guns. Still, knowledge of the new regulations (especially *F.u.G.*) often seemed lacking. There were still too many fundamental mistakes in types of combat, such as the "delaying defense," which were thoroughly covered in *F.u.G* or *A.V.I.* In terms of fire defense, there was still much work to be done, especially in fire protection for advancing infantry. Very often infantry left cover too hastily, without adequate fire support, and often without even light machine gun fire. Such infantry would be "cut to pieces" in real combat. But Seeckt expected the army to pay greater attention to this problem in the coming year. He did see progress being made in the use of terrain and in the employment of more appropriate battle formations: "Nearly everywhere one saw the thin lines made necessary by hostile fire." But in some cases this went too far: "Individual riflemen advanced to the assault." Even in a war of movement, "a certain attacking power was required to execute the assault and take advantage of its success."[38]

Seeckt was happy to see that the concept of reliance on the machine guns had become "the common property of the army." But here too there had been excesses. In trying "to oppose only machine gun fire to the enemy and to conduct the attack in as thin formations as possible," companies sometimes carried out attacks with only a few light machine guns deployed well forward. Umpires had to make troops aware that such behavior was a mistake, by imposing losses, machine gun jams, and depleted ammunition. Riflemen had to be reminded that they had the right to open fire on their own.[39]

Cavalry

Seeckt welcomed the increase in the "offensive spirit" of the horse arm, a subject to which he would return again and again in the 1920s. But the horses were often in poor condition, and Seeckt advised "sparing" them during the maneuvers. There were other areas of concern: close reconnaissance had failed several times; the cavalry had not echeloned its attacks in sufficient depth; and mounted firing, both carbine and pistol, left much to be desired.[40] Although a certain dissatisfaction is evident here, it is equally clear that Seeckt still saw cavalry as an important component of a modern army.

Artillery

Once again, the weight of Seeckt's comments had to do with cooperation with the infantry. Artillery support for the infantry had to be strong and continuous. Unsupported infantry must never be exposed to hostile fire. Inasmuch as the *Reichswehr's* complement of artillery was so small, close cooperation with the infantry required frequent changes of position by the batteries, in fact often by individual sections. This always had to be done by echelon (i.e., some guns firing while others moved). Especially in the retreat, it was wrong to limber up the whole battalion at once and leave the infantry without assistance until the guns reached the next firing position.[41]

Observations of the Chief of the Army Command
Based on His Inspections in 1924

The *Observations* for 1924 contain appreciation at the progress the army had made, along with disappointment at continuing mistakes.[42] Individual training had improved to a great degree, as had instruction at the importance of combined arms. Now it was the task of the coming year to train "the leaders of all grades, as well as the specialists." But Seeckt also offered a warning: every kind of military training was ultimately in vain if the improvement of the morale of the troops did not keep pace with it. The "fundamental principle" of every army was its morale, its character. In its search for technical proficiency, the *Reichswehr* must not fail to take note of the "various dangers and temptations that surround us."[43]

As always, he began with the maneuvers. The preceding year's suggestions about the design and planning of the exercises had borne good fruit. The problems seemed more ingenious and instructive, and the situations confronted a leader with a choice among several decisions. This not only secured the leader's interest, but enlivened the maneuver for all the participants. The maneuver director had to take care not to go too far, however, because a dizzying succession of changing problems would eventually reach the point of no instructional value. Seeckt also warned against deploying one battalion as the enemy in regimental exercises. Not only did this mean that the regimental commander saw one battalion fewer on this day, but it also prevented him from showing his leadership of all the battalions "in their proper regimental relationship."[44]

Maneuvers on the divisional level had been perfectly satisfactory in terms of organization and conduct. Indeed, the *Observations* singled out one unnamed division (probably the 1st Infantry Division, stationed in East Prussia and often regarded as the "elite" unit in the *Reichswehr*) as a model: "Without any protracted preparations, . . . the parties soon gained contact. An engagement developed, interesting to its very close, that required no forcible intervention" by the umpires. All the troops in this maneuver actually became engaged in the combat, "were fresh and interested in the cause, and learned much accordingly."

Reichswehr maneuvers were supposed to be short and crisp, and prolonging was to be avoided—particularly in bad weather, when a long maneuver hurt more than it helped. Weary troops did not learn anything. If maneuvers were to stretch out over several days, commanders should arrange for a break. Once again, Seeckt returned to the subject of orders. Feeling that perhaps he had not expressed himself clearly in the past year's *Remarks,* he now went more deeply into the topic. There were, he wrote, two kinds of orders: the informal, verbal order to subordinate leaders, and the formal command. If there was time, a commander should call a personal conference with his officers. And the result of such a gathering had to be a definite order, not "I'll leave it to your judgment." Such a phrase "does not exist in the language of command." The more urgent the situation, "the sharper and more concise the order should be."[45]

Another area in which there was obvious room for improvement was that of surprise. In the only italicized sentence in six years of *Observations,* he wrote that "the troops must guard themselves against surprise in every situation."[46] When they were halted temporarily or resting within contact distance of the enemy, they had to be careful that an enemy attack would not find them unready—grouped in an unfavorable manner, for example. On one maneuver, this very point imposed considerable losses on a force taking a break. Likewise, for instance, in foggy weather, troops had to be ready so that they would not be caught unaware if the fog suddenly lifted.

Again, there was discussion of modern weapons. The hated gas mask had remained almost completely unused, despite Seeckt's recommendation from the previous year. The problem of protection from aerial attack still required a solution, and he had once again to remind the *Reichswehr* that "in all maneuvers the presence of hostile airplanes must be taken for granted on principle. . . . This is valid not only in combat but also in marching and bivouacking."[47]

His last word on maneuvers was directed at the umpires. He was still unhappy that they were not following their regulations. In particular, they had no right "to interfere in the tactical dispositions or decisions of commanders." He warned insistently against the umpires' giving "binding instructions" to the commanders that determined how the combat exercise was to proceed. For example, on one occasion in the past year, an umpire had decided not to allow an attacking party to go beyond a certain sector because of the combat planned for the next day:

> However the commander drove the attack forward. The umpires then resorted to desperate means: the assumption that a strip of woods known and ascertained to be unoccupied was strongly occupied; the assumption of overpowering hostile machine gun fire, of which nothing was to be heard; and the assumption of a scarcity of ammunition for the troops, which had not yet fired a single shot that day. The troops do not understand such assumptions, and resent them.[48]

The *Observations* section on the infantry highlighted the relationship of fire and movement. Fire protection for troops in the approach march was still often lacking. In particular, the advance guard often lacked the heavy machine guns that would have enabled them to crush any resistance they encountered. Support fire from machine guns on heights in the rear was common, but the troops seemed to be taking less care to push the machine guns forward in echelon. All too frequently machine gun company commanders received only general instructions to see to "the fire protection of the battalion in its advance." But it was the responsibility of the battalion commanders to coordinate the movement of the infantry companies and the machine gun platoons covering them (e.g., through overhead fire, firing through gaps, cross-firing). After consulting with the machine gun commander, the battalion commander had to give "definite combat instruction" to the heavy arms.

In the attack support fire not only protected the advancing troops, it was responsible for keeping the defenders pinned down. Fire and movement always had to be closely combined. Seeckt, though, was distressed to see attacks proceeding at a very halting pace, alternating fire and advance, or even with "single skirmishers working their way forward without any assured fire protection." Seeckt blamed it first of all on "the fact that younger troops had no wartime experience to teach them better." The solution was the careful training of all commanders, especially junior officers, who had to learn, above all, that "fire is not incidental to the attack, not something by itself."[49] Support fire existed only to help one's own forces overcome their moment of weakness, that is, while on the move.

The discussion of cavalry offered a mixed picture. It was becoming increasingly obvious that despite his attachment to the arm, its use on the maneuver field was becoming confused. Alhough cavalry exhibited a new determination to remain in the saddle as long as possible to derive all possible benefit from its mobility, Seeckt had to warn that "the [mounted] cavalry attack . . . must not fall into oblivion." Dismounted attacks were also too weak owing to the great dispersion with which cavalry had to approach the battlefield. Seeckt believed that the future of the arm lay in cooperation with motorized units, and thus frequent exercises with armored cars took place. But alongside this modern view there was a touch of the romantic in Seeckt's assessment of the horse arm:

> Our cavalry troopers must learn even more than heretofore, on field ser-
> vice to carry themselves as hunters, for instance, cautiously adapting
> themselves to the terrain, leaving the cover only after the surroundings
> have been carefully inspected; closely observing everything possible
> from the rising dust and smoke and hoof tracks; misleading the enemy in
> every way by tricking him and leading him wherever possible into a
> trap.[50]

But in fact—and by now a number of his own officers recognized this fact—this was no more possible in 1924 than it had been in 1914 (or 1870, for that matter). As Seeckt himself admitted, German cavalry was now an arm consisting of understrength units riding overage mounts. Even though its existence was mandated by the Treaty of Versailles, the cavalry did not deserve the time or attention lavished on it in *Reichswehr* exercises. The cavalry's world view was simply not suited to modern warfare. It seems the height of military folly when the supreme army commander must waste space in his yearly instructions to the troops to warn the cavalry against the practice of collecting horses of the same color in individual squadrons or to discuss how to grip the saber to achieve its correct position when drawn (for the record, with the ball of the thumb resting on the upper thigh).[51]

Neither was the artillery performing particularly well. Batteries were often not quick enough for the war of movement, and were lax in opening fire in acute situations. Opening fire did not require lengthy preparations and long telephone conversations, or using directional circles to lay the guns; rather, the most important thing was for artillery to fire quickly, to show friendly infantry that it was there. Too often battery commanders wasted time seeking precise information that they could gather later (e.g., inquiry about the shortest ranges, possibility of lateral oscillation, flanking fire, presence of friendly machine guns) The "most important and indis-pensable thing," was shortening the time required to open fire. "We still have much to learn in this matter," he concluded.[52]

Observations of the Chief of the Army Command
Based on His Inspections in 1925

The 1925 *Observations* were the last Seeckt would issue. After Seeckt re-signed in 1926, however, his successor Gen. Wilhelm Heye would release a large—in fact, downright unwieldy—compilation of all the *Observations* from 1920 to 1925. They were necessarily general and thus nearly useless.[53]

Seeckt felt obliged to begin the 1925 *Observations* by once again criticizing the predilection of units, both large and small, to carry out their maneuvers stereotypically. He issued a general warning against this error and urged a "thorough study of the spirit and nature of tactical operations" as a remedy. Still, despite a great deal of bad weather, the men were generally "fresh and full of zeal." The situations were well interpreted and forced officers and men to act independently.

These *Observations* showed a greater tendency toward higher ideas and concepts instead of the minutiae of tactical detail. To Seeckt, the maneuvers proved that the *Reichswehr* was beginning to free itself "from the chains of positional warfare under which it is still laboring." Mobility, he said, was the "prime requirement of our army." Training had to conform to this requirement. And there followed what was for Seeckt an unusually interesting rumination:

> We shall proceed calmly and steadily along the path we have trodden. Basic changes are not necessary. The principal thing now is to increase the responsibilities of the individual man, particularly his independence of action, and thereby to increase the efficiency of the entire army. . . . The limitations imposed by exterior circumstances cause us to give the mind more freedom of activity, with the profitable result of increasing the ability of the individual.

By now, the litany was familiar. For the best training results the maneuver problems had to remain simple, and once again simplicity had not always been present. The "whys, wheres, and wherefores" only had a place in the maneuver problem insofar as they were of decisive importance to the combat leadership. Anything beyond this was "not only superfluous, but detrimental." Every participant in an exercise—down to "the last train driver and horse orderly"—should be able to follow the exercise carefully, which was impossible if the problem required long study to be grasped. The purpose of a field exercise was not, after all, to solve tactical problems. You did not need troops for those, just a table, chair, map, and compass. The purpose was to train the troops and to practice leadership on the battlefield, to transform the will of the leader into action by the troops. Anything else "diverts us from the proper road." Commanders should closely examine their maneuver problems beforehand to see what could be left out as unnecessary. They should not answer the large number of questions subordinate officers were sure to ask. As a rule, answering them in detail only caused confusion. The commander should simply reply "That does not concern you" or "You would not know that in war, either."

There were two types of maneuvers, Seeckt wrote, and each was of value. One put the commanders and the troops out in the field and left them to find a solution on their own, influenced by the terrain and the enemy. The other linked the troops to a hazy and indefinite main force, perhaps as a flank guard, and thus forced them to follow orders from a higher authority. In either case, the best sort of maneuver dealt with an order that handed the unit a mission (*Auftrag*), then left the means of fulfilling it up to the unit itself. It was also advisable that after drawing up an order, the commander ask himself whether he had ever seen a similar situation during the war. Such an exercise would "perhaps restrain him from suppositions which are too fantastic."[54]

Again Seeckt discussed support weapons, in this case tanks. Tanks were represented in insufficient numbers, he complained, while insisting that "use be made of the adopted models at all the larger exercises." Officers must study the question of tanks from the theoretical standpoint. Starting off with sandbox wargames, "the employment and combat of tanks must become a matter of common knowledge throughout the army."[55]

The 1925 *Observations* included a number of recommendations to officers. There was no need to be too far out in front of the troops. In fact, the command post was better located to the rear where reports from all sectors could easily be assembled. But the commander should ride out from his command post to reconnoiter the ground in front: "No report, no matter how good it is, can replace personal observation." The leader should neither lurk to the rear, nor involve himself in impetuous charges. "Steadiness and thoroughness" should be his hallmarks. The commander should never include the phrase *Eile geboten* ("haste is imperative") in an order; he should expect all his orders to be carried out with rapidity. He should not issue so many orders based on maps; maps were never there in an emergency. For small unit maneuvers, errors were more likely in a map-based order than one based on the terrain. Above all, the commander should keep in mind the necessity of having a battle *Schwerpunkt*. This could come about through means discussed in previous *Observations* (narrowing the combat sector, concentration of fire, employment of the reserves). Only these—not rigid orders—could give the battle its distinctive character.[56]

In the section dealing with individual arms, Seeckt was pleased that the previous year's comments on fire protection had had their effect. He noted "unwarlike methods of attack" (i.e., without proper fire support) occurring much more seldom.[57] Nonetheless, the combination of infantry and light machine guns required more thorough attention; the interrelationship of fire and assault (as well as their inherent differences) was not always brought out. For example, riflemen did not always open fire promptly when the light machine gun jammed (as it inevitably would). The rule was that the light machine gun did not break through the enemy lines, but its fire fixes the enemy during the advance of the riflemen.

Seeckt also noted the tendency to form *Kampfgruppen*, consolidating infantry, light machine guns, and heavy weapons into one. Although he approved of such "independent action," he did not want to see it become stereotypical. *Kampfgruppen* should only be formed if a "certain tactical purpose" called for it (e.g., against a newly identified point of resistance). The principal organization for combat was the infantry platoon, consisting of rifle squads and light machine guns under the command of the platoon commander.

He also warned against breaking off the exercises after the attack had penetrated enemy lines: troops gained a false impression of actual combat, which involved extending the attack into the depth of the enemy's defensive zone. World War I had taught that the most vulnerable moment for assaulting infantry was just after it had broken through the enemy line, and exercises had to model that lesson.[58] He was disturbed once again to see no use of the gas mask. Further, there had been little improvement in air defense. The idea that friendly aircraft made air protection unnecessary was false. Passive measures (e.g., camouflage) were also indispensable.[59]

With regard to infantry support weapons, Seeckt was pleased to see that indirect fire seemed to be improving with both heavy machine guns and trench mortars, and that needed to continue. But there was neglect in other areas. Something as basic as choosing a secure fire position for the machine gun often seemed ignored. Deploying the piece on a ridge or near a conspicuous point made the maneuver easier to follow; it would be deadly in actual combat. Firing from under shelter as recommended in the regulations, certainly possible from a technical standpoint, occurred but rarely; usually this was due to the maneuver directors not allowing the machine guns sufficient time to prepare. Seeckt recommended another look at the problem.[60]

Seeckt now turned to the cavalry. "I do not demand as much from any other arm," he wrote. It not only had to know how to ride, it had to be as adept at combat as the infantry. But where was the German cavalry headed? Did it have a future? He criticized its lack of practice in mounted firing (both pistol and carbine); overly quick evolutions on the training ground; its failure to practice sufficiently with the lance (!); faulty reconnaissance and security; its habit of offering a target for enemy fire by exposing itself on ridges; its unfortunate habit of "galloping to the nearest woods" when airplanes appeared, which to Seeckt betrayed more information to the aviator than if the troop simply halted;[61] and the tendency for the mounted staff to be too large and unwieldy. But there was more. The cavalry was most effective when it struck the enemy's flank and rear. But Seeckt noted that it often failed to bring along sufficient artillery. He also noted a recent disturbing urge to fight in forest. This was a dangerous development, in that commanders had a very difficult time maintaining control over their squadrons. It was also very tough in such a situation to protect the cavalry column's very vulnerable flank. All in all, he had little positive to say, beyond a few recommendations for the delaying defense.

There was little of note in the 1925 *Observations* regarding artillery. He did warn of stereotyped developments in the use of the motorized battery: in maneuver after maneuver, commanders trundled it off to lay down fire against the enemy flank. This was not wrong in and of itself, but there was too little concern about the dangers facing the battery, primarily its extreme vulnerability and total exposure. Once again, the vast majority of his observations had to do with the employment of artillery in a war of movement (changes of position, withdrawal, liaison with the infantry).[62]

The Influence of Seeckt's Doctrine on the Reichswehr

The "Observations," as comprehensive as they are, still raise one crucial question: How carefully did the *Reichswehr* read these comments? In any army, or any hierarchically structured organization for that matter, the implementation of doctrine rests not only on the publication of new manuals by the higher leadership, but also on the "reception" accorded those manuals by the lower ranks, who have to take the new message to heart, internalize it, and reorder their own behavior according to its precepts.[63] How, we might ask, did officers and men "receive" Seeckt's new gospel of mobile warfare?

In July 1926, the U.S. military attaché in Germany, Col. A. L. Conger, sent the War Department a report dealing with this very question. As one German officer had told him, "These 'Observations' by our chief are our rule and guide for the year's work of training."[64] Every officer down to and including the rank of captain received a copy. Each company commander was responsible for making them known to and understood by the men under his command.

Conger saw convincing evidence that this was so. With regard to Seeckt's criticism of "stereotypical execution of certain forms of combat," for example, he saw an unmistakable effect. During his stay at Arys in May 1926, he had personally witnessed a number of maneuvers in which the noncommissioned officer arranged his combat groups on a certain pattern that was not suited to the terrain. Invariably, an officer ran up, studied the ground, and gave orders to reconfigure the unit. The umpires also repeatedly intervened when a set form of attack did not appear to conform to the situation. Seeckt's emphasis on the short, concise maneuver problem was being followed. Conger was "struck by the ability of every officer and NCO, upon hearing the problem read once, to repeat it verbatim to his subordinates." Seeckt's command to include more tanks was in evidence. Conger saw tanks in every maneuver he had attended, save for one nighttime exercise. Seeckt's call for wargaming of tank tactics was also having its effect. Conger described one, a typical "sandbox wargame," in which the opposing sides maneuvered its units on a realistic representation of the terrain:

The sandbox instruction referred to in this paragraph refers to wargames played by the officers and non-commissioned officers, as well as by privates, on relief maps constructed on sand tables, and that map I was shown made on one was the most carefully made and realistic wargame relief map I have ever seen The scale was approximately 20 inches to a mile. Woods, streams, roads, bridges, houses, individual trees were all shown with the most painstaking detail. Plowed fields, standing crops, and stubble fields were represented, as also different colored earths. Strings overhanging the map enabled airplanes to be suspended . . . for a discussion of air defense measures. The troops signs employed were lead blocks with various arrows to represent . . . every kind of infantry weapon and unit, light and heavy machine guns, light and medium mine throwers, infantry guns, etc.[65]

Conger also noted the effects of Seeckt's *Observations* on the choice of command posts and on the earnest attempt by each commander to discriminate between situations calling for quick action and those that required methodical preparation. Virtually all German commanders showed skill in improvising attacks, but when there was sufficient time the commander studied and planned every detail of the attack or defense, placing every weapon for maximum effect. Conger never saw a hint of "excitement or undue haste." In a situation calling for action, the commander left the choice of means up to his subordinates, trusting to their best judgment rather than dictating their behavior by strict orders.

In numerous other areas Conger saw the army following Seeckt's observations almost to the letter. He heard the word *Schwerpunkt* used frequently in discussions between German officers, though he never saw it used in a combat order. Instead of defining the *Schwerpunkt* in an order, the commander simple deployed his forces in the proper way so as to arrive at it. Seeckt's orders on the coordination of rifles and light machine guns also had had an effect. Rifle fire was now to be seen when the light machine gun had jammed or was withdrawing. He also confirmed that men and officers tried to fulfill Seeckt's demand for more realistic maneuvers. An umpire accompanied every platoon and whenever it came under hostile artillery fire, he would throw more bombs (giant firecrackers, really) and smoke canisters. The constant use of these two weapons gave the maneuver field a very realistic battle appearance.[66]

Seeckt's impact on the *Reichswehr* is also clear from German military writings of the period, in innumerable articles and books written by the German military community. In 1923, Gen. Friedrich von Taysen, wartime commander of the 94th Infantry Regiment (Grossherzog von Sachsen, 3rd Thuringian), and one of Germany's most prolific military writers in the interwar period, penned a long essay that appeared in the journal *Wissen und Wehr* and that dealt with the war of movement. It began with the fundamental change that had taken place on the wartime battlefield. Both sides had perfected certain arms (the machine gun, artillery, the airplane), and invented others (gas, smoke, tanks). Taysen saw an unhappy result: "the factor of preponderant importance in combat is no longer the man, but the machine and material," even though such mechanical devices still had to be "galvanized into life by human energy."[67]

Like Seeckt, Taysen placed emphasis on the combat role of supporting weapons—artillery, trench mortars, and machine guns—in modern combat. He was a particularly strong advocate of the heavy machine gun: "Anyone who has seen the harassing effect of concentrated fire of heavy machine guns upon infantry will come to the conclusion that no trouble is too great in placing this fearful arm in correct position."[68] It should be elevated, or if that were not possible, deployed so as to be able to fire through the gaps in one's own infantry. Given the tiny amount of artillery allowed to the *Reichswehr*, the heavy machine gun would have to take over many artillery tasks—but the basic principle of the use of the heavy machine gun was still subordination to the infantry. Taysen deplored the infantry's overreliance on machine gun fire in the previous war. Many units had become so dependent on it that the soldiers forgot completely about their own rifles: "The purpose of the heavy machine guns is to assist the infantry companies in executing the attack. In many cases the attack is out of the question without their support. Therefore it is necessary that they work in closest agreement with the infantry." The gun's support would be closest if the heavy machine gun platoon were under the orders of the infantry company (i.e., functioning as the fourth platoon of the company).[69] Taysen concluded by urging all German officers to instill the "spirit of attack" in their men. Spirited troops working in close cooperation with their auxiliary arms and "mechanical devices"—was the essence of modern, mobile combat—a concept practically indistinguishable from Seeckt's own.

Another article from 1923, this one by Maj. Paul Hausser (commander of the 3rd Jäger Battalion of the 13th Württemberg Infantry Regiment), devoted itself entirely to the role of the heavy machine gun.[70] It began with a discussion of indirect fire. Hausser recalled that prewar training and tactics for the gun had made almost no provision for unobserved fire. Machine gun companies made quickly for hills or knolls, lined up two paces apart, and began blasting away at observed targets. Of course, the guns' large armored shields made them easily visible from afar. But the demand for indirect fire became insistent once the war began, and there were many reasons for this. Enemy artillery, with its improved optical instruments, sorely pressed the machine guns when they fired. The war of position demanded suppression of targets that were invisible, but whose position was known. With the development of the light machine gun, the heavy developed more and more into a long-range weapon, and it found long-range fire impossible without its own laying devices and optical equipment. The British and French had led the way in this, with the British actually working out complicated plans for massed machine gun barrages at Passchendaele.[71]

Hausser now turned to the present. There was an urgent need for more indirect fire, which would bring the following advantages:

1. The placement of the heavy machine gun would be hidden from enemy sight.
2. Surprise, always desirable in war, would be complete when the machine gun opened fire.
3. Machine gun fire could proceed without harassment from enemy fire, thus minimizing losses. The laying device (*Richtmittel*) and aiming mechanism (*Richtgerät*) would also be more precise, leading to greater fire efficiency.
4. Since the firing position would be undetected, the gun could occupy it for a longer period of time. A machine gun engaging in direct fire attracted the enemy, and often had to relinquish its position.
5. Using indirect fire, the heavy machine gun could make use of ranges up to 2,000–3,500 meters and thus supplement (or even in certain circumstances replace) artillery fire.
6. Indirect fire could still take place at night, or in mist or smoke; in fact, it was the only means of attaining success in these conditions.[72]

Hausser took a balanced view, however. Direct fire, since it was the quickest method of destroying a hostile target, was still preferable in most cases, despite the dangers it entailed. There were also definite disadvantages to indirect fire:

1. It was often difficult to observe the effect of indirect fire. Artillery and trench mortar observers could see the fall of every shot, then correct their aim accordingly. It was much more difficult for the heavy machine gun, even with high-caliber rounds.
2. Since the trajectory of the heavy machine gun was very flat, it was possible to use indirect fire only for ranges exceeding 1,000 meters. The flatter the trajectory, the harder (and more dangerous) it was to fire over the heads of friendly troops.
3. Laying devices could be inaccurate when improperly used. Combined with special features unique to machine gun (wobbly stands, worn barrels, insufficient water for the cooling mechanism), accuracy could be a great problem.
4. Indirect fire required a tremendous output of ammunition; resupply of the weapon would not be possible in every battle situation.[73]

For all these reasons, indirect fire would never completely replace direct as the machine gun's primary mission. Still, there were a number of situations where it would be appropriate. In preparing for an attack, it could help protect the assembly, deployment, and extension of the unit, especially if artillery was not available. At the outset of an assault converging fire could protect the light machine guns as they advanced. During the attack indirect fire from the rear would help sustain the momentum. Finally, if the enemy retreated, "it is mainly the machine guns further to the rear whose duty it is to inflict injury on the enemy with their far-reaching indirect fire."[74] There were also a number of defensive situations where indirect fire was called for: supporting the withdrawal of combat outposts, for example, or harassing the attacker in his assembly areas, but these received much less attention than the role of the machine gun in the attack. Once again, Seeckt's influence is noticeable.

Perhaps the strongest evidence of Seeckt's influence dates from the fall of 1924, when the *Militär Wochenblatt* began publishing a set of tactical exercises. Composed by Lt. Col. Friedrich von Cochenhausen of the Army Training Section (*Heeresausbildungsabteilung*), section four (T-4) of the *Truppenamt*, the exercises may thus be considered more or less "official" in character. Once again, the subject was the war of movement.[75] To be specific, they dealt with the handling of an infantry division or reinforced infantry regiment "in open warfare during a continuous campaign." Their aim was to give the officer using them an opportunity to practice making tactical decisions and giving orders. Cochenhausen's solutions were not to be taken as perfect answers to the problems posed, but merely "to indicate suitable methods of working out such problems."[76] He recommended them to officers preparing for examinations or for a *Führerreise*, or to anyone seeking to improve his tactical training.

The eleven exercises began by describing a wartime situation (*Lage*). In the first one, the Weser River formed the boundary between a "red" state in the west and a "blue" one to the east.[77] As a result of political tension, both have placed their armies on a wartime footing and ordered a heightened watch on their border districts by customs officials and local garrison units (*Landsturm*). Blue's II Army Corps received the mission of preventing any crossing of the Weser. According to reports from friendly aviators, a long column of unspecified vehicles was approaching the river; there were also reports of enemy planes violating blue airspace.

The commander of blue's II Corps now sent orders to his left-wing division (the 6th Infantry) to move up to the Weser between the 5th Infantry Division on his right and the 3rd Cavalry Division on his left. The divisional commander also received a communication from the 15th *Landsturm* Regiment to the effect that a red crossing of the Weser was imminent. Red patrols had already endeavored to cross, but the regiment's 1st Company had beaten them back. There had also been fighting near the town of Ohsen, and the bridge over the Weser there had been destroyed. A rather long column of cavalry had also been spotted on the far bank. Red was clearly superior in the air and seemed well equipped with modern heavy artillery and tanks. The exercise required the commander of blue's

6th Infantry Division, first, to give his estimate of the situation and the terrain, and second, to issue the appropriate specific orders.

With regard to the battle situation, including the terrain, Cochenhausen's solution began with the obvious. Reports concerning enemy movements made it plain that red units were advancing toward the river in strength and preparing for a crossing. It was apparent that red units intended to force a crossing by reconnaissance detachments and cavalry first, and appeared to have chosen Ohsen as the operational *Schwerpunkt*. While air reconnaissance had detected only two columns of red vehicles, it was probable that strong forces of all arms had reached the Weser bank by night marches. The columns, for example, might have been the supply train of a unit that had already reached the jumping-off point for its river assault.

The key question for blue forces, then, was which immediate measures to take to prevent the crossing. According to the commander of the local *Landsturm* unit, defending Ohsen was a problem. Cover on the far bank served to protect the red approach march and assembly, there was only a tiny blue garrison in the town, and, contrary to reports, the bridges there were only damaged, not destroyed. If red forces could establish a bridgehead by this evening, it would be difficult to force them back. Blue forces therefore had to dispatch a strong force to Ohsen at once. It would be a hard march for troops who were just now in the process of moving up to the Weser, but exertion now might save them from difficult fighting later on. Available troops included 6th Division's advanced units (1st Battalion of the 16th Infantry Regiment, half of the 6th Reconnaissance Regiment, and the 4th Battery of the 6th Artillery Regiment).

The deployment of the rest of the division depended on what happened at the Weser. One possibility was that the units rushed forward so hastily would fail to throw red forces back across the river. In that case, the main body of 6th Division would have to ready itself to launch a counterattack on the red bridgehead. A second possibility (the more probable one) was that the entire near bank of the Weser would be in blue hands tomorrow. In that case, the division had to form up in depth in order to be ready to oppose any new attempt to cross the river, even by strong enemy forces. The division commander could best meet both of these scenarios by concentrating his division a few kilometers away from the river bank, at Lauenstein. Divisional staff, Cochenhausen stressed, should draft both orders at once, so as to be ready to move quickly.

In posting units on the Weser bank, Cochenhausen saw two danger spots. One was Ohsen, already mentioned; the other, a series of westward bends in the river at Ohr and Hajen-Hehlen. Ohr was protected by a series of wooded heights; no enemy advance was possible here, even if he successfully crossed the river. But Hajen-Hehlen was a different story. The enemy could find sufficient cover on the far bank by using the village of

Hajen and the forest west of it. He could also take the defender under fire from the heights to the south of Hehlen. Moreover, the terrain on the near bank was open and would permit a rapid advance. From these observations, Cochenhausen advised that first-rate troops hold the bridge site at Ohsen and Hajen-Hehlen in strength. Weaker forces would suffice along the rest of the river bank.

Cochenhausen's solution went on to list the specific orders that the blue 6th Division commander should draw up. They included the formation of a reinforced battalion-sized "task force" consisting of the advanced units mentioned above; the partitioning of the divisional battle area into sectors; and the creation of a reserve. Orders were to be clear and direct: "Any attempt of the enemy to cross is to be nipped in the bud by immediate counterthrust by the sector reserves, which are to be strongly equipped with heavy weapons."[78]

This, then, was the basis upon which the next ten exercises rested. All are impressive to the modern reader, primarily for the care and precision with which Cochenhausen formulated them. They seem "real," even to the point of having moments of excitement. They instructed the officer performing them in a wide variety of tactical problems. Problem no. 2, for example, began with red forces over the bridge (incompletely destroyed, as feared) at Ohsen. Blue forces counterattacked them there, led by 1st Battalion and a cyclist company.[79] Using the advantage of surprise, and cooperating with fire from the 4th Battery, the blue attack succeeded in driving red forces out of Ohsen. Sixty prisoners, belonging to the red 4th Dragoon Regiment, were taken, along with six machine guns and two armored cars. The enemy "streamed back across the bridge in disorder, suffering heavy losses," and the bridge was again demolished, this time permanently. But red units had also crossed the river at Haven and also in the sector of the 3rd Cavalry Division at Börry. Red troops took the village, which was garrisoned by *Landsturm* units, and then drove on into the blue interior. At this point, 3rd Cavalry Division sent a frantic wire to the blue 6th Infantry Division, requesting assistance. The problem was this: "What answer does the commander of the infantry of the 6th Division give to the commander of 3rd Cavalry Division (word for word)?"[80]

Characteristically for a *Reichswehr* officer, Cochenhausen's solution was for 6th Division to plan a flanking attack from the north on the enemy force just across the river. The cavalry could assist first of all by not panicking, and then by establishing a defensive line to prevent any rapid eastward movement by red forces. In this way, the red crossing force could be pinned in place and enveloped by the 6th Division swooping down from the north.

The next two exercises examined the preparation and execution of this flanking maneuver by the 6th Division. Cochenhausen stressed that "all available forces had to join in it, and that it had to strike the enemy's flank unexpectedly."

At 10:50 am the 2nd Battalion, 6th Artillery, the 16th Trench Mortar
Company, and all available heavy machine guns of the 16th Infantry Regiment threw a violent burst of fire lasting for five minutes on the enemy's
covering troops north of Börry, while at the same time the 16th Infantry
gun battery took them under point blank fire from concealed emplace-
ments in the woods. Then the 16th Infantry dashed to the attack with two
battalions in the front line. The 1st Battalion, advancing on the right,
headed for Börry, overran the enemy's sentries and penetrated, almost
without fighting, into the village, which was filled to overflowing with
vehicles. When the foremost portions of the battalion reached the south-
western exit of the village, two of the enemy's batteries which were in
position west of Kleine Hill were bringing up their limbers to change position. They were overwhelmed by fire and captured after a brave resistance. In the meantime, the 2nd Battalion had advanced beyond Börry in
a more southeasterly direction, likewise meeting with only slight resistance, and struck unexpectedly in the flank and rear of the foe engaged in
combat southwest of Bessinghausen. Three to four hundred pioneers, six-
teen machine guns, and several infantry guns and trench mortars were
captured. The enemy sought to escape by fleeing to the south, but suffered heavy losses in doing so.[81]

The passage shows Cochenhausen's talent for concocting realistic battle
scenarios. The learning benefits of playing through such a simulation were
tremendous.

But the exercises did not end here. The division to the right of the blue
6th Infantry, the 5th, had launched a poorly executed counterattack of its
own against red troops that had crossed in its sector. Heavy casualties had
shattered the unit, which was now in full retreat. The blue 6th Division
now had a new dilemma: press on to the river bank and ensure the total destruction of red forces already beaten at Börry, or fall back with the 5th Division to cover the left flank of its retreat. The 6th Division's commander
decided to disengage from the enemy and fall back, which formed the
heart of exercise no. 5. When the flight of the routed blue 5th finally came
to a halt, the 6th Division once again turned about for an obstinate defense
of a wooded ridge (exercise no. 6).

Exercise no. 7 began a new situation, with the blue I Corps in full retreat toward Hanover via Minden and Rintelen, after unsuccessful battles
west of the Weser. The exercise dealt with the arrival of a new division into
the theater of war, in particular preparations for the billeting of the unit. But
exercise no. 8 found Cochenhausen "back on the attack," as it were, forcing
the officers taking the exercises to employ the newly arrived unit (3rd Infantry Division) in an assault on the flank of the advancing Red army. This
counterattack formed the basis for exercises no. 9 through no. 11.[82]

This series of exercises stands as a superb example of tactical training in Seeckt's *Reichswehr*. Within the boundaries of these eleven situations may be found virtually everything a modern commander might encounter: defense against a river crossing, the initiation of flanking attacks,

protecting the flank of a neighboring unit in combat; disengagement; retreat; the stubborn defense of a ridge line; insertion of new units into an ongoing battle. Cochenhausen's "Tactical Exercises in a War of Movement" demonstrates conclusively that the military art had survived Germany's defeat in 1918 and proves once again how ineffectual the Treaty of Versailles was in preventing the eventual rebirth of German military power.

Conclusion:
The Reception of Seeckt's Doctrine in the *Reichswehr*

Seeckt's doctrine did not go unchallenged in the 1920s. His vision of a small, professional army, highly mobile and trained in the offensive, brought forth three principal schools of opposition. The "defensive school," led by Gen. Walther Reinhardt, argued that modern weaponry and the rise of mass armies had elevated the defensive to a nearly impregnable position. Thoughts of grandiose breakthroughs were mere fantasies. The "psychological school," exemplified in the writings of young wartime officers like Ernst Jünger and Kurt Hesse, rejected all the traditions of the Prussian-German army, including the supposed monopoly of military wisdom possessed by the General Staff. Such writers held a romantic image of war. Only troops inspired by "a frenzy of faith in Folk and Fatherland, blazing out from any rank of society" could bring victory on the future battlefield. Then there was the "people's war" school, rejecting Seeckt's view of the *Führerheer* (army of leaders) in favor of the *levée en masse* concept, the mobilization of the whole people in the manner of the French revolutionaries of the 1790s. Lt. Col. Joachim von Stülpnagel is a good example, calling in 1923 for a popular uprising and guerrilla warfare against the Franco-Belgian occupation of the Ruhr. It was certainly not an era free from controversy.[83]

Yet Seeckt's vision prevailed. Attack was stressed in the doctrine of the *Reichswehr*, which was led by a General Staff disguised as the *Truppenamt*, and was restrained from any fantastic adventures such as those envisioned by the "people's war" school, adventures that would have surely brought disaster to not only the army, but to Germany as well. And as the representative sampling of professional military literature we have analyzed in this chapter shows, Seeckt's views on war found acceptance among the great body of German officers under his command. It is clear that the principles of Seeckt's new manuals—especially *F.u.G.* and *A.V.I.*—did filter down to the rest of the army. Mobility, the close cooperation of all arms, flexibility on the part of men and leaders, adherence to the overall mission balanced by independence in the choice of means, determination to settle for nothing less than total breakthrough and destruction of the enemy—these were the characteristics that Seeckt succeeded in imprinting on the *Reichswehr*.

Notes

1. For the preservation of the General Staff in the form of the *Truppenamt*, see Waldemar Erfurth, *Die Geschichte des deutschen Generalstabs von 1918 bis 1945*, 2nd edition (Göttingen: Musterschmidt Verlag, 1960); for German military activity in the Soviet Union, see Manfred Zeidler, *Reichswehr und Rote Armee 1920–1933: Wege und Stationen einer ungewöhnlichen Zusammenarbeit* (Munich: R. Oldenbourg Verlag, 1993). Seeckt's handling of the "pledge of tradition" that each battalion and company in the *Reichswehr* took to an old imperial regiment is discussed in Harold J. Gordon, *The Reichswehr and the German Republic 1919–1926* (Princeton, NJ: Princeton Unviersity Press, 1957), pp. 305–306; for the experience of individual *Reichswehr* units, see Wolfgang Paul, *Das Potsdamer Infanterie-Regiment 9*, 1918–1945 (Osnabrück: Biblio Verlag, 1985), pp. 20–25, and Gerhard Lubs, *Aus der Geschichte eines Pommerschen Regiments 1920–1945* (Bochum: Berg-Verlag, 1965), pp. 28–29.

2. The *Observations of the Chief of the Army Command* for the various years are found in English translation in *United States Military Intelligence Reports: Germany, 1919–1941* (Frederick, MD: University Publications of America, 1983), microfilm reel XV, frames 106–150. In shorthand notation, the above document would be labeled USMI, XV, 106–150. For the 1922 *Observations,* see USMI, XV, 539–624; for 1923, USMI, XV, 807–846; for 1924, USMI, XV, 151–180; and for 1925, USMI, XVI, 657–680. A copy of the original German text for the 1923 *Observations* is found in *Stück* (item) 133 of the Seeckt *Nachlass*, a microfilmed copy of which is on deposit in the National Archives, microcopy number M132, microfilm reel 21. In shorthand notation, these documents would be listed as Seeckt Papers, M132, 21, 133.

3. These included Gen. Friedrich von Taysen's supplement for the infantry (USMI, XV, 107–114), Gen. Max van Poseck's for the cavalry (USMI, XV, 115–119), General von Bleidorn's for the artillery (USMI, XV, 1201–1227), General von Klotz's for the pioneers (USMI, XV, 128–131), Gen. Erich von Tschischwitz's for the motor and wagon transport (USMI, XV, 132–139) and Gen. Georg Wetzell's for the signal troops (USMI, XV, 140–150).

4. *Observations of the Chief of the Army Command Based on His Observations in 1921*, section 2. In shorthand notation, the citation would be *Observations 1921, 2.*

5. *Observations 1921, 4* and 5. See also section 46.

6. The term is *Waffen-Partikularismus, Observations 1921, 10.*

7. Friedrich von Rabenau, *Seeckt: Aus seinem Leben, 1918–1936* (Leipzig: von Hase und Koehler, 1940), p. 510.

8. *Observations 1921, 13–14.* See also section 25.

9. Ibid., 48.

10. Ibid., 18–19. See also section 40.

11. Ibid., 39. In his supplement appended to Seeckt's *Observations* General von Taysen makes a similar comment (see note 2, above).

12. *Observations 1921, 21.*

13. Ibid., 26–28. For the comment on corps artillery, see section 34.

14. Ibid., 52–54.

15. Ibid., 61.

16. Ibid., 62–68.

17. Ibid., 69–75.

18. Ibid., 99–110. The quote is from section 100.

19. Ibid., 111–125.

20. See Peter Gay, *Weimar Culture: the Outsider as Insider* (New York: Harper & Row, 1968). Walter Laqueur, *Weimar: a Cultural History* (New York: G. P. Putnam's Sons, 1974) covers much the same material in a very different fashion. For the best discussion of the "mystique of youth" in the Weimar Republic, see Detlev J. K. Peukert, *The Weimar Republic: The Crisis of Classical Modernity* (New York: Hill and Wang, 1992), pp. 86–106.

21. *Observations of the Chief of the Army Command Based on His Observations in 1922* is found in USMI, XV, 539–624; see especially sections 1–3. In shorthand notation, the citation would be *Observations 1922, 1–3*.

22. *Observations 1922, 5–6*.

23. Ibid., 8–9.

24. Ibid., 11.

25. Ibid., 14.

26. Ibid., 30 and 32.

27. Ibid., 39.

28. Ibid., 43 and 48.

29. Ibid., 54.

30. *Observations of the Chief of the Army Command Based on His Observations in 1923* (hereafter *Observations 1923*) is found in USMI, XV, 807–846. The crisis year of 1923 has been the most closely scrutinized in the history of the Weimar Republic. Still the best narrative of those bewildering months is found in Erich Eyck, *A History of the Weimar Republic, Vol. 1* (Cambridge, MA: Harvard University Press, 1962), pp. 227–302. The accounts in E. J. Feuchtwanger, *From Weimar to Hitler: Germany, 1918–33* (New York: St. Martin's Press, 1993), and Peukert, *The Weimar Republic*, are also quite useful. The Hitler *Putsch* in Munich is the subject of a monograph by Harold J. Gordon Jr., *Hitler and the Beer Hall Putsch* (Princeton, NJ: Princeton University Press, 1972).

31. *Observations 1923*, sections 4–5.

32. Ibid., 8–9.

33. Ibid., 15–16.

34. Ibid., 18.

35. Ibid., 55.

36. Ibid., 28–33.

37. Ibid., 34–35.

38. Ibid., 57–68. The quote is taken from section 59. For a related discussion on the need stength in the assault, see *Ausbildungsvorschrift für die Infanterie* (hereafter *A.V.I.*), volume I, section 112 (in shorthand notation, *A.V.I.*, I, 112) and *A.V.I.* II, 247.

39. *Observations 1923*, 60. See also *A.V.I.*, II, 52.

40. *Observations 1923*, 69–79.

41. Ibid., 80–93.

42. *Observations of the Chief of the Army Command Based on His Observations in 1924* (hereafter *Observations 1924*) is found in USMI, XV, 151–180.

43. *Observations 1924, 5–6*.

44. Ibid., 10–11.

45. Ibid., 15–16. The 1st Infantry Division in East Prussia (headquartered in Königsberg) had an impressive list of commanders over the years, including later

Chief of the Army Command Wilhelm Heye and later Defense Minister Werner von Blomberg.

46. Ibid., 21.

47. Ibid., 32.

48. Ibid., 40.

49. Ibid., 48–49.

50. Ibid., 63–89; see especially sections 65 and 80.

51. For the warning against collecting horses of the same color, see Observations 1924, 84; for the correct position of the drawn saber, see Observations 1924, 88.

52. Ibid., 93.

53. *Observations of the Chief of the Army Command Based on His Observations in 1925* (hereafter *Observations 1925*) is found in USMI, XVI, 657–681. For Heye's compilation, see USMI, XVI, 044–209.

54. *Observations 1925,* sections 1, 3–4.

55. Ibid., 6.

56. Ibid., 9–10, 13.

57. Ibid., 27.

58. Ibid., 30–31.

59. Ibid., 23–24.

60. Ibid., 35–43.

61. Ibid., 44, 49.

62. Ibid., 56–76.

63. The same issue affects religious doctrine; the Catholic Church, for instance (the classic model of the hierarchical institution), has always distinguished between the *promulgation* of doctrine on the one hand and its *reception* by the faithful on the other—no doctrine can ever become part of the Church's official teaching unless it is accepted by the whole body of believers.

64. Colonel A. L. Conger's report, *Influence of the "Observations of the Chief of the Army Direction" General Oberst von Seeckt on the Regimental Training,* is found in USMI, XVI, 706–712; the quote is found in USMI, XVI, 706.

65. Conger, *Influence,* USMI, XVI, 707.

66. Ibid., USMI, XVI, 709.

67. Friedrich von Taysen, "Über die Formen des angelehnten Angriffs und die Verteidigung im Bewegungskrieg," translated as "Regarding the Force of Supported Attack and Defense in a War of Movement," USMI, X, 316–417. The quotes are taken from X, 318, 320. They are quite similar, nearly word for word, in fact, to Seeckt's own ideas. See, for example, Hans von Seeckt, "Moderne Heere," reprinted in *Gedanken eines Soldaten* (Leipzig: K. F. Koehler, 1935), p. 56.

68. Taysen, "Supported Attack and Defense," USMI, X, 339.

69. Ibid., USMI, X, 382.

70. Maj. Paul Hausser, "Das schwere Maschinengewehr: Seine schiesstechnische und taktische Verwendung auf Grund der Erfahrungen des Weltkrieges," translated as "The Heavy Machine Gun: Its Firing Methods and Tactical Utilization on the Basis of the Lessons Learned in the World War," found in USMI, X, 795–861. Hausser would go on to military greatness as one of the leading armor commanders of the *Waffen*-SS in World War II. For a biographical sketch of his career, see Robert M. Citino, *Armored Forces: History and Sourcebook* (Westport, CT: Greenwood Press, 1994), pp. 242–243.

71. Hausser, "Heavy Machine Gun," USMI, X, 797–798.

72. Ibid., USMI, X, 799–802.

73. Ibid., USMI, X, 802–803.

74. Ibid., USMI, X, 804.

75. Lt. Col. Friedrich von Cochenhausen, *Taktische Aufgaben aus dem Bewegungskrieg mit Lösungen,* translated as *Tactical Exercises in Open Situations with Solutions,* found in USMI, XII, 482–555.

76. Cochenhausen, *Tactical Exercises,* USMI, XII, 483.

77. "Tactical Exercise #1" is found in Cochenhausen, *Tactical Exercises,* USMI, XII, 484–493.

78. Ibid., USMI, XII, 492.

79. "Tactical Exercise #2" is found in Cochenhausen, *Tactical Exercises,* USMI, XII, 493–497.

80. Ibid., USMI, XII, 495.

81. "Tactical Exercise #3" is found in Cochenhausen, *Tactical Exercises,* USMI, XII, 497–501; "Tactical Exercise #4" in USMI, XII, 501–510. The descriptioni of 6th Division's flanking maneuver is found in USMI, XII, 502.

82. Tactical Exercise #5" is found in Cochenhausen, *Tactical Exercises,* USMI, XII, 510–517; "Tactical Exercise #6" in USMI, XII, 517–522; "Tactical Exercise #7" USMI, XII, 522–528; "Tactical Exercise #8" in USMI, XII, 528–535; "Tactical Exercise #9" in USMI, XII, 535–540; "Tactical Exercise #10" in USMI, XII, 540–546; "Tactical Exercise #11" in USMI, XII, 547–555.

83. The best discussion of the various schools of military thought in the *Reichswehr* is found in James S. Corum, *The Roots of Blitzkrieg: Hans von Seeckt and German Military Reform* (Lawrence, KS: University Press of Kansas, 1992), pp. 51–67.

CHAPTER 4

The Reichswehr as Military School

The *Reichswehr* never fought a battle (unless one considers its pacification campaigns against Red forces in the Ruhr, Saxony, and Thuringia). It has no Austerlitz to its credit, or Waterloo for that matter. Its importance lies not in any list of battlefield triumphs, but in the way in which it taught an entire generation of young German soldiers a new doctrine of warfare. This new doctrine wasn't *Blitzkrieg*, or "lightning war" (that term will arise later), but *Bewegungskrieg* (the war of movement) with combined arms. During the period from 1921, when the new field service regulation *Führung und Gefecht der verbundenen Waffen* (F.u.G.) appeared, to the formation of the Hitler cabinet in 1933, the *Reichswehr* served primarily as a school. It instilled new military values in its charges and prepared them for the day when the international situation would permit German rearmament and army expansion.

The attempt to build an "army of the future" required a great deal of military imagination from all concerned. Staff, officers, and men all had to assume the presence of weapons the *Reichswehr* did not, in fact, possess. Plans had to be made for campaigns that the current army would never be able to fight. Despite the fact that the *Reichswehr* was basically a light infantry force, for example, emphasis on supporting arms and heavy weapons was a constant feature of the era. This emphasis went well beyond current weapons like trench mortars and machine guns; heavy artillery, tanks, aircraft—all were represented to an impressive degree in *Reichswehr* maneuvers, although none could be physically present. Operational doctrine, stressing the envelopment and destruction of the enemy, also stood far above the current material abilities of the army.[1]

The problem, therefore, was to instill the same vision of warfare shared by the higher leadership of the army in all of the ranks. It was largely a question of education, and the way in which it was solved is perhaps the greatest achievement of what one French writer called this "great army in miniature."[2]

73

Defense District Examinations, 1921

In the 1921 Defense District examination (*Wehrkreis Prüfung*), administered to all officers, the questions for both infantry and cavalry dealt with
the importance of the supporting arms. Infantry officers had to answer
questions on the appropriate mission for the light trench mortar (*Minenwerfer*) and discuss future trends in the weapon's development. Cavalry
officers had to write an essay criticizing the equipment of machine gun
units in the present-day cavalry unit, as well as give a critique of the organization of the machine gun units themselves. For artillery, officers had
to analyze the use of shrapnel and time-shell for the light guns; pioneer officers had to discuss details of building a field bridge and an auxiliary
bridge for the crossing of an infantry division. There were also questions
for the signal services and for motor and wagon transport. Officers had
two and one-half hours to complete the exam. After grading the examinations, the training section of the *Truppenamt* published the official answers
in early 1922. They were, the army stressed, by no means "school solutions, but were merely guides to the correct answers."[3]

With regard to infantry and the trench mortar, the solution began by
examining the mission of the weapon. It was to augment the fire of infantry and machine guns against targets that the infantry could not destroy,
and to augment the fire of artillery batteries when the latter could not be
brought to bear with full effect. Thus the trench mortar was "a kind of accompanying artillery" working in close cooperation with the infantry.[4] It
had to be able to destroy targets as quickly as they could be identified, especially resistance nests and enemy machine guns. It also had to be able to
pin enemy infantry as long as possible during an assault by one's own
forces and fire at short range at targets behind hills and slopes that the artillery was unable to hit because of its flat trajectory fire. In close terrain,
the trench mortar was a replacement for artillery that was limited in its observation. Finally, the trench mortar had to be ready to battle tanks encountered in combat by the infantry.

Given these various missions, there were six technical requirements of
the trench mortar:[5]

1. High mobility. The light trench mortar had to be able to enter all
   sorts of terrain and to keep up with infantry in the advance, the assault, and the pursuit.
2. Precision fire. It had to be effective against live targets, chiefly
   through the fragmentation of its projectile. Effectiveness against
   tanks was secondary.
3. Limited range. Its chief mission was engaging targets at very close
   range. Increased range was therefore of little use. Nevertheless, its
   range should be long enough to engage enemy machine guns in

open terrain, while remaining outside the machine gun's range. Slightly increased range might also be of use in other situations, allowing the trench mortar to strike targets more deeply in the enemy's zone of deployment.

4. High-angle and flat-trajectory fire. The mission of the trench mortar embraced both types, demanding the ability to switch from one to the other. In addition, the trench mortar should be suited to both direct (observed) and indirect (unobserved) fire.

5. Rate of fire and fire readiness. It had to be effective quickly against designated targets. It therefore required a high rate of fire as well as the ability at any moment to engage newly designated targets.

6. Traverse. Since the trench mortar had to be able to switch its fire rapidly from one target to another, it had to have a quick traverse.

Comparing these technical demands to the actual ability of the trench mortar, the Training Section made the following observation. Mobility was not a problem. The trench mortar on its flat-trajectory carriage was capable of following the infantry into almost any terrain and in fact could even be drawn by the men, if necessary. Its fire showed little dispersion in either type of trajectory (plunging or flat). But it did require uniform projectiles and powder charges. Currently the burst had about the same effect as a field shell, but that too could be improved by the adoption of a more sensitive detonating cap.

The range of the light mortar, using high-angle fire, was from 300 to 1,300 meters; using flat-trajectory fire it ranged from 500 to 1,100 meters. These ranges made it impossible for a trench mortar to engage a machine gun in open terrain. The principal improvement recommended by the Training Section was to improve the range of the piece to approximately 2,500 meters, without increasing the weight of the weapon or lessening its accuracy.

The trench mortar was capable of both high- and flat-trajectory fire. However, in order to change from the latter to the former, it was necessary for the gunners to remove the carriage wheels, a costly proposition in terms of time. Thus, it would be most advantageous if the trench mortar were able to deliver high-trajectory fire from its wheeled mount, though this would have to be accomplished with no increase in weight.

The mortar's rate of fire was certainly sufficient, at least when delivering high angled fire—about 10–15 rounds per minute. The rate was slower in flat fire, and improvement was possible here. Likewise, the traverse of the trench mortar (accomplished by shifting the train manually) was sufficient, but a great improvement could be effected by the installation of an automatic traversing mechanism.[6]

The solution to the infantry test question concluded by stating that the light trench mortar was an "extraordinarily effective auxiliary arm of the infantry in attack as well as in defense."[7] An increase in its range would make it even more useful. But such an increase should not lead to the mortar being deployed farther to the rear. Its mission required it to be at the front, with the infantry, where it could "conform to the vacillations of the battle." Only in the front could it best take quick advantage of any targets that offered themselves.

The solution to the cavalry question, dealing with the organization of machine gun units assigned to the cavalry, began by pointing out the role of the Great Powers (and the Treaty of Versailles) in all questions relating to German military organization. Equipping a cavalry regiment with only four heavy machine guns (organized into a single machine gun section) was obviously insufficient. Since each cavalry platoon was stationed far from the others, there was no uniformity in training.

Again, the place to start was with the mission of the cavalry. It alone had the ability "of rapidly and suddenly producing a strong firepower against sensitive points" in the enemy position.[8] Reconnaissance, rapid occupation of key points, operations against the flank or rear of the foe, screening the movement of friendly units, flank protection, leading the pursuit or protecting the retreat—these were the unique tasks of the cavalry, and each of them required machine guns. Even when fighting dismounted, cavalry's firepower was limited. But even the smallest cavalry unit (the troop) had to be able to break minor resistance rapidly. Any reconnaissance detachment without machine guns lacked the essential element for driving back the enemy. Despite the occasional mounted charge, cavalry was today useful only in so far as it could deliver fire at the enemy. And the machine gun, far from existing merely as an auxiliary arm, was today "the undisputed backbone of the firefight."[9] Moreover, cavalry had to be ready to fulfill any role played by the infantry. From this, it was logical to conclude that the machine gun was not a luxury for a modern cavalry formation, but an absolute necessity.

The solution now turned to the most suitable organization for machine gun units in the cavalry. Smaller units (patrols and troops) obviously required the most mobile machine gun, the light one. Since they would have to make frequent use of cross-country riding, vehicle transport was inappropriate. Carriage by pack animals was the answer. Larger units (regiments or brigades) required both mobile (light) and heavier pieces; motor transport made more sense here.

In terms of numbers, the solution recommended that six light machine guns (on pack animals) be attached to each cavalry troop; one machine gun troop of twelve heavy guns on vehicles (with crew mounted on horseback) to each regiment; and one machine gun battalion of twelve heavy machine guns on vehicles (men riding on vehicles) to each brigade.

The solution concluded by stating that the use of cavalry was by no means a thing of the past. Increased firepower on the battlefield and the greater importance of motorized vehicles had not changed the need for first-class cavalry. But the high demands placed on cavalry meant that it could not suddenly be created in wartime; it required thorough and uniform training now. It had to be able to fight mounted or dismounted. It must never sink to the level of mounted infantry, "riding badly and shooting badly." To achieve all this, cavalry had to have the correct armament and equipment "as taught us by the experience of the war."[10]

Combat School for the Infantry (1924)

Supporting arms also formed the basis for a number of battalion drills drawn up in 1924 by Colonel Stollberger, a staff officer in Defense District VII (Munich), and published as *Combat School for the Infantry* (*Kampfschule für die Infanterie*). Based on both *Leadership and Battle (F.u.G.)* and *Training Regulations for the Infantry (A.V.I.)*, these exercises offered a number of scenarios in which infantry had to react to the presence of modern weaponry.[11] Exercise No. 1, for example, dealt with the employment of an infantry battalion in the presence of enemy aircraft.[12] The situation was this: friendly (blue) forces in battalion strength were on the march south through the drill ground of Grafenwöhr, when sirens heralded the approach of hostile aircraft. Umpires informed the companies that an "escadrille" was coming in from the east, just 5–10 kilometers away. As it approached the battalion it descended to 1,000 meters of altitude, then began dropping bombs and strafing. Blue antiaircraft guns had no visible effect. The battalion had been expecting an air raid. Its order of march had been 1st, 2nd, 3rd Company, each with an attached machine gun platoon. A few noncommissioned officers and sharp-eyed men were accompanying the battalion on bicycles, searching the sky for aircraft. They moved in groups from one hill to the next, maintaining liaison with officers in the column. As soon as the spotters announced the presence of hostile aircraft, the noncommissioned officers informed their company commander. The battalion commander then gave the order: "Battalion command—formation against airplane units."[13]

Now the battalion broke up. The first company hustled forward, the second to the right, right face, the third to the left, left face. The companies simultaneously broke up into small units, then smaller still, so as not to offer the flyers good targets. The light machine gun and antiaircraft machine guns went into position to fire. Ammunition wagons sought cover, or if that was not possible, stayed in the open while maintaining great distances from one another and from the riflemen. The machine guns (and in some cases the riflemen as well) now engaged the enemy aircraft, aiming for the first plane of the formation, presumably containing the commander. Fire was executed in bursts. After every burst, the gunners established a new aiming position in front of the leader. Meanwhile, patrols and spotters kept scanning the sky for more enemy aircraft, and the ground for enemy troops.

In discussing this maneuver, Stollberger stressed the importance of the marching column anticipating an enemy air attack, even when far away from the enemy. If aviators forced the column to leave the road, they could count it as a great victory, "even if they have not disabled a single man or horse."[14] They will have greatly delayed the advance and discomfited the marching troops. The infantry had to learn how to behave in such circumstances; it certainly could not be expected to move across country in deployed formations or to march only at night. Neither could it rely solely on the antiaircraft and machine guns for protection. The employment of "air scouts" was helpful, but enemy air squadrons could be over the column within moments of being spotted. Scouts were therefore only of value if their information was reported promptly, and if a single short command sufficed to disperse the troops. Often events would move so fast that there would not be time even for a short command. In this case, companies would have to take the appropriate action on their own initiative, clearing the road by having even-numbered companies turn to the right, odd-numbered to the left. If vehicles were unable to leave the road, they had to utilize the freed-up space to spread apart as much as possible. If due to the narrowness of the space (mountain defiles, for example), infantry units could not disperse into small groups, they would have to seek cover in ditches by the side of the road.

To Stollberger, enemy air attack against narrow defiles were probable, and represented a special problem. In such a case it was the duty of antiaircraft guns to secure safe passage for the troops, and the guns' fire must not be wild and aimless. Light and heavy machine guns firing armor-piercing ammunition were to attack enemy aircraft at altitudes under 1,000 meters, concentrating all fire on the lead plane (as in a battle at sea). Fire was to occur in bursts aiming at a point ahead of the previous one. Constant fire would always lag behind the target. Such a technique required skill and practice, but did offer significant hope of success.[15]

Other maneuvers in Stollberger's *Kampfschule* continued the emphasis on support weapons. One, for example, examined the deployment of an infantry battalion under long-range fire by enemy artillery, another the same maneuver while under heavy machine gun fire.[16] In the latter, friendly artillery and light machine gun units were to go immediately to the front in order to screen the movement of the infantry.

A particularly interesting maneuver tested an organized attack from a distance of 4,000–2,000 meters.[17] As a blue infantry battalion marched north, it received scouting reports from cavalry and aircraft that a red force was in position on both sides of the road facing south. What was most significant about the exercise was the total domination of the battlefield by the firepower of the supporting arms. Red machine guns halted the blue advance, then were themselves silenced by blue artillery. Each attacking blue company had its own platoon of heavy machine guns and trench mortars. One of the companies infiltrated the red position and established a position for flanking fire, which was carried out by the heavy machine gun. Here was infantry battle as envisioned by *A.V.I.*—fire and movement working in harmony, fire making movement possible, movement increasing the effectiveness of fire.

All told, the *Kampfschule* was a comprehensive series of exercises for every situation that wartime infantry might encounter. It included defensive exercises along with attacks (all highlighting the role of support weapons), river crossings during combat (suitably covered by artillery and machine gun fire), the insertion of reserves by the regimental commander, breaking off combat (in which heavy machine gun fire played a prominent role), pursuit of a routed enemy by a battalion, delaying defense (the *hinhaltendes Gefecht* of *F.u.G.*), enveloping attacks, and infantry-cavalry encounters.[18] All operations were mobile, stressing flexibility and the rapid shifting of support fire from one spot to another on the battlefield. They indicate the highly advanced state of tactical thought in the Germany of the 1920s.

Defense District Examinations, 1924

Further examples of Defense District examinations, this time from 1924, show the emphasis on mobility and envelopment characteristic of the Seeckt era.[19] The first problem dealt with the organization of small detachments on the battlefield. It began with a blue army becoming engaged in combat with a red army advancing from the southwest. After two days of fighting, the blue army had to withdraw its right wing behind a small creek in the battle sector. This wing consisted of an infantry division (the 1st), that had already been roughly handled. Once behind the water barrier, however, it managed to repel repeated crossing attempts by red units. Two days after its withdrawal, the division received news that another division, the still-fresh 2nd, was advancing from the north. Its orders were to advance south, turn the red forces' western flank, and thus compel a complete red withdrawal.

But as the van of the 2nd Division, consisting of the reinforced 6th Infantry Regiment, approached the battlefield, it hears that the red army had already begun its own attack, crossing the creek and crashing into the right flank of the exhausted 1st Division. The 1st Division commander had reported being under heavy fire from guns on the south bank of the creek, and had ordered the bridges in the area destroyed. The problem for the examinee was whether to continue on with the original plan of outflanking

red forces, or instead to seek to reinforce the hard-pressed 1st Division before it melted away.[20]

The solution began by giving an estimate of the situation.[21] First of
all, blue forces had orders to carry out a flank attack against red forces.
The commander of the 6th Division could deviate from this mission only
for very weighty reasons. The solution did not consider such reasons to be
evident. True, red forces had achieved success by crossing the creek, but
with the bulk of the red guns still on the south bank and with vehicles only
able to cross the creek at the bridges, the red army was not going beyond
its crossing points anytime soon. Should the 6th Regiment veer off course
to support the 1st Division, it would certainly help relieve the endangered
unit, and probably bring the enemy attack to a standstill. At the same time,
it would mean losing the chance for a decisive flanking victory over the
red army. Pausing at the creek itself, in order to decide whether to engage
red forces on this or that side of the water, was also unwise in terms of the
original mission. The regiment would almost certainly find itself engaged
on the north side of the creek by advancing red forces. Splitting off a small
detachment to screen the regiment's movements and to harass the red advance with flanking fire represented a diversion of effort and should be
avoided.

No, the only course of action was for the 6th Regiment to push on
rapidly with strong combat units, force passage of the creek, and crash into
the red left flank. This would give the enemy as little time as possible to
organize a defense. In terms of the 2nd Division's orders, the entire unit
would eventually take part in the flank attack: "No man should be with-
drawn from this principal task." The 6th Regiment was not an independent
unit, but there was no time to wait for divisional orders. The regimental
commander had to make the decision, after due consideration of the divisional mission and the intentions of the divisional commander. It was self-
evident, the solution declared, that turning aside to come to the aid of the
1st Division would be a "false movement."

Indeed, the best way for the 6th Regiment to rescue the hard-pressed
1st Division would be to launch a decisive attack on the red flank. This
would provide direct support to the 1st by driving red forces from the battlefield. As for the present, even if red forces succeeded in pushing back
the 1st Division and in getting their guns over the creek, it would have no
impact on the overall battle. In fact, the further north red forces got, the
more vulnerable their flank would become.

The key to the operation now was for the blue army to thrust its mobile units toward the south to seize intact the bridges immediately to the
west of the operational area. In fact, until blue detachments had secured
the river crossings, the solution stated that "it would be premature now to
issue orders for deployment, for preparation for attack . . . or to indicate
remote points for attack." The approved decision (*Entschluss*) was to

continue the march to the south for a drive into the enemy's rear, throwing forward mobile forces (machine gun platoons, artillery) in order to take possession of the crossings at Raaben and Sasterhausen. Weaker detachments were to be sent forward as flank protection.[22]

Based on this decision, the commander of the 6th Infantry Regiment drew up his orders. They began with verbal instructions to the advance guard leader, with the artillery commander present, to send his machine gun and artillery platoons forward to seize the crossings at the two villages and "hold them open for the regiment." The rear company of the advance guard was to move at once to occupy a position on the left of the advancing regiment. This would establish liaison with the 1st Division and also provide flank security for the advance. Verbal orders to the main body sent the mounted machine gun platoons and artillery to trot ahead at once along the road, passing to the left of the infantry. Both were placed under the command of the advance guard leader.

The first noteworthy characteristic of this solution was the German intention to maneuver in small units of all arms, in this case an infantry regiment reinforced with a heavy artillery battery, a battalion of field artillery, a half-company from a reconnaissance detachment (armored cars, bicycles, and cavalry), pioneers, and a bridging train. It was designed to be capable of launching a powerful attack on its own, and of fighting independently for a considerable period. The flexibility of German organization is worth noting. Terms like "regiment" or "division," in fact, seem increasingly obsolete when discussing this sort of operation. The commander of the 6th Regiment created a "task force" or "battle group (*Kampfgruppe*)" on the spur of the moment to seize and hold the bridges over the creek. Artillery and machine guns were taken from their own commanders and given to the leader of the advance guard. The order of march, with artillery in the rear, found itself completely turned around with the dispatch of the artillery to the front.

Under Seeckt, the *Reichswehr* had come to view war as a series of missions—unique and ever changing. The duty of the officers was no longer simply to carry out incredibly detailed orders from on high. Instead, as the behavior of the 6th Regiment commander had shown, he was to keep the mission foremost in his mind. The method of achieving it was more or less up to him.

A second characteristic of the solution was its aggressive nature. It called for ignoring a clear danger (as well as the panicky cries of the 1st Division) in order to win a greater success. It labeled as clearly wrong the conservative decision (going to the defense of a unit in trouble) in favor of the riskier flank operation. This is not to say it encouraged foolhardiness. The 6th would have ample flank protection and artillery support as it came forward. But it was a risky move just the same.

The other examination questions dealt with different missions, but always with the same stress on the flexibility of means. Problem no. 2, for instance, began with the retreat of a corps-sized formation, and then posited a reinforced infantry regiment acting as the rear guard for its division.[23] The problem specified the regiment's organization—giving it bicycles, a mixed complement of artillery, armored cars, pioneers, and antiaircraft guns, though the troops were "considerably fatigued after the exertions of the last few days."[24] It posed the question of whether the rear guard should defend against an enemy attack passively or launch an attack to hold it up. Characteristically, the solution called upon the regiment to attack. Other problems looked at a reinforced infantry regiment foiling a flanking attack against a friendly division, not by defending but by taking the flankers in their own flank.[25] Again, the emphasis was on task force organization, with the regimental commander throwing forward a mixed unit of artillery and machine guns to launch the assault. And, like all these problems, this one laid great stress on establishing antiaircraft defenses.

An officer trained in this system would have many positive qualities. He would be bold on the battlefield and flexible in the organization of his forces, shaping them and reshaping them as the situation demanded. Most important, he would constantly strive for nothing less than total victory— though always within the context of his higher unit mission.

On the negative side, there was the possibility that an officer trained in this way might have a bit too much independence of thought; that quality had not always been beneficial to the German army on the battlefield. Gen. Alexander von Kluck's decision to wheel north of Paris in 1914 is the classic case.[26] It may have been the right thing to do; it may not have been. But it indisputably meant the abandonment of the Schlieffen Plan and Germany's chances for total victory early in the war. During the East Prussian campaign of August 1914, Gen. Hermann von Francois's unilateral decision to advance I Corps to meet the invading Russian 1st Army under Rennenkampf led to a premature engagement at Stallupönen, which overthrew the entire German plan for the campaign.[27] Had things gone just a little worse for the Germans there, no opportunity for a Tannenberg would have arisen; East Prussia might have been lost. Thus, pumping up each officer into a "mission-driven" and more or less independent entity held dangers as well as opportunities for the Reichswehr.

A second, even more critical problem was that the German army through its educational programs was essentially training technicians. The entire thrust of Reichswehr training under Seeckt was tactical and operational. Strategy, grand strategy, and even military history were almost entirely absent. German officers as high as colonels and generals spent far more time in the 1920s thinking about the use of the trench mortar in combat than about Germany's overall strategic situation in the event of any conceivable future war. This is not to advocate "sensitivity training" for officers in place of military tactics. But as West Point, to its great credit, had recognized from the start military history (and history in general) is an indispensable part of the training of a well-rounded officer. The German tradition, jealously guarded by Seeckt, was to educate its officers in a vacuum of pure technique that viewed war essentially as a technical exercise, devoid of any strategic context.[28] In fact, Seeckt insisted that his army refrain from political discussion or involvement. In the land of Clausewitz, who preached that "war is merely the continuation of policy by other means," this was an inexcusable failing.[29]

The Divisional School in the German Army

The strictly technical approach of German staff training is apparent in a report by U.S. military attaché Conger regarding the school of the 3rd Infantry Division, stationed around Berlin. Once again, the tactical training was impressive. In one of the tactical problems administered by the staff to the officers, red troops were advancing westward on a broad front, driving the blue *Landsturm* before them. By the evening of May 1, the situation was as follows: the blue *Landsturm* was defending the Oder River line on both sides of Glogau. Reinforced by active troops, *Landsturm* forces hoped to hold until the evening of May 2, then retreat into prepared positions behind the lower Neisse River. But to the north, red forces amounting to four or five divisions have seized the road bridge at Frankfurt on the Oder. The Küstrin-Berlin railroad had been cut, and red forces had already constructed a number of bridges over the Oder. Meanwhile, the blue 1st Army, consisting of six divisions, had attacked red forces north of the Küstrin railroad and succeeded in driving back the red northern (right) wing. The blue army now decided to rail the newly formed II Corps into position to attack the southern (left) flank of the advancing red army.[30]

The exercise proceeded from the point of view of the commander of the blue 3rd Infantry Division (attached to II Corps) as it advanced to battle. The division was partially motorized, and split into a reconnaissance detachment, an advance guard, and a main body. As the division approached the battle zone, however, the commander received disturbing news. It is quoted here in full not for the reader to follow in a tactical sense (that would require the detailed—perhaps overly detailed—1:100,000-scale maps of the Oder-Neisse region carried by German officers), but merely to give a flavor for the level of detail reached in such an exercise:

He [3rd Division commander] learns that:

1. The 4th Landsturm Brigade is retreating with heavy losses before strong enemy forces with much artillery. The right wing is supposed to be at Bergenbrück; the left wing is at present halting east of Neuendorfe im Sande and north of Hp. Neuendorf-Buchholz. The power of resistance is now only very slight owing to constant and heavy artillery

fire. The situation with the neighboring brigade is unknown. The enemy is said to already be in Beerfelde.

2. II Corps HQ, with which the communications are at present cut off, communicated from Kagel 1/4 of an hour ago that the 4th Division was marching forward undisturbed. The Landsturm, it is reported, has lost Müncheberg and is there holding the eastern edge of the Müncheberger Forst. The 4th Division will attack over the line Beerfelde-Schönfelde in its support. The combat is going well with the 3rd Army Corps north of Müncheberg. This corps hopes to be able to proceed to the attack at noon. No communications exist with army headquarters.

3. The 1st Cav Division has thus far withstood attacks of strong cavalry in the Markendorfer Forst and at Hohenwalde. At Neubrück an enemy reconnaissance detachment broke through to the west early today. The passage has been closed again behind it. On the roads from Frankfurt to Petershagen and Jacobsdorf there is constantly heavy traffic.

4. A pursuit airplane, hard-pressed by enemy airplanes, landed on the Fürstenwalde flying field at 9:45. He reports "We intervened in the ground combat with several squadrons on the northern wing at 9:00 am. The advance is doing very well there. Many prisoners and guns have been taken. At the time we entered into action the Blues were in the line Neu Trebbin—Alt Lewin-Güstebiese."

There is isolated dispersion fire on Fürstenwalde.

Our own airplane activity is very much hampered by enemy air superiority and dull weather. Enemy airplanes repeatedly flew over the march column of the division.

The divisional commander now had to make his decision as to how to proceed (and list the reasons), provide the report he would give to corps headquarters (including the full wording), and draw up specific orders to execute his decision.[31]

Conger attended the discussion of the problem and later sent Washington a detailed report. It gives a vivid impression of some of the world's best tactical minds at work, as well as the intensity that the *Reichswehr* could bring to what was, after all, merely a paper exercise. Leading the discussion was General Otto Hasse, at the time commander of the 3rd Infantry Division, and soon to be head of Army *Gruppenkommando* I (in other words commander of I Corps, consisting of the 1st, 2nd, and 3rd Infantry Divisions, as well as the 1st and 2nd Cavalry Divisions). Hasse was, therefore, operational commander of all German forces east of the Elbe, and his presence at an officer training exercise reinforces the gravity with which the army approached its work.[32]

He began by defining the difference between two relevant terms: *Beurteilung* and *Begründung*. The first, meaning "estimate of the situation," called for a complete study of the battle situation, the terrain, and all possible courses of action open to both sides. The *Begründung,* on the other hand, simply called for the commander's decision together with the reasons for its adoption or for the rejection of other courses of action. "In this problem," Hasse stated, "it is necessary first of all to determine the mission of the division. In order to do that, we have, first of all, to put ourselves in the Red commander's situation and discover his view of the problem." And then he proceeded to do just that. Conger was very impressed with this part of the proceedings: "It was extremely interesting to me to observe the intensity with which the instructor put himself, in the discussion which followed, which lasted some twenty-odd minutes, into the enemy's situation." Further, he noted how Hasse delivered the enemy's estimate of the Blue force and situation "as though he were himself a completely dyed-in-the-wool Red." Conger discussed the interesting psychology of this performance: "It need only be recalled that the Reds are in this case the Poles who have only a hundred-odd kilometers to go from their frontier to reach Berlin." The problem under discussion, therefore, was not merely plausible; virtually every officer in the room, Conger observed, believed it was "likely to happen within a few years." Adding a further element of realism was the fact that the *Reichswehr's* 3rd Division to which these officers belonged, stationed as it was near Berlin, might one day be called upon to carry out in reality the paper exercise now under discussion. "Hence the realistic way in which the instructor threw himself into the enemy's estimate of the situation with all his force and power of imagination could not but arouse admiration."

Reconstructed from Conger's notes, Hasse's talk went something like this:

> On the Red side we are invading Blue territory and have just broken across the line of the Oder at Frankfurt and to the north with four divisions. In the first place, it must be asked if it be possible with this as a base to make an attempt to reach Berlin. [At this point, reported Conger, Hasse asked several members of the assembly their opinions on this point. Some answered yes, others no.] Hasse went on: It is decidedly impossible for the point of an advanced guard flanked on both sides by hostile forces to capture a great city. Even if such a feat were to be attempted, examination of the map will show the many obstacles to be encountered in between the present apex of the Red line and Berlin, namely numerous chains of lakes and watercourses. Hasse then paused to point these out in detail on the map, and showed how easily small forces might defend these water lines. Thus we see that it is impossible for us (referring here to the reds) to hope to capture Berlin without being able to cross the Oder on a much broader front than has yet been possible.

Still using the first person plural, Hasse went on to declare:

> We have one of two choices. The first is to parry the counterattack now being made on our north wing, where we are now losing ground. The second is to attack the exposed flank of Blue forces defending the line of the Bober with a view to gaining a broader front west of the Oder and enabling us to continue our operations. But before reaching a decision in

this matter, we have first to consider (from the Red viewpoint), What are the Blue intentions? The Blues must realize that we cannot achieve the complete object of the campaign without gaining a broader front west of the Oder. However, the best way to achieve this is to strain every nerve to take from us the ground we have already gained west of the Oder, while preventing any widening of the breach. Hence, we (as Reds) are bound to expect, in connection with the movement against our right flank, that the enemy (Blue) is likely to attempt some similar movement from the south . . . as the surest means of preventing a widening of the breach over the Oder.[33]

With this in mind, Hasse went on, red was bound to use its available reinforcements not to try to push the "point" of its advance further westward, but to strengthen the right flank of its advance west of the Oder. Red must also maintain a reserve to ensure the possession of Frankfurt; since their position west of the Oder depended only upon military bridges, it would be "anything but secure" without the city.

Hasse now returned to the blue side. The blue 3rd Division commander had "one all-important mission to perform," he said: to get across the Spree River that day and enter the fray against red forces; otherwise, the division might find itself cut off from the rest of its corps. Held up from crossing the river by a red detachment, the 3rd Division would find itself "unable to participate either in an attack or, if the enemy withdraws, in a pursuit." But once that had been done, there was still the question of what axis of attack the division should take. Unfortunately, Hasse observed, the 4th *Landsturm* Brigade was in trouble. Placed by circumstances in the center of the line, it required support against heavy red attacks, which included a great deal of artillery. The 3rd Division, therefore, would have to enter combat against the left wing, not the left flank, of the red line. The terrain in this area was also more favorable for the attack. A battalion of the main body would have to be left as a rearguard over the Spree bridges, in case the fight did not go well. Once again, a *Reichswehr* exercise tempered boldness of maneuver with sensible caution.

Conger also sent back other instructional exercises for the 3rd Division staff.[34] One was a map problem, written by staff officer Major Bohnstedt. Taking part in the exercise and the subsequent critique were the chief of staff, Col. Kurt von Hammerstein, and General Hasse. Accompanied by a 1:100,000 map, it began with Czech (red) forces crossing the German frontier into Saxony and engaging blue forces there. The blue 3rd Army, deployed for protection of Silesia, had begun its approach from east of Liegnitz and was acting in cooperation with blue frontier guards (*Grenzschutz*) occupying the ridge of the Riesengebirge. On the evening of March 25 elements of the army's right wing (I Corps, to be specific) were in action.

The corps consisted of the 15th and 25th Infantry Divisions. Both were standard *Reichswehr* divisions reinforced by the following: one heavy artillery battalion with one 10 cm battery and two heavy field howitzer batteries; one antiaircraft battery (all guns horse drawn); one airplane observation squadron with three observation planes; one artillery observation squadron with two airplanes; 16th Cavalry Brigade, consisting of the 10th and 11th Cavalry Regiments, reinforced by one cyclist company and a motorized light machine gun company two mounted batteries. The corps troops included one heavy artillery regiment, including a battalion of two motorized 10 cm batteries; one battalion of two horse-drawn heavy field howitzer batteries; one antiaircraft battalion of two motorized batteries; one motorized pioneer battalion; one motorized machine gun battalion; one observation squadron of four airplanes; and one artillery observation squadron of three airplanes.

The border guard regiment protecting the Riesengebirge consisted of three battalions, two mountain artillery pieces, and two platoons of motorized trench mortars. The problem did not describe red forces in the same detail, other than to say they were equipped with "modern" weapons, a description presumably referring to heavy artillery, aircraft, and tanks.[35]

The problem forced the participants to act as chiefs of staff to the corps commander. Specifically, the situation dealt with the 15th Infantry Division of I Corps. While the 25th Division was already in the field, unspecified delays had held up the 15th, and it had not finished detraining until noon on March 25. The question, then, was which route would concentrate the two divisions in the quickest and most secure fashion? A secondary question was the correct employment of the 16th Cavalry Brigade. Discussion on this point was lively among the twelve officers taking part in the exercise.[36] Some recommended sending it across the border for raiding purposes; others sent it to assist II Corps to the west, now bearing the brunt of the red attack. Major Bohnstedt did not favor any of these courses of action. In the first place, "a few squadrons of cavalry could not accomplish any appreciable good attempting a raid behind the enemy's front." Second, the problem had not given any specific information about II Corps, and sending it assistance was tantamount to operating without adequate reconnaissance. Too little was known. What was II Corps's actual situation? Did it need assistance? Above all, where was the assurance that I Corps would get its cavalry back, if needed?

Bohnstedt instead pointed out the dire straits in which the border guard unit found itself. The cavalry brigade alone might not be strong enough to stop the red assault force here, but with reinforcements from the corps troops (the motorized machine gun battalion, for example), it just might do the trick. A cavalry brigade-machine gun battalion task force "might well succeed in holding back or at least seriously delaying even a whole division for a whole day in the rough country" on the border.

Bohnstedt took this opportunity to discourse on the role of the cavalry. "It is a mistake," he said, "to think of a modern cavalryman in terms of the warfare of the last century. The cavalrymen is a mounted rifleman, nothing more." The horse got him to the battlefield more quickly, but upon his arrival he was a rifleman or a machine gunner, "the same as any infantryman." Therefore, the supposition that cavalry could not operate in mountainous terrain, which had shown up in the various proposals for employment of the 16th Brigade, was wrong. Horses could deliver the men more quickly and with less fatigue to the mountains just as well as they could to flat terrain. Once the cavalry arrived, it was just as valuable as it was anywhere else. Thus, Bohnstedt concluded, the nature of the frontier country was "no reason for keeping the cavalry back from it."

Bohnstedt's comments were followed by those of Colonel Hammerstein, who chose to highlight the role of the border guard unit. Many of the officers present had wondered why, after the unit had seen its position penetrated, it did not simply retreat and rejoin the main body of regular forces in the interior. In answer, Hammerstein pointed out that it was border guard doctrine, when attacked in force, to disappear and stay invisible for three hours. This would allow the main body of the hostile column to pass, at which point the border guard unit would "reappear and fire on every detached officer, man, messenger, ammunition column or supply column that attempts to penetrate the frontier zone." That, he said, was the expected role of the border guard unit, and it must play it indefinitely, "until the enemy is forced back across the frontier." It was therefore "not unreasonable" to assume that the main ridge of the Riesengebirge was still in the hands of the border guards even if the enemy had broken through in two or three places.[37]

Divisional commander Hasse then spoke. He had found the problem to be of great interest and had studied it for over two hours before arriving at his own solution. He disagreed with many of the solutions he had read, which called for a night march by both infantry divisions preparatory to a daylight attack on red. Bohnstedt's solution, for example, had the 15th Division on the road at 11 P.M. and the 25th Division at 3 A.M., so that they could rendezvous for an attack at 8 A.M. Hasse's experience was that "troops cannot be expected to fight all day after a march begun before midnight." He saw a 3 A.M. start as reasonable for both divisions. "You can get troops up very early in the morning and march them to the battlefield and they will fight very well. But if you start them earlier than that you either have to make an embarrassing halt somewhere when you can ill afford to do it, or else they will give out on you in combat." The 15th Division would arrive late, meaning that the attack would have to be put off several hours. Better a carefully planned attack at full strength than one hastily thrown together. Again, this exercise married a high degree of boldness in execution (in this case a counterattack against superior forces) to a healthy dose of battlefield caution.

Hasse ended with a nod to the specialist troops, in this case the engineers. He noted that most of the participants had used them like any other body of infantry, for example as advance guards. This happened often in maneuvers, he said, and unfortunately it happened in wartime as well, since pioneers were very useful in fixing roads and bridges, making them more easily accessible to the main body of infantry. But it was "a great mistake, because engineers are the most valuable troops we have," the most difficult to train and the hardest to replace. Even though it went without saying that a commander could always throw them into combat in a critical moment, "this must be the exception and not the rule, and certainly they should not be put to the front at the beginning of the combat."[38]

Colonel Conger went on to describe the wargames he had witnessed that were staged by officers and men of the 3rd Division.[39] One game on 13 February 1928 dealt exclusively with river crossings; it was preceded by a lecture from one of the younger instructors, defining the various types of river crossings and the various means of defending a river line. For the actual game itself, classroom tables were arranged in an open square, three on a side, with extra tables to the rear. The director of the game sat at the center table on one side with two student assistants beside him, both of whom kept notes; but Conger observed that the Director did not once consult the students or their notes. The director seemed to be keeping his own. On the other side of the room were tables for the principal players (representing the divisional commander, his chief of staff, and the divisional artillery commander). The rest of the student participants sat on the table to the director's right; the table on the left was reserved for Conger and Major von Obstfelder, the division's senior instructor. Because it had to command more troops, the red side was larger than blue (seven officers to five). The remaining two members of the class took part as assistant umpires. As the director called each side into the room, the other party would leave, taking along their maps and papers.

Conger noted that no large-scale map was present; each officer taking part had the 1:100,000-scale map in two sheets. The mention of specific terrain—the name of a farm or a numbered hill—therefore necessitated a great amount of searching. The men usually defined the location with reference to some larger feature.

The game began at 9:15 A.M. with a preliminary discussion between the director and the Red team (including the issue of orders, it took over an hour). He then called in the blue team; this session took fifty-five minutes. The red team then returned for a more detailed discussion of the crossing and stayed for an hour and 10 minutes. In the course of this meeting members of the blue party (excepting the division commander and his chief of staff) were summoned, in order to hear the red team's description of the crossing. By now, it was 12:20 P.M. The blue division commander and chief of staff now returned to hear the discussion and draft their orders, this taking forty minutes. At 1 P.M., the director gave his impressions of the game (twenty minutes) and then the senior instructor did the same (twenty more). The game thus totaled about four and one-half hours.

Conger was impressed with the game, particularly with the "earnestness and enthusiasm shown by all the officers taking part." The director questioned each officer in turn and kept every man "busy and interested." Young lieutenants had played the role of division commanders on both sides; they were "keen and well-instructed." While their decisions were grounds for discussion and even considerable criticism, the lieutenants received "far more praise than blame" from the director and senior instructor. But for two exceptions, the senior instructor had taken part in the game until its conclusion. Once he interrupted the game to ask the red officers to write out brief orders to their artillery. These notes, consisting of just a few lines, were then assembled and brought to him. The second interruption occurred during red operations to bridges which the director had allowed to be finished on time. The senior instructor had then intervened to say that although bridges might be built that quickly in peacetime maneuvers, such rapid construction was not to be expected in actual war. To this the director responded by saying that he had been present at the German assault on the Marne on 15 July 1918 (the Second Battle of the Marne), and that on that occasion the engineers had all the bridges up and functioning ahead of the scheduled time. The senior instructor then withdrew his objection.[40]

The situation examined in this game was an interesting one. As the red situation report described it, a red army had penetrated deep into Germany from the southwest, reaching the Werra and Fulda rivers on 14 February. Blue forces appeared ready to defend on the northern bank of the Werra. The red reinforced 1st Cavalry Brigade was already up to the southern bank, screening the approach of the rest of the army, and the red 1st Infantry Division was acting as an army reserve behind the right wing. On 16 February the division staff received orders from army headquarters, and was to plan a surprise crossing of the Werra early on 18 February and gain the heights north of the river in order to advance on 19 February in support of an attack by the southern wing of the army (identified in the orders as the *Schwerpunkt* of the attack). The red 1st Cavalry Brigade would screen the division's movements and crossing preparations. A motorized supply column from I Corps would arrive on 17 February with smoke and gas ammunition—1,000 shells for the light field howitzers, 600 shells for the heavies, divided evenly between smoke and gas (identified by blue and green crosses on the shells, respectively).

Rounding out the red situation report was a list of various details of importance to the game:

Condition: Troops have not yet been in combat; rested.
Weather: Clear; sunshine; no wind.
Air situation: For Blue, only a few observation airplanes have thus far shown themselves; strong antiaircaft defense for Blue; seven Red pursuit planes missing since February 14.

Population: Inclined to acts of sabotage.
Sunrise: 0745. Sunset: 1722.
Terrain: Forest tall and thin. Road dry. Werra 50m broad, 2m deep.
1m/sec velocity of current.

The director also provided the red side with a detailed order of battle
for the 1st Pioneer Battalion, which would assist in the crossing:

Organization of the 1st Pioneer Battalion
   a. Staff and Signal Troops.
   b. 1st, 2nd, 3rd Companies. Horse drawn. Strength of each company:
      5 officers, 250 non-commissioned officers and privates. 6 large and
      3 small rafts. 4th Company, motorized. Strength: same as 1st, 2nd,
      and 3rd Companies. Men loaded on 10 trucks, equipment on 3
      trucks.
   c. Illumination (searchlight) platoon.
   d. Bridge column:
   1st Detachment: Pontoon Bridging Equipment
      1st Platoon: 2 trestles, 13 pontoon wagons.
      2nd Platoon: 2 trestles, 13 pontoon wagons.
      Assigned: 4 trestles, 26 pontoon wagons.
   2nd Detachment: horse-drawn.
      3rd Platoon: 17 bridge wagons drawn by 6 horses each, with 4
      large raft bags and superstructure equipment for about 100 meters
      of light, raft-column bridge, capable of bearing up to 2.5 tons.
      4th Platoon: rapid bridge platoon. Bridge wagons drawn by 7
      horses. Wagons 1–6 each carry 5 foot-bridges each 5 meters long
      and 10 small raft bags, or 25 meters of rapid construction bridge
      each (for pedestrian traffic and weapons up to heavy machine
      gun). Wagon 7 carries spare parts.[41]

Blue's situation report indicated that it intended to go beyond a mere
passive defense. In fact, the blue 1st Army was preparing to attack. But red
operations on the Werra threatened the left flank of the army. The blue 3rd
Division was assigned the task of defending against what was sure to be a
red crossing of the Werra. The 3rd was a standard *Reichswehr* division reinforced by a heavy artillery battalion (of two heavy field howitzers and a
100mm battery), a squadron of three aircraft, and unspecified (though apparently powerful) antiaircraft assets.[42]

The instructor began the game by announcing to the red side the
weights that could be borne by the various types of bridges in use, as well
as the time of construction for each type (one to five minutes per meter,
depending on the method used). He called on the red commander for an assessment of the situation, including the terrain, then turned to the commander of the engineers for his estimate of the terrain and his recommendations. Finally, it was the turn of the red aircraft commander; he had to
describe the measures he had taken for air reconnaissance, the times and
missions for each sortie.[43]

The wargame began with the 16 February evening turn. The red side sent out air reconnaissance at 7 A.M. on 17 February and every two hours thereafter during the day, scanning the roads to the Werra for enemy troops. The director promptly described the information gleaned by these flights and the time it was received. The division commander could then give fresh orders based on the new intelligence. At noon on 17 February, red aviators had definitely located the 3rd Division in Göttingen, behind the Werra, and one of the red brigade commanders was called on to make his recommendations to the divisional commander about the crossing. The report was brief and crisp, only about 10 minutes. The director ordered the division commander to give his estimate of the situation, in light of this new information, and then dismissed the red team, which left to formulate detailed plans for crossing the Werra.

The blue team now entered the room and received a briefing on its *Landsturm* troops, then holding the Werra line (the "Göttingen *Grenz-schutz* Brigade"). The Director described the unit as being made up of men up to 55 years of age and organized into two regiments. Each company had two light machine guns, augmented on the battalion level by six heavy machine guns; each regiment had a "howitzer company" consisting of just two light and two heavy trench mortars, for which there were only 150 shells per gun. Conger found this description interesting in terms of the kind of troops likely to be detailed to border guard duty "in the next war."[44]

The director now asked the blue commander whether he wanted to reinforce this sector. The latter decided to dispatch one infantry battalion as a central reserve for the border guards, and then designated one of his team as the battalion commander, whom the director immediately called upon to step forward and give his dispositions. The rest of the evening was taken up by the blue force in air reconnaissance, which revealed nothing of a detailed nature. The blue 3rd Division, meanwhile, was on the road, the division commander originally having planned a halt at midnight, but deciding to press on at that point. There was an interesting psychological touch added at this point: "The infantry commander was told that on the march at 2 A.M. both regimental commanders came to him with the report that the men were suffering severely from cold and begged for a halt to enable them to get warm. The infantry commander replied that he was sorry but he could not change the division commander's order and that they should increase the pace and enable the men to warm up in that way." The blue division reached its cantonments between 3 and 4:30 A.M.

The director now recalled the red team and heard the division commander's "preparatory order," a very lengthy and detailed description of the intended crossing, which called for a simultaneous operation by two independent columns. There was a great deal of discussion in the room as to whether the order could be shortened. The director agreed that in some cases, a short verbal order would suffice for a river crossing, but that in this case, with defenders in prepared positions, there was reason for making the orders as complete as possible. There was also the question of what to do after crossing the river. The red commander envisioned forming a number of "reinforced detachments" to carry out various tasks once over the river. These, taks were included in the order. The time of the crossing was not specified, listed simply as "X-hour," but was later set for 7:15 A.M., a quarter of an hour before sunrise.

The blue commander and chief of staff were now called into the room and given the reports the commander had received at 7:30, 7:45, and 8:00 A.M. The commander took no action on the first two; they were sketchy and very short on specific information. By the time of the 8:00 A.M. report, however, it was clear that the red force was crossing the Werra. The blue commander immediately ordered his whole division to advance and attack the enemy forces as they made their crossing. At this point, the game came to an end.

Both teams now met to hear the director's critique. He approved of the blue commander's dispatch of reinforcements to his border guard, but would have recommended a whole regiment rather than a lone battalion. He criticized blue force's failure to do any more than reconnoiter artillery positions along the river, which was all that had taken place before the red attack. He approved of blue dispositions in general, but was very critical of blue movement into position: the march should have started earlier on the 17 February, affording the men a good rest and leaving them fresher for the next day's combat. As to the red handling of the situation, he approved of the decision to cross the river in two columns, but urged that the crossings should have been more widely separated. The senior instructor then spoke, emphasizing the critical importance of artillery and machine guns in forcing a river crossing.[45]

Conger witnessed another of the 3rd Division's wargames on 25 February 1928. Devised and conducted by one of the students, it analyzed the course of a combat in which a division, after making an attack, had to revert immediately to the defensive. But this game was not altogether successful.[46] The senior instructor was highly critical of the situation, which featured overly complex, even stylized, maneuvers by the units involved, and once again featured troops rushed into day-long combat after all-night marches. The problem also failed to tell the division commanders where they might reach their respective corps headquarters. Overall, the problem was not well conceived, requiring entirely too much "umpire control," robbing both teams' commanders of their initiative and thus reducing the instructional value of the game. Still, Conger saw reason to be impressed: "The wargame was well-played and orders were well-given; in fact, it might be said the high state of training of the class was all the more clearly demonstrated by their carrying on so well in spite of the insufficiency of the umpiring."[47]

Conger also drew up a lengthy report on the 3rd Division's officer training school.[48] He had requested an opportunity to visit one and finally received an invitation from Colonel Liebmann of the *Truppenamt*. Liebmann had orders to let Conger see "absolutely everything without reservation," but there was one qualification. Inasmuch as the officer training schools and their curricula were still matters of controversy with the Allied governments, he asked Conger to tell no one that he had visited the school, or even to admit to knowledge that such schools existed. Liebmann went on to explain the difficulties that the Versailles military restrictions placed in the way of training officers along "General Staff lines." With the old *Kriegsakademie* abolished after the war, the fourth department of the *Truppenamt* (T-4), called the *Heeresausbildungsabteilung* (Army Training Section), was responsible for this activity. Every year it chose a "class" of officers from each of the *Reichswehr's* divisions for a two-year course of training. In this way a large percentage of Germany's officers were given General Staff training and stood ready to fill these posts in the expanded German army of the future.

Conger now paid a visit to General Hasse, the 3rd Division commander, in the latter's headquarters on Kurfürstenstrasse. The general and his chief of staff welcomed him and promised to show him any part of the divisional schools he wished to see, but repeated their request that he not mention the schools to anyone in Berlin. After giving his assurances, Conger received his *Ausweis* (pass) and was introduced to the director of the schools, Major Obstfelder.

The training of the German officer for General Staff duty began with classes of senior first lieutenants and junior captains.[49] For all officers of these ranks who had not yet attended one of the schools, there was an annual examination, the *Wehrkreis Prüfung,* which corresponded to the prewar entrance exam to the *Kriegsakademie*. Officers who passed the exam were accepted for a two-year course at their divisional headquarters; the course aimed to make the candidate a staff officer, though the army had to use the official euphemism *Führergehilfe* (command assistant). Classes stretched from October to May (28 weeks). The first year dealt with a reinforced infantry regiment; the second with a division.

During the first year, classroom instruction added up to 22 hours per week, not including the wargame or other form of map or tactical exercise one day a week.

Divisional School: First Year (D-1)

Subject	Hours per week
Tactics (reinforced infantry regiment	6
Military history	4
Supply/quartering of combatant troops	considered in tactical problems

Air protection	1 hour every two weeks
Technical instruction in the various arms	1 hour every two weeks
Special artillery instruction	1 hour every two weeks
Engineer service	1 hour every two weeks
Motor transport service	1
Signal service	1
Sanitary service/health of troops	10 hours altogether
Veterinary service	10 hours altogether
Judge Advocate's department	10 hours altogether
Foreign language	2 hours per week
Physical training	2 hours per week
Horsemanship	3 hours per week

[The second year amounted to about 24 classroom hours per week, though the same comment applied regarding the weekly wargame or exercise.]

Divisional School: Second Year (D-2)

Subject	Hours per week
Tactics (Division)	6
Technique of command	2
Military history	4
Army organization	1
Supply/quartering of combatant troops	1
Army transport service	1 hour every two weeks
Air protection	1 hour every two weeks
Special artillery service; chemical warfare	8 hours altogether
Motor transport service	1 hour every two weeks
Signal service	1 hour every two weeks
Army administration	12 hours altogether
Foreign language	2 hours per week
Physical training	2 hours per week
Horsemanship	3 hours per week

Conger also appended the weekly schedule in his report. From it we can see clearly the tactical and technical emphasis of the division officer training school.

Monday
8:15–9:00 Foreign Language (French, Russian)
9:15–11:00 Tactics (Cpt. von Fumetti)
11:15–12:00 Command Technique (Cpt. Mieth)
12:15–2:00 Physical Training (Sports Instructor Dörr)

Tuesday
8:00–8:45 Riding (Lt. Grolig)
9:15–11:00 Army Organization (Maj. von Obstfelder)
11:15–1:00 Military History (Cpt. Mieth)
1:15–2:00 Foreign Language (English)

Wednesday
Open, devoted to special assignments

Thursday
9:00–10:00 Lectures in Reichswehr Ministry
10:15–12:00 Tactics (Maj. von Obstfelder)
12:15–1:00 Foreign Language (French, English, Russian)

Friday
8:00–8:45 Riding (Lt. Grolig)
9:15–10:00 Army Transportation (Cpt. von Tippelskirch) or Motor Transportation
   (Lt. Pick)
10:15–12:00 Military History (Cpt. Mieth)
12:15–1:00 Air Protection (Maj. von Freyberg) or Communications (Cpt. Gerke)
1:15–2:00 Special Artillery Service (Maj. Heidrich) or Administrative Service
   (Dr. Kunz)

Saturday
8:00–8:45 Riding (Lt. Grolig)
9:15–11:00 Tactics (Maj. von Obstfelder)
11:15–1:00 Supply/quartering of combatant troops (Cpt. Niedenführ)

The Friday classes bear some explanation. The sessions in motor transportation and army transportation alternated every week, as did the classes in the special artillery service and administration. The course in air protection went from October to the end of December. Communications then started with the new year and went to the end of March. Thereafter, these classes also alternated weekly. Finally, there was a wargame every other Saturday, in place of supply and quartering.

Conger estimated that there were currently 15 officers enrolled in D-2 (the second year of instruction). If the other divisions had schools of equal size, there would be a total of 105 officers, or 2.6 percent of the entire officer corps, limited by the Versailles treaty to 4,000 men. Assuming there were similar schools for the cavalry, of perhaps slightly smaller size, Conger arrived at an estimate of 140 officers per year, about 3.5 percent of the officer corps. Comparing this with the prewar German army, a *Kriegsakademie* class consisted of a bit over 400 officers, less than 1.0 percent of the pre-war officer corps. "One can only admire that the German army with its officer corps reduced to 1/15 of its former number is nevertheless able to turn out for training in general staff work 1/3 of the actual number previously detailed for such training," he noted.[51]

Turning to a discussion of each individual class, Conger noted that the course on tactics was based on "the pre-war opinion that the subject could best be mastered by the study of very simple combinations of the arms," one or two battalions of infantry, one or two artillery batteries, a smattering of tanks, cavalry, and motorized infantry, and a reconnaissance detachment. Thus, while the U.S. Army in its postwar tactical training at Ft. Leavenworth had eliminated the study of the reinforced infantry brigade from its former central role, the Germans still devoted one whole year to it "and continue to regard that as the most important year of the officer's tactical education." The study of tactics, in fact, received the greatest emphasis during the first year's study; there was relatively little time spent on actual General Staff training, the formulation of orders, or the problems of supply. In fact, as far as Conger could tell, the division was the smallest unit in the *Reichswehr* that operated with formal orders—and as some of the maneuvers had shown, sometimes even divisions dispensed with them. The second year course on division tactics concerned itself with the larger problems confronting the divisional commander and his staff: When and how is the division to be divided? What should be the strength of its various detachments? If the mission called for forcing a river, how large should the columns be? Where exactly will they cross? Where will the artillery be deployed? During the river crossing wargame the director had dismissed the actual crossing in two words: "It succeeded." More detail than this (the small unit maneuvers of the various detachments) was considered to be out of place in a division-level game.[52]

Also interesting was the course on military history. The first session attended by Conger discussed a problem, previously handed out, dealing with the situation of the Prussian army facing the Austrians on 6 August 1866, after the victory at Königgrätz. Discussion centered on strategy, the possibilities open to both opposing armies in the campaign, and the strategic principles involved. When one student raised the question of whether or not the Prussians should have marched on Vienna, the instructor, Captain Mieth, dismissed his suggestion "as something which, while in vogue in the years of Friedrich and Napoleon," had no application in modern strategy. The problem of pursuing the retreating Austrian forces took up much of the class, and the instructor compared the situation with Napoleon's pursuit of the Prussian army after Jena in 1806, still obviously regarded in the *Reichswehr* as the textbook case.

The history class lasted two hours, the first being devoted to discussing solutions to the assigned problem. The various measures adopted by each student were carefully discussed, pro and con. The second hour dealt with the next steps to be followed by the Prussian army as it drove to the south. Each student located the individual divisions of both armies on their maps with red and blue pencils, marking off their daily movements. There would then be pauses to discuss the various strategic possibilities opened up by the day's events. The Austrian view of the campaign was as much a part of the discussion as the Prussian; there was full discussion of the reasons for the various Austrian moves. There were also occasional references to strategic situations in the world war, especially the campaigns of 1914.

At the end of the class, the instructor handed out topics for individuals in the class to investigate, all dealing with situations in the world war. The principal assignment for the next session, however, was a continuation of the 1866 discussion. Conger noted that the entire two hours had dealt with strategy—the movement of armies. This formed, in his mind, a useful complement to the coursework on tactics, "the idea seeming to be that instruction in the two subjects, strategy and tactics, should go hand in hand."

The atmosphere of the class had been pleasantly relaxed. The instructor had related an incident in which a little known colonel by the name of Blumenthal had written an indiscreet letter criticizing the strategy of the great chief of staff, Moltke. It had somehow been made public, to Blumenthal's great embarrassment, and published in a Viennese newspaper. The instructor's reading of the criticism "caused merry laughter on the part of the class."

The second class Conger attended brought the 1866 war up to the armistice that ended it. Again, it dealt with a day-by-day account of divisional movements, all duly noted on the maps. A main topic was the concentration of the army in the direction of Pressburg (Bratislava), with the instructor calling on the students to estimate the time required for such a concentration. They also had to decided a suitable date for attacking Pressburg, given the superior weight of Austrian forces there.

This time Conger's reactions were mixed. On the one hand, the German system of this level of staff training seemed superior to the U.S. Army's in that it began to teach the young lieutenant from the start the outlines of strategy at the same time as he was studying tactics. Thus, strategy and tactics went hand in hand, unlike the U.S. system that tended to separate them. On the other hand, however, the study of military history itself seemed to be "very superficially conducted" and limited almost exclusively to technical questions, "which may account for the badly written histories which have hitherto been published by the German General Staff."

His negative impression on this point found confirmation in the second hour of the class. It featured a lecture on the evolution and employment of cavalry, illustrated by six maps that were handed out to the class. The first three dealt with the handling of the cavalry in 1866, with one of them devoted to Schlieffen's recommended employment of a cavalry corps in that campaign. Another illustrated the handling of the cavalry in the 1870 campaign west of Metz. The lecturer described the use of cavalry in the advance on Sedan and Paris and also mentioned the use of cavalry in 1914, although he did not discuss the latter point substantively. The lecturer was a young cavalry lieutenant attending the school, whose talk seemed "neither interesting nor valuable" to Conger: "He merely described what cavalry had done, without bringing out any principles regarding its employment."[53]

Conger also attended one session of the course in army organization that proved to be quite interesting.[54] The instructor, Captain von Fumetti, began by observing that modern war depends for success on correct organization: he said that Clausewitz had pointed out the necessity for economy of force in war 100 years ago. Since no nation could supply a preponderance of force all along the line, it was necessary to organize so as to have the superiority of force at the decisive point. In fact, Fumetti stated, military leaders could take a lesson here from industry: he called attention to a standard business text, Taylor's *Principles of Management,* describing it as "the most important book which has appeared since Clausewitz on this subject." Although it dealt with business and production, its basic points were equally applicable to national organization for war.[55]

But it was Fumetti's next topic that made Conger's ears perk up. According to his notes, Fumetti said that

> the United States has since the war done more than any other nation in the matter of organizing its industry for the next war. Such organization must precede the organization of the army itself because the army cannot hope for success without proper organization of its ammunition and supplies and unless the vital necessities of the nation during the war are themselves provided for. Such an organization would be very difficult for Germany, bound as it is by the Versailles Treaty. Nevertheless, place for its rapid accomplishment has to be made if success in the next war is to be achieved.[56]

Conger was unsure how much of this talk reflected actual opinion in the German officer corps and how much was staged for his benefit. He did note, however, that Fumetti's bearing, characterized by a "great force and earnestness," indicated that he was serious.

Conclusion

In the conclusion to his report Conger painted a mixed picture. While most methods of instruction had not changed since the war, the Germans had made great progress tactically. Tactics and methods of instruction were ahead of the Americans, and far ahead of the French. "They themselves speak laughingly about postwar French tactics and orders," he wrote.[57] According to one German officer, even though the French said they believed in open warfare and the war of movement, they sought to conduct it with methods that had evolved from the trench warfare stalemate of the Western Front and that were in fact only possible in such a situation. With their lack of highly trained officers in the lower grades, the French had had to adopt a "system of elaborate plans and highly centralized control in the hands of the higher leaders."

The Germans, however, had had a completely different wartime experience. They had seen trench warfare on the Western Front, to be sure, but they had also had a significant amount of fighting on other fronts, like Turkey, Russia, Rumania, and the Balkans. Nearly every German officer had fought in one or another of these places and had gained experience in open warfare, with rapid movement and widely dispersed forces, where close control from above "was neither possible nor desirable." Thus the Germans aimed at the same sort of control and coordination over the battlefield as the French, but went about it in a completely different manner— by developing tactical proficiency in all officers and men, "encouraging individual enterprise and initiative," and keeping orders from superiors to an absolute minimum. For success, the same officer said, we look not to the commanding officer's tactical genius executed by an elaborate mechanism of clockwork orders, but to "the individual initiative and right action of subordinates at the front who take advantage of every local opportunity." The role of the high command was to exploit each one of these local successes, reaping the full benefit by the timely employment of reserves.[58]

It was now beyond question that the Germans planned to fight the next war with mobile warfare methods exclusively. The men Conger had encountered at the division school knew that in the event of a war "they would have to submit to having their country invaded." Lacking the forces to engage the enemy frontally, they would have to resort to employing frontier guard formations and hastily raised levies to defend the frontiers and perhaps carry on some sort of guerrilla (or, in the American term, "bushwhacking") operations. The regular army would fight only to gain a decisive result, either offensively or defensively. If that were no longer possible, it would "retreat to a position in readiness and there await a more favorable opportunity regardless of the loss of territory or the strategic consequences." He had heard "no other possibility discussed by any responsible officer or instructor."[59]

There had been both good and bad in the classes he had seen. The courses in supply of troops in the field had been full of "methodical minuteness and precision."[60] Instruction in all matters of technique, such as the issuing of orders and weapons instruction, was very proficient. But the course in strategy had been very weak, really nothing more than an exercise in "grand tactics."[61] Rather than examine the underlying political, economic, and psychological grounds by which war is waged (i.e., a true course in strategy), the Germans concentrated on the technical considerations related to the movement of corps and armies in a particular theater of war. Comparing the strategy and history classes for the U.S. Army at Ft. Leavenworth, Conger felt the German courses were "extremely weak and backward." His analysis closed with words that today appear prophetic, even chilling:

> To sum up the impressions gained, I infer that in the next war the Germans will be tactically and technically a most formidable fighting force, but that the leaders of the army, in so far as they are trained in these schools, will suffer from the same defects which nullified to so great an extent the efforts of the German commanders in the field in the world war

in that they will again lack a correct understanding of the lessons taught
by military history and also lack an understanding of the broader principles of modern strategy, including its political and economic, as well as
its military, aspects, unless some self-made leader comes to the fore who
. . . gains for himself in some way a correct understanding of war in its
broader phases.

The appearance of that "self-made leader" was just around the corner, although Conger could scarcely have imagined how correct his prediction
would be.[62]

Notes

1. The realization of the fantastic nature of much of their training seems to
have filtered down through the ranks of the *Reichswehr*. Thinking back on his
training in antiaircraft and antitank tactics, one soldier wrote, "Die Durchführung
war etwas problematisch, weil diese Waffen für Deutschland verboten und nicht
einmal in Nachbildungen vorhanden waren. Oft mussten Belehrungen und Fantasie
die praktische Anschaulichkeit ersetzen" "Carrying out [our training] was somewhat problematic because these weapons were forbidden to Germany, and never
present in training. Often lessons and imagination had to replace practical clarify."
See Gerhard Lubs, *Aus der Geschichte eines Pommerschen Regiments 1920–1945*
(Bochum: Berg-Verlag, 1965), p. 20.
2. Jacques Benoist-Méchin, *Histoire de l'Armée Allemande* (Paris: Editions
Albin Michel, 1938), quoted in Friedrich von Rabenau, *Seeckt: Aus seinem Leben,
1918–1936* (Leipzig: Von Hase und Koehler, 1940), pp. 454–455.
3. The examination was published under the title *Die Werhkreis-Prüfung
1921* (Charlottenburg: Offene Worte, 1921), translated as *Extracts from Defense
Military Examination 1921* in *United States Military Intelligence Reports: Germany, 1919–1941* (Frederick, MD: University Publications of America, 1983), microfilm reel X, frames 418–444. In shorthand notation, the above document would
be labeled USMI, X, 418–444. Officers who had been transferred from one branch
of the service to another had an option as to which question to answer.
4. *Military Examination 1921,* USMI, X 423.
5. Ibid., USMI, X, 423–424.
6. Ibid., USMI, X, 424–426.
7. Ibid., USMI, X, 426.
8. Ibid., USMI, X, 427.
9. Ibid., USMI, X, 428.
10. Ibid., USMI, X, 429.
11. Colonel R. Stollberger, *Kampfschule für die Infanterie* (Charlottenburg:
Offene Worte, 1924), translated as *Combat School for the Infantry,* USMI, X,
525–686. The volume includes thirty-four exercises in all.
12. "Maneuver #1" is found in Stollberger, *Combat School,* USMI, X, 529–532.
13. Ibid., USMI, X, 530.
14. Ibid., USMI, X, 531–532. See also *Ausbildungsvorschrift für die Infanterie* (hereafter *A.V.I.*), vol. I, sec. 146 (in shorthand notation, A.V.I., I, 146) and
A.V.I. II, 247.
15. "Maneuver #1," USMI, X, 532. See also *A.V.I.,* I, 153, 155 for the ability
of machine guns to engage enemy aircraft.

16. The infantry battalion deploying under long-range artillery fire is found in "Maneuver #2," Stollberger, *Combat School,* USMI, X, 532–534. Deployment under the fire of heavy machine guns is the subject of "Maneuver #3," Stollberger, *Combat School,* USMI, X, 534–543.

17. "Maneuver #4" is found in Stollberger, *Combat School,* USMI, X, 543–550.

18. Two maneuvers in the *Combat School* (#11 and #12) deal with the "delaying attack"; two with the "delaying defense" (#13 and #14).

19. The examination was published under the title *Die Werhkreis-Prüfung 1924* (Charlottenburg: Offene Worte, 1924), translated as *The Defense District Examination 1924: With Solutions by Certain Officers,* in USMI, XVI, 409–447.

20. The first problem is found in *District Examination 1924,* USMI, XVI, 410–417.

21. See "Solution" to the first problem, *District Examination 1924,* USMI, XVI, 413–417.

22. Ibid., USMI, XVI, 414–415.

23. The second problem is found in *District Examination 1924,* USMI, XVI, 418–426.

24. Ibid., USMI, XVI, 420.

25. The third problem is found in *District Examination 1924,* USMI, XVI, 427–434.

26. The best study of the Marne—and Kluck's fateful "wheel"—is found in Correlli Barnett, *The Swordbearers: Studies in Supreme Command in the First World War* (New York: Morrow, 1963). See also Robert B. Asprey, *The First Battle of the Marne* (Philadelphia: Lippincott, 1962); Georges Blond, *The Marne* (London: MacDonald, 1965); and Wolfgang Paul, *Entscheidung im September: Das Wunder an der Marne 1914* (Esslingen: Bechtle, 1974). A work by a later *Reichswehr* minister is still quite useful: Wilhelm Groener, *Der Feldherr wider Willen: Operative Studien uber den Weltkrieg,* (Berlin: E. S. Mittler & Sohn, 1931).

27. For Tannenberg, see Francois's memoirs: Hermann Karl Francois, *Marneschlacht und Tannenberg: Betrachtungen zur deutschen Kriegsführung der ersten sechs Kriegswochen* (Berlin: A. Scherl, 1920). The definitive work is the recent monograph by Dennis E. Showalter, *Tannenberg: Clash of Empires* (Hamden, CT: Archon Books, 1991).

28. Arguing along these same lines are David N. Spires, *Image and Reality? The Making of the German Officer, 1921–1933* (Westport, CT: Greenwood Press, 1984), and Michael Geyer, "German Strategy in the Age of Machine Warfare, 1914–1945," in Peter Paret, ed., *Makers of Modern Strategy: From Machiavelli to the Nuclear Age* (Princeton, NJ: Princeton University Press, 1986), pp. 527–597. For a dissenting view, see James S. Corum, *The Roots of Blitzkrieg: Hans von Seeckt and German Military Reform* (Lawrence, KS: University Press of Kansas, 1992).

29. Carl von Clausewitz, *On War,* ed. and trans. Michael Howard and Peter Paret, book 1, ch. 1, no. 24 (Princeton, NJ: Princeton University Press, 1976), p. 87.

30. Colonel A. L. Conger, *Third Division Officers' School,* 7 March 1928, USMI, XIV, 374–408. See, especially, "Tactical Problem No. 1," appended to Conger, *Officers' School,* USMI, XIV, 375.

31. "Tactical Problem No. 1," in Conger, *Officers' School,* USMI, XIV, 376–377.

32. "Discussion of Map Problem I," appended to Conger, *Officers' School,* USMI, XIV, 378–379.

33. Ibid.

34. Colonel A. L. Conger, *Staff Instruction, 3rd Division, German Army: Tactical Map Problem*, 27 February 1927, USMI, XIV, 365–368.

35. Conger, *Staff Instruction*, USMI, XIV, 366.

36. "Discussion by Major Bohnstedt," appended to Conger, *Officers' School*, USMI, XIV, 367–368.

37. Ibid., USMI, XIV, 368.

38. Ibid.

39. "Wargame of February 13, 1928," appended to Conger, *Officers' School*, USMI, XIV, 383–384.

40. Ibid., USMI, XIV, 384.

41. "Situation for red," appended to *Wargame of February 13*, USMI, XIV, 385–386.

42. "Situation for blue," appended to *Wargame of February 13*, USMI, XIV, 387–388.

43. "Course of the Exercise," appended to *Wargame of February 13*, USMI, XIV, 389–390.

44. Ibid., USMI, XIV, 389.

45. Ibid., USMI, XIV, 390.

46. "Report of the 3rd Division Schools: Wargame of February 25, 1928," appended to Conger, *Officers' School*, USMI, XIV, 391–399.

47. Ibid., USMI, XIV, 399.

48. See the body of Conger's report on the *Third Division Officers' School*, USMI, XIV, 400–408.

49. Conger, *Officers' School*, USMI, XIV, 401.

50. The curriculum chart is found in Ibid., USMI, XIV, 402.

51. "Estimated Number of Officers Undergoing General Staff Training," in Conger, *Officers' School*, USMI, XIV, 403.

52. "Course in Tactics," in Conger, *Officers' School*, USMI, XIV, 403–404.

53. "Course in Military History," in Conger, *Officers' School*, USMI, XIV, 404–406.

54. "Course in Army Organization," in Conger, *Officers' School*, USMI, XIV, 406–407.

55. For the influence of "Americanism," "Taylorism," and "Fordism" on contemporary German social and economic life, see Mary Nolan, *Visions of Modernity: American Business and the Modernization of Germany* (New York: Oxford University Press, 1994). Apparently, such concepts had also entered German military thought in the 1920's.

56. "Course in Army Organization," Conger, *Officers' School*, USMI, XIV, 406.

57. "Conclusions," paragraphs 1 and 2, in Conger, *Officers' School*, USMI, XIV, 404–406.

58. "The Difference Between French and German Postwar Tactical Procedure (as Related by a German Officer)." The document is signed by Colonel Conger, but its date is unclear, as is its exact source. USMI, XIV, 595.

59. Conger translates *Bewegungskrieg* as "open warfare." See "Conclusions," paragraph 3, USMI, XIV, 407.

60. Ibid., paragraph 5.

61. Ibid., paragraph 4.

62. Ibid., paragraph 7.

CHAPTER 5

Exercises and Wargames

Since the days of the elder Helmuth von Moltke, no army in the world had taken wargames, exercises, and maneuvers as seriously as the German army.[1] This tradition received renewed emphasis during the Seeckt years. The *Reichswehr's* military simulations came in a variety of types.[2] The most important kind was the commander's wargame (*Führerkriegsspiel*), that simulated the movement and combat of available forces on the map. Played on a sand table, replete with terrain undulations, its purpose was to place officers and commanders in the midst of a realistic wartime situation, force them to decide on the appropriate action given the forces available, and express their decisions in clear orders. Such games usually involved two teams, with Germany as the blue and an enemy power as the red, but a three-sided game was also not out of the question, with Germany facing off against a western enemy (France, often represented as yellow) and an eastern one (Poland, red). Conducting the game was a direction staff (*Leitungsstab*, or simply *Leitung*). It worked out the war scenario (*Lage*) well in advance, carried out the movements as they were ordered, determined the outcome of individual battles, and most important, conducted a final discussion (*Schlussbesprechung*), bringing out the game's lessons for both sides and evaluating the sides' performance. This analysis, often quite lengthy, of the strategic and operational questions involved was much more important than any notion of "winning" or "losing" the game.

Of course, a wargame is not war. Problems could arise, for instance, with regard to intelligence. Having the *Leitung* umpire the game and actually carry out the movement of units for both teams, only allowing one team in the gameroom at a time, and covering the table with a large sheet of paper all contributed to keeping each side in the dark about the other's moves. But even with these precautions, breaking up the continuous activity of war into "turns" often led to anomalies on the gameboard. Even more regrettable was the necessity of having one's own officers command the teams representing other nationalities. With German officers, trained in

105

a certain system and imbued with a certain spirit, commanding the "French" or "Polish" armies, the game often degenerated into three "German" armies maneuvering around the map. This problem was essentially unsolvable, however, and it was left to the *Leitung* to urge events into a direction that would be most instructive to the participants.

The army also participated in a number of staff tours (*Führerreisen*). Usually overseen by the chief of the Army Command (General von Seeckt until 1926, followed by Generals Heye and von Hammerstein), the tours dealt with concrete defense problems in a given geographical area. They typically involved higher staff officers of the two army Group Commands (*Gruppenkommandos*), divisional commanders, and officers of the disguised General Staff (*Truppenamt*) in actual tours of the "battlefield." Their purpose was not only to impart a more realistic training in the problems of actual war than was possible in the classroom, but also to familiarize officers with terrain over which they might one day have to fight.

Finally, there was the field exercise (*Übung*) and the maneuver (*Manöver*). Involving actual units in the field, these were typically concerned with training, the testing of tactics and equipment, and the overall battleworthiness of the army, rather than the broader questions of strategy and operations. The principal difference was one of scale. The *Übung* involved smaller units up to regimental level; the *Manöver* involved one or more divisions or even corps. Both occupy an extremely important place in German military planning in the interwar period. Given the severe constraints placed on the army by the Treaty of Versailles, the *Reichswehr* command felt that it was necessary to get the men into the field as often as was humanly (and materially) possible, if only to preserve their fighting spirit.

Umpire Regulations, May 1921

The foundation for *Reichswehr* maneuvers was the manual *Regulations for the Umpire Service During Troop Maneuvers* and its appendix "Guiding Principles for Judging the Efficiency of Arms," issued by General von Seeckt in May 1921 and revised in both 1923 and 1924.[3] The *Regulations* began with a discussion of the umpire's main goal, which was to provide "the impression of actual war" that peacetime maneuvers invariably lacked. It was up to the umpire to force both sides to realize the importance of both individual action and of combined arms. He had to take action to prevent unrealistic situations. He also had to take into account the effect of weapons that Germany did not then possess—not just tanks and planes, but items such balloons and poison gas, for instance. He was to take into account moral, as well as material, factors in rendering his decisions. The job required independent tactical judgment, knowledge of all arms, energy, foresight, and the ability to make prompt decisions and to bear responsibility for them.[4]

In terms of organization, the umpire service's first requirement was a large number of men, both officers and experienced, older noncommissioned officers: "Economy in this case easily results in the purpose of the maneuver not being attained and is therefore a mistake."[5] It was also advisable to use officers from all branches of the army taking part in the exercise, including machine gun, trench mortar, and Signal Corps personnel. During the maneuver, the officers would be responsible for reporting to the headquarters on situations peculiar to their own branches, information that would allow the head umpire to gain a truer impression of the overall operation. Besides these special assistants, it was advisable to attach an officer of the umpire service to every unit taking part (e.g., battalion, battery, cavalry squadron, signal company), as well as one to each sector of the battle (e.g., one for the blue right wing and red left wing, another for the center, a third for the blue left wing and the red right).[6]

All the umpires were to meet with the commanding officer before the exercise. They were to learn the instructional purpose, the intentions and initial orders of the leaders on both sides, and the contemplated course of the exercise. They would be instructed on such things as how aircraft and balloons were to be represented (and their effect on operations), whether gas shells had already been fired to suppress the artillery of one side or another, and whether heavy artillery was present (and the level of its ammunition supply). They might receive special maps or sketches.[7] They would have recourse to a full complement of mounted messengers, cyclists, and signal and observation equipment, as well as a "neutral" (i.e., not available to either side in the maneuver) telephone net.[8]

Wearing a white band on his cap and sleeve, an umpire first had to select a favorable position with a good view of the "battlefield." The senior umpire moved as little as possible during the proceedings: his activity was never to betray the movements of one side's troops to the enemy. During the action, his principal task was to inform the troops continuously of the kind and effect of enemy fire, and insofar as would be possible in a real war, the effect of their own fire. As a rule, an umpire never made a decision until an action had been completed. Then came the time for his decision.[9]

Evaluation of enemy fire had to be prompt, and the umpire was never to err on the side of caution. He should not hesitate to report the effect of enemy fire, even if he only had a "reasonable supposition of its presence" and even if he "has not been fully informed regarding the movements of the other side." He simply had to risk the error. Only in this manner could the troops avoid unrealistic maneuvering within range of enemy guns.[10]

It was the umpire's responsibility to designate which troops were killed, injured, or taken prisoner. All units were to be trained to consider surrender "disgraceful." Should a unit be taken, "the umpire must always look into it and see whether there was not even the smallest chance for the unit to fight its way through the enemy." He was then to impress his findings upon the unit. All units taken out of action designated themselves by

having their troops turn the lining of their caps inside out. Individual soldiers were to remain where they were at the time of the umpire's decision;
they were then collected at intervals and led back to their unit's initial assembly points. Affected machine guns and trench mortars were turned
around and marked with a yellow flag. Finally, the umpire had to make a
split-second decision at the moment troops were fighting hand to hand.
The results here were simple, direct, and brutal, for example: "The Red infantry in sector x—y is annihilated. The Blue attack was therefore a success." If the umpire had observed the prior activities of both sides, he
should already have reached a conclusion regarding success or failure. The
victor was then allowed the opportunity to follow up his victory. There was
no artificial separation of the troops as in the pre-war maneuvers: a natural
separation between the victors and the defenders falling back would result,
anyway, since the pursuing force had to prepare its own position for counterattacks and reorganize his troops in depth for the pursuit.[11]

In judging an attack the umpire had to take a number of factors into account. They included the condition of the attacking troops (the demands
placed on them during previous march and combat, their state of rest and
nourishment); the nature of the terrain and weather; the effect of enemy aerial reconnaissance; the measures adopted for antiaircraft defense; the preparation and execution of friendly reconnaissance, both ground and air; the actual start of the attack (whether the defenders took advantage of the terrain,
whether they assembled in depth, as well as the resulting reduction in the effect of defensive fire); the cooperation of the various arms—the grouping
and observation of artillery targets, the manner and time required for artillery preparation, and the effect of flanking fire; the state of communication and signal services; the initiative of the leaders and striking power of
the troops; uniformity in execution of the attack; the care taken to establish
superiority at the decisive point; the use of envelopment and surprise; quickness in preparing the newly won ground against enemy counterattack or fire;
the conduct of the troops during enemy counterattacks; and the state of ammunition supply and measures taken for replenishment.[12]

Similar points were important for the umpire's judgment of a defensive effort. As in the case of an attack, the condition of the troops, protection from enemy air reconnaissance, communications, the level of cooperation of all arms, and the effect of flanking fire were all important. There
were also points, however, that were unique to the defense: the use and
strengthening of the terrain; the depth of the defensive position; and the
timing, direction, and impetus of the counterattack. During a maneuver,
the construction of defensive works would seldom actually take place, due
to the great damage caused to property. Most terrain preparations would
simply be declared. The umpire would then inform the defenders whether
or not there was time and manpower to finish their contemplated work. He
might, for reasons of the overall maneuver, forbid the work entirely due

to "high ground water" or "impenetrable rock," or "lack of construction materials." He would immediately transmit this decision to the concerned troops.[13]

Maneuvers, 1922

The *Reichswehr's* most effective peacetime training method was the maneuver in the field. That was true of the old Imperial Army, as well, but there were essential differences. Seeckt took great pains to avoid the isolation of the various arms that had characterized the prewar era. Opinion within the *Truppenamt* was strong that the *Kaiserheer* had erred in trying to perfect each arm separately and had ignored the fact that the perfection of each arm was only to be found in full cooperation with the others.

A 1922 article by an active *Truppenamt* officer discussed the point at length.[14] The lesson of World War I was that infantry was still the principal battlefield arm. The foot soldier—bayonet in hand, crashing into the enemy position—was still the essence of battlefield victory, and the mission of the other arms was to support the advance of the infantry. Open warfare was "the kernel of modern strategy," since it alone made possible the accomplishment of strategic victory. A more or less permanent "confinement in trenches" was a "degenerate form of warfare." It was precisely a failure of the supporting arms that brought offensive movement to a standstill and led to positional warfare.

But auxiliary arms could only do their job once they were thoroughly acquainted with the tasks of infantry in a large-scale engagement. Thus, the determining characteristic of modern training had to be the mixed training of troops at regular intervals, as well as the instruction of the officers of the supporting arms in the tactics of the infantry. Battle training for all arms should take place at maneuver camps designed for the purpose. Unit inspections had to be held frequently, and should ensure that troop units met wartime standards. After the inspection, exercises of all arms were to be held, infantry, artillery, and other arms training together in exercises of all kinds—including range firing.

Battle situations in the exercises should be "simple and ordinary" and communicated to the units as they left their billets. "Anything which affects the general course of the action must be represented as in actual battle, or reported in messages or orders." This would, of course, require the services of a large number of umpires and assistants.

The choice of the battle situation faced one great difficulty, however. In the modern world of mass armies, a situation in which companies or battalions would have a chance to act alone belonged to the realm of fantasy. The battle scenario would have to make clear that the small units were integral parts of some larger action. For instance, a company could be designated as the advance point for an entire division or as part of an advanced battalion operating on a flank. These sorts of situations arose constantly on the modern battlefield. If only small units were mentioned in the maneuver problem, "the minds of the men [would be] impressed with something which no longer exists." Small-unit commanders would have to gain their instruction elsewhere, in frequent *Führerreisen*, for instance. The troops, however, were to be shown "only that which actually occurs in a modern battle, i.e., the fighting methods of large units."[15]

Another serious maneuver problem arose at the moment the enemy front was penetrated. Maneuvers had formerly tended to end at this point: in the immediate prewar years, this was the moment when the directors gave the signal to halt, held a critique, and reorganized and separated both sides. The exercise then resumed, with an intervening distance between the two sides, by allowing the defeated side a half-hour head start. These maneuvers had ignored the decisive moment when the defender launched the counterthrust with his reserves, a hard lesson learned by all sides in the previous war. Heavy fighting had invariably taken place inside the defensive position at the moment the enemy front was ruptured. When the attacking force was fatigued and disorganized, its foothold precarious at best, a skillfully conducted operation by the defenders might repulse it altogether. Representing this decisive element in battle would teach the attacking force some important lessons: it had to advance in well-ordered formations, and keep strong reserves available for support in any possible emergency. Fighting and attacking in echelon was also an important requirement, rather than throwing in the last reserves the moment the enemy line was penetrated.[16]

Numerous small-unit problems could be studied in such an exercise. Safety measures would have to be in place, but firing exercises and maneuvers must never be separate. Small units such as companies might hold their preliminary shoots separate from other exercises, but all firing exercises had to assume battle conditions, and there was to be no more firing at targets. This was not to say that live ammunition had to be used—blank ammunition with the same ballistic effect was perfectly suitable, especially for artillery.

In executing attacks against an enemy represented by targets, the effect of fire should be ascertained by repeated examination, and the actions of the attacker modified if necessary. The signal to suspend fire should be given, then the umpires would examine the targets. As a matter of principle, the survival of a single enemy machine gun nest should be cause to discontinue an infantry attack, and the attacker was to first call in fire from support arms to silence the machine gun. If, as was formerly done, the attack was simply allowed to continue, the result would eventually be a well-worn target (shredded by rifle fire at close range), but no real lessons learned. It was medium- and long-range hits that actually permitted an infantry advance to take place.[17]

The article ended with a discussion of the umpire service and labeled it the decisive element in staging a realistic maneuver. Umpires were responsible for bringing out the best in the individual and combined arms and for excluding anything not appropriate to a real battle. Only experienced officers should be called on, though younger officers and noncommissioned personnel could serve as assistants.

The commander of the maneuver was responsible for all the umpires. He had to discuss the maneuver with the umpires, making sure they were familiar with the terrain and all possibilities that might arise. Each side was to have its own umpire staff with numerous assistants. Once a chief umpire had taken up position between the two sides, all reports from both umpire staffs were to come to him, usually via telephone. He and he alone supervised the entire maneuver by personal intervention, based on the reports he had received. His decisions would then be subject to criticism by the commander of the maneuver during the final discussion (*Schlussbesprechung*) that formally closed the proceedings.[18]

Guiding Principles for Judging the Effect of Weapons, 1924

The most important segment of the umpire regulations was the annex, "Guiding Principles for Judging the Effect of Weapons"[19] Here were the *Reichswehr's* own guidelines for the tactical efficiency of various arms on the field of battle. Although the guidelines were intended to guide the umpire's decisions in a maneuver, they also offer a great deal of insight into German tactical doctrine.

We begin with infantry weapons (rifles, light and heavy machine guns, trench mortars, and infantry guns).[20] To be most effective, they had to work in combination—both with each other and with artillery and tanks. Their effect was determined by four things: the number of pieces firing, the direction of the fire, the efficiency of the riflemen or crew, and the accurate installation of the heavy machine gun or trench mortar for indirect fire. Beyond these were a number of target factors such as the distance, height, width, depth, thickness, and recognition factor of the target, and the nature of the ground (which might affect the possibility of observing hits, or the conditions for impact and burst, or the inclination of the target to the line of sight) around the target. In addition, the effect of enemy fire, the influence of the weather and lighting, and the possibilities of ammunition replenishment all had to be taken into account. And, of course, range was decisive. When firing at a high target, a heavy machine gun with sights set at the highest elevation could expect success up to a range of 2,500 meters for direct fire; up to 3,500 meters for indirect fire. For the light machine gun and rifle, the effective range was 1,200 meters. Out to

800 meters, rifles and light machine guns could expect to achieve an "annihilating effect."

During an attack, groups of riflemen advancing without cover would begin to suffer "considerable losses" at long ranges from unmolested enemy infantry and especially from its machine guns. Losses became "heavy" at medium range, and increased with the density of the target. With the addition of a flanking machine gun, the effect increased to "annihilating." Thus uninterrupted movement within enemy line of sight and without cover was out of the question. Advance was only possible if one's own infantry cleverly worked itself forward, making careful use of the terrain and under the protection of artillery as well as heavy and light infantry weapons. Against low targets, "well-nestled in the terrain," a heavy machine gun could have good success out to 1,200 meters. The fire of light machine guns and rifle groups against such targets would be fully effective only out to 600 meters.

Infantry rifle fire had other uses as well. It could be very effective against targets appearing suddenly at close range (a soldier lifting his head, for example), though such fire required "a good, observant, and quick acting rifleman."[21] Infantry could also paralyze the movement of artillery and hinder its fire by engaging it from the front. It could not, however, expect to silence a battery in this manner: the riflemen would have to take the artillery in the flank, especially with light and heavy machine gun fire. Sudden, well-planned fire was necessary.

The fire effect of small arms could be especially devastating against mounted machine guns and limbered artillery. But machine guns in position—with or without shields—were difficult targets to hit. Even the loss of a crew member or two had little appreciable impact on a machine gun's firepower. What was required was the combination of machine gun fire from various directions, if possible in cooperation with light trench mortars and, especially, direct fire artillery. And before such destructive fire could be called in, individual sharpshooters could at the least hinder an enemy machine gun at ranges up to 800 meters.

Flanking fire was effective at all ranges and against all targets, most of all when carried out by machine guns. Even in darkness or fog, light machine gun fire up to 800 meters and heavy machine gun fire up to 1,200 could do a great deal of damage. Fire from light machine guns could also be effective against aircraft at ranges (not altitude) of up to 600 meters; a heavy machine gun might even be able to bring down aircraft at 1,000 meters, if its fire was aimed along the special antiaircraft sight at the front of the weapon.

The "Principles" discussed heavy machine guns in some detail.[22] It was a weapon with multiple uses: it could lay down direct fire on an observed target; indirect fire on a target observed by a third party; and finally, direct or indirect fire on invisible targets, that is, upon zones or areas. With good distribution of fire and accurate data, a heavy machine gun using area fire was capable of laying down a field of fire extending some 200 meters into the enemy's position. While care had to be taken in firing over or through the gaps in one's own troops, the sudden appearance of heavy machine gun fire in an engagement always had an appreciable moral effect and greatly increased the chance of victory.

The trench mortar (*Minenwerfer*) was useful, as well. The crucial fact to be kept in mind was the time it took to be brought into action. Therefore, in judging the effectiveness of its fire, one had to determine the available time, the position of the gun when firing, the position of its observation post in relation to the gun, the duration of the fire, and the ammunition supply. Also important were the distance from the target, the target's size, visibility and position, and the wind (capable of having a great impact on high-angle fire by a light mortar). Contamination of the friendly firing position by enemy gas shells might also be a factor; it could reduce the effectiveness of trench mortar fire or make it altogether impossible. Mortars also had a special ability of hitting targets behind steep slopes, villages, tall woods, and in trenches; they could also hit targets screened from direct artillery fire by the close proximity of friendly infantry. Owing to the accuracy of their fire and their close liaison with the infantry, the mortars were often the weapon of choice for hitting enemy machine gun nests and advanced observation stations. Light trench mortars could also fire from what the Germans called an "open position," using direct fire on a flat trajectory. This could be devastating against enemy skirmishers advancing in dense groups or lines from about 1,000 to 150 meters, especially if used in conjunction with flanking fire. Used in a high-angle mode, such fire was effective from 1,100 to 325 meters (and impossible at closer ranges).

When used against artillery, trench mortars could not be counted on for decisive results. But light mortars could make it impossible for artillery to maneuver, even when under cover. The mortars could thus impede its fire activity and even force it to cease fire temporarily. Trench mortars were to endeavor whenever possible to shell enemy artillery while it was limbering or unlimbering. Trench mortars could also be effective against machine guns, both limbered and unlimbered, though against a heavy machine gun in firing position, mortars required very careful fire preparation. Against tanks, trench mortars were not effective, though the mortars could hinder an advance by directing their fire against enemy infantry accompanying the tanks.[23]

The "Principles" then turned to cavalry. The horse arm was to fight mainly with its firearms, while using the horse to increase its mobility. Therefore any evaluation of its combat effect revolved around the number of infantry weapons it brought to bear. The fire effect of its skirmishers was the same as that of infantry, although cavalry skirmishers would have "more frequent opportunities than infantry for attacking from the rear and flanks." Mobility was the edge that made cavalry fire more effective. The only way cavalry could operate mounted was in the context of a mixed attack that succeeded in completely suppressing enemy fire—or through surprise. In a meeting engagement of two mounted forces, "the one which charges the enemy with leveled lance without hesitation" would be the victor. But under hostile infantry fire mounted action as a unit was totally impossible: "Only single horsemen and small patrols can move, riding skillfully at a rapid gait." Under hostile artillery fire mounted units had to "ride rapidly and in a thin formation" if they were to avoid terrible losses.[24]

By far the largest portion of the "Principles" dealt with artillery fire.[25] As always, the starting point was the same: "the performance of artillery is measured by its direct and indirect usefulness to the infantry." It must never fire simply for its own sake. Preparation for delivering effective support to the infantry took time and required correct data on the target, good reconnaissance and signaling equipment, and useful maps. It was most effective when firing from a concealed, surveyed, and unexpected position, carefully protected from air surveillance. Further factors to be taken into account included the types of projectiles and fuses to be employed; the distance, position, size, and discernibility of the target; the enemy's use of terrain and diversion; the ability of friendly forces to observe the shot; the question of who had mastery of the air, and so forth. Finally, the question of close cooperation with the infantry and trench mortars was of crucial importance. Artillery fire was by far the most complicated factor in modern warfare.

The manual recommended firing as close as possible during battle to the friendly infantry "without endangering it in any way." The better the opportunities for observation, the shorter this distance might be. But "in critical moments, the infantry had better suffer being hit by a few rounds which have fallen short than renounce effective artillery support."[26] In an attack, the element of decisive importance was the speed with which artillery fire arrived to support the infantry. The "Principles" also told umpires to take into account the psychological effect of artillery, the nerve-racking sound of its detonation, and the uncertainty of knowing where the next round might fall. Such qualities might have a devastating effect on shaken or poorly trained infantry.

Specific guns were appropriate to specific targets. Field guns, for example, were best when used against live targets in the open with no overhead protection, against tall shelters, or against any lightly protected targets. Effective range was 9 kilometers. Cannon mounted on armored cars could be used in situations requiring a sudden, rapid fire, out to an effective range of 7 kilometers; the cannons' mobility enabled them to escape enemy counterbattery fire. Infantry guns were useful for laying down single accurate rounds up to 4 kilometers. Mortars, due to the penetration of their burst, were best suited for action against prepared positions, installed batteries, and weak concrete shelters. Also, "a single shot from them versus assembled troops has an annihilating effect." The "Principles" laid down detailed instructions for all the other types of guns in the German arsenal (and some that were forbidden by the Versailles Treaty)—mountain guns, light field howitzers, antiaircraft guns, heavy field howitzers, medium and heavy cannon.

In fighting enemy artillery, prospects for success were best when using observed fire against an enemy battery on the move. All calibers were capable of achieving good effect in this way. Artillery unlimbered in the open was also very vulnerable, but once deployed in an emplacement or pit, it was vulnerable only to heavy caliber fire. At any rate, complete suppression of hostile guns was rare over the long term, particularly if batteries made use of the terrain and deployed in long, winding, or irregular formations. The guns' destruction required planning—a "carefully conducted, observed destructive fire at an effective combat range" was necessary. Air observation could play a crucial role. A battery under ground cover, but observable from the air, might as well be in the open.

The "Principles" ended its artillery section with a few comments regarding its effect on infantry. All troops in close formations suffered heavily under artillery fire. A well-placed barrage on troops forming up for an attack could break up the assault before it even started. Even loose-order skirmishers presented a good target, whether they were on the move or prone, and light-caliber guns could be particularly effective against them. Infantry's best protection was still the spade. The deeper and cleverer the infantry dug, "the less recognizable its works, the more irregularly they are laid out," the lower would be its losses to artillery fire.[27]

The "Principles" ended with a discussion of air power and armor, present in German maneuvers if not in the *Reichswehr* itself. Aircraft were important support weapons for the other arms. In carrying out their primary mission, reconnaissance, the crucial factors were not only the quality of the plane and the training of the crew, but also the weather, visibility, and protective measures taken by the other side. The aviator's orders had to be clear; he had to be told exactly what kind of information the commander wanted to know. From the ground perspective, three factors were useful in foiling air reconnaissance: the troops' skill in combating aircraft, the clever use of disguising terrain, and measures taken to fool and mislead the enemy. Guns, and machine guns, and their crews could fight off airplanes, but required the appropriate mounts, sufficient ammunition, and special training. Finally, troops on the ground should also adapt to the terrain and split up into smaller units.

The effect of an air attack could be decisive: the "moral effect" of the appearance of enemy aircraft was "in most cases greater than the actual performance of the weapons." A unit already exhausted by combat might be completely dispersed by air attack, especially if caught in close formation or in a defile, and most especially if it contained cavalry or wagons. Repeated bombing attacks, often staged by night, might produce severe moral effects on the target unit.

As for tanks, even poorly led armored units were capable of annihilating unprotected infantry. But the "Principles" identified problems with the tank as well, in a section worth quoting in full.

> The gun work of tanks will be considerably limited by their movements, the shaking and swaying wide in movement, and also by the limited field of view. For that reason, good work with them can be done only at ranges up to 200 meters. Their greatest range is 600 meters. The tank is therefore a close range combat weapon, and it cannot be used as artillery at long ranges.[28]

Due to insufficient height tanks were incapable of firing over the heads of their own troops, and they also vulnerable to enemy artillery fire. Even infantry, operating at close range and equipped with antitank rifles, flamethrowers, and demolition charges, represented an antitank threat. Tanks also had to be careful about obstructions (e.g., ditches, water wider than 3 meters, barricades, fallen trees, minefields) The delay caused by such obstructions made tanks vulnerable to planned enemy fire. Clearly, the German army did not consider the tank some sort of wonder weapon.

The comments on armor attack were perceptive, and deserve attention. Presaging the development of the *Blitzkrieg*, the "Principles" stated that success with armor was only possible through a "sudden launching of tanks en masse on a broad front and in a deep formation." A massed armor attack "splits up the work of the defenses, especially artillery." Employment of armor on a narrow front (or in a small number) would succeed only in concentrating upon itself all enemy fire in the vicinity: far from being an effective support for the infantry, in this case tanks were a positive danger. Above all, they should never be used individually.[29]

Signal Troop Exercises, 1922

Given his great stress on mobility, Seeckt regarded the signal troops as a crucial component of the modern army. In August 1922, 1st Group Command, headquartered in Berlin, held the first signal exercise of the interwar era, testing the *Reichswehr's* wireless facilities; use of carrier pigeons, telephones, and messenger dogs; as well as its techniques of visual signaling. The goal was to give the signal troops practice in their craft in conditions approaching what they were likely to encounter in the field. The exercise's war situation was an attack upon Germany from the east (Poland and Czechoslovakia), with German forces having been pushed back but in the process of mounting a counteroffensive. Signaling services and equipment from at least three divisions were involved in the exercise.[30]

The exercises yielded some interesting findings. Orders tended to be much too long, leading the umpires to stress clarity and brevity in all messages. Officers tended to rely far too heavily on the telephone, ignoring other forms of communication (e.g., wireless, motorcycles, riders). Often, the advance of the troops was held up while engineers constructed a trunk line for telephones.[31]

But other signaling methods also showed problems. Coding and decoding messages was a time-consuming affair (and prone to error due to lack of trained personnel). Messages carried by automobile often encountered delays, for example, on roads blocked by troops or in such a poor state of repair that they were nearly impassable. The result of such delays was that one division (the 2nd Infantry) was "lost" for one whole day, that is, it was out of communication with its high command.[32] When telephone communications were finally reestablished, they lasted for only a few moments, and then were lost again. The chief of the exercise's direction staff (the *Leitung*), Gen. Georg Wetzell, reminded all concerned that just as it was the responsibility of the high command to maintain contact with its subordinate units, it was equally the responsibility of the subordinate unit to seek out its commanders when contact had been broken. Apparently, the 2nd Division did not appear sufficiently upset at having been lost in the exercise.

The directors also noticed a tendency to overreact. When a weak enemy force was encountered (an advance guard of bicyclists or cavalry, for example), friendly signal troops went into service much too hastily, establishing, among others, an extensive branch telephone net, sections for flash signaling, and wireless transmitters. By the time such an elaborate net was ready the battle was over, the enemy dispersed, and a great deal of equipment readied to do nothing in particular. As a result telephone equipment was often not available in areas where it was really needed. Erecting and dismantling a telephone net was hard work, and dangerous under fire. It was only to be undertaken, Wetzell instructed, when it was really necessary.[33]

The *Leitung* also was highly critical of the performance of the wireless troops. On the one hand, messages were all too often sent *en clair*, which would have given valuable information to the enemy, "even if he paid only the slightest attention." On the other, signal personnel needed to be reminded of the difficulty of wireless transmission, coding, and decoding. Sending messages of over 100 words, which took place more than a few times during this exercise, was "nonsensical," said Wetzell.[34]

Finally, a word about dogs and pigeons. Wetzell was pleased with the performance of the former. The dogs proved loyal and dependable, though often they were distracted by "too much play with the men" and fatigued by the long marches. "A strict prohibition against playing with the dogs is necessary," he stated. Pigeons had had some successes in the war; the French, for example, had used them to good effect at Ft. Vaux in the battle of Verdun.[35] But they were total failures in this exercise: there were delays, lost messages, and vehicle crashes in which pigeons were killed. Clearly, this was not a method of communications upon which the *Reichswehr* could rely.

Maneuvers 1923: 1st Infantry Division

The first interwar maneuver for which we have a detailed description took place in the fall of 1923.[36] *Reichswehr* Minister Otto Gessler invited the U.S. military attaché, Col. A. L. Conger, to East Prussia for field exercises involving elements of the 1st Division. They took place on 10–11 September in the area between Johannisburg and Sensburg, close to the Polish frontier. The units taking part in the exercise were the 2nd Infantry Regiment, one battalion of artillery, one *Minenwerfer* company, and one regiment of cavalry (*Reiterregiment*).

The exercise was based on the historical situation of 1914, a continuous operation extending over a period of six days. The German forces took the part of a detachment pushed out from a northern red army invading East Prussia from the east (equivalent to Rennenkampf's 1st Russian Army of 1914). Its mission was to move around the southern end of Lake Spirding and establish communications with another red army (Samsonov's 2nd Army) that was advancing from the south along the axis Ortelsburg-Bischofsburg. The detachment was to move from the 1st Division training ground at Arys via Johannisburg, to the south of Lake Spirding, and then to advance on Sensburg and drive out any hostile forces there. At the same time, its orders were to establish communications between the left wing of the northern red army through Nikolaiken and the right wing of the southern red army that was passing through Willenberg, Ortelsburg, and Bischofsburg. The chief umpire would have to determine whether this connection had indeed been made.

The use of this campaign as a training tool is indicative of Seeckt's overall strategic vision. The battle of Tannenberg, in which the Germans saved East Prussia by crushing one invading army and then turning to maul the other, was perhaps the ultimate example of an encirclement battle, a "Cannae," in German military parlance.[37] The victory had largely been due to the Russian's failure to establish communications between their two invading armies. The Germans had thus been able to deal with one army at a time. The exercise of 1923 attempted to show that it was possible for two armies, one from the south and one from the east, to cooperate in an invasion of East Prussia. In 1923, however, the territories from which these armies would invade was Polish. One may therefore view the 1923 maneuver as a test of the feasibility of a Polish invasion of Germany's isolated eastern province. For the record, the detachment did establish communications between the two invading armies, which then pressed on to take Königsberg.

Colonel Conger was quite impressed with what he saw of the *Reichswehr*. In his report to the War Department, he remarked that all the equipment seemed well cared for, the animals were in excellent condition and well groomed, and the men were alert at their work and looked fit. The officer directing the exercise remarked to him that "we can depend on the troops of this division." All officers seemed thorough and conscientious. Conger's general estimate of morale and efficiency was "far above average."

More specifically, he was impressed with the mobility and march discipline of the troops. Carrying their "light field packs" weighing about 60 pounds, the troops still managed an average march of 28 kilometers on Monday, 10 September. The mounted troops went much farther due to the nature of their work. One of the battery commanders told Conger that he had ridden his horse by nightfall a full 75 kilometers. In spite of this distance, however, Conger noted no signs of undue fatigue on the part of the infantry or any of the animals he observed. At day's end he concluded that both men and animals were in good, hardened condition.[38]

Conger also reported on the use of the *Minenwerfer* in the combat. Each company contained three medium mortars (17cm) and nine light ones (7.6cm). The medium piece was amounted on a carriage and pulled by a team of four horses, while the light one required a two-horse team. When the pieces went into position, the wheels were simply removed and the platforms placed on the ground. But these weapons were not completely satisfactory, he felt. Everywhere he heard repeated the slogans of offensive, maneuver-oriented warfare. Numerous officers had told him they viewed trench warfare as "degenerate" and repeatedly pointed out the limitations of the medium *Minenwerfer:* "A very frequent remark made by the umpires was: 'I am no friend of the Minenwerfer.' On account of their very short range the difficulties of keeping them near enough to the front to be effectively used in an attack was apparent even in the maneuvers."[39]

The exercise also demonstrated Seeckt's success in training the men in techniques of infantry assault. Conger described the method by which German infantry advanced over dangerous ground. As the infantry advanced to the front, heavy machine guns were placed in position and advanced by echelons so that there were always some in position to fire in case the enemy showed himself. Light machine guns moved forward with their units until opposition was actually encountered. "It is a fixed principle that the machine guns must furnish the small arms firepower and that the infantry must close to the assault. The firing is of secondary importance and he is not permitted to use his rifle except at good targets at very close range."[40]

These comments indicate how closely the *Reichswehr* was following the new tactical manuals that Seeckt had written, in particular *F.u.G.* and

A.V.I. The assault by highly mobile infantry remained the logical culmination of battle and it was characterized by the use of combined arms and support fire from the heavy weapons, especially light and heavy machine guns. Again, to Seeckt, these were the lessons of World War I, not the supposed invulnerability of the defense.

Conger also discussed the activities of the umpires. They did not, under any circumstances, make tactical decisions; that was the province of the actual troop commanders. If a unit leader wanted to lead a dense column assault over 1,000 meters of open terrain into the teeth of twelve enemy heavy machine guns and artillery, that was his prerogative (though it should be added that German officers took these maneuvers very seriously and were hardly the sort to be too frivolous with their tactics). The umpire merely transmitted information. He was to be seen riding back and forth across the battlefield, reporting to both sides, providing information, in Conger's words, "such as projectiles of the enemy would give in actual battle." He would, for example, impose losses on a particular unit that had exposed itself to incoming fire or order a delay in a unit's movement. But umpires were not permitted to give information regarding the enemy. The only way to get that was through reconnaissance. As a result, much of the maneuver day passed in very long delays. One umpire told Conger, however, that there was nothing wrong with that: "War is more than half made up of waiting."[41]

Maneuvers, 1924

The 1924 fall maneuver featured elements of the 2nd and 3rd Infantry Divisions, as well as the 2nd Cavalry Division.[42] It took place along the Oder near Küstrin. The *Leitung* of the maneuver specified three goals for the exercise: to practice and solve problems in a war of movement, with the very limited means permitted to the *Reichswehr*; to give as much experience as possible to all officers and troops in warlike conditions, using as many commanders and staffs as possible for practice in troop command and tactics; and to specialize in flanking operations. According to the U.S. military attaché, Col. Allen Kimberly, no illegal weapons (aircraft, balloons, gas, heavy artillery, tanks, antitank or antiaircraft guns) were actually used, and the number of machine guns was limited. But the Germans did simulate all these weapons in the course of the exercise. In place of actual warplanes, for example, an officer (generally an ex-aviator) with special markings rode unhindered on a motorcycle through and around enemy lines. Upon his "landing," he reported in writing to the umpire; the umpire then decided how much of this report was in keeping with an actual aerial reconnaissance and transmitted all or part of it to the commander sending out the "aviator." Antitank guns were constructed of wood and pipe, although Kimberly noticed that the sights appeared to be real. There were no military aircraft in the *Reichswehr*, of course, but commercial craft en route to Königsberg or Poland circled the field daily, and were targets for simulated machine gun fire. Dummy tanks made of light wood and canvas also appeared, camouflaged and pushed by men inside the tanks.[43]

Kimberly spent much of the five days of the maneuver in the company of his guide, Maj. Walter von Reichenau.[44] He was furnished with all relevant documents and maps and was permitted to visit any part of the field he wished. He did not attend the final discussion (*Schlussbesprechung*)—no foreign observer did—but his report is as complete a picture as we are likely to get of the German army in the Seeckt era.

The first maneuver problem dealt with a German (blue) counterattack against a Polish (red) drive toward Küstrin. Both sides had access to aerial reconnaissance, and both strove in three days of action to find and attack the enemy flank. Cavalry played a key role, working in union with aircraft and machine gun units to seize strategically important positions. A major feature in this maneuver was the blue's storming of red positions on Vossberg Hill outside Küstrin.[45]

The second problem dealt with blue forces using an infantry and cavalry division to strike a counterblow at a red force crossing the Oder River below Küstrin. The operation called for an envelopment by blue forces of the left (south) wing of the enemy as it crossed the river. Red plans were to cross the Oder and envelop the right (north) wing of the blue defenders. Thus both sides had the task of attacking one enemy flank while simultaneously guarding their own. The climax of this operation was a charge by a brigade of blue cavalry against the flank of two red artillery batteries. Before the blue troopers could carry out the destruction of the red guns, they were in turn taken in the flank by a red assault force including tanks. Detachments of blue cavalry managed to save the day, however, by getting around the flank of red advance guard and launching an attack on the enemy's rear.[46] At this point, the maneuver ended. It had been a busy two days, and a good practice for all concerned in the exhilaration—and difficulty—of mobile warfare.

Kimberly had been impressed with the staff officers he had observed. They gave orders very efficiently in both oral and written form and saw to it that they were transmitted promptly to the troops. This gave the troops time to carry out detailed reconnaissance before executing their orders. The orders themselves followed a regular scheme: a first paragraph describing enemy movements and intentions, a second and third giving the friendly plan of attack, and a fourth giving the location of the commander issuing the order.[47]

The men had also acquitted themselves nicely. Infantry carried out its attacks skillfully, maintaining its communications laterally and to the rear and making good use of machine guns in both the advance and the retreat. There was little use of the rifle in the advance, although rifle fire did come into play during the assault, along with fire from the heavy machine gun.

Transport for the latter consisted of a sled with handles in front and rear or a light wheeled carriage if the ground permitted it. The machine guns, firing blank ammunition, appeared to operate well. There was always a sufficient amount of ammunition. The blank cartridges had hollow wooden bullets, and the machine gun muzzle had an apparatus attached to reduce its size and increase recoil. The result was a splintering of the bullet, making it harmless just a few feet away. Fire control was very good for both machine guns and trench mortars. Targets were clearly identified, with heavy machine guns seldom firing at ranges beyond 1,600 meters and light machine guns 600 meters. Rifle fire, too, was carefully sighted and effective.

March discipline was very good as well, with troops keeping to the right side of the road. Infantry seemed very concerned about maintaining overhead cover. Since compasses were limited to officers, troops had a tendency to become disoriented at night or in fog. Nonetheless, they did reconnoiter the ground before an attack as much as time and the situation permitted. All men seemed to be thoroughly acquainted with the object of the attack or defense.[48]

The artillery presented a mixed picture. Kimberly was certainly not impressed with the equipment. Most pieces were 77mm field guns and 105mm howitzers from the World War I. Still, firing positions and observation posts were skillfully chosen; communications between them were good. Almost all fire was indirect. Artillery was close to the front, "taking every opportunity to get into action." Liaison with infantry seemed to be a pressing concern, and each infantry regiment had an artillery liaison officer with signalmen from his own unit.[49]

Cavalry operated in both mounted and dismounted modes. Kimberly noted that both horses and equipment were kept in good condition, especially those of the officers. The cavalry's armament consisted of rifles, sabers, and lances. Once again, security from enemy air activity was stressed; for example, riderless horses were tied up against houses, where they would be harder to spot from the air. The cavalry proved skillful in both patrolling and screening operations, its principal tasks.[50]

The greatest weakness of the five-day proceedings, he felt, was the treaty-mandated absence of modern arms and technical auxiliaries. The entire maneuver, therefore, had an "antiquated" air: "An army commander cannot adopt a method of combat fully coinciding with realities if he must do without modern weapons."[51] The lack of such equipment could not be made up through "assumption or study." Many serious question remained. How long would it really take to get heavy artillery into action? What were the real strengths and weaknesses of tanks? Most seriously, what impact would air power have had in this battle if the shooting had been real? There was no effective substitute for real aircraft in a maneuver.

A further problem, he felt, was the large amount of cavalry forced on Germany by the treaty—eighteen regiments versus just twenty-one of infantry.[52] He was especially interested in problem no. 2, which was supposed to demonstrate the use of a cavalry division in modern warfare. There seemed to be a great deal of uncertainty among the Germans about how to employ the arm. Throughout the maneuver, the cavalry failed to make maximum use of its mobility, even with a screen of fog, and it missed numerous opportunities for carrying out deep raids that would have resulted in a great deal of damage to the enemy. (As far as Kimberly was concerned, the exercise proved only that a cavalry division had no business at all on a modern battlefield.)

Kimberly ended by rating the *Reichswehr* according to U.S. Army standards:

1. Training: above average
2. Discipline: above average, especially in light of no military tribunals being allowed since the attempted revolution
3. Fighting efficiency: above average
4. Staff work and high command: superior
5. Orders: superior
6. Machine guns: above average
7. Clothing of men: below average (poor quality, not uniform in color due to the necessity of using up war stocks)
8. Clothing of officers: average
9. Equipment: average (but old)
10. Transport: above average
11. Endurance and capacity for hard work: above average

With regard to tactics and weaponry, Kimberly noted that the problems that functioned as the basis for the maneuvers bore no real similarity to the experiences of the previous war. He felt that the Germans evidently did not see the positional warfare of that era, "whereby the higher command exercised considerable influence upon the very smallest units" as the type of combat likely to take place in a future war. Instead, these exercise problems stressed high-mobility warfare, with the subordinate leader's judgment and action playing a prominent role. The main purpose of this exercises, indeed, seemed to have been to create a situation in which small-unit leaders had to make quick decisions in the face of rapidly changing conditions. Thus large forces were assumed to be on the flanks, allowing the small-unit commander considerable freedom of action. The lessons of the world war, Kimberly noted, were almost completely ignored.[53] In his closing he noted that Germany was to all intents and purposes disarmed according to the Versailles Treaty. "Her brains," however, were "far from disarmed."[54]

Maneuvers, 1925: The 1st Infantry Division

A much larger maneuver of the 1st Infantry Division took place near Marienwerder in September 1925. It consisted of three distinct problems, each of which postulated a Polish invasion of Germany.[55] The first had a blue (Polish) invading force (the "I Army Corps") advancing from the south about 5 kilometers west of Deutsch Eylau, opposed by a single red (German) corps. The second tested the ability of two German forces to converge on an invading Polish detachment and destroy it. German forces had air support, but it was limited to reconnaissance activity only. The third also postulated a corps-strength (three infantry divisions) Polish invasion of East Prussia. The centerpiece of this situation was an assault by a Polish infantry division against an entrenched German Border Guards (*Grenzschutz*) unit.

In all three problems the German force was able to achieve its mission. The corps defending East Prussia in the first situation encircled and defeated the Poles. (Given relatively even numbers, the Germans were confident of their ability to deal with a Polish invasion.) In the second, a smaller German force, making good use of maneuver and employing its cavalry to good effect, managed to seriously disrupt a Polish advance into East Prussia. The Border Guards unit in the third exercise not only repulsed the Poles but was able to launch a counterattack later in the day.

Tactically, the exercise showed the primitive level of motorization achieved by the German army. Colonel Conger described one encounter between red and blue forces just north of Marienwerder. Each side had two armored cars with machine guns. The red commander also had a 77mm field gun placed in a naval mount on a truck between his two armored cars. All four armored car detachments were preceded by motorcycle scouts, which at one point ran into one another in a bend in the road. In the general confusion, the motorcycles neglected to send word back of the presence of hostile vehicles. When both sides' armored cars moved up in support of their motorcyclists, they all ran into each other at the bend. For the most part thereafter, the armored cars roamed about in the enemy's rear areas, but played no role in the main operations.[56]

Another encounter illustrates the trouble that the troops had with the new technology. The blue commander had posted his reserve of two battalions and a detachment of twelve camouflaged tanks in the wood for a counterattack that was successful in driving back the enemy. The tanks were employed in three lines about 100 yards apart, consisting of five, four, and three tanks, respectively. This was the first time the Germans had used these camouflaged tanks, and the infantry seemed baffled by their presence. In one company the platoons formed up in columns behind the tanks, in another they marched parallel with the tank, and in another company they preceded it. These problems must have been ironed out overnight, because on subsequent days the infantry kept clear of the tanks so as neither to obstruct their fire nor come under hostile artillery fire directed against the tanks.[57] It was from the improvised solutions to such situations that the Germans would develop their later, fearsome armored expertise.

On one level, the exercise seemed to prove that with superior leadership, mobility, and coordination, a smaller German force was capable of holding off a larger Polish invading force. Most significant in this context was the excellent performance of the blue cavalry, which held up the advance of the red Starogard detachment just long enough to prevent it from participating in a simultaneous, concentric attack on Wandau. The similarities to the battle of Tannenberg, where Rennenkampf's army was delayed long enough for Samsonov's to be destroyed, and which seemed to have become a paradigm for Germany's military planners, are obvious.

When the exercise ended at 2:00 P.M., 8 September, the commander of the 1st Division, Lt. Gen. Wilhelm Heye, could be fairly proud of his troops. A wide variety of tactical, operational, and strategic problems had been analyzed during the six days of maneuvers, and the units involved had demonstrated that Germany once more had an excellent army. Colonel Conger was certainly impressed. "The maneuver was more like real war than any I have ever seen," he wrote at the beginning of a lengthy report. Rather than concentrate on the strategy involved in the exercises, however, he was more interested in the tactical capabilities of the individual arms of the *Reichswehr.* The cavalry, he observed, was still armed with lances and had actually used them in the maneuver. It also carried carbines, either slung or with the butt resting in a boot on the back of the saddle. (He had heard talk of a proposal to arm the cavalry with the bayonet as well as the carbine.) Cavalry troopers also carried entrenching tools.

Tactically speaking, he was impressed with the cavalry's ability to pass itself off as infantry. "Their horses were never in evidence from the side of the enemy and they produced quite as much racket of machine guns in proportion to their numbers as did the infantry." They also made good use of artillery; often a single gun was to be seen accompanying a patrol of fifteen to twenty-five men. "This flexibility of the cavalry," he wrote, "made it impossible to tell, when one heard the rattle of the machine guns and the sound of artillery in a certain location, whether it was a reinforced cavalry patrol, or an infantry battalion or brigade that was holding the line."[58]

The infantry, which bore the brunt of the fighting throughout the maneuvers, was "the backbone of the German army," wrote an obviously impressed Conger. The men appeared "hardy, very young on the average, and well disciplined." On the road the infantry marched in columns of squads, but as it approached the enemy went into columns of files, covered by the trees along the road. Conger noted that "no movements were made of troops in larger units than a squad" when the unit was moving forward, deploying, or moving up as part of the support or reserve, although at very long distances, and outside the range of enemy air observation, he did spot a few platoons.

Conger also took note of the *Reichswehr's* new style of attack. During deployment there was no attempt to observe sector lines between units.

If there were woods in the area to give cover, supporting troops took advantage of them, then later on would "trickle back, a squad at a time, into their sector." Squads advanced in a staggered arrangement, and the men in each one marched irregularly. The idea was not to form a rigid firing line, but "to take the best advantage of cover and avoid offering a target either for artillery or machine gun fire."[59]

Finally, there was the crucial role of the machine gun. Conger witnessed little fire by the advancing infantry at any but very close range, but he did see machine guns firing constantly. When attacking troops reached a ridge, or high ground, machine guns would halt and open fire from the ridge while the infantry continued the advance. On forward slopes or in exposed spots the squads would fan out even more and, if there was enemy fire, make a series of very short dashes of 5 or 10 yards, on the assumption that any movement would attract machine gun fire. The moment the machine gun opened, the infantrymen would drop to the ground. When the infantry reached assaulting distance they fixed bayonets and made the charge with a yell. "In all phases of the maneuver," he wrote, "the infantrymen took the keenest interest and were very quick and alert in all their movements of rising, running forward, and dropping to the ground."

The machine guns' firepower was the cutting edge of the infiltrating infantry. It is clear from Conger's report that whether on the offensive or the defensive, the Germans relied almost exclusively on the machine gun for fire support. Seeckt would have been proud to read that "the general impression given by the German troops is that of machine guns everywhere firing, and almost never visible from the side of the enemy. The machine gunners seemed so well-trained that they were rarely given orders as to their position or target."[60]

Finally, in what was a ritual in reports on German maneuvers in the 1920s, Conger described the dummy tanks he had seen. It is clear from his observations that the German army was still a long way from what was to become *Blitzkrieg* in 1925, although he was impressed with at least the appearance of reality:

> The tanks used in the maneuvers were mounted on a pair of bicycle wheels, made of canvas properly camouflaged, and resembled the Renault tank with a turret and a heavy (dummy) gun at the top, and slits for machine guns lower down in front. A man in front of the tank walking along can, and some of them did, actually fire a machine gun from the front which aided in giving the tanks a semblance of reality. The tank is actually operated by two men inside at the back of the tank, who push it forward. The back of the tank is left open for the convenience of these men. These tanks trundling along over rough ground on their two bicycle wheels, which are, of course, inside and out of sight, progress with all the mannerisms of movement of real tanks.[61]

In his evaluation, Conger gave the *Reichswehr* high marks, in a curiously American way: "The officers and men of the 1st Division seemed to be of excellent morale, and to be well-trained. The majority of the German soldiers seemed very young but did not look essentially different from our own men in the 2nd Division in San Antonio."[62] He also praised the close relationship between the army and the civilian population in the area. The description he gives is quite different from that of historians who write of the hostility between the *Reichswehr* and the nation:

> The population of East Prussia was as much interested in the maneuvers as were the troops. . . . Many children were present also and, from the ages of 8 to 18, seemed to take the same zest in observing the conduct of the operations and learning how the various movements were made as did the ex-officers and soldiers.[63]

Maneuvers, 1925: The 4th Infantry Division

We also possess detailed records for the 1925 maneuvers of the 1st Infantry Division (East Prussia) and the 4th Infantry Division (Saxony), investigating the possibility of Polish and Czechoslovak invasions of Germany, respectively.[64]

A detailed reconstruction of this mock battle among the mountains and tiny villages along the Czechoslovak frontier would require a 1:100,000-scale map to track down the obscure place names. Short of that, we can state that a superior attacking red force, consisting of two infantry regiments of the 4th Division (the 11th and 12th), along with two regiments of cavalry and a host of auxiliary units succeeded in driving back a lone blue infantry regiment supported by one cavalry regiment and a reconnaissance detachment.

The chief of the maneuver *Leitung* was Gen. Friedrich von Lossberg, head of Group Command I. Under him was a chief umpire (also a general officer), with two assistants, a chief umpire for red forces and one for blue. There was also an umpire staff, with one umpire attached to each regiment, battalion, and company. The system was quite flexible, with umpires being transferred from unit to unit as necessary. Wearing white bands on their forage caps and sleeve, they were supplied with army vehicles or requisitioned civilian ones in order to move quickly from one part of the field to another. The entire area was also connected by an efficient telephone net combining army equipment and local lines. Umpires on both sides appeared to be in constant communication with each other.[65]

Both red and blue forces were supposed to be part of large, multicorps armies, and flags and guidons were used to represent phantom units. Flags were usually in the shape of a pennant and either made of metal or framed so that they always stood out flat. In the case of headquarters units, the flag was then stuck in the ground pointing to the spot or the house where the headquarters was located. Blue and red imaginary companies were indicated by a cloth of the appropriate color, stretched over a frame about 18 inches square and stuck in the ground on a small shaft. Imaginary machine gun companies used checkered cloth of blue and yellow or red and yellow. Heavy machine gun companies were indicated by cloth rectangles of 18 by 24 inches.[66]

U.S. Colonel Conger was full of praise for the exercise and the troops he observed. The *Reichswehr* troops "were the 100,000 best soldiers on the continent." It was a "first-class fighting machine, thoroughly trained in all its elements." Equipment and arms were "first class in model and condition." Infantry seemed to be particularly well versed in the use of automatic weapons, not surprising given the emphasis placed on the auxiliary arms since 1920. The troops were also "possessed of a high morale, perhaps too aggressive for future peace," and were often heard singing while marching back to billets.[67]

In combat every unit maneuvered in the attack, seeking to take advantage of the terrain and trying to attain surprise. There were numerous flanking attacks with highly mobile units like cavalry and armored cars. There was no list of objectives or a timetable; this was complete *Bewegungskrieg*. Divisions received only general missions, and "no effort was made to restrict the intention of the commanders." The defense, too, was mobile, and featured frequent counterattacks. Both attackers and defenders spent most of the maneuver off the road and well concealed.

Staff work was particularly well done, Conger noted. Orders were always plain and intelligible, without stepping on the prerogatives of subordinate officers. He had never, he said, seen a wider distribution of maps at a military exercise: even those officers who had not been issued maps bought them for their own personal use. Troops appeared well supplied, with field butchers operating as far forward as possible.[68]

Conger had special praise for the infantry and supporting arms. In the attack units were always protected on their flanks by combat patrols. The men were skilled in the use of their rifles as well as light machine guns, which always seemed to be in the forward position. Heavy machine guns were used on the flanks or in overhead firing. He noted that the machine guns never had a fixed position, but were instead constantly on the move to avoid return fire. After firing a few bursts the crew would pick up the gun and carriage, run at top speed to the flank (perhaps 100 meters away), and then go into firing position again. This operation was carried out repeatedly and rapidly, Conger said with admiration, typically without orders from the platoon commander. He called the mobility of German machine guns "one of the most noticeable features" of the maneuver.[69]

Another noteworthy point made by the U.S. attaché was the presence of about 200 Saxon security police, who were constantly present on the maneuver field, mounted and fully equipped with pistols, sabers, and maps. Although they did not actually take part in the maneuver, Conger saw their groups of four to five men everywhere, led by their own officers. A member of the *Truppenamt* told Conger that these police officers were ex-army officers. Conger was not surprised: "They carried themselves as such." It was clear that these men "could readily step back into the *Reichswehr* as commissioned officers." The enlisted personnel, too, "were all high-grade men," capable of an immediate return to active duty. On Sunday, the last day of the maneuver, he noted about 100 men, "uniformly dressed, though not in military uniform," marching through the town of Tharandt in perfect columns of four, behind a military band. Again, they seemed capable of being taken back into the *Reichswehr* on very short notice. He estimated, however, that although the number did not appear to be computed in any scientific fashion, Germany was capable of quickly and easily expanding the *Reichswehr* to 300,000 men "without any great loss of efficiency."[70]

Spectators at the maneuvers were numerous and followed the action eagerly. They were of all ages, from the elderly to school children (who appeared to have been given time off from school to attend), men and women. Many of the men were evidently former officers; they talked and joked with active *Reichswehr* officers and even criticized this or that aspect of the maneuvers. A large percentage of the observers carried Zeiss or Goertz military-style binoculars and even were seen following troop movements on their own maps. Although the spectators did indeed interfere with the maneuvers—Conger himself said at times it was difficult to distinguish them from the troops—the officers made no complaint. They were "apparently very glad to encourage interest in the maneuvers by the citizenry."[71]

A few last points are worth mentioning. First, German experimentation with the armor forbidden by the treaty was still primitive. The 4th Division maneuvers featured a group of eight dummy tanks, similar in appearance to a French Renault, and very much the same as those he had seen used in the 1st Division maneuvers of 1925. The one time Conger saw the tanks used, they arrived behind their attacking infantry and were deemed "too late to be of any value."[72]

Second, Conger discussed the state of German air power. In accordance with the treaty restrictions no military aircraft had taken part in the maneuver. But he also observed that Germany's highly developed commercial aviation, with its vast number of trained pilots and supporting industry, was capable of creating an air force rapidly. Interestingly enough, there was an incident involving aircraft during the maneuver. On the first day, while the troops were moving into position, a Czechoslovak military biplane had to make a forced landing because of engine trouble. Its pilot had evidently been sent to reconnoiter the German maneuver, but was left unharmed and sent back to Czechoslovakia. But the incident put the Germans in a state of "very active indignation," wrote Conger.[73]

Finally, Conger was able to observe both Defense Minister Otto Gessler and General von Seeckt during the course of the exercise. The general had assumed a position from which he could best observe the maneuvers. Gessler, he said, was a Bavarian "endowed with an easy and friendly manner, not at all pompous, a description often given for von Seeckt." The latter was "very slight and military in carriage and very smartly uniformed." But Conger was struck as much by his cold and unbending manner as by his distinguished appearance:

"He was surrounded by a staff from the *Reichswehr* Ministry. They never engaged him in conversation except to make a report. Reports were made to him by officers as cadets on parade. I have even seen Lieutenant-Generals speaking to General von Seeckt with their heels together and certainly not very much at their ease." Nonetheless, Conger admitted, Seeckt was a figure of "great prestige," both inside and outside the army. Many officers, in fact, seemed to be affecting a monocle for the sole reason that Seeckt wore one.[74]

Troop Exercises, 1926: Döberitz

Foreign observers attended a large number of troops exercises in 1926. In March, at Döberitz training ground outside Berlin there was a maneuver involving an infantry and a cavalry regiment on either aside. These troops were part of the 4th Cavalry Regiment (Potsdam), the 9th Infantry Regiment (also Potsdam), and the 5th Infantry Regiment (Stettin). The cavalry brigade was split into red and blue forces, each made up of two regiments (of four troops each). Broken up into phases, the maneuvers embraced: (1) a nighttime and early dawn engagement between two regiments of cavalry; (2) the attack of a red infantry regiment against a blue cavalry screen; (3) a delaying withdrawal by a force of cavalry; and (4) a turning action and envelopment by cavalry on a force of attacking infantry. The cavalry performed well in this maneuver. In the second phase, a very thin line of cavalry deployed over a broad front of 9 kilometers was able to hold up an infantry attack for several hours. The cavalry line was amply reinforced with machine guns, roughly one heavy and two light machine guns every 100 meters. The defenders deployed their machine guns in concealed positions well back in the woods. The attackers, coming forward in two columns, came under machine gun fire at about 800 meters from their objective. But the infantry reacted as trained, going to ground until almost no man was visible. Attacking machine gun crews now worked their way forward under cover of a low ridge. In the words of one observer, "There came into play machine gun after machine gun until the attacker had in operation practically double the number of machine guns available to the defenders' side." With fire superiority on the side of the attacker, the cavalry eventually had to retreat.[75]

Cavalry was also the star of the fourth phase. The cavalry had disengaged by this time and ridden far to the south out of contact with the red attackers. But the red infantry regiment had now committed itself to an attack on the main blue position (occupied by an infantry regiment), which covered about 200 meters in depth and consisted not of a line, but of an interlocking series of heavy and light machine guns nests, covered by another series of light machine gun nests 500 to 800 meters in front. The ground for this combat was very broken, with small patches of woods and a great deal of second-growth underbrush, meaning the attackers could find cover from long-range fire almost anywhere they chose. The early approach therefore went very quickly, until red forces reached the blue outposts. But as red approached blue's main line of resistance, they suddenly came under machine gun fire deep into their right flank. The blue cavalry had ridden around the red flank and then come into dismounted action against the supporting troops and reserves of the attacking red force. Conger described it as "spectacular."

In fact, the whole maneuver had been a "great tribute to the cavalry arm" and a very clear indication that as far as the Germans were concerned, "the cavalry is by no means an extinct arm in the battle of maneuver of the future." Conger compared the advantage of cavalry over infantry to that of the high-speed battle cruiser against the slower moving battleship "in being able to choose the time, place, and direction of its attack or defense, and being further able to break off the battle at will."[76]

Troop Exercises, May 1926:
The 2nd Infantry Regiment, Arys

In May, the 2nd Infantry Regiment conducted four days of maneuvers at the Arys training ground in East Prussia.[77]

The first day's exercises involved the regiment's 1st and 3rd Battalions. Each was stationed on the flank of its own division, the red side on the right wing and blue on the left, and each had been reinforced. Commanded by Major Gercke, the red side consisted of the 1st Battalion, one infantry gun, and a platoon of five dummy tanks. He posted his formation in two patches of woods lying about 1 kilometer east of the right wing of his division. Here he waited for reinforcements that he knew were on the way, another company of infantry (3rd Company), the remainder of his machine gun company, and another platoon of tanks. The blue side, commanded by

Major Berg, consisted of the 3rd Battalion, two infantry guns, a platoon
of trench mortars, four cavalry men, and the 7th battery of the 1st Artillery
Regiment—and was posted behind the left wing as the divisional reserve.
Its mission was to attack the red right wing and was already on the approach march southeastward.

When the attack came, it was made by two infantry companies side by
side, covered in the front by light machine guns and supported by two
heavy machine guns firing over the heads of the frontline troops. The artillery was posted on the right flank of the attack, supporting it from a
range of 2,300 yards. Trouble soon developed, however. The two companies advanced more or less independently of one another, with the advance
of the company (the 11th) on the right being very rapid and unconcerned
with cover. As a consequence, the umpire had to intervene and rule back
the 11th. This left the other attacking company "in the air" without much
support. A red counterattack, spearheaded by its five tanks, was thus able
to develop. But this decision, too, turned out to be faulty, with all five
tanks running head-on into direct fire from the Blue artillery battery and
being destroyed.[78]

In fact, the umpires found fault with much of this maneuver. The red
infantry gun had been deployed in a spot where it was exposed to fire from
the blue main position. The blue attack, particularly the quick charge of
the 11th Company, had been entirely out of place in a situation that called
for careful reconnaissance and a methodical advance. Red tanks had been
squandered, used much too quickly in a haphazard fashion. They should
have waited until blue forces had advanced further, which would have
made the tanks' entry decisive; instead, they merely forced back the enemy
attack rather than crushing it, as they could have if the counterattack was
timed better.

The second day's exercise again pitted two flank battalions against
each other. The blue battalion was posted in the rear of the blue right
flank, on a position known as the Schweykonen-Höhen, a series of hillocks
of 30 to 40 feet in elevation, with orders to secure that flank. The red
force, reinforced by one field artillery battery and a trench mortar company, had orders to attack and seize that same position.

The maneuver opened with the blue force occupying the heights and
blue patrols active in the patches of woods immediately to the northeast.
The center of the red position was a height called Hill 134. Here it deployed its trench mortars and artillery. The red attack went in at 8:30 A.M.,
with two columns in the advance. One attacked frontally, the other sought
an envelopment on the blue right flank. But after sweeping over the first
few hills "in a most dramatic manner," red forces attempted to continue
the advance in the teeth of blue machine gun, mortar, and artillery fire. At
this point, the umpires had to suspend the exercise to point out to all concerned the disastrous nature of such an attempt. Ninety percent of the

attacking troops were ruled dead. The teams eventually replayed the game in a more methodical manner.[79]

Once again, there is much to be impressed with in this series of exercises. The situations and play had all been realistic and had forced the small-unit commanders to make difficult decisions in a rapidly changing battlefield situation. There was a real effort to treat it like real war. On the fourth maneuver day (7 May), Captain Strack, commanding the blue 1st Battalion, received a message "to be opened at 3:15 A.M." Since it was only 3:05, he gave it back to the orderly saying "Give it to me again please in 10 minutes." What followed should suffice to illustrate the skill of the commanders and the intensity with which the 2nd Infantry Regiment carried out its maneuvers:

> He (Captain Strack) waited until 3:15 before he would receive it. He then sent for his company commanders and requested the regimental staff officer, who had brought the order, to open it and read it to him and the company commanders. He did so, Captain Strack and his officers studying each his own map with the aid of an electric candle as the order was read. As the order was finished, Captain Strack said to the staff officer, "See now if I understand it correctly," and then repeated the order verbatim without a mistake from beginning to end, still throughout studying his map.[80]

These maneuvers were not particularly modern; in terms of weaponry, except for a platoon of dummy tanks, they could have been performed in the prewar era. But they give us a glimpse of a tactically proficient force, one with excellent training and high morale. And why not? As Colonel Conger observed, "Practically every officer from the grade of first lieutenant up has a more or less brilliant war record."[81]

The *Reichswehr* also seemed to have succeeded in simplifying its system of battlefield command. Conger was able to overhear a battalion, company, and platoon commander all give orders for a formal attack, and no one giving or receiving these orders used a map. The battalion commander dictated his, but the others did not. All three commanders, though, gave the orders with "clarity and precision, ample time being taken for the explanation of the situation and the complete orienting of subordinates." The orders themselves were exceedingly simple, on the pattern of "order to attack—direction of attack—sectors—starting time." Likewise, all command messages in the maneuver were given verbally to the man closest at hand, who then repeated the message word for word before starting out.[82] Finally, concerning the particular East Prussian troops that had taken part, Conger noted that with the danger of war with Poland being so great in the province, "Every time a battalion marches towards the frontier, they never know whether they are going through or not—but if they do it would not surprise anybody."[83]

A concept discussed repeatedly by German officers at these maneuvers was that of the *Harmonika* (accordion in German). The attacking forces stretched out in great depth during the advance. Then, when it came upon an obstacle that could not be overcome by the leading elements, the accordion closed until a wave was formed dense enough to overcome the obstacle. Then the advance resumed, and the accordion stretched out again, developing maximum firepower and automatically forming a defense in depth against enemy counterattacks.[84] Even though *Harmonika* might not be as familiar a term as *Blitzkrieg,* the German army would continue to use this tactic throughout World War II.

Group Command Maneuvers, 1926

The Seeckt era reached its climax with the maneuvers of the two Group Commands (*Gruppenkommando*) in September 1926.[85] These were the first maneuvers in postwar Germany to involve more than a division of troops. The exercises of the 1st Group Command took place in north-central Germany, in Brandenburg north of the Harz Mountains and west of the Elbe River. Taking part were the 2nd Infantry Division (headquartered at Stettin) and the 1st Cavalry Division (Frankfurt on the Oder) on the red side, and the 3rd Infantry Division, with a troop of cavalry attached, for the blue. Each side had an imaginary division of infantry attached; the 1st red division operating on the red right flank, and the 4th blue division on the blue left.

Blue forces had the mission of defending the line of the Elbe River against a red advance. According to the "General Situation" given to both sides at the outset, "A Blue army is withdrawing behind the Elbe, with north wing via Stendal, before a superior Red army advancing north of the Harz Mountains."[86] Each side then received a "Special Situation," a view of the battle from its own side's perspective. For the blue side it included the fact that, in the course of its retreat, the blue force had crossed the Elbe on 12 September without being pressed by the enemy, and now intended to defend the Elbe line stubbornly. Up to this point only weak patrols of red cavalry had cautiously felt their way up to the river; they had been followed by long columns of red forces about a day's march behind. At least a corps of red units was marching toward what looked like an eventual crossing of the Elbe at Wittenberg. Blue forces intended to oppose such a crossing with its II Corps, recently arrived from the east, composed of the 3rd and 4th Infantry Divisions. But the red cavalry was too quick, seizing crossing points over the Elbe on 12 September and pressing ahead into Perleberg on the blue side of the Elbe.[87]

The red "Special Situation" stated that in the pursuit to the Elbe, the red army had concentrated strong forces on its north wing to force a crossing of the Elbe near and north of Stendal. The I Army Corps, with 1st Cavalry Brigade, had received orders to cross the Elbe at Wittenberg to advance against the northern flank of blue forces on the right bank of the Elbe. By 12 September units of the 1st Cavalry Brigade had swum the Elbe at Wittenberg to protect the construction of a military bridge, and then had pressed on into Perleberg a few miles past the right bank of the Elbe.[88]

This was not purely an infantry exercise. Both sides had air forces. Although the red side had superiority in the air, blue air activity had increased as the fighting drew deeper into Germany—and so far the Red side had been either unable or unwilling to bomb targets east of the Elbe. Both sides also could call upon armored and motorized forces. The organization chart for the blue 3rd Division, for instance, included (besides the obligatory three infantry regiments) a *Staffel* of six observation planes, a company of fifteen tanks, a detachment of four armored cars, and a troop of cavalry. At this point, the *Reichswehr* made a distinction between *Panzerkampfwagen* units (tanks) and *Panzer* units (armored cars); in fact, the armored car formation in this maneuver was identified as the 3rd Panzer-Abteilung. The red 2nd Division was similarly constructed, though its observation squadron included nine planes. The red 1st Cavalry Brigade also had a motorcycle platoon as one of its organic components.[89]

The maneuver concentrated on the approach march of each side to the Elbe. The red main body was just coming over the Elbe, while its cavalry probed aggressively past Perleberg; blue forces had orders to march on Perleberg and evict any red forces found there. Especially important was the combination of cavalry and air power in carrying out both short- and long-range reconnaissance. Divisional orders for both red and blue sides gave detailed orders for this cooperation, as well as the usual organizational instructions for the march. The red division was advancing in a single column toward a crossing of the Elbe; the blue approach was being carried out in two columns. Both commanders had complete liberty of action according to their respective corps orders.[90]

Some fairly interesting action was the result. The blue left column encountered red cavalry outside of Perleberg and drove it back. The blue column was then driven back in turn by a red infantry regiment just over the Elbe. Meanwhile, the blue right column was finding the going tough as it encountered resistance from a complete red infantry regiment. Both columns now began calling on the division commander for reinforcements—to be specific, the third regiment, which was up to that moment being held in reserve. Rather than commit forces to either column, though, and risk having his entire position compromised by the collapse of the unsupported column, the blue commander merely shifted the reserve to cover the gap between his two columns more effectively.

In a continuation of tactical developments that had been going on since the war, there was no real battle line, but rather a zone about 800 meters deep on both sides, consisting of mutually supporting machine gun nests with interlocking fields of fire. Heavy machine guns fired indirectly over the heads of their own troops; this appeared by now to have become standard German practice, despite the danger attendant on it. Although the U.S. military attaché was informed that an officer had been killed in a previous exercise by a "short," those to whom he talked here said "it is one of the things that has to be done," even though it was extremely unpleasant to have bullets whizzing by just over one's head.[91] Tanks also made another appearance, these being constructed on a framework of light steel tubing, covered with camouflaged canvas and mounted on two bicycle wheels. They were operated by two men on foot inside the apparatus. Antitank defenses were in evidence, often consisting of isolated field guns emplaced to command stretches of open road. Where guns were not present, there were numerous roadblocks and abatis.

Air defense, however, seemed to be the highest priority. As in every German maneuver of the period, the umpires constantly reminded both sides of the effect of enemy air by giving them assumed air situations. Aircraft were sometimes represented by toy balloons of various colors, sometimes simply assumed. Men and officers tried to achieve concealment from air observation by cover of camouflage; if that was not possible, then they tried dispersion of men and materiel.

In the critique at the end of the day, the commander of the First Group Command, General von Lossberg, was critical of the blue division's deployment into two columns, which he said was insupportable by the local road net. He also noted that the two columns were too far apart for mutual support, a fact born out by the haste with which both had to call for reinforcements. While Lossberg felt that the red dispositions were correct, he criticized the commander for moving too slowly and not taking advantage of the wide dispersion of blue forces. If the red forces had moved more quickly, the blue side would have suffered an even worse defeat.

Seeckt followed these comments with "a sweeping denunciation of the employment and handling of the cavalry." First of all, he felt that the red command had erred in using cavalry as a holding force at Perleberg. Cavalry might delay the advance of infantry, but it was improper to commit it to holding any individual position in which it might be exposed to severe losses. Second, he was visibly upset that in the latter part of the day the cavalry was tied down protecting the flank of the red division, rather than being turned loose against the flank and rear of the blue force. His comment: "The handling of the cavalry in this maneuver takes us back to the times of Frederick the Great, when the cavalry was habitually posted on the flanks of the infantry in the order of battle. Such a procedure is out of date and a foolish use to make of modern cavalry."[92]

The second and third days' maneuvers themselves contained little that was new from a tactical point of view.[93] Red forces continued to push back the blue, but a constant downpour kept either side from trying anything too complicated. Nonetheless, there were some points of interest. One observer described the red commander, General von Tschischwitz, issuing his orders. There was no attempt to formulate a precise written order; Tschischwitz merely gave one instruction after another in "a clear and forceful manner." It was all done much too quickly to be taken down word for word. His staff took notes of the instructions, however, and at once dispatched subordinate officers to execute them. Tschischwitz himself spent most of the day on the move, trying to get as far forward as possible to follow events more closely. All commanders on both sides kept in constant telephone communication with one another. All headquarters seemed to function on the simplest level possible. There were, said an observer, "many more messages coming back from front to rear than orders going from superiors to subordinates. They were all playing a game thoroughly understood, with assurance that each was perfectly at liberty to do the best he knew how without asking anybody and completely confident that superiors, subordinates, and commanders of adjacent units would play the game."[94]

Taking part in the exercises of 2nd Group Command were the 7th Division (Munich) and the 5th Division (Stuttgart), colloquially known as the "Bavarian" and "Württemberg" divisions, respectively. Units of the 6th Division (Hanover) were also present. The maneuvers took place in a spot accessible to all three divisions by rail, in Franconia. This is the northwestern corner of Bavaria, near the town of Würzburg, a piece of terrain with which the U.S. Army has become quite familiar since 1945. The maneuvers investigated two problems, though in both, a German army (blue) was defending against an invasion by a French (red) force attacking northward through the Rhine Valley. The division designated as red formed the right wing of the advance. In each problem, the red side had complete superiority in the air; the blue side had no air force at all.[95]

These would be the last maneuvers at which Seeckt presided. Already, there was a hint of change in the air, with newly elected President Paul von Hindenburg present and very much the center of attention at the proceedings. According to the U.S. assistant military attaché, Major McLean, he arrived wearing the full uniform of a German field marshal and took up his position on a hill commanding a view of the proceedings, where all the foreign observers (from the Nordic countries, the Netherlands, Switzerland, Hungary, Bulgaria, Russia, Argentina, Chile, Peru, and the United States) were brought to meet him. It might here be noted that Germany had invited no observers from Great Britain, France, or Italy, these three nations still being represented on the Interallied Control Commission and thus still in some sense "hostile" powers.[96]

Never was Hindenburg's role as a kind of "surrogate Kaiser" so obvious. A report in the *Lokal-Anzeiger*, for instance, waxed poetic at the sight of the "old field marshal in the glorious times of yore at the combat post of his army." Here he was again, "Germany's first soldier," just as in the days, "which through him became immortal." The Würzburger *General-Anzeiger* went on in a similar vein, describing the reception for Hindenburg at the town of Mergentheim:

> In the show windows of stores predominates the picture of the old Field Marshal. For all persons there exists just one objective: "Mergentheim," and only one question: "Have you seen him?" The maneuver . . . has become a secondary affair. Hundreds of people jammed the streets in front of Hindenburg's hotel, serenading the old man with the *Deutschlandlied*, weeping, holding up their infants to catch a glimpse of him.

"A new wave rolls over the German land," said the newspaper. "One feels it on the maneuver grounds, where one may observe a thousand times that love of the soldier and our army is again awakened." The "strongest German feeling" seemed concentrated in Hindenburg's person, allowing the ordinary German once again to have the feeling that "there is someone who is watching over us." The people's veneration for Hindenburg "is touching, is holy, and the faith in him knows no limits."[97] McClean's comments on the maneuver dealt extensively with civil-military relations. He noted large crowds from all classes of the population, even when he arrived on the maneuver field at 3:00 A.M. Many well-dressed, well-educated types were there, evidently ex-officers, following along with maps and binoculars. He talked to a number of German teenage boys, obviously very enthusiastic about the army ("therein lies the great danger," he wrote). He noted generals from the old imperial army too numerous to count—General von der Schulenberg, Prince Hohenlohe, and many others. *Reichswehr* officers seemed to make a special attempt to be agreeable to the civilian crowd, a very different attitude from what would have been shown before the war. For example, one of the maneuver directors was explaining the situation to the crowd of official foreign guests. "He noticed a group of civilians approaching, apparently very eager to hear also. He stopped his talk and beckoned to them to come so they could hear his exposition of the situation." Both Seeckt and Gessler were there, and they too made a special attempt to be pleasant to civilians.

All this added up to a threatening atmosphere, wrote McLean. The spirit of the German army was "aggressive." The *Reichswehr* was actively fostering the sentiment among the people that Germany had been treated unjustly by the peace treaty and was only waiting for "an opportune time to disregard the military clauses of the Treaty of Versailles. One cannot perceive the spirit of Locarno in the army or in the people."[98]

Tactically, these exercises, like the ones in Brandenburg, showed an impressive use of combined arms. Once again, a large variety of auxiliary weapons augmented the infantry. The organization charts of the 7th Infantry

Division included a motorized headquarters platoon, a "reconnaissance battalion" of armored cars, motorcycles, and cavalry; and a motorized artillery battery (belonging to the 17th Cavalry Regiment). The 5th Infantry Division had similar assets attached. Neither was a "motorized" division, but the German army was clearly moving in that direction (within the limits set by the Versailles Treaty).[99]

In terms of defensive deployment, the *Reichswehr* once again demonstrated its belief in depth. The front line was merely a series of outposts, designed to make the enemy force deploy into battle formation and cause it serious losses while it did so. Of the twelve heavy machine guns per battalion, perhaps one or two were deployed here. The principal defensive zone was composed almost entirely of light or heavy machine guns, perhaps seven or eight of the heavies. They were positioned in spots offering concealment and protection, as well as opportunities to flank the ground over which an enemy would have to advance. Riflemen played almost no part in the defense of a position, being employed mainly to carry out counterattacks should the enemy break into the position.[100]

Conger later combined his comments on the 1st Group Command exercise with McLean's on the 2nd in a confidential report to the War Department.[101] The strategic basis for the two maneuvers had been the German assessment of the course of the next European war, assuming it broke out in the next few years. The Germans apparently conceded that the French army could easily break into Germany, seize the Rhine Valley, and penetrate the Black Forest into Württemberg, with the aim of cutting off Bavaria from the rest of the country. Given the good defensive terrain on either side, it was north of the Harz Mountains and along the Elbe that the French attempt to cut off Bavaria would have to be met. This was the scene of the 1st Group Command maneuvers, which were held under conditions of high security. Apparently, the government had forbidden the press to cover the event (in sharp contrast to the 2nd Group Command exercise). Conger saw scores of policemen in their distinctive green uniforms, and heard that numerous plainclothesmen were also present, to prevent unauthorized persons from witnessing the first maneuver.

Conclusion

The army Conger witnessed in action had achieved a high degree of proficiency in training. But he was not at all convinced that training, no matter how skillfully conceived or carried out, was capable of making up for such severe material deficiencies. An army without an air arm, poison gas, tanks, heavy artillery, modern light artillery, or even adequate stocks of light and heavy automatic weapons—how effective could it possibly be in a war? He was also doubtful about the prospect of every man in the

Reichswehr being able to take over an officer's commission should the army
have the opportunity to expand. The intelligence of many of the enlisted
men, he felt, was simply not sufficient, although the possibility did exist of
calling back to the colors the many officers the Versailles Treaty had forced
the army to discharge. All in all, he certainly did not see the German army
as "a threat to the peace of Europe," as Major McLean had called it.[102]

He also disagreed with McLean's assessment about the "aggressive
spirit" of the army. German officers with whom he had come into contact
seemed to realize their complete inability to make war "owing to a complete lack of the necessary materiel." In fact, they seemed more aware of
this than the German people themselves. "I have yet to meet a German officer either anxious or ready to make war now or in the near future." He
certainly did not believe that the army was encouraging political sentiment
either among the soldiers or the population at large. His experience was
that German officers would talk about almost anything, until the subject of
politics came up: "They at once evince a lack of interest."[103]

Conger's assessment of the German army echoed those of many German officers. In 1924, Lt. Col. Joachim von Stülpnagel, head of the Army
Department (*Heeresabteilung*) of the *Truppenamt*, had delivered a paper to
officers at the Defense Ministry entitled "Thoughts on the War of the Future." Although conflict with France was inevitable, he wrote, to start a
war today and for the foreseeable future "would be a mere heroic ges-
ture."[104] The seven existing infantry divisions, he pointed out, had just
enough ammunition for precisely one hour of combat! Seeckt saw the
Reichswehr as a nucleus of the expanded army of the future, but many of
his own officers were now thinking in different terms: How could the army
best defend the country now, with the weapons and personnel at hand?

Notes

1. For wargames and their role in German army planning before World War I,
see Arden Bucholz, *Moltke, Schlieffen, and Prussian War Planning* (Providence,
RI: Berg, 1991); for the interwar era, see Robert M. Citino, *The Evolution of
Blitzkrieg Tactics: Germany Defends Itself Against Poland, 1918–1933* (Westport,
CT: Greenwood Press, 1987).

2. For a detailed description of the various types of exercises, written by a
participant, see Adolf Reinicke, *Das Reichsheer 1921–1934: Ziele, Methoden der
Ausbildung und Erziehung sowie der Dienstgestaltung* (Osnabrück: Biblio Verlag,
1986), especially pp. 220–236, "Methoden und Mittel der Gefechtsausbildung."

3. The 1923 version of the *Regulations for Umpire Service on Troop Maneuvers* is found in English translation in *United States Military Intelligence Reports:
Germany, 1919–1941* (Frederick, MD: University Publications of America, 1983),
microfilm reel XV, frames 681–712. In shorthand notation, the above document
would be labeled USMI, XV, 681–712. The 1924 version is found in USMI, XV,
657–667.

4. *Regulations for Umpire Service, 1924,* sec. 1–2, USMI, XV, 658.

5. Ibid., sec. 3,USMI, XV, 658.

6. Ibid., sec. 5, USMI, XV, 659.

7. Ibid., sec. 9, USMI, XV, 660.

8. Ibid., sec. 10, USMI, XV, 661.

9. Ibid., sec. 11–12, USMI, XV, 661–662.

10. Ibid., sec. 15, USMI, XV, 662.

11. Ibid., sec. 15, USMI, XV, 662–663.

12. For "Judging an Attack," see *Regulations for Umpire Service, 1924,* sec. 27, USMI, XV, 665–666.

13. For "Judging a Defense," see *Regulations for Umpire Service, 1924,* section 28, USMI, XV, 666–667.

14. Prepared for the Military Intelligence Division of the U.S. War Department, *Sketch of Modern Maneuvers in the* Reichswehr is found in English translation in USMI, XIII, 809–812. The author was "an active officer of the German General Staff who was present at the 1921 maneuvers of the 5th *Reichswehr* Division." He requested "that the material contained therein not be communicated to any but American officers." USMI, XIII, 809.

15. Sketch of Modern Maneuvers, sec. 5, USMI, XIII, 810.

16. Ibid., sec. 7, USMI, XIII, 810–811.

17. Ibid., sec. 8–9, USMI, XIII, 811.

18. Ibid., sec. 10, USMI, XIII, 811–812.

19. The manual, *Anhaltspunkte für Beurteilung der Waffenwirkung,* is found in English translation as *Guiding Principles for Judging the Efficiency of Arms* in USMI, XV, 667–680.

20. *Judging the Efficiency of Arms,* sec. 1–18, USMI, XV, 667–670.

21. Ibid., sec. 4, USMI, XV, 668.

22. Ibid., sec. 10, USMI, XV, 669.

23. Ibid., sec. 11–16, USMI, XV, 669–670.

24. Ibid., sec. 19–23, USMI, XV, 670–671.

25. Ibid., sec. 24–32, USMI, XV, 671–676.

26. Ibid., sec. 27, USMI, XV, 672.

27. Ibid., sec. 29, "Material Effects", USMI, XV, 673–675.

28. Ibid., sec. 47, USMI, XV, 679.

29. Ibid., sec. 51, USMI, XV, 679.

30. See *Report Regarding the Signal Exercises in August 1922 in the Area of the 1st Group Command, under the Direction of the Inspector of the Signal Troops* in USMI, XIV, 20–78.

31. "Part III: Experiences," in *Signal Exercises August 1922,* USMI, XIV, 40–43.

32. "Automobiles and Motorcycles," in *Signal Exercises August 1922,* USMI, XIV, 51–52.

33. "Part III: Experiences," in *Signal Exercises August 1922,* USMI, XIV, 44.

34. "Wireless Service," in *Signal Exercises August 1922,* USMI, XIV, 47.

35. See the sections "Messenger Dogs" and "Carrier Pigeons" in *Signal Exercises August 1922,* USMI, XIV, 50–51.

36. See the lengthy report, *Subject—Field Exercises 1923, German Army,* Berlin, 15 October 1923, in USMI, XV, 713–718.

37. For a discussion of "Cannae," see, for example, General Wilhelm Groener's *Das Testament des Grafen Schlieffens* (Berlin: E. S. Mittler und Sohn, 1927); for Seeckt's views on the double envelopment as an "ideal battle," see his article, "Schlagworte," reprinted in Hans von Seeckt, *Gedanken eines Soldaten* (Leipzig: von Hase und Koehler Verlag, 1935), pp. 9–18.

38. *Field Exercises 1923*, USMI, XV, 717.

39. Ibid., USMI, XV, 715.

40. See the sec. entitled "Tactics" in *Field Exercises 1923*, USMI, XV, 716.

41. See the sec. entitled "Umpires" in *Field Exercises 1923*, USMI, XV, 716.

42. Major Allen Kimberly, acting U.S. military attaché, to War Department, Berlin, 23 September 1924, *German Army Maneuvers, September 4th to 9th, 1924*, in USMI, XVI, 210–258. A translation of the German regulations for the maneuver is found in USMI, 259–290.

43. "Simulation of Forbidden Equipment," in Kimberly, *German Army Maneuvers*, USMI, XVI, 214.

44. "September 3rd Preliminaries," in Kimberly, *German Army Maneuvers*, USMI, XVI, 216. Reichenau would go on to win a field marshal's baton in World War II, commanding the 10th Army in the invasion of Poland and the 6th Army during the Western campaign in 1940 and Operation Barabrossa in 1941; in December 1941, he took over Army Group South after Hitler's great purge of senior commanders. He died in an airplane crash in 1942.

45. "First Problem," in Kimberly, *German Army Maneuvers*, USMI, XVI, 217–220.

46. "Second Problem," in Kimberly, *German Army Maneuvers*, USMI, XVI, 233–238.

47. "Observations: Staff," sec. 1–3, in Kimberly, *German Army Maneuvers*, USMI, XVI, 239.

48. "Observations: Infantry," sec. 1–4, 8, in Kimberly, *German Army Maneuvers*, USMI, XVI, 240–241.

49. "Observations: Artillery," sec. 1–6, in Kimberly, *German Army Maneuvers*, USMI, XVI, 245.

50. "Observations: Cavalry," sec. 1–4, in Kimberly, *German Army Maneuvers*, USMI, XVI, 247.

51. "Remarks: Leadership," in Kimberly, *German Army Maneuvers*, USMI, XVI, 254.

52. "Remarks: Cavalry," in Kimberly, *German Army Maneuvers*, USMI, XVI, 254.

53. "Remarks: Tactics and Weapons," in Kimberly, *German Army Maneuvers*, USMI, XVI, 254.

54. "Conclusions," in Kimberly, *German Army Maneuvers*, USMI, XVI, 258.

55. Colonel A. L. Conger, U.S. Military Attaché, to War Department, Berlin, 16 September 1925, *Maneuvers, First Division*, in USMI, XIV, 184–233. This lengthy report contains maneuver problems and orders for both sides taking part, comments on the maneuvers for all five days, and general comments, as well as Conger's answers to a Department of the Army questionnaire.

56. "Comments on the Maneuver of the 1st Division," in Conger, *Maneuvers*, USMI, XIV, 187. In addition to armor, air power was also represented at the maneuver—indicated by the raising and lowering of red, white, blue, and green toy balloons, 14 meters in diameter, to mark the presence of combat planes, observation planes, pursuit planes, and bombers, respectively. Whether the aircraft was hostile or friendly was indicated by a red or blue pennant attached to the cord near the end of the balloon, USMI, 14, 222–223.

57. See "Maneuver Exercise on 4 September," in Conger, *Maneuvers*, USMI, XIV, 189.

58. "General Comments: Cavalry," in Conger, *Maneuvers*,, USMI, XIV, 223–224.

59. "General Comments: Infantry," in Conger, *Maneuvers*,, USMI, XIV, 224–225.

60. "General Comments: Machine Guns," in Conger, *Maneuvers,* USMI, XIV, 225–226.

61. "General Comments: Tanks," in Conger, *Maneuvers,* USMI, XIV, 226–227.

62. "General Coments: Personnel," in Conger, *Maneuvers,* USMI, XIV, 228.

63. "General Comments: Observers," in Conger, *Maneuvers,* USMI, XIV, 229.

64. See the comprehensive report, "Fall Maneuvers of the German 4th Division," in USMI, XIV, 234–279. Again, it includes the maneuver problem, unit orders, and comments from U.S. and foreign observers.

65. "Comments on Fall Maneuvers of the 4th Saxon Division: Umpire System," in USMI, XIV, 270.

66. "Comments: Flags and Guidons," in Conger, *Fall Maneuvers,* USMI, XIV, 271.

67. "Comments: General," in Conger, *Fall Maneuvers,* USMI, XIV, 277.

68. "Comments: Command," in Conger, *Fall Maneuvers,* USMI, XIV, 269.

69. "Comments: Infantry and Other Trooops," in Conger, *Fall Maneuvers,* USMI, XIV, 269–270.

70. "Comments: Security Police," in Conger, *Fall Maneuvers,* USMI, XIV, 271.

71. "Comments: Spectators," in Conger, *Fall Maneuvers,* USMI, XIV, 270–271.

72. "Comments: Tanks," in Conger, *Fall Maneuvers,* USMI, XIV, 276. Apparently, the use of armor made no special impression on the observers; Conger's report actually devotes more attention to a discussion of messenger dogs.

73. "Comments: Czech Military Airplane Incident," in Conger, *Fall Maneuvers,* USMI, XIV, 277.

74. "Comments: General," in Conger, *Fall Maneuvers,* USMI, XIV, 278–279.

75. See Conger's *Report of German Maneuvers on March 20th, 1926,* USMI, XIV, 538–540.

76. "Observations," in *German Maneuvers on March 20th,* USMI, XIV, 540.

77. See Conger's report, "The Four Days of Maneuvers of the 2nd Infantry Regiment," USMI, XIV, 541–573.

78. For the first day's maneuver, see "Maneuver, May 3, 1926: Development of the Exercise," USMI, XIV, 544.

79. For the second day's maneuver, see "Maneuver, May 4, 1926: Development of the Exercise," USMI, XIV, 546–547.

80. "Maneuver, May 7, 1926: Development of the Exercise," USMI, XIV, 562.

81. There is a series of "general comments" included in Conger's file on the 2nd Infantry Regiment's maneuvers, USMI, XIV, 572.

82. "Maneuver, May 5, 1926: Development of the Exercise," USMI, XIV, 555.

83. "General Comments," USMI, XIV, 572.

84. "Manuever, May 3, 1926: Tactics," USMI, XIV, 545.

85. Details of the maneuvers of both Group Commands are available in Conger, *Fall Maneuvers, 1926,* USMI, XIV, 664–771. For the 1st Group Command, see *Maneuvers of the 1st Group Command (1st Army Corps) North of Harz Mountains and West of the Elbe River, September 13th to 15th,* USMI, XIV, 666–711.

86. "General Situation: 1st Group Command Fall Manuvers, 1926," USMI, XIV, 671, 681.

87. "Blue: Special Situation," in *Maneuvers of the 1st Group Command,* USMI, XIV, 671–673.

88. "Red: Special Situation," in *Maneuvers of the 1st Group Command,* USMI, XIV, 681–683.

89. The organization for the blue 3rd Division is found in USMI, XIV, 674–675, the red 2nd Division in USMI, XIV, 684–685, both in *Maneuvers of the 1st Group Command.*

90. See "blue: Division Order for the Advance on September 13th," USMI, XIV, 677–678; "Blue: Special Instruction for the Advance on September 13th, USMI, XIV, 679–680; "Red: Division Order for the Advance on September 13th," USMI, XIV, 686–687; and "Red: Special Instruction Regarding Divisional Order No. 1," USMI, XIV, 688–689. All are found in "Maneuvers of the 1st Group Command."

91. "General Comments on the 1st Group Maneuver: Indirect Machine Gun Fire," USMI, XIV, 706.

92. "Maneuvers of September 13th," in *Maneuvers of the 1st Group Command*, USMI, XIV, 668.

93. For the second and third days, respectively, see "Maneuvers of September 14th," USMI, XIV, 694–695, and "Maneuvers of September 15th." USMI, XIV, 703–704, both in *Maneuvers of the 1st Group Command.*

94. "Maneuvers of September 14th," USMI, XIV, 695.

95. See *Fall Maneuvers 1926: Maneuvers of the 2nd Group Command (II Army Corps) South of Würzburg,* USMI, XIV, 713–771). See also the report *Maneuvers of the 2nd Group Command, German Army, in Bavaria, Southwest of Würzburg, September 17th to 21st, inclusive, 1926,* in USMI, XIV, 596–663, which includes translations of the actual maneuver problems.

96. "President von Hindenburg," in "Confidential Appendix to Report on German Maneuvers," USMI, XIV, 767–768.

97. For the *Lokal-Anzeiger* article, see USMI, XIV, 622–623; for the report from the *General-Anzeiger,* see USMI, XIV, 624–626.

98. *General Remarks: Maneuvers of the 2nd Group Command,* USMI, XIV, 596–598.

99. "Organization of the 7th (Bavarian) Division," USMI, XIV, 632; "Organization of the 5th Division," USMI, XIV, 636; both in *Maneuvers of the 2nd Group Command.*

100. "Remarks Concerning Tactics and Equipment," USMI, XIV, 600–601, in *Maneuvers of the 2nd Group Command.*

101. "Confidential Appendix," USMI, XIV, 758–771.

102. "Estimate of the German Army," in "Confidential Appendix," USMI, XIV, 760–761.

103. "The Spirit of the Army," in "Confidential Appendix," USMI, XIV, 761.

104. Stülpnagel's essay, "Gedanken über den Krieg der Zukunft" ("Thoughts About the War of the Future") is found in *Bundesarchiv-Militärarchiv N 5/10.* Heinz Hurten, ed., *Das Krisenjahr 1923: Militär und Innenpolitik 1922–1924* (Dusseldorf: Droste, 1980), pp. 266–272, contains an extract of the document. It has received its share of attention from historians. See Michael Geyer's monograph, *Aufrüstung oder Sicherheit: Die Reichswehr in der Krise der Machtpolitik, 1924–1936* (Wiesbaden: Franz Steiner Verlag, 1980), pp. 81–82, as well as his "German Strategy in the Age of Machine Warfare, 1914–1945," in Peter Paret, ed., *Makers of Modern Strategy: From Machiavelli to the Nuclear Age,* pp. 527–597 (Princeton, NJ: Princeton University Press, 1986); Edward Bennett, *German Rearmament and the West, 1932–1933* (Princeton, NJ: Princeton University Press, 1979), p. 50; James Corum, *The Roots of Blitzkrieg: Hans von Seeckt and German Military Reform* (Lawrence, KS: University Press of Kansas, 1992), pp. 63–64; and Wilhelm Deist, "The Road to Ideological War: Germany, 1918–1945," in Williamson Murray, MacGregor Knox, and Alvin Bernstein, eds., *The Making of Strategy: Rulers, States, and War* (New York: Cambridge University Press, 1994), pp. 352–392.

German troops prepare to embark. Some are wearing farewell flowers on their tunics.

Training in wooded terrain before the war or shortly after its outbreak.

A soldier poses with his MG34 in a farmer's field. Note the camouflage on the gun and helmet.

German soldiers in line, displaying their equipment.

Troops with a light early-war PaK (*Panzerabwehrkanone*, an antitank gun).

On the Eastern Front, German soldiers pose with a knocked-out Soviet light tank.

Three Waffen SS junior squad leaders. All hold the Iron Cross; one (left) holds the Infantry Assault Badge and Iron Cross, First Class.

A prewar or early-war Panzer Mk III.

A group of soldiers takes the oath of loyalty.

Artillery training.

CHAPTER 6

The Changing of the Guard

The Departure of General von Seeckt

Seeckt's departure from the *Reichswehr*, which was a result of his ill-considered decision to allow the Hohenzollern crown prince's son to take part in a *Reichswehr* maneuver, is perhaps more relevant to a political history of the Weimar Republic than a military one.[1] But the passing of Seeckt certainly was the end of an era. He had rebuilt the army from the ruins of 1918; taken it in hand after the Kapp putsch and formed it into a disciplined, elite force; and had imbued it with a spirit of movement and attack, despite its small numbers. Although treaty restrictions on armaments made the *Reichswehr* unsuited for use in an actual war, Seeckt had done all that was humanly possible to keep alive the flame of German military excellence. The sudden return to military power after 1933 was due more to the groundwork laid by Seeckt than to any alleged military genius on the part of Adolf Hitler.

Seeckt had his blind spots, to be sure. He seemed detached from the problem of how actually to defend Germany should a war break out. During the Russo-Polish War following World War I, he had suggested simply allowing Soviet forces to overrun East Prussia as a way of forcing Allied intervention on Germany's behalf.[2] With regard to a French invasion, he had no real plan of defense save for a retreat behind the Weser River, perhaps as far as the Elbe. "The road from Dortmund to Berlin is not long," he once stated to the British ambassador at the height of the Ruhr crisis, "but it leads through rivers of blood."[3] But whose blood would that have been? Many, if not most, of the officers around Seeckt felt that he ought to be doing more about the problem of developing a strategy for national defense (*Landesverteidigung*).

Another of his blind spots was the continued support for the cavalry arm. He once wrote that the flurry of talk about the "obsolescence of cavalry" was simply a canard, repeated by laymen loudly enough until it had

145

acquired the ring of truth.[4] Certainly he knew that the age of the decisive
cavalry charge was over; the development of firepower had brought an end
to the days of huge, closed bodies of cavalry. But he still saw numerous
battlefield roles for the cavalry. Close reconnaissance was still its main
task; using its superior mobility to find and strike the enemy flank was another. The development of air power, he was certain, had simply augmented, not replaced, the cavalry in this respect: "In union with the air
squadron, the cavalry division finds a new strength."[5] Likewise, motorization of the army did not mean that the age of cavalry was over. Even
though some "prophets" were predicting that in the future entire armies
would be deployed in armored vehicles, he wrote, that was not the situation at present. Roads, bridges, and mountains were simply not suited to
the use of massed combat vehicles; Germany also lacked the materials to
build them. Although fighting vehicles were growing into a separate arm
alongside the infantry, cavalry, and artillery, they were unlikely ever to replace those arms. In fact, transport vehicles, used rightly and in good mea-
sure, meant an increase in the strength of the cavalry division.[6]

Seeckt said that he never regretted the Versailles Treaty's inclusion of
so much cavalry (three out of a total of ten divisions). An inordinate
amount of time and energy was devoted at maneuvers to the insertion of
cavalry—complete with lances and sabers—into situations where it was
impossible to imagine it having an effect in a real battle. He had to admit
that battlefield firepower forced mounted cavalry into such a state of dispersion that its dismounted attacks lacked all force, that it seemed lost
when enemy aircraft appeared overhead, that its troopers always seemed to
dismount too early.[7] He would have been better off training it as infantry,
despite the Versailles restrictions.

Keeping the timeframe in mind is important here. Seeckt left the army
in 1926. He wrote a long article proclaiming the continued importance of
cavalry ("Neuzeitliche Kavallerie") in 1927, just twelve years before the
onset of a war whose outcome was determined almost exclusively by
clashes of huge mechanized formations and in which cavalry played almost no part.[8] None of this is to condemn him unfairly for developments
that took place after he left his post and that he perhaps could not have
foreseen. It is simply to suggest that in the crucial question of motorization
versus cavalry, Seeckt was much more a remnant of the past than a har-
binger of the future.

Seeckt's political attitudes have been seen as controversial. That this
"Guards officer of the old school" had no love for a republican form of
government is obvious; equally obvious is that he had no intention of allowing the *Reichswehr* to stage a coup to overthrow it, or to restore the
monarchy.[9] He had received emergency powers from the government during the crisis of late 1923; he handed them back when the crisis was past.
The most infamous statement attributed to him, that "the *Reichswehr*

stands behind me," given in answer to President Friedrich Ebert's question about the *Reichswehr*'s loyalty to the republic, was probably a figment of his overly enthusiastic biographer's imagination.[10] There is little evidence that Seeckt ever uttered anything of the kind. In 1923, he moved against threats from the Right and the Left (e.g., the so-called Buchrucher uprising in Küstrin in October, and the Hitler putsch in Munich in November). In fact, not a few old comrades from the Kaiser Alexander Garde-Regiment refused to speak with him anymore, so convinced were they that he had "gone republican." Although many on the Right waited for a "putsch of the *Reichswehr*," it never came. He stayed out of the "political demi-monde" that called for a national uprising, even though his sympathies indeed lay with the Right. To Seeckt, thoughts of a coup might have been suitable to "some comic opera South American republic" but were unworthy of Germany's military tradition.[11] His dressing down of the candidates at the Ohrdruf officers school, many of whom had taken part in Hitler's failed attempt to overthrow the government, indicates that Seeckt was no political adventurer. "For the first time in my life," he hissed at them (monocle glittering icily, we may imagine), "I am speaking to mutineers."[12] There followed a severe reprimand to the cadets, who were forced to stand at attention throughout.

Seeckt was certainly not a warm or lovable individual, but he did inspire a considerable amount of loyalty in his men. "We were proud of him as the representative of the new army," one officer wrote.[13] His portrait was often to be found not only in the corridors and meeting halls, but in the personal quarters of NCOs and privates as well.

The feeling toward his successor, Gen. Wilhelm Heye (1926–1930), was nowhere near so favorable. Heye, in an attempt to be less imperious and more "democratic," announced that his door was open to any soldier who desired to see him.[14] To many soldiers this smacked of an invitation to bypass their immediate superiors, and they made little use of his offer—and for obvious reasons it played poorly with the officers. His tenure as chief did see one important initiative: a trip to the United States and new contacts with U.S. officers and industry. But he was never quite taken seriously, and his unmilitary appearance was cause for many jokes among the men.[15]

The next chief of the High Command, Gen. Kurt Freiherr von Hammerstein-Equord (1930–1934), fared better. His men regarded him as a clever unit commander, capable of leading an army, as well as a modern thinker in political terms. Occasionally, in the years before 1933, he had to face the possibility that armed intervention might be necessary if Hitler tried to overthrow the government. In mid-October 1932, at the Jüterbog training ground, Hammerstein spoke to about 100 officers on the current domestic situation. Carrying on Seeckt's tradition, he demanded complete political neutrality from the army, and went on to say that "if Herr Hitler believes he can politicize the *Reichswehr*, a few bullets flying around his ears will someday demonstrate that the *Reichswehr* is not to be politicized."[16]

Seeckt's successors brought about no radical departures from his policies in terms of training and tactics; the principal difference was the *Reichswehr's* new emphasis on national defense (*Landesverteidigung* or *Landesschutz*). Ever since 1923, when the French occupation of the Ruhr in 1923 laid bare Germany's complete military impotence, many officers had been dissatisfied with Seeckt's focus on the *Reichswehr* as an "army of leaders" for the expanded force of the future. They felt it was necessary to look at the reality of the present-day military situation, and from it develop a policy of national defense that spoke to actual conditions. Led first by Lt. Col. Joachim von Stülpnagel, head of the *Heeresabteilung* (later promoted to general and given command of the 3rd Infantry Division in Berlin), the circle included others such as Col. Werner von Blomberg, head of the *Truppenamt* in 1927 (later promoted to command of the 1st Infantry Division in East Prussia), and Col. Kurt von Schleicher (later a general), head of the new *Ministeramt*, the army office in charge of liaison with the civilian government.[17] There was a general feeling among all these officers that Seeckt was training an army that was dangerously out of touch with reality, playing with weapons it no longer possessed or had yet to devise. They were convinced that Seeckt's depoliticization of the *Reichswehr* was unsustainable in the long run, and believed that a closer relationship with the state was essential to developing a coherent strategy of national defense. The assistance of the government was indispensable to rearmament, especially the economic problems sure to be associated with it. Schleicher, due to his political contacts, became a figure of enormous importance for that reason.

Groener as Defense Minister

Another figure of crucial importance here was the new defense minister after Otto Gessler's resignation: Gen. Wilhelm Groener.[18] He, too, saw the necessity of building a new civil-military relationship in the interests of national defense, and more so than Gessler, who survived by agreeing with everything Seeckt said and did, was in a unique position to help bring it about. A *Vernunftrepublikaner* (one who tolerated the republic as a necessary expedient) rather than an enthusiastic democrat, he had a strong interest in politics, though he lacked the romantic outlook of many former imperial officers. In 1918, he had had the courage to tell the kaiser that the war was lost and that the army was no longer loyal, an act of bravery that had won him the hostility of a significant body of his fellow officers. It was he who advised the government to sign the Versailles Treaty in the summer of 1919. He had even held a cabinet post in the early years of the republic, as minister of communications, which enabled him to put to civilian use his considerable expertise with railroads.

At the same time, his military credentials were impeccable. As head of the Railway Section of the General Staff in 1914, he had overseen the entire process of rail mobilization, and it is no exaggeration to say was the one operation on either side in the whole war that actually proceeded according to plan. In 1917 he received a field assignment as commander of the 33rd Infantry Division in France: in 1918 he traveled east to assume the post of chief of staff to the Kiev Army Group; and in November of that year he succeeded Gen. Erich Ludendorff as first quartermaster general.

After resigning from the cabinet in 1923 he had turned to his first love, writing military history. His major works, *Feldherr wider Willen* (about the younger Helmuth von Moltke) and *Das Testament des Grafen Schlieffens*, dealt with the relationship between the supreme command and the army in the field. He was a great admirer of Schlieffen, but his portrayal of Moltke's unfortunate role in the early days of World War I was brutal.[19] He was also an essayist of some note, and wrote widely about the effects of the new technology on warfare.[20] His words still carried the *gravitas* of a former General Staff officer, even if his "republican leanings" made him suspect to many in the *Reichswehr's* old guard.[21]

The broader view that Groener brought to military affairs was evident as early as April 1928, when he ordered the dispatch of an unofficial military attaché to Poland. Before 1928, German military intelligence had relied upon officials of the legation in Warsaw as well as upon the intelligence services of the Baltic states. Groener was unsatisfied with the intelligence he had about the Polish military and thought that the transfer of an officer to Warsaw would result in more reliable and timely information. An associate described Groener's opinions on the subject:

> The dispatch of a Polish military attaché to Berlin has raised the question of whether a German attaché ought to be sent to Warsaw. He [Groener] felt that an attaché had no worth outside of Warsaw. Poland was the single land, he declared, that interested us militarily. . . . He would even be satisfied if an inactive officer with no connection to the *Reichswehr* were attached to the legation as counsel or secretary. That would satisfy him fully, and would be of great worth to the Defense Ministry, since the intelligence supplied by the agents was not sufficient.[22]

By May 1928 Groener had decided on Richard Du Moulin as the military attaché to Warsaw. Groener felt that to send a regular officer to Poland might appear provocative to the Allies, so Du Moulin, a former officer with a broad knowledge of military affairs, was an ideal choice. In order to prepare him for his task, Groener assigned Du Moulin to the Defense Ministry for three months; in addition, the future attaché participated in the army exercises at Döberitz and the maneuvers of the 1st Infantry

Division in East Prussia.[23] The attaché arrived in Warsaw in September, and he quickly became Groener's most trusted source of information on Polish military affairs. He was especially helpful in informing Berlin about Polish war plans about which the Germans previously had received little information.

Further evidence of Groener's broader view was his emphasis on naval affairs. Seeckt had had little interest in naval questions. Under Groener, naval planning began to assume a major place in German strategy, and questions of naval policy played an important role. And almost immediately upon the assumption of his office, he became embroiled in the *Panzerkreuzer* affair.

In 1928, the navy had decided to build a new type of armored cruiser, or *Panzerkreuzer*, which would represent a significant step forward in German naval technology. The new design was fast and heavily armed, and to meet the Versailles Treaty tonnage restrictions the designer sacrificed armor in favor of guns. The ship was thus fast enough to hunt down anything afloat, even much smaller ships. It was also powerful enough to defeat enemy cruisers in combat, but speedy enough to run away from most enemy battleships. Construction of this new ship would mean German domination of the Baltic Sea, at least against Poland alone. The only problem with the armored cruiser was its enormous cost, and the debate over financing *Panzerschiff A*, as the first ship in the series was called, came to dominate the proceedings of the *Reichstag* during the spring of 1928. The parties of the Left were against funding the ship, declaring it to be a waste of Germany's scarce resources as well as a threat to peace.[24]

Although Groener pointed out that the construction of the ship would give new life to Germany's depressed shipbuilding industry, the economic question was not the decisive factor in building the ship. Instead, he saw the cruiser playing a major role in his new naval strategy toward Poland. In November 1928 Groener drafted a memorandum on the need to build the *Panzerschiff*.[25] He observed that the armored cruiser had become a matter for public debate, and political maneuvering had only served to confuse the public. It was now time to rescue the cruiser question from the resulting "fog of opinions" and discuss the matter clearly. He asked four questions: What were some likely war scenarios for Germany? Which tasks would the navy have to fulfill? Would these tasks be easier to carry out with the new armored cruiser? Were there any further reasons for building the ship?

Groener saw two possible cases in which Germany might become embroiled in a war: defense against a sudden *coup de main* or the protection of German neutrality in a conflict between foreign powers. The navy would have an important role to play in either one. In the first case, Groener saw the strong possibility of a Polish strike against East Prussia. The crucial battles of this campaign, of course, would be on land, where

Germany would have to fight under grave disadvantages because the enemy would possess superior force. Any attempt by German forces to break through the Polish Corridor was bound to fail, and East Prussia would very shortly face a crisis of supply, especially in munitions.

In Groener's opinion, only the navy could help to offset these disadvantages, particularly the problem of supplying East Prussia, because the replacement of personnel and munitions was only possible by sea. Moreover, the navy had other tasks should the Poles invade East Prussia, such as defending coastal areas and protecting land forces against hostile sea power. This would free the army from worrying about its flank and rear and free coastal artillery for use in other areas.

The second case was a war between foreign powers that threatened German neutrality. This would present the navy with two tasks: protecting German home waters and preventing the use of German ports by a belligerent power. If Germany should nevertheless have to enter the war, then the navy would have the crucial task of transporting raw materials from Scandinavia.

Having outlined the navy's likely wartime missions, Groener turned to the question of whether building the armored cruiser would allow the navy to accomplish its mission more efficiently:

> The fleet can only accomplish its mission in Case I if it dominates Poland in the Baltic. This is today the case against the forces which Poland possesses. It will not be possible against the Polish fleet with which we may have to reckon in the future. Poland is today strengthening its fleet in two ways. The construction of modern destroyers and submarines is proceeding in foreign shipyards. The second method of strengthening its naval forces is by a treaty with France. In this agreement, France has promised to support Poland in a war by dispatching a cruiser squadron to the Baltic. This squadron can fly the Polish flag, so that France does not have to enter the war. We are at the moment inferior to any such fleet.

Groener then discussed the means by which Germany could redress the naval imbalance it was likely to find in the Baltic. A modern warship, he wrote, must possess the quickness to cooperate tactically with cruisers and to do battle with enemy battleships. At the same time, it needed the firepower to battle both cruisers and ships of the line. Finally, a warship should be as secure as possible against attacks from submarines or aircraft. The present German fleet of pre-World War I vessels, he argued, had none of these qualities. The new type of "pocket battleship," however, was both quick and powerful enough to destroy any ship of equal size or smaller. Again, Groener left no doubt against whom the new ship was intended:

> It remains to be seen whether Poland, through the use of submarines and battleships, can overcome the superiority of our new armored cruiser. The effect of submarines is limited. Their use in the Baltic has a practical

limit—the shallow depth of the water. The danger for German transports will be less if an armored cruiser accompanies them. They can then make the crossing from Swinemünde to Pillau by day, and they will therefore be safe from the most dangerous submarine tactic, the night attack. At the end of the last war, it must be noted, methods of defense against the submarine had to a great degree overcome the threat of submarine attack. The pocket battleship also has the ability to fight the battleship. The probability of large battleships entering the Baltic is small. Poland has neither docks nor repair facilities for battleships. The cost of building these from scratch would be enormous.

In a speech before the *Reichstag* on the armored cruiser Groener summarized the ship's significance to Germany: first, it increased the strength of the German army by freeing it from concern about its seaward flank; second, it would give Germany freedom of action in the Baltic. Groener took history seriously, and in his view history had shown conclusively the importance of a strong naval presence. It was Germany's deficiency in this vital area, he thought, that had lost the war, and Germany must never enter another war without a powerful navy.[26] Groener's arguments eventually prevailed, and the Reichstag approved the construction of two pocket battleships. The first of these, the *Deutschland*, was launched in May 1931.

Preparations for National Defense

To most German officials, both civil and military, a future war would involve the German nation's very struggle for existence. Thus it was not enough simply to prepare military forces for it. The experiences of the world war, in which Germany based everything on the preparations of the General Staff, showed that it was necessary to do more, to prepare the entire forces of the nation. This broader concept of national defense far surpassed the tasks of the armed forces: it embraced "the unified and systematic action of all sources of national strength for the goal of defending the Reich," as one government minister put it. There was no area that the state could ignore in terms of the preparation and conduct of a future war. It was not simply the task of the Defense Ministry, but of all the ministers, and especially the chancellor. The cabinet should draw up broad directives, draw up the spheres of responsibility for the various departments, and decide differences of opinion that might arise between them.

The transition from the "army of the future" to "national defense" came about very abruptly with Seeckt's departure, indicating the broad support in the army for such a move. A cabinet meeting in February 1927 (i.e., while Gessler was still in the defense ministry) dealt extensively with the topic. Then, in October, Gessler sent a series of reports on *Landesverteidigung* to Foreign Minister Gustav Stresemann, penned by then-colonels Schleicher and Freiherr von Fritsch, along with Defense Ministry recommendations.[27]

Using the term "national protection" (*Landesschutz*), Schleicher defined it as "the defense of the Reich's borders as well as the protection of the lives and property of the population from enemy attacks and from acts of violence on land, on sea, and from the air." Any such comprehensive strategy required "trustful cooperation between the civil authorities on the one hand and military officials on the other," he wrote. The army had to go beyond mere operational measures—seeking a battlefield victory was in any case impossible, given Germany's current enforced military weakness. "The goal of our preparations is to be ready to prevent a *Tatbestand* [*fait accompli*] that could prejudice a decision of the League of Nations or another international court of arbitration."[28] To that end, he listed a series of recommendations:

1. Preparation of an air defense scheme (*Reichsluftsschutz*)—both civil and military—for the entire nation, including special measures to protect the civilian population from gas attack from the air. This would fall under the purview of the Ministry of the Interior, and in terms of gas protection could consist of sanitary and building inspection measures.
2. Preparations for the evacuation of civilians from the border regions in case of war, an obvious case of a task requiring civil-military cooperation.
3. Protection of the national boundaries against hostile incursions (that is to say, a renewed emphasis upon the formation of *Grenzschutz* units).
4. Preparation for the transition of the peacetime army into a field army under the protection of the border defense forces.
5. Preparation, by civilian authorities, of sources of supply and replacement for personnel, materiel, and reinforcements, in cooperation with the military authorities.
6. Protection of stores of weapons, munitions, and army equipment.

It was obvious, wrote Schleicher, that the army alone was incapable of carrying out such measures. They required the active cooperation of the state authorities, and this was particularly true for border defense, the creation of which required a trained body of replacements, and that was only possible by registering and training the entire population capable of defense duties (*die wehrfähigen Bevölkerung*).[29]

Border defense, Schleicher went on to say, only made sense if it was ready at a moment's notice. Peacetime measures were therefore necessary to train its leaders in command techniques and its troops in the technical aspects of weapons use. The question of training replacements for such a force was also important—it was no longer possible to look to former wartime soldiers as a ready reserve because that pool was shrinking from year to year. Military preparations, even military training itself, for border defense had therefore become an urgent necessity, and something had to be done about it.

Schleicher was confident that the task was feasible. He mentioned, in fact, that negotiations between the Defense Ministry and the Prussian Ministry of the Interior were already underway to deal with the instruction of border defense commanders and weapons training. But he made clear that neither these measures, nor any of the others he had listed were in any way preparations for war in the sense of being mobilization plans. They were simply emergency measures (*Notwehrmassnahmen*) designed to let the army carry out the task allotted to it by the Versailles Treaty—the protection of Germany's borders—and to avoid developments such as the Polish occupation of the Lithuanian city of Wilno (Vilnius) in 1920.[30]

Commenting on behalf of the army, the chief of the Army Section of the *Truppenamt* (designated T-1), Fritsch, agreed that the government should undertake whatever the "most sober judgment" of Germany's foreign and domestic situation, as well as the nation's own strength, would permit.[31] In foreign policy terms, this meant that there could be no question of border defense measures in the west: here Germany would have to rely upon the 1925 Locarno Conference guarantees. National defense was essentially an issue in the east, to hinder any sudden move by Poland or to win time in a crisis. Defensive measures were not a goal in themselves, but had to stand in the service of foreign policy. On the domestic side, there was no room for private initiative in the assembly of recruits or materiel, as had occurred in the past. The new approach had to have a purely official character, and be completely neutral in a partisan political sense.

Above all, it was necessary to establish that national defense was not the prerogative of a single minister, or even of the foreign minister and Foreign Office together. It was the affair of the complete cabinet, and, once it had reached its decisions, the chancellor of the *Reich* would have to act as liaison with the governments of the various states (*Länder*), especially Prussia.[32]

It was self-evident, Fritsch said, that any such measures were violations of the Treaty of Versailles, Article 175, to be specific, which forbade Germany to undertake any mobilization measures. It was therefore necessary not only to hide them from the outside world, but to use the greatest circumspection when dealing with officials inside the country as well. Written orders, especially, were to be avoided whenever possible.

It was inevitable that the Allies would eventually uncover these activities. Germany would be able to defuse Allied objections most effectively, however, by justifying its actions with the right of every country to defend itself. Another important strategy was to cloak every national defense activity in some disguise that looked harmless to the outside world.

Fritsch then commented on Schleicher's specific suggestions. The Versailles Treaty did not forbid either the preparation of air defense, nor the drawing up of evacuation measures for certain districts in time of war. But with regard to the formation of a border defense force, such as already existed in East Prussia, the incompatibility of such a notion with the Treaty of Versailles was obvious. The same could be said for Schleicher's call for the establishment of stores of weapons and replacement sources for personnel, materiel, and reinforcements. Though Fritsch did not disagree with any of Schleicher's recommendations, he was surprised at the Defense Ministry's equanimity as it contemplated such systematic and comprehensive violations of the treaty, while the footprints of the recently departed Interallied Military Control Commission (IMCC) were still fresh on German soil.[33]

The Foreign Ministry's response to Schleicher's recommendations was mixed: on the one hand, Stresemann realized the "fundamental need for certain measures" in this area[34]; on the other, there were regrets that the army might be moving too fast. One foreign ministry official, Gerhard Köpke, drafted a detailed response to the Schleicher plan.[35] He felt that it was understandable for the Defense Ministry to look with concern on Germany's military situation, a situation created above all by the Versailles Treaty, but the Foreign Ministry had to evaluate the problem from the standpoint of the primacy of foreign policy. Before the world war, Germany had had an incredibly powerful army; if something had threatened Germany's foreign policy interests the country could always go to war, confident in its ability to defend itself. Today the situation was totally different. Today, avoiding a war through foreign policy was Germany's only defense. If that failed and war came, there was no hope that the army could defend the country against such vastly superior armies. This did not mean that the army should not prepare itself for special situations, even if such preparations went beyond the Versailles Treaty. But it did mean that all rearmament activities had to be evaluated by their diplomatic implications, and cease if they were overly disruptive of the sphere of foreign policy.

It was from this point of view that the Foreign Ministry had the "sad duty" to urge discretion on the Defense Ministry in its plans for national defense.[36] After all, the IMCC had only left Germany at the beginning of 1927. The Allied powers had only sold that move to their peoples by stating that they had transferred the military control to the League of Nations; it was a fiction, but its maintenance was important. It was essential at this delicate time, that the League not be empowered to carry out arms inspections in Germany. If it did receive such authority, and actually found preparations of the sort envisioned by Schleicher, Germany could no longer say that it was simply the ill-will of its former enemies that was responsible. This would be a neutral authority, not the Allies, now accusing Germany of treaty violations. Thus, for the time being, Germany had to avoid any activities that might give rise to Allied suspicions.

The effect of the Schleicher plan on the disarmament talks in Geneva would also be catastrophic. Germany's goal there was to achieve peaceful change, based on its portrayal of the situation of a defeated, disarmed Germany surrounded by the heavily armed victorious powers. It would be a very slow and strenuous process, to be sure, before Germany achieved success; the Great Powers that held the decision in their hands had shown no desire to give up their military supremacy over Germany. But Germany had to take care not to display a contradictory attitude to the disarmament proposals under discussion.

Köpke could not simply condemn the Schleicher proposal. The Foreign Office shared his concern about sudden *faits accomplis* on the eastern border: "We cannot and do not want to accept the responsibility for a policy in which the government sits with folded hands in the face of such a danger." The fact that national defense activities violated the Treaty of Versailles did not disturb the Foreign Office, either. But Köpke urged caution: "We must, however, limit the necessary preparations for national defense so that Germany's vital interests are not endangered. These preparations should not put the whole into danger."[37] Defense measures had to be strictly and lastingly subordinated to general policy, and their extent should be limited to what was absolutely necessary. They had to remain secret for as long as possible, and when the Allies did find out about them, as was inevitable, "harmless reasons" had to be ready to justify them. Finally, they had to be the program of the whole federal government, in cooperation with the *Länder*, and strictly on the official plane.

Köpke also pointed to the severe domestic opposition such a plan was sure to encounter. He referred back to a September cabinet meeting that had foundered on the opposition of Prussian Minister-President Otto Braun. Since then, in contrast to Schleicher's view, little progress had been made between the Defense Ministry and the Prussian government, and it was unlikely that there would ever be "totally convinced cooperation" between them. Negotiations between Braun and the chancellor would have to take place before any agreement was possible.

Köpke also commented on the various points of the Schleicher plan.[38] It was true that the Versailles Treaty contained no objections to civil air defenses. But measures in the military sphere required close oversight, especially with regard to naval aviation. Likewise, planning for the evacuation of the civilian population did not run contrary to Versailles. But it was important to leave it in the hands of the civilian authorities alone to avoid the appearance of mobilization measures. The Foreign Office recognized the need for a border defense. Training the population of the border districts was necessary to a certain degree, and so was preparing stocks of weapons, especially machine guns. But the Foreign Office found it regrettable that the Defense Ministry intended to draw up actual lists of personnel and select certain individuals for weapons training. Machine gun exercises in the border districts would be impossible to keep secret, especially from Poland's espionage service. Great problems in the diplomatic area were bound to be the result. As to the establishment of a border defense in the west, Köpke agreed with Fritsch: it would be impossible from the foreign policy point of view, and useless to boot. Regarding the establishment of a replacement pool throughout the *Reich* for personnel and materiel, the Foreign Office also recommended extreme caution. Discovery of such a plan (and it would be discovered, maybe even denounced by someone inside the country) would lead to immediate trouble with the Allies. The same thing needed to be said about plans to establish stocks of weapons throughout the country.

Köpke finished by saying that it would be extremely regrettable if the *Reichswehr* felt that it could use preparations for national defense as a means of achieving rearmament. The only hope for rearmament lay in the foreign political sphere. Trying to achieve it in secret would not only lead to great trouble politically, it would be of little use to the army.

The Era of Civil Military Cooperation: Wargames

Easing these suspicions on the part of the Foreign Office now became a priority of the army. After all, cooperation with the civilian authorities was the bedrock of the national defense concept. In November 1927, the *Truppenamt* invited Foreign Office personnel to attend an operational wargame based on "the present condition of the German armed forces and a politically possible case for conflict."[39] The Foreign Office accepted the invitation enthusiastically; it simply never would have occurred during the Seeckt regime.[40] The game, which took place at Defense Ministry offices on Königin Augustastrasse, began on 11 January 1928, and lasted until the end of February, with subsequent meetings being held on 18 and 25 January, and 8, 22, and 29 February.[41]

The first day of the game postulated a crisis over an unnamed issue that had led to tension between Germany and Poland in the summer of 1927.[42] Bilateral negotiations had failed to resolve the issue and were broken off. The result was a great increase in anti-German propaganda in Poland. By mid-September, with Polish propaganda continuing unabated, the German government requested action from the League of Nations. An armed conflict was possible. The League took no action, and the end of the month saw another German appeal to the League for quick action to avert a war. On 30 September the League decided to form a commission to investigate the disagreement, which would begin its work in the middle of October. But that evening Polish insurgents broke into East Prussia, Polish planes bombed Allenstein, and there was shooting across the German-Polish border in many sectors. Both sides declared their borders closed.

At noon on 1 October, the German government made a number of crucial decisions. It declared an immediate, nationwide state of emergency. It empowered the authorities in East Prussia and the civilian population of the border areas to form a volunteer border defense force. (The insertion and employment of these troops, however, was to require the approval of the national government.) It had the German ambassador in Warsaw demand an explanation from the Polish government; he also delivered a formal protest against the violation of East Prussia by armed Polish bands. The German government sent a telegram to the League protesting against the border violations. Finally, insofar as it was possible, the government intended to seek a peaceful solution to the crisis and to avoid further military measures until it had received responses from Poland and the League.

That afternoon the East Prussian authorities ordered the formation of a military border defense. That evening the ambassador in Warsaw wired Berlin that his attempt to secure information from the Polish government had failed. Polish officials denied that they were responsible for the insurgents; the behavior of Germany itself had led to this "movement" among the Polish people. The government was no longer in the position to influence public opinion. The results, and the consequences still to come, were the fault of Germany's intransigence in negotiations. In Warsaw itself, noted the ambassador, there was a great deal of war enthusiasm and talk of the annexation of East Prussia. He did not expect a formal declaration of war.

Late on 1 October, the chief of the Army Command reported to the cabinet that Polish cavalry (of the regular army) was assembling on the East Prussian border, and that a Polish invasion of East Prussia and the *Reich* seemed imminent. Given this grave situation, the cabinet now moved to put Germany on a wartime footing: it handed overall authority to a "chief of the Armed Forces" (*Chef der Wehrmacht*). It deployed all available forces in East Prussia for the defense of the province and authorized the commanders there to do everything necessary to keep the province in German hands. Naval units in East Prussia were subordinated the commanders for this purpose. In effect, this order made East Prussia an independent command. It also extended the formation of a border defense to the entire eastern frontier, put the armed forces into a state of march readiness, and ordered additional divisions to be formed inside the country.

These preparations took place just in time. On the night of 1 October, Polish (red) naval forces opened hostilities at sea, carrying out a blocking operation against the East Prussian port of Pillau, in concert with heavy bombing raids on the port itself. On 2 October, officials in East Prussia ordered the deployment of all available forces, and the callup of a border defense force throughout the eastern frontier regions commenced.

That same day, however, the government received a telegram from the president of the League of Nations High Council. "Seek to avoid hostilities," it ran. "Abstain from a violent solution to this conflict. The League Council has been called into immediate session."[43]

That evening, the chief of the Army Command received a telegram from the chief of the Armed Forces: "The introduced measures are progressing. We have thrown back enemy forces that had crossed the borders of the *Reich*. It is now important to establish whether and where active enemy forces are taking part in the fighting. Our own forces may not, for the time being, cross the border."[44]

He did not have long to wait. By 4 October, it was clear that regular Polish troops had invaded East Prussia and Germany proper. On the morning of October 5, Germany's two army commands, *Feldoberkommando* I and II, received orders from their chief: "Since active Polish troops have now crossed the German border, the previous restriction of the battle to German territory is no longer in effect."[45]

It was the diplomatic developments that were of primary interest to the Foreign Office participants. On 4 October, the Lithuanian government declared its neutrality in the German-Polish conflict. The Germans had been counting on Lithuania, still angered over the loss of Wilno, to put pressure on Poland from the east. But of even greater significance was the game's inclusion of the United States. On the morning of 4 October, Polish gunfire sank a U.S. merchant steamer in the locks of the Holtenau Canal near Kiel; several U.S. lives were lost. That afternoon the American government lodged an official protest with the Polish government.[46]

The Defense Ministry was interested in the opinion of the Foreign Office on the likelihood of the entire scenario, but particularly its analysis of the U.S. ship episode. In general, the diplomats saw the situation as unlikely: "A German-Polish war without the participation of France or other powers, seems improbable."[47] Nevertheless, since Poland had attacked Germany, the entry of France into the war on Poland's side would be a clear violation of the Locarno Treaty, and thus demand Britain's intervention on behalf of Germany. That situation also seemed unlikely, but it was possible that a French attack would lead to severe differences of opinion between France and Britain. Thus French intervention would probably not take place in the first phases of such a conflict. The German government would be able to make good use of this interval by appealing to the League, exactly as it had done in the game.

As for the Soviet Union, the Foreign Office felt that the nation's active participation in a conflict like the one postulated in this game was unlikely. There was a possibility, however, of getting the Soviets to make a demonstration against the Polish border. It could consist of a sharpening of the diplomatic tone, or perhaps even certain troop movements in the border regions, and would certainly tie up some Polish forces.

The Foreign Office also looked to internal events to weaken Poland's offensive strength. The unwillingness of the national minorities would probably unhinge mobilization; in fact, the government would probably have to call out reliable troops to oversee mobilization. Such tension might lead to acts of terror and sabotage, and almost certainly to a Ukrainian uprising, which could call upon 40,000 to 60,000 irregulars in eastern and central Galicia (though this might not occur in the first few days). It would certainly require strong, mobile Polish forces to put it down. There might also be a smaller uprising in Belorussia.

With regard to the sinking of the U.S. steamer, the Foreign Office labeled it a clear breach of international law that requiring reparations—but the United States would probably limit itself to demanding a monetary payment. Only if Poland refused to pay would further measures come into consideration, such as breaking off diplomatic relations.

The Foreign Office was most emphatic in stating that "the most effective action that the government could take to impede, delay, or weaken the Polish attack, lay without a doubt in the area of the League of Nations." According to Article 11 of the League Covenant, not only each war, but each threat of war, was the affair of the entire League. The red attack at sea on the evening of October 1, as well as the land attacks in the following days, were clear violations of the covenant, and raised the possibility of economic sanctions against Poland. However, given the international situation, these sanctions would probably have little effect. The Soviet Union was not a member of the League; action by Poland's neighbors such as Czechoslovakia and Hungary could not be expected to be decisive; a blockade of the Polish coast by Britain and France was not very likely. Still, the success of Germany's appeal to the League was not to be judged by whether it caused an immediate cessation of the Polish attack, but whether in the long run it led to the weakening of Poland's political position. The Foreign Office was reminding the army that with the conflict unwinnable in a strictly military sense, victory could only lie in the realm of politics and diplomacy.

The situation postulated in the game formed the basis of the *Truppenamtreise* of 1928.[48] By the end of October, Polish troops had overrun all of East Prussia save Königsberg. Despite the efforts of border defense troops and hefty counterattacks by the regular army on the Oder, all of Pomerania and Silesia had also fallen into Polish hands. Both sides had up until then respected the neutrality of the Free City of Danzig.

At this point, insistent urging from Germany and strong pressure from Britain led to the intervention of the League of Nations, which ordered Poland to suspend hostilities and drew a line of demarcation between German and Polish forces, to be in force until the completion of peace talks. In East Prussia, the line ran southwest of Brandenburg-Kreuzburg-Uderwangen-Tapiau-Deime River (the bridges over the river had already been destroyed). In other words, the truce left virtually all the province outside of the Samland peninsula and Königsberg in Polish hands. In the *Reich* proper, the line ran along the Oder River from the sea to the bend in the river south of Fürstenberg, then south along the Görlitzer Neisse. In other words, the German wargame of 1928 reckoned with a Polish occupation of

Germany up to the Oder-Neisse line—a fact not without a certain irony. The bridges over the Oder were destroyed, those over the Neisse were not. Furthermore, Germany and Poland had signed a truce agreement that included the following provisions:

1. The line of demarcation was to block all trade, as well as flights by aircraft.
2. On both sides of the demarcation line, there was to be a zone of 50 kilometers in which each nation was permitted to have only security garrisons. The size of these garrisons was not to exceed one division per every 30-kilometer stretch in the zone. Neither side was to build fortified positions anywhere inside the zone.
3. At sea, Polish warships and aircraft were not permitted west of Kolberg. German vessels and airplanes were not allowed east of Arkona. German shipping to Königsberg was limited to necessary imports of foodstuffs, and would be monitored by the League.
4. The intention to end the agreement required a 24-hour notice.

In the course of the winter of 1927–1928, the Soviet government succeeded in cleverly diverting domestic discontent into war fever against its hated Polish neighbor. Moscow spent weeks preparing for war, then invaded Poland at the beginning of April. Rumania immediately intervened on the side of Poland.

On 8 April, the negotiations in Geneva were suspended as useless; they were canceled altogether in early May. The sharp tension between France and Britain that had been so obvious within the League had abated perceptibly since the Soviet invasion. The French press continued to urge action on behalf of Poland. But all of Germany's remaining neighbors (with the exception of Belgium) had declared neutrality.

On 9 April, the Germans learned that the Soviets had won a great victory over the Polish 1st Army at Baranowitschi. The next day a note from the Soviet government demanded immediate German action against Poland, and made it clear that in the absence of a German response the Soviets themselves would decide the fate of Poland. Germany's "Chief of the Armed Forces" now informed the government that the military buildup had progressed far enough to entertain a hope of success against Poland. But it would be absolutely necessary to use all forces against Poland; the political leadership would have to keep other states—Britain and France above all—from active intervention against Germany. This was all in light of Germany's dependence on overseas imports for its war economy.

The wargame showed that there were sharp differences between the Defense Ministry and the Foreign Office. The Foreign Office disagreed with the fundamental premise of the game, stating that "a situation in which Germany and Russia go to war with Poland, without France and

Britain making an appearance, is politically unthinkable."[49] But disagreement between diplomats and soldiers is never surprising. What is most remarkable about this exercise was the degree to which the military and civilian authorities were now participating jointly in the formation of policy.

The military also redoubled its efforts to ease the fears of the Foreign Office about the former's national defense activities. In February 1928 Foreign Minister Gustav Stresemann, Defense Minister Groener, and Blomberg as head of the *Truppenamt* met to discuss the question, especially the formation of border defense units. Blomberg stated that the registration for enlistment of suitable personnel, which the Foreign Office worried would be impossible to keep secret, was only to take place in limited districts near the border, and it would be under the control of the Prussian Interior Ministry. Such a program already existed in East Prussia, and had run smoothly (there had also been similar preparations in Pomerania). The Foreign Office also was hesitant to approve machine gun exercises, but Blomberg assured it that they would take place only under very strict limits and with great care. Stresemann expressed concern about such training exercises, which he said should only take place within the framework of Germany's frequent civilian shooting matches. But he urged that there must be no participation by *Reichswehr* officers or noncommissioned officers as instructors, a point with which the army agreed. The meeting ended with a promise by Groener to meet with Prussian officials, in particular Minister-President Braun, to ensure civilian oversight over any further defensive preparations, and he invited Foreign Office representatives to attend.[50]

None of this is to suggest that the Defense Ministry and the government of Prussia, which was dominated by the Social Democrats, had suddenly began to see eye to eye on preparations for defense. Groener complained that Braun and Interior Minister Carl Severing were dragging their feet on the issue, and that in fact they had reneged on a series of agreements they had made with Gessler, his predecessor. The fundamental problem between army and Prussia, said the Foreign Office, was that the Prussian government drew a sharp distinction between border defense (to which it raised no substantive objections) and national defense. Border defense activity was to take place only in the border districts and involve only the local population. But it wanted national defense outside the border regions limited only to a limited stocking of arms.

To the Defense Ministry, however, this meant that in the event of an invasion, the border population would be more or less on its own, without hope of replacements from the interior of the country in either the material or manpower sphere. This was unacceptable. National defense was pointless from the start if it was excluded from certain areas (i.e., not truly national). And telling the border population that it had to fend for itself without the support of the rest of Germany was a recipe for disaster.

The Foreign Office declared on the side of the Defense Ministry in this argument. The *Reich* cabinet had already decided on the necessity for national defense preparations. It made no sense to limit the preparations to the small zone of the border: certainly defense activities in the country at large required care and a certain reserve, but that did not mean that such preparations should not take place at all.[51]

The Foreign Office was also represented at both Naval and Army Command (*Marine-* and *Heeresleitung*) wargames in the winter of 1927–1928. In his letter inviting civilian officials to his game, Chief of the Naval Command Admiral Hans Zenker declared that he wanted to "work together with the Foreign Office in a frictionless manner and with great sensitivity on all points of common interest."[52]

Dirk Forster and a number of other individuals from the Foreign Office also attended the Army Command wargame that winter.[53] The game assumed that in September of Year X (compatible with the force levels and international situation of 1927) negotiations between Germany and Poland over an unnamed issue had suddenly turned acrimonious. A strong anti-German movement had arisen in the Polish population, either with the toleration or encouragement of the government. Germany raised objections in Warsaw against anti-German propaganda, and when it got no satisfaction it took the issue to the League of Nations. Toward the end of the month the situation in Poland worsened. By the beginning of October it was clear that the Polish government was planning some sort of blow against Germany. It aimed to seize East Prussia without mobilization or a declaration of war, and to support this move by a drive into the *Reich* proper. Poland deployed its army, strengthened by keeping the yearly class of reserves with the colors, in three groups: one on the East Prussian border, a second in the Polish Corridor, and the third southwest of Posen, ready to attack toward Breslau and Glogau. The advance guard consisted of irregular bands. Given the weakness of its own forces, the German government now had to decide whether to sacrifice East Prussia and withdraw behind the Oder or put up a fight for East Prussia and the entire eastern border. It decided on the latter course. Filling out the situation was the status of the Great Powers most likely to intervene, France and the Soviet Union. The game assumed that German relations with France had progressed to such a point that French intervention in this war was unlikely. The internal situation in the Soviet Union had deteriorated so far that it represented no threat to Poland.

It was thus to be a bilateral conflict between Germany and Poland, described by Forster as "an extraordinarily favorable situation for us."[54] Nonetheless, in a pregame discussion that he attended, Germany's army commanders gave a very pessimistic analysis of the situation in terms of manpower, armaments, replacements, and air and border defense. Despite the favorable international situation, the generals evidently believed that

Germany was entering a hopeless conflict. In fact, so gloomy was the assessment that Forster believed it was intended partly to convince the government of the need for further measures in the realm of national defense.

Conclusion

It is easy to overestimate the impact of these wargames. They have certainly elicited their fair share of attention from historians, with no less than two full-length monographs devoted to them.[55] The games did not include any real innovation in terms of German military strategy, nor do they represent "operational planning" in any real sense. They were not simply unreal fantasies spun by the army to justify its own existence.[56] But in terms of the history of the *Reichswehr*, they do mark a new era of close cooperation with the civilian authorities, and are thus a dramatic departure from the "nonpolitical" army of Seeckt. The army had not suddenly become a buttress of the republican order, but it had recognized the importance of the Foreign Office and the civilian authorities in waging a modern war.

It was also at this time that the army began inviting Foreign Office representatives to exercises and maneuvers. In April 1928 Heye sent the Foreign Office a schedule of troop training exercises for that summer, saying that he would be pleased if members of the office decided to attend one or another.[57] He also invited Foreign Office representatives to the large maneuvers of 1st Group Command in September "in order to win a general overview." Finally, he offered the army's services to brief the Foreign Office on topics being discussed at the disarmament talks in Geneva. It might not have been a "move to the left" on the part of the army, but it was clearly a new age in German military history.

Notes

1. For the best—if relatively unknown—account of the crisis, see the chapter entitled "Die Prinzen-Krise" in Wolfgang Paul's regimental history, *Das Potsdamer Infanterie- Regiment 9, 1918–1945* (Osnabrück: Biblio Verlag, 1985), pp. 43–50; it was the 9th Infantry Regiment's maneuver that caused the uproar. See also the memoirs of Defense Minister Otto Gessler, *Reichswehrpolitik in der Weimarer Zeit* (Stuttgart: Deutsche Verlags-Anstalt, 1958), for the view of the man who dismissed Seeckt. For other accounts of what Seeckt's biographer calls the "firing" (*die Entlassung*), see Friedrich von Rabenau, *Seeckt: Aus seinem Leben, 1918–1936* (Leipzig: von Hase und Koehler Verlag, 1940), pp. 533–577; Hans Meier-Welcker, *Seeckt* (Frankfurt am Main: Bernard & Graefe Verlag für Wehrwesen, 1967), pp. 501–523, calls it a "resignation" (*der Abschied*). Other worthwhile accounts include Harold J. Gordon, *The Reichswehr and the German Republic 1919–1926* (Princeton, NJ: Princeton University Press, 1957), pp. 261–268; F. L. Carsten, *The Reichswehr and Politics 1918–1933* (London: Oxford University Press, 1966), pp.

245–250; Gordon A. Craig, *The Politics of the Prussian Army, 1640–1945* (London: Oxford University Press, 1955), pp. 421–423; Rainer Wohlfeil, "Heer und Republik," *Handbuch zur deutschen Militärgeschichte 1648–1939*, VI: *Reichswehr und Republik* (Munich: Bernard & Graefe Verlag, 1979), pp. 283–285; J. W. Wheeler-Bennett, *The Nemesis of Power: The German Army in Politics, 1918–1945* (London: Macmillan & Co., 1964), pp. 152–153; Walter Goerlitz, *The German General Staff* (New York: Praeger, 1953). pp. 248–250; S. W. Halperin, *Germany Tried Democracy: A Political History of the Reich from 1918 to 1933* (New York: Norton, 1946), pp. 409–410; and Erich Eyck, *A History of the Weimar Republic*, vol. 2 (Cambridge, MA: Harvard University Press, 1962), pp. 86–92.

2. The only comprehensive account of Seeckt's inaction in 1920 is Robert M. Citino, *The Evolution of Blitzkrieg Tactics: Germany Defends Itself Against Poland, 1918–1933* (Westport, CT: Greenwood Press, 1987), pp. 15–33.

3. "Der Weg von Dortmund nach Berlin ist ja nicht weit, aber er führt durch Ströme von Blut." See Rabenau, *Seeckt: Aus seinem Leben*, p. 324.

4. For Seeckt's views on the continuing utility of cavalry, see Hans von Seeckt, "Neuzeitliche Kavallerie," reprinted in *Gedanken eines Soldaten* (Leipzig: K. F. Koehler, 1935), pp. 99–116.

5. "In der Verbindung mit dem Fluggeschwader findet die Kavallerie-Division eine neue Stärkung." See Seeckt, "Neuzeitliche Kavallerie," in *Gedanken*, p. 101.

6. "Die Transportwagen können und sollen, richtig und mit Massen verwandt, den Kavallerie-Division einen wesentlichen Kraftzuwachs geben." Seeckt, "Neuzeitliche Kavallerie," in *Gedanken*, p. 102.

7. For the many problems that arose in trying to integrate cavalry into *Reichswehr* training and maneuvers, see the numerous references in Seeckt's "Observations of the Chief of the Army Command, expecially "Observations 1921," section 100; "Observations 1923," 69–79; "Observations 1924," 63–89; and "Observations 1925," 44, 49.

8. The article originally appeared in the *Militär Wochenblatt*, the semiofficial German military weekly, no. 6, 11 August 1927.

9. According to F. L. Carsten, *The Reichswehr and Politics 1918–1933* (London: Oxford University Press, 1966), German officers saw Seeckt as "a 'substitute for the monarch who filled 'the void' created by the abdication of the Emperor" (p. 107); see also Michael Geyer, *Aufrüstung oder Sicherheit: Die Reichswehr in der Krise der Machtpolitik, 1924–1936* (Wiesbaden: Franz Steiner Verlag, 1980), p. 81.

10. For the original quote, see Friedrich von Rabenau, *Seeckt: Aus seinem Leben, 1918–1936* (Leipzig: von Hase und Koehler Verlag, 1940), p. 342. For a trenchant criticism of Rabenau's use of the sources, see Hans Meier-Welcker, *Seeckt* (Frankfurt am Main: Bernard & Graefe Verlag für Wehrwesen, 1967), pp. 9–12.

11. See Adolf Reinicke, *Das Reichsheer 1921–1934: Ziele, Methoden der Ausbildung und Erziehung sowie der Dienstgestaltung* (Osnabrück: Biblio Verlag, 1986), pp. 269–270.

12. Ibid., p. 270.

13. Ibid., p. 269.

14. For the transition from Seeckt to Heye, see Rabenau, *Seeckt*, pp. 540, 547; Gordon, *The Reichswehr and the German Republic*, pp. 267–268; and Carsten, *The Reichswehr and Politics*, pp. 253–254, which places it in the context of an alleged "move to the left" on the part of the *Reichswehr*. Heye

15. Reinicke, *Das Reichsheer*, pp. 270–271; Carsten, *The Reichswehr and Politics*, paints a much more favorable portrait of Heye, praising his forthcoming and conciliatory policy toward the republican regime: "He even accepted part of

the responsibility for the constant friction with the Prussian government. All this would have been unthinkable under Seeckt, who would never have admitted any fault of his own" (p. 267). For Heye's trip to the United States, see the documents found in *Akten des Auswärtigen Amtes* (Records of the German Foreign Office). A microfilmed copy of these documents is found in the National Archives, Washington, DC, Microcopy T-120, reel 5168, serial K1796, frames K446 647–736. For microfilmed records from this collection, the following sequence will be used hereafter: AA (standing for *Auswärtiges Amtes*), to be followed by reel, serial, and frame numbers. Under this system of abbreviation, the above document would be cited as AA, 5168, K1796, K446 647–736.

16. For the transition to Hammerstein, see Carsten, *The Reichswehr and Politics*, pp. 325–328 and Reinicke, *Das Reichsheer*, p. 271.

17. Geyer, *Aufrüstung oder Sicherheit*, pp. 78–100, offers the best analysis of this *fronde* of younger officers that led the opposition to Seeckt's policies in the years after the Ruhr occupation. In the Seeckt years, he writes, "it was difficult to distinguish between future-oriented training and mere escapism from reality" (p. 80). For Geyer, it was not the failure at the Marne in 1914 or the ultimate defeat of November 1918, but the complete inability to oppose the French march into the Ruhr that marks "a decisive break in the continuity of the Wilhelminian General Staff" (pp. 84–85).

18. The best single-volume history of Groener's tenure as defense minister is Johannes Hürter, *Wilhelm Groener: Reichswehrminister am Ende der Weimarer Republik, 1928–1932* (Munich: R. Oldenbourg Verlag, 1993), although it focuses more on Groener's domestic political activity and relationship to the Weimar Republic than on his military significance. The biography of Groener written by his daughter is still quite useful, as well: Dorothea Groener-Geyer, *General Groener: Soldat und Staatsmann* (Frankfurt am Main: Societäts-Verlag, 1954). For Groener's impact on military planning, see Robert M. Citino, *The Evolution of Blitzkrieg Tactics: Germany Defends Itself Against Poland, 1918–1933* (Westport, CT: Grenwood Press, 1987), pp. 144–194, and Geyer, *Aufrüstung oder Sicherheit*, pp. 198–236. Gaines Post, Jr., *The Civil-Military Fabric of Weimar Foreign Policy* (Princeton, NJ: Princeton University Press, 1973), pp. 94–100, focuses on the "new realism" among German officers in the wake of Seeckt's resignation.

19. Wilhelm Groener, *Der Feldherr wider Willen: Operative Studien über den Weltkrieg* (Berlin: E. S. Mittler und Sohn, 1931), and *Das Testament des Grafen Schlieffens* (Berlin: E. Mittler und Sohn, 1927). See also Groener's correspondence with the Reichsarchiv in the microfilmed copy of the Groener Papers, reel 8, National Archives, Washington, DC.

20. See, for example, the essay "Gedanken über die Entwicklung des Kriegswesens," Groener Papers, reel 25, pp. 1–29. See also, on the same reel, "Stichworte für grössere gemischte motorisierte Verbände."

21. For a dissenting comment on Groener's alleged political "moderation," see Peter Gay, *Weimar Culture: The Outsider as Insider* (New York: Harper & Row, 1968), p. 25n.

22. Erich Zechlin, Foreign Office, "Aufzeichnung," Berlin, 18 April 1928, AA, 3527, 9182H, E645 778–889.

23. Herbert Dirksen, Foreign Office, "Aufzeichnung," Berlin, 16 May 1928, AA, 3527, 9182H, E645 788.

24. See Gordon A. Craig, *The Politics of the Prussian Army, 1640–1945* (London: Oxford University Press, 1955), p. 525.

25. Groener, "Das Panzerschiff," Berlin, November 1928, Groener Papers, reel 25, pp. 1–29.

26. Groener's speech to the Reichstag is found in the Groener Papers, reel 25,

pp. 1–21.

27. "Vortrag vor dem Herrn Reichsaussenminister über Landesschutz," Defense Minister Otto Gessler to Foreign Minister Gustav Stresemann, Berlin, 25 October 1927, AA, 3613, K6, K000 300–304.

28. "Vortrag über Landesschutz," p. 1, AA, 3613, K6, K000 301.

29. Ibid., pp. 2–3, AA, 3613, K6, K000 302–303.

30. Ibid., p. 4, AA, 3613, K6, K000 304.

31. "Mündlich Erläuterungen des Obersten Freiherrn von Fritsch," AA, 3613, K6, K000 305–308.

32. Ibid., section III, AA, 3613, K6, K000 305–306.

33. Ibid., section IV, AA, 3613, K6, K000 306–308.

34. Post, *Civil-Military Fabric*, p. 182; see also Foreign Minister Gustav Stresemann to Defense Minister Otto Gessler, Berlin, 25 November 1927, AA, 3613, K6, K000 316–317.

35. See the report from Gerhard Köpke of the Foreign Office, "Aufzeichnung über die Pläne des Reichswehrministeriums betreffend den Landesschutz," AA, 3613, K6, K000 309–315.

36. Ibid., section II, AA, 3613, K6, K000 310.

37. Ibid., section III, AA, 3613, K6, K000 311–312.

38. Ibid., section V, AA, 3613, K6, K000 312–315.

39. Col. Werner Blomberg, Chief of the Truppenamt, to State Secretary Karl von Schubert, Berlin, 12 November 1927, AA, 3613, K6, K000 318.

40. Foreign Minister Gustav Stresemann to Defense Minister Otto Gessler, Berlin, 25 November 1927, AA, 3613, K6, K000 319.

41. Col. Werner Blomberg, Chief of the *Truppenamt*, to State Secretary Karl von Schubert, Berlin, 22 December 1927, AA, 3613, K6, K000 332.

42. Col. Werner Blomberg, Chief of the *Truppenamt*, to State Secretary Karl von Schubert, Berlin, 14 January 1928, contains a detailed narrative of the game, especially appendix (*Anlage*) 1, *Zeitliche Entwicklung der politischer Ereignisse bei Blau*, AA, 3613, K6, K000 337–340.

43. *Zeitliche Entwicklung,* section entitled "Am 2.10. 2,00," AA, 3613, K6, K000 339.

44. Ibid., section entitled "Am 2.10. 5,00," AA, 3613, K6, K000 339.

45. Ibid., section entitled "Am 5.10. 8,00," AA, 3613, K6, K000 340.

46. Col. Werner Blomberg, Chief of the *Truppenamt*, to State Secretary Karl von Schubert, Berlin, 14 January 1928, Appendix 2, "Versenkung eines amerikanischen Dampfers bei Holtenau," AA, 3613, K6, K000 341.

47. Taken from an unsigned document headed "Vormerk" (probably written by Dirk Forster), AA, 3613, K6, K000 342–344.

48. Col. Werner Blomberg, Chief of the *Truppenamt*, to State Secretary Karl von Schubert, Berlin, 8 February 1928, "Die Lage baut sich auf dem Winterkriegsspiels des Truppenamtes auf," AA, 3613, K6, K000 347–350.

49. Unsigned handwritten note. Again, the author is probably Forster, AA, 3613, K6, K000 350.

50. The minutes of this important meeting are found in AA, 3613, K6, K000 367–368.

51. Dirk Forster, "Bemerkungen über Landesschutz," prepared for a meeting between the new defense minister, Gen. Wilhelm Groener, Prussian Minister-President Otto Braun, and Foreign Minister Gustav Stresemann, Berlin, 13 April 1928, AA, 3613, K6, K000 370–372.

52. Chief of the Navy Command, Adm. Hans Zenker, to State Secretary Karl von Schubert, Berlin, 20 April 1928, AA, 3613, K6, K000 320–321; State Secretary Karl von Schubert to Chief of the Navy Command, Adm. Hans Zenker, Berlin, 20

April 1928, AA, 3613, K6, K000 322.

53. Dirk Forster, "Aufzeichnung über das Kriegsspiel der Heeresleitung im Winter 1927/28," AA, 3613, K6, K000 329–331.

54. Ibid., section II, AA, 3613, K6, K000 330.

55. Geyer, *Aufrüstung oder Sicherheit;* and Post, *Civil-Military Fabric.*

56. This is the thesis argued by Geyer, *Aufrüstung oder Sicherheit:* "Nicht die Übungstechnik also, sondern der Unwille, politische und militärpolitische Alternativen zur unmöglichen Kriegführung anzuerkennen, führte zu einem Zustand, in dem Phantasie und Realität hoffnungslos vermischt wurden" (p. 192). In relation to the intervention of the League of Nations in the wargame scenario and the subsequent German-Soviet attack on Poland, "Der Völkerbundeingriff hatte nicht nur einen Niederlage abgefangen, sondern der Reichswehr gleichzeitig zu einem Krieg verholfen, den sie zu führen wünschte, aber nicht führen konnte" (p. 193). Geyer is correct in describing the "unreality" of the wargame situation. But he fails to discuss a related point. What would be the point of a wargame that assumed the strength and armament of the 100,000-man Versailles army? What lessons could it possibly teach the participants? That a 100,000-man army was insufficient to continental defense, even against one of the medium powers like Poland? Most officers already knew that fact.

57. Chief of the Army Command, Gen. Wilhelm Heye, to Foreign Office, Berlin, 20 April 1928, AA, 3613, K6, K000 374–377.

CHAPTER 7

The Army and the "New Objectivity"

The *Reichswehr* has been the object of a great deal of scholarly research, but there has not yet been an attempt to integrate its history into the broader cultural history of the Weimar Republic. It has become common-place among cultural historians to divide the republic into two phases: a stormy, Expressionist-dominated experimental beginning (characterized in Peter Gay's phrase as "a revolt of the sons against the fathers") and a less flashy but more solidly creative phase (the period of Walter Gropius's Bauhaus and the plays of the mature Bertolt Brecht), described as the "new objectivity" (*Neue Sachlichkeit*).[1] What is perhaps surprising is how closely the history of the *Reichswehr* follows this scheme. From its origins in the collapse of the old order, through the storms and stresses of its infancy (participation in antirepublican activity such as the Kapp and Hitler putsches), under the leadership of a man who thought much more in terms of the army of the future than in terms of the actual situation, the *Reichswehr* had by 1927 left behind the dreams of its youth to come to grips with its most pressing task: devising a strategy of national defense (*Landesverteidigung*). In the military, as well as the architectural or artistic realm, it was the age of the new objectivity.

Civil Military Cooperation, 1928

As mentioned earlier, the *Truppenamt* had used the results of the 1927 wargame as the basis for a General Staff tour (*Truppenamtsreise*) at Bautzen and Bad Salzbrunn in Silesia, in the spring of 1928. Combining a wargame with a tour of the actual terrain over which the game was taking place, the staff tour had been a staple of the Seeckt years. Again, Blomberg invited participation of the Foreign Office. Since this was to be a ten-day affair (17–27 April), however, he recommended attendance on the last two game days and the final critique (23–26 April), if participation in the entire tour was impossible.[2]

The sudden invasion of East Prussia, Pomerania, and Silesia had found Germany lacking in manpower and materiel. The munitions situation was perhaps most serious of all. The new situation postulated that the League of Nations' enforced cease fire in late fall had enabled both Germany and the Soviet Union to increase the level of their military preparations. Thus, by the resumption of hostilities, Poland faced a strengthened Germany in the west and a war-ready Soviet army in the east. Neither Britain nor France had as yet entered the war, although France appeared to be preparing for an invasion of Germany.[3]

From the start of the tour, the Foreign Office advised the *Truppenamt* that such a situation was "practically unthinkable." The *Truppenamt* agreed, but it also wanted to give its commanders practice in large-scale operations, which required that the opposing forces be more or less equal. Dirk Forster of the Foreign Office agreed that the operations had been interesting from the military standpoint, featuring a Soviet attack on Poland and a French drive into Germany. He also had the opportunity, in the course of the many long automobile rides, to form some personal impressions of Germany's military leaders: General von Blomberg, chief of the *Truppenamt,* Colonel von Fritsch, Colonel Muff, and Major Wever, as well as Colonel Stülpnagel (at that time head of the Army Personnel Section) and Colonel Kühlenthal, head of the Statistical Section (responsible for intelligence on foreign armies).[4] General Heye was also present. Forster's overall impression, based in part on the extreme politeness with which he was treated, was that the men of the *Truppenamt* really did desire closer relations with the Foreign Office. He was happy to see a "sober judgment" of Germany's military and political situation by the army that placed limits on the *Truppenamt's* operational and strategic objectives. Again and again he had heard the phrase "turning away from romanticism," although he had the sense that it had occurred more in the army than in the navy. The *Truppenamt* apparently felt that any military-political activity abroad would be inadvisable at this time, and it would greet any attempt to draw closer to another power with great reserve. For example, the notion of closer military cooperation between Germany and Italy—then a staple of Italian foreign policy—was received with coolness. Likewise, most German officers recognized the essential unreliability of an alliance between a communist and a capitalist power.

Forster found some interesting ideas about relations with France, however. Many officers expressed the opinion that the army's dislike of France might some day have to give way to developments in the political sphere. It was all part of what he called a "new outlook" in the armed services. Heye had installed a number of bright young officers in leading positions, and with no little pride, they viewed themselves as a "young generation," ready and willing to accept new conditions. Although Forster was mainly interested in how this new outlook would affect foreign policy, he admitted it very well might have implications in the purely military sphere as well. He had even heard officers say that the radical disarmament clauses of the Versailles Treaty had been a benefit to the army, forcing it to get rid of not only old materiel but also outmoded institutions and ways of thinking.

The leading figure, "the spiritual leader of the new army," was General von Blomberg, Forster felt. The entire officer corps respected Blomberg's "personal qualities and military capabilities." The personal impression he made was all the greater due to his above-average education and background. When not discussing the disadvantages of the medium trench mortar in mobile warfare, or the use of indirect fire by the heavy machine gun, he could also discuss and analyze in great detail modern German, French, and American literature. And he had personally told Forster that the *Heeresleitung* desired the participation of as many Foreign Office representatives as possible in future wargames and General Staff tours.

In May 1928, the *Reichswehr* Ministry formulated a series of directives on national defense, based on Schleicher's memorandum of the previous year.[6] They discussed in greater detail the principal points of the former document:

1. Caches of weapons, which were now being supervised by the civil authorities (in cooperation with the local *Wehrkreiskommando*).
2. Border defense forces, organized in sufficient depth and supported by a signal organization in the border regions. Special measures in this area included the preparation of defense zones, instruction of officers in the terrain, theoretical instruction on border defense battles, preparations of defensive works and demolitions, weapons training (at first only in East Prussia, designated here as *Grenzschutz Ost*), and cooperation with the civil authorities.
3. Preparation for the expansion of the peacetime army into a march-ready field army, including the fleshing-out of the peacetime divisions and the establishment of a reserve pool.
4. The necessary statistical work, again supervised by the civil authorities, to evaluate Germany's situation in terms of manpower and materiel.

Close civil-military cooperation was essential for achieving these goals. The men responsible for it in the most direct sense were the *Wehrkreis* commander and the *Oberpräsident* of the province. There was to be no private participation in military affairs. In particular, the various paramilitary *Verbände* and *Vereine* (a few on the Left, the vast preponderance on the Right) had no place whatsoever in this system. The *Reichs-*

wehr would assume no responsibility for them, or for private weapons camps not officially registered with the authorities. The *Reichswehr* could call on civilian specialists in various areas, but only with the written approval of the states' executives. For their part, civilian officials had to agree to secrecy in these matters, and to use all the authority of the state to protect it.[7]

Again, the Defense Ministry submitted the document to the Foreign Office for comment. Forster advised that it was in compliance with Article 160 of the Versailles Treaty, permitting Germany to take the necessary measures to protect its borders.[8] In its present size and condition the *Reichswehr* was incapable of defending German territory from foreign attack, and would remain so as long as Section V of the Treaty (dealing with German rearmament) was in effect. Since a change in the treaty did not seem likely in the near term, it was necessary to undertake certain preparatory measures throughout Germany to enable the army to protect the border against a sudden invasion and to prevent any *fait accompli*. But these measures had to be of limited scope, and must not appear to be paving the way for any sort of general rearmament. They also had to be strictly subordinated to Germany's foreign policy.

The Foreign Office therefore supported the efforts to establish a more viable national defense posture and was ready to work toward that end. But Forster went on to point out that such measures were also in clear violation of Germany's treaty obligations, specifically Article 178, which required Germany to refrain from any and all mobilization measures. Individual details were the prerogative of the *Reichswehr* Ministry, but the Foreign Office demanded that no activities be approved that compromised Germany's foreign policy, and deciding what did or did not was the final prerogative of the Foreign Office.[9]

This answer was apparently satisfactory to the Defense Ministry. Groener approached Forster at the cornerstone laying ceremony for the new Chancellery (*Reichskanzlei*) building in June to discuss the various issues involved, and followed up that contact with a note.[10] Groener had observed in the recent wargames how difficult it could be to construct a game on a realistic foundation, and felt that it would be advantageous to both his officers and the participating Foreign Office personnel to set up some sort of diplomatic game (*diplomatischen Übungsspielen*), based on the current actual diplomatic and military situation. He had taken a first step in this direction by inviting Foreign Office representatives to the past winter's games. But a common game on a larger scale would be even more beneficial to both sides.

Further cooperation was in evidence at the 1928 fall maneuvers in Silesia and the winter wargame of 1928–1929.[11] A high point of sorts was reached in the last game when the *Truppenamt* asked the Foreign Office to allow a diplomatic operative to play the role of German foreign minister. The game began, in fact, with discussions between the "minister," Blomberg as the *"Chef der Wehrmacht,"* and the chiefs of the Army and Naval Command. Their discussion formed the basis for the military events in the game (a simultaneous invasion of Germany from east and west, and the period of tension leading up to it). Another Foreign Office representative took part in the team directing the game (the *Truppenamt*, interested in a fresh outlook, requested that he be young).

Operational Planning: The Attack on Gdynia

The late 1920s also saw the beginning of realistic operational planning—against Poland. Up until this point German plans for war had been purely defensive. Army maneuvers analyzed the possibility of a Polish invasion of East Prussia or Silesia, either alone or in conjunction with a grand French offensive from the west. Naval maneuvers concentrated largely on controlling the waters of the Baltic Sea against the tiny Polish navy (sometimes reinforced by a French squadron), as well as maintaining sea communications between the *Reich* and East Prussia. To the chief of the Naval Command, Adm. Erich Raeder, the maneuvers of 1928–1929 had demonstrated conclusively the importance of the Polish port of Gdynia.

The Poles had built Gdynia in the early 1920s out of concern over their access to the Baltic. Although the Treaty of Versailles guaranteed Poland the use of the Free City of Danzig, Poland had soon found this arrangement unsatisfactory: in 1920, with the Red Army advancing on Warsaw, German dockworkers in Danzig had gone on strike and refused to unload shipments of war materiel sent from the West to aid the Poles.[12] There was no guarantee against a repeat of this occurrence should Poland once more go to war, especially with Germany as a potential adversary. The Poles therefore saw the construction of alternative port facilities on the Baltic as a pressing need.

Work on Gdynia began in 1921, and the port was in operation by 1923. As a German report from 1929 put it, "At great expense—a preliminary estimate puts it at 52 million gold francs—Poland has succeeded in creating, where once stood nothing but an insignificant Pomeranian village, a Baltic seaport that now threatens to surpass Danzig in importance." With good protection from the weather, favorable water depth, numerous inlets into the harbor, and modern rail and coaling facilities, Gdynia could handle ships of up to 16,000 tons with ease.[13] Steamer lines from Britain, Denmark, and the United States put Gdynia on their routes.[14] Not only did its commercial traffic soon exceed that of Danzig, but its military significance soon became obvious. As Poland's only real access to the sea Gdynia was also by necessity a naval base, and the Poles had equipped it with heavy guns and air cover. It included the Baltic's only repair facilities for

Polish and friendly vessels.

By the end of 1929 the *Truppenamt* was considering operations to neutralize Gdynia at the outbreak of a war, at first, wanting a sudden blow either during peacetime or as a counter to a Polish attack upon Germany. Such an operation would require forces large enough to crush all Polish resistance within twenty-four hours. A rapid operation would limit the political repercussions as well as present Poland with a *fait accompli* before Polish mobilization was complete.

The *Truppenamt* envisioned three operational targets for German planners: Gdynia's port facilities; the seaplane stations at Puck and Rewa, along with the air base at Rahmel; and Gdynia's land and sea batteries, including the heavy batteries on the fortress of Hel.[15] The *Truppenamt* viewed the first target as the key, although it was complicated by the presence of Danzig. If Poland occupied Danzig and used it as its principal Baltic base, then the entire plan would be called into question. An attack on Gdynia with the limited goal of removing the coastal batteries and the airfields would not be worth the cost.

The *Truppenamt* had initially envisioned an army operation. Problems soon arose, however. According to German military intelligence, a company of marines, a battery of coastal artillery, and a railroad battery were all deployed in or around Gdynia. A marine battalion had recently arrived in the port, but it appeared that the purpose of this 900–man force was to fill empty billets on the ships in the harbor, not to act as a land defense force. There were air bases at Puck, Rewa, and Rahmel, but none of them had sufficient military personnel to form an effective defense. The headquarters of the Polish 8th Cavalry Brigade was at nearby Starogard, but the only field units there were the 2nd Light Infantry Battalion and the 2nd Cavalry Regiment. There was another light infantry battalion, the 1st, at Chojnice to the southwest and an infantry battalion, the 2nd of the 65th Infantry Regiment, at Mewe to the south. Although the Poles had planned for some time to strengthen their forces in the Polish Corridor to six light infantry battalions, four cavalry regiments, one horse artillery battery, one antiaircraft battery, and two armored battalions, this reinforcement had not yet occurred.[16]

German estimates were that these forces, led by the truck-mobile light infantry, could react within eighteen hours of an attack. According to reports received by German intelligence, the light infantry battalion at Chojnice had orders to take up a defensive position west of town immediately upon the outbreak of hostilities between Germany and Poland. This force would therefore be in a position to upset the intended twenty-four-hour timetable for the German assault.

In addition to the regular forces, there were also some ten battalions of irregular border defense forces (both police and civilian units) near Gdynia.[17] In the event of mobilization, the Germans expected these to form two distinct groups, one at Koscierzyna of six battalions and one at Chojnice of four battalions. Each battalion contained about 350 men, organized into three or four companies. Finally, the Poles had available at Puck and Neustadt a battalion-sized force of irregulars. All told, the Poles could call on 10,000 men for the defense of Gdynia, far more than the Germans could assemble for an attack on the port.

The terrain around Gdynia also made the *Truppenamt* wary of a land attack.[18] The region is basically flat, though with occasional undulations, but there were woods with thick undergrowth around the city, impassable to all but small bodies of infantry. At the time, few good roads existed; lateral east-west roads, that is, those which an attacking German force would have to use, were in particularly bad condition—so movement of large bodies of troops off the roads would be impossible. Small roadblocks by Polish cavalry detachments could therefore seriously hinder the operation. Like the manpower balance in the region, the terrain made it unlikely that land forces could achieve the quick decision required by the *Truppenamt*.

This disinclination to use land forces received further reinforcement from the commander of Defense District II (*Wehrkreiskommando* II) in Stettin. In June 1928, the Defense Ministry had ordered General Schniewindt, commander of the 2nd Infantry Division, to draw up plans for an attack on Gdynia.[19] This "Stettin Plan" drew a distinction between an operation by the field army and a rapid coup (*Handstreich*) by special forces assembled for this purpose. Only the military and political situation of an actual war could determine the shape of field army operations. It was impossible to say, for example, what forces the army might be able to spare from the main theaters of war. Peacetime preparations could therefore only be of the *Handstreich* variety, similar to the blow against the Belgian fortress of Liège in the opening days of World War I. Such an operation could only begin after the fighting had already broken out elsewhere. According to Schniewindt, "political considerations preclude a coup before the outbreak of war," although he added that "the sooner after the start of war the coup takes place, the more favorable its chances of success."[20]

Nonetheless, the difficulties facing such an operation were daunting. The Stettin Plan called for three advancing columns. The middle column had the task of seizing Gdynia; it would march on its objective via Neustadt. As a minimum strength for this column, the plan called for two infantry battalions, made more mobile by bicycles, motorcycles, and trucks, and receiving fire support from infantry guns; one reconnaissance battalion, with a squadron of armored cars; two artillery batteries; pioneer units; communications troops; and marine demolition units. The northern column would drive on the air base at Puck and the Hel fortifications. It would consist of a mobile infantry battalion, an artillery battery, and pioneer troops. The mission of the southern column was to protect the flank of the main column. Its strength was equal to the northern column, plus a platoon of armored cars. Rounding out the "task force" was the reserve: five infantry battalions, a reconnaissance detachment with armored cars, a cavalry regiment (also with armored cars), and four artillery batteries.

Protecting the main column's southern flank was crucial, and keeping Polish reinforcements out of Gdynia was an absolute necessity. To assist the southern column, Schniewindt planned to use agents and saboteurs to destroy railroads, roads, and communications in the Polish Corridor prior to the attack. Noisy concentrations of border defense units in the area would also help to draw off Polish reserves heading for Gdynia. Because of the poor quality of these irregular forces, he had no intention to use them in the advance. Finally, Germany's meager air assets would keep watch over the southern approaches to the Corridor.[21]

The manpower requirements of Schniewindt's plan apparently convinced the *Truppenamt* that a land drive on Gdynia was out of the question.[22] A response to the Stettin Plan from *Truppenamt* chief General von Hammerstein, written in January 1930, listed many reasons why the plan would not work. Given the fact that the march route from Lauenburg to Gdynia was roughly sixty kilometers, an attacking force was looking at a thirty-six-hour march if unopposed. Polish border defense activity could stretch that out to forty-eight or even sixty hours, and any opposition by regular Polish formations might prevent the Germans from reaching Gdynia altogether. Should the attacking force arrive, the situation in Gdynia was by no means clear. The outbreak of any war, even one following a short period of tension, would almost certainly find Gdynia with an increased garrison. The Poles recognized the importance of Gdynia and would make its land defense one of the cornerstones of their strategy. Any attacking force would therefore be outnumbered. The manpower imbalance meant that an arriving German force would most likely find itself in a bloody battle for possession of the port, a battle it was by no means sure to win. Further, the ability of the attacking force to actually destroy the port facilities within twenty-four hours (and destruction of the port was essential, as opposed to merely blocking it) was doubtful.

While Hammerstein was rejecting the army plan, the navy had been conducting its own studies for an attack on Gdynia. This was the genesis of "Study Gdynia" (*Studie Gdingen*), the navy's operational war plan against Poland.[23] Along with two other operational studies worked out under Raeder, "Study Baltic Sea Defense" (*Studie Ostseeverteidigung*) and "Study Commerce Protection" (*Studie Schutz der Zufuhr*), it was essentially a defensive plan, to be put into effect only if Germany were attacked.[24]

In April 1929 Raeder circulated a questionnaire to various departments in the navy, asking "which measures are to be taken at sea against Poland in the event of a sudden outbreak of war?"[25] The purpose, he said, was to determine which countermeasures Germany might take against a sudden Polish attack (e.g., an occupation of East Prussia). The assumption was that there would be no time to mobilize or reinforce, since only a short period of tension (three days) was presumed to precede the conflict. Germany would have to act with the means at hand. Since the initial fighting was of a localized nature between Germany and Poland, Raeder left French forces out of the picture for the time being.

In order to proceed with the planning, Raeder felt he needed more detailed information on Polish naval forces and dispositions. What forces would Poland have available at sea, in the air, and on land? What sorts of reinforcements could Poland expect in case the war dragged on? Would Poland attempt to improve its strategic position by occupying Danzig?[26]

These questions led to a companion series of questions about the *Reichsmarine*. What naval forces would Germany have at its disposal? What should be the navy's strategic goals in the event of a conflict with Poland? Should it concentrate on destroying Gdynia as a base? Preventing the use of Danzig? Destroying Polish naval forces? Or perhaps adopting a defensive posture in order to protect Pillau, East Prussia's only useful port? Finally, did Germany's naval strength suffice to meet all these goals or, indeed, any of them?

The answers Raeder received to these questions were mixed. On the one hand, there were many officers in the *Reichsmarine*, with Raeder evidently among them, who were confident of their ability to control the Baltic in a war with Poland, and even to strike an offensive blow against Gdynia.[27] On the other hand, there were those like Fleet Commander Adm. Iwan Oldekop, who labeled any thoughts of attacking Gdynia "fantasy" because of Germany's material and numerical weakness.[28]

After analyzing these reports and conducting an in-depth study of the port's defenses, Raeder and the Naval Command concluded that Gdynia was vulnerable. Polish surface naval units were insignificant, and the port lacked strong artillery defenses. The greatest danger to any strike on Gdynia was the Polish air force, especially since the Germans had no combat aircraft of their own. Polish airpower could pose a grave threat to the *Reichsmarine's* light surface forces. Polish planes would be operating close to their bases, and the narrowness of the sea area would restrict German maneuverability to a great degree. German naval leaders had confidence in their antiaircraft gunners, but recognized that the most effective defense against a Polish air attack were warplanes of their own.[29]

Studie Gdingen, as it eventually evolved, contained four steps: shelling the port, clearing mines, landing troops, and demolition. It would have to be a lightning strike. Therefore, the study recommended the preparation of a "light task force," equipped with on-board munitions, just for this mission. It was to consist of two cruisers, two torpedo flotillas with flak guns, and mine boats.

This force would have to arrive at Gdynia within hours of the outbreak of hostilities. It had three missions: locating mines in Gdynia harbor;

preventing a breakout by Polish naval units; and protecting the larger German units to follow. It would be guided by intelligence gleaned by German reconnaissance aircraft flying sorties during the tense prewar period. Since the planes were unarmed, these flights would have to cease when the war began.

Within twenty-four hours of the arrival of the light task force, heavy units, including the four battleships, would arrive. One cruiser would shell the town of Puck, north of Gdynia, to prevent use of the airfield there. Three of the four battleships would shell targets in the harbor from medium range, while the fourth would stand guard outside the harbor to repel any attacks by Polish forces sailing toward Gdynia. Under the protection of the heavy guns, minesweepers would then go in to clear a path for the marine infantry landing vessels. After disembarking, the marines would carry out demolitions in the port. Following demolition, the marines would reembark and leave the area. The final stage of the operation involved mining the harbor and sinking blockships to close Gdynia permanently.[30]

Although the balance of forces in 1939 would render this operation unnecessary in a strategic sense, it would be the guns of the German navy—fired by the obsolete battleship *Schleswig-Holstein* against Polish positions on the Westerplatte—which would announce on 1 September, 1939 that the world was once again at war.

Group Command Maneuvers, 1927–1928

At first, the *Reichswehr's* field maneuvers reflected little new thinking. Both the 1927 and 1928 fall maneuvers of the Group Commands, for example, used cavalry in a leading role. The former, held near Paderborn near Westphalia, featured a cavalry division attempting to cover the retreat of a friendly infantry division; the 1928 maneuvers pitted these units against each other.

The 1927 maneuvers featured the troops of 2nd Group Command, commanded by General von Reinhardt.[31] Red forces consisted of the 3rd Cavalry Division (including the 7th, 8th, and 9th Cavalry Brigades) and a reinforced motorized infantry regiment (the 15th). The brigades were a provisional form of organization, consisting of two regiments each; the formal table of organization and equipment for a German cavalry division simply listed six regiments. The red side also had air assets, represented by hydrogen balloons. Blue forces included the 6th Infantry Division (16th, 17th, and 18th Regiments), reinforced by armored car platoons, horse artillery, and tanks. It too had a balloon "air force."[32]

The war situation assumed an invasion by a hypothetical Red nation across the Rhine to the upper Weser River. A blue (German) army, the 1st, was approaching from the east. Its deployment along the Weser was to be covered by the 16th and 26th *Landwehr* Brigades (their presence was assumed) and the 6th Infantry Division. The red II Cavalry Corps was acting as a screen for the movement of the main force (designated "Northern Army") as the latter approached the Weser. It also had orders to break through blue screening troops and disrupt the concentration of 1st Army in cooperation with bombing attacks. Basically, then, this was an infantry-cavalry engagement.[33]

At the post-exercise critique (*Schlussbesprechung*) of the first day's action, presided over by Reinhardt and attended by twenty-one foreign attachés, the general was highly critical of the advance of the cavalry patrols. They had neglected their cover, he said, pointing out what excellent use might have been made of the trees on the side of the road. Small bodies of cavalry, he said, "should advance in columns of twos, each trooper being taught to march directly under the trees, leaving the center of the road clear." He also criticized the continued use of the lance. There was no longer such a thing as "mounted action," and the lance was merely an encumbrance as well as being a nuisance for the horse holders. He pointed out that this, happily, was the last maneuver of the *Reichswehr* in which lances would be used.[34]

According to Col. H. H. Zornig, acting U.S. military attaché, both red and blue sides had performed credibly. Both had made "excellent dispositions for holding a position." The troops seemed particularly skilled in placing light machine guns where they could be fully supported by other weapons. Machine gun fire was far more prevalent than rifle fire. In one instance, Zornig saw a corporal take a light machine gun and advance it about 50 yards to a haystack, which he flattened out on top of a few boards as a base and "set up his gun so that it was invisible from any angle." Zornig saw similar advantage being taken of tombstones in small cemeteries, farmer's wagons, and bell towers of small churches. The machine gun, he felt, was "the essential weapon of the German army." It was a weapon of great tactical potency and "each machine gun unit displayed great skill, the result of long and careful drills."[35]

The third day of the maneuver began with all the attachés being taken at 5:00 A.M. to a hill overlooking the battlefield. Here they witnessed the blue horse artillery in action covering the retreat of the blue 6th Division's three regiments. The retreat was orderly, proceeded by battalions, and took every effort to use trees or other camouflage against enemy air observation. If neither cover nor camouflage was available, the units dispersed as much as possible so as not to offer a target, either to aerial bombardment or to long-range artillery directed by aircraft. The blue artillery, for example, was not under cover but deployed in the open in an irregular checkerboard formation, batteries being posted over an area about 300 yards wide and deep. Hostile aircraft would not have found a single target comprising more than a single caisson and gun. This did, of course, cause great problems in terms of fire control, especially in rapid shifting of fire from one target to another, as well as command control. But the purpose, so Zornig heard, was to test a new style of camouflage netting.

Later the attachés witnessed the advance of the red 15th Infantry Regiment (motorized). The *Reichswehr* seemed highly interested in problems of motorization, and was therefore service testing a large number of trucks and cars. Infantry rode in a 3.5-ton truck. Horse artillery was also transported, apparently some sort of experiment (harnessed horses three to a truck, gun and caisson loaded on a single truck). The purpose was to allow the horse artillery to keep up with the motorized infantry, yet have all of the advantages of ordinary horse artillery when crossing fields.[36]

The critique for this day's action featured all of the officers of both the red and blue forces, collected in a hollow square around Defense Minister Otto Gessler, chief of the Army Command Heye, and General Reinhardt in the center. French attachés were in attendance, as were a number of photographers from leading newspapers and cameramen from the Signal Corps, snapping pictures of the many diverse individuals and uniforms. Gessler and Heye each spoke briefly, congratulating the men on their excellent performance. Reinhardt then spoke for two hours, going over the entire maneuver from first day to last. A main theme of his address was the importance of indirect fire by heavy machine guns, especially the usefulness of having it deployed in positions to the rear and firing over the heads of friendly advancing infantry.[37]

Zornig closed his report to the War Department with some general comments. First, with regard to mechanization, the lack of tanks, gas, heavy artillery, and aircraft meant that these German maneuvers "had a great unreality attached to them, more so than any maneuvers held anywhere else in the world." The participants had to imagine the existence of airplanes, tanks, and all the other forbidden equipment, taxing the young German soldier's powers of creativity.

Still, it appeared to this observer that the German army had progressed in motorization and mechanization about as far as was humanly possible, given the material constraints. The treaty had forced the Germans into a position where they were "beginning to look upon huge numbers of armed men as an encumbrance" rather than an advantage. Quickness of movement along roads and across country, and the launching of sudden attacks followed by equally rapid evasion—these seemed to be the aim of Germany's new army. At no time, Zornig stated, did he witness "the rigidity of the old German military tactics": instead, "the utmost elasticity" seemed to be the new watchword. The motorization of the army, along with its diminished size, reduced the importance of railroads and increased that of good roads (especially those lined with large protective trees). The treaty set no limits on German road building, and Zornig predicted that the German government would continue to take advantage of this loophole (a prediction later fulfilled by Hitler's construction of the *Autobahn* system). These roads would afford Germany "the possibility of concentrating an adequate force of great striking and penetrating power." All dismounted troops in the maneuver, for example, had ridden trucks from their quarters to the maneuver area. No railroads had been used at all.

Germany seemed to be training an army of technicians, and the design of technical equipment was a prime consideration. Zornig had heard a great deal of talk about air power, to give just one example. After World War I, most specialists were concerned with building even larger aircraft engines, but the smaller engines allowed to Germany for her civil aviation (*Lufthansa*) had proven just as efficient. Even though civil and military aviation were not the same, such crucial areas as the training of pilots, radio operators, and mechanics, as well as the development of metallurgy, were continuing unabated in Germany.[38]

Zornig saw little that was new in terms of infantry. He noted that each company of infantry contained three platoons of two light machine guns and one rifle group each, thus reinforcing the supremacy of the machine gun in German infantry tactics. Enlisted men were young and in fine physical shape, and there was a noticeable absence of "the old and fat NCO," so much a part of the prewar German army.[39]

His overall impression of these German maneuvers was that of an army that was serious about motorization. Armored cars were used in abundance, though due to their age they often experienced breakdowns. Isolated field guns, posted at crossroads, were the main defense against them. Small dummy tanks were also used, and for the first time were mounted on a small, one-cylinder motor car (the Hanomag). A Mercedes-Benz "reconnaissance car" also made its first appearance, with a six-cylinder water-cooled engine. It had eight-wheel drive (two on each aside of the double rear axles) and operated in plowed fields at high speed without becoming bogged down.[40]

The 1928 maneuvers of 1st Group Command continued in the same vein. Even the *Militär Wochenblatt* had to admit that there was strong similarity to the 1927 exercise in that a cavalry division was fighting an infantry division.[41] The article went on to say that the resemblance was only superficial, however, since this time the assumption was that the divisions were fighting separate from their respective armies. While this gave them greater freedom of action, it also made it much more difficult for the maneuver directors to control the exercise, in particular to keep the units on the desired terrain.

The situation postulated that a superior red army, enjoying control of the air, was driving into Silesia from the southeast (i.e., from Czechoslovakia). The red 2nd Cavalry Division had just repelled a blue cavalry division and was pushing it to the north. The red division was formed for purposes of the maneuver into two brigades (of three regiments each). In addition to these regular units, the division had been reinforced by a regiment of horse artillery (two detachments of three batteries each), by a number of armored cars (*Strassenpanzerwagen*), by brigade units, and by a "7th (Motorized) Infantry Regiment" (actually a battalion of infantry from the 1st Infantry Division in automobiles, a motorized artillery battery, a number of dummy tanks, and motorcycles).

The blue army was retreating in a westerly direction into Silesia, but it intended to give battle on a line extending eastward from Löwenberg, screening the important city of Breslau. The blue 4th Infantry Division was ordered into the gap between the Bober and Queis rivers, where strong red cavalry forces (the 2nd Cavalry Division) were reported to be advancing. The blue 4th Division, besides its standard three regiments and one pioneer battalion, had assigned to it the 4th Reconnaissance Detachment (three squadrons of cavalry with machine guns, light cannon, armored cars, and bicyclists), plus two batteries and motorcycle units.

The maneuver, essentially a meeting engagement, was not particularly well done. The *Militär Wochenblatt* criticized the action on the grounds that "there was more maneuvering than fighting" and that "such reciprocal castle moves" would hardly be possible in real combat. On day one, the red 2nd Cavalry Division came out almost unscathed. The next day it retreated suddenly for no apparent reason. Nonetheless, there were moments of interest. Cavalry made its appearance for the first time *sans* lances and appeared reinvigorated. Troops of all the services gave an impressive appearance and looked as fresh at the end as they had at the start.

Maneuvers of the 1st Infantry Division, 1928

Far more impressive that fall were the maneuvers of the 1st Infantry Division in East Prussia.[42] The 1st had by now acquired a reputation as the elite unit in the *Reichswehr*, stationed on what was expected to be the "front line" in any future war and defending the land many avid nationalists considered to be the birthplace of the German nation. The maneuvers took place in the Masurian Lakes country near Lötzen from 3 to 8 September 1928, and were attended by a large number of foreign attachés, as well as by General Heye, 1st Group Command leader General von Tschischwitz, Chief of the Army Personnel Office Stülpnagel, and the inspectors of cavalry, artillery, and the signal troops—all in all a very impressive turnout for a divisional maneuver. Divided into two parts, the exercises of 3–4 September simulated a meeting engagement, breaking off combat, and the transition to a delaying action by a red detachment as it slowly fell back on its main force. The red side, led by the commander of the Königsberg garrison Colonel Spemann, consisted of an infantry regiment (the 2nd), a battalion of infantry, the 1st Cavalry Regiment, a company of signal troops, and a smoke platoon. The blue side was led by Colonel Fleck (commander of the 3rd Infantry Regiment, 1st Division), and consisted of two infantry regiments (the 1st and 3rd), an artillery regiment, the 2nd Cavalry Regiment, a machine gun company, and an armored car platoon.

Both blue and red forces were moving to take possession of a narrow defile between two lakes, intending to hold it open for the passage of their respective armies.[43] Red cavalry arrived first, blocking passage on a long, thin front, and then had to hold it against attacks from the superior blue force. In a well-planned assault, the blue side sent its cavalry squadrons and bicyclists forward first, screening the approach of its main infantry body. Two more blue squadrons erode around the lake to the west, in an attempt to turn the red right flank. The superior weight of blue infantry began to tell in the course of the day's fighting, and pushed the red force back.

After a break for lunch (if only this happened in a real war!), red forces had orders to break off the combat, retreat to the northeast, and then turn and offer resistance in another lake defile. Blue units were to keep their attack moving and gain a rapid and decisive victory. They decided to build bridges over one of the lakes, and by crossing the infantry at that point, turn the entire red position. Pioneer units built two bridges, usable by all arms, on the evening of 3 September. One was constructed of pontoon boats. Blue forces successfully crossed the lake by 8:00 A.M. on 4 September, and launched an attack on the red right flank. This was the situation when part one of the maneuvers ended.

The first two days had offered interesting tactical problems in the combined use of infantry and cavalry, and forced the commanders into some difficult situations. On the first day, for example, both sides had to insert infantry into a battle where cavalry was already fighting, then withdraw and regroup the cavalry for service elsewhere. It basically came down to liaison between the overall detachment commander and the cavalry commander who was already engaged in the combat. The director of the maneuver, General Fett (infantry commander for the 1st Infantry Division), was not totally pleased with this aspect of the maneuver. It was "best accomplished," he stated, by "riding ahead, joining him [the cavalry commander] temporarily, and having a personal interview with him at the front." As always in the *Reichswehr*, the commander was expected to exercise personal leadership.[44]

After a break of one day, part two of the maneuvers began on 6 September. It opened up with the red side, already formed up for the advance, having to retreat behind a screen of its own cavalry. Then, on 7 September, it was the turn of the blue force to retreat, and the reinforced red forces to pursue and attack. The first day began with another meeting engagement. Because neither side commanded assets for a reconnaissance, they blundered into each other unexpectedly. Red forces won the advantage in the first few moments by being in possession of the high ground, but with these forces on a strategic defensive at this point, it decided not to press the advantage against the superior blue force. Nevertheless, by threatening the blue flank, red cavalry was able to tie up one and a half battalions of infantry (out of a total of five battalions), "an illustration of how troublesome is its [cavalry's] mere appearance on the flank." On 8 September, a greatly strengthened Red force launched a river crossing against a prepared Blue position.[45]

In his critique of the maneuver, U.S. Military Attaché Col. Edward Carpenter was first of all struck by the hard demands it had placed on officers and men alike. The action had gone on day and night, and both sides were given extremely tough march requirements. The smart and enthusiastic appearance of the men on their postmaneuver parade march belied the fact that they had been on their feet for three days and two nights straight. There had also been challenges for the commanders. The exercise had attempted to give the lower commanders and troop leaders experience in decisionmaking under conditions of mobile warfare. Carpenter had heard officers use the phrase "commanding into the uncertain," i.e., making decisions on partial and ever-changing information. He felt that this was the aim of the maneuvers, not the solution of specific operational or tactical problems.[46]

Contributing to the sense of realism were the umpires, who made the difference between an instructive, intense maneuver and a waste of time. The Germans, Carpenter admitted, had few peers in this area. Their organization was complete, with a chief umpire for each part of the maneuver; the partition of the maneuver ground into two sections (the blue's left wing and the red right forming one section, the blue right and the red left the other). There was an umpire for each sector. A plethora of officers and noncommissioned officers functioned as subordinate umpires. At least one mounted umpire served each battalion of infantry, field artillery regiment, and cavalry regiment. Two senior NCOs were assigned to each company of infantry, and one to each troop of cavalry and platoon of artillery. A separate telephone system for the umpires covered the entire area; it was clearly marked, and considered neutral and unavailable for use by either the Red or Blue side.

According to regulations, umpires were not allowed to order or recommend a course of action to a specific unit: they could neither permit nor disallow any activity. If a *Reichswehr* officer insisted on forming his men into a Macedonian-style phalanx, for instance, that was his choice (although his career would probably be over). The umpire was only to inform the commander of the situation: "You are under machine gun fire from the east" or "artillery fire from the heights to the south." It was the prerogative of the unit commander to decide on a course of action, exercising his own initiative and taking the proper steps to avoid losses.[47]

The cavalry, as it had in the Silesian maneuvers, appeared without lances. Mounted cavalry rode in small groups, keeping to the sides of roads, making use of all available cover, but still staying mounted. Along with the discarding of the lances, this had a positive impact on the cavalry's mobility. Cavalry, in fact, had been more active in these exercises than in any previous one, though Carpenter did note a tendency to ride the horses to excess. He attributed this to the fixed ending date of the exercise: the rider knew it would be over in five days, and then he and his horse would have a long rest.[48]

The principal problem areas were in the realm of materiel. First was the lack of air power, which caused both sides to operate "blindly," as it were: a great deal of blundering around was the result. The meeting engagements in the lake defile, for instance, could have been avoided altogether by the presence of air reconnaissance. Second, Carpenter noted that the German heavy machine guns lacked the mobility to support the advancing infantry, their principal task. The replacement of the heavy machine gun by the light trench mortar seemed like a possibility. Third, no tanks at all had taken part in the maneuver.[49] Although the *Reichswehr* had superb manpower, its lack of real weapons was an insoluble problem.

Mountain Infantry in the *Reichswehr*

In areas where a lack of heavy weapons and aircraft was not decisive, the *Reichswehr* continued to make progress. Training of mountain infantry, for example, had begun under Seeckt, who ordered one battalion per division to be trained as *Jägers* (light infantry) and provided with mountain equipment.[50] He also formed a mountain trench mortar company and two mountain batteries. A July 1924 decree had established two types of mountain units: units specially trained and equipped for high-mountain (alpine) work, and those with special equipment for mountains of medium height. Alpine troops included the regimental staff of the 19th Infantry Regiment (stationed in Munich), the 3rd Battalion of the 19th, two trench mortar companies and an artillery battalion (the 2nd of the 7th Bavarian Artillery Regiment, Munich), a pioneer platoon (from the 7th Bavarian Pioneer Battalion, Munich), two signal platoons, and two transport battalions. Equipment for medium mountain work was assigned to a number of units, mostly in the 7th Infantry Division (Bavaria).

The alpine troops trained year round. The winter training period lasted from the middle of December to the beginning of April, and it included individual alpine training, skiing, combat, and firing exercises. The summer training period began in May with Alpine exercises lasting four weeks, scheduled this early to avoid interfering with the tourist traffic. The exercises began with military alpine training, firing within the company or battery, and finished with several exercises of all the alpine troop, including marching, reinforcement, and combat. Following these, autumn was a time of continued individual training, with an emphasis on patrol. All this was, of course, in addition to the men's standard training on level ground, and at times it seemed as if there were not enough months in the year.

An article in the *Militär Wochenblatt* showed how seriously the Germans took this subject. Those states whose defense force was restricted by the Treaties of Versailles and St. Germain, it stated, naturally took special interest in mountain warfare for the reason that, as Captain Simon of the French Chausseurs Alpines rightly said in his 1910 *Principes de la Guerre Alpine,* "the Alps reduce the importance of the mass and increase that of the elite." The mountains were the only terrain on which the ideal war could still be carried on. There, numbers meant little, the worth of the troops everything. According to Napoleon, "the attacker is at a disadvantage" in the mountains; Clausewitz had called them "a veritable refugee of the weak."[51]

The 3rd Battalion held its first maneuvers in May 1928, and the *Reichswehr* invited several foreign attachés to observe.[52] Held at Oberammergau, the maneuvers were directed by Colonel Wilhelm Adam, commander of the 19th Infantry Regiment (the 3rd's parent unit). It was apparent from the start, at least from the point of view of Colonel Conger, the U.S. observer, that German mountain training was still in its infancy. He watched the 12th Machine Gun Company try to ascend the Kosel (a hill of some 1,300 meters rising above Oberammergau). "It needed no apologist," he wrote, "to say that this was its first day this year in the mountains." The unit struggled upward, apparently without any "intelligent supervision" by commissioned or noncommissioned officers who understood mountain operations. Equipment appeared improvised and technique shoddy: "Some of the horse leaders walked on the inside of the trail, others outside; some ahead with loose reins, others with hand on bit." As the observers were passing the unit, a horse toppled over and "went rolling down, crossing the zig zag path below some three times before he was lost to view behind some bushes." Meanwhile, the men in the path below made no real effort to get their animals out of the way of the falling horse; they "seemed glued to where they stood." The fact that the falling animal did not hit other horses and totally destroy the ascent was due to good luck and, unfortunately from a purely tactical point of view, gaps in the column below. Endurance was also a problem, As the day wore on, Conger saw ammunition boxes and equipment taken off exhausted horses and strewn about the path. The entire scene conjured up a hasty retreat, rather than the route of advance of a well-trained unit. Once the summit had been reached, however, the training of the machine gun company reasserted itself. In assembling, posting, and concealing their weapons, the troops were excellent. Still, the establishment of liaison and communications between the battalion and company headquarters and the numerous detachments along the ridge was a problem never satisfactorily solved.[53] Engineer troops had also done a less than sterling job of preparing the trails. The trench mortar company had an especially difficult time. It used pack mules, while the machine gun company used small pack horses. The "trail" prepared by the pioneers was a foot trail only and unsuitable for animals in many places. The bridges were narrow, constructed of poles 4–5 inches in diameter laid lengthwise, and often they had to be covered with sod to give the animals a footing. On one occasion, when this was not done, a pole snapped, badly wounding a mule. When queried about the poor state of the trails, Colonel Adam admitted that although the eight-man engineer detachment was large enough to have done a better job, "the trouble was they had gotten lost and spent most of their time preparing the wrong trail."[54]

Overall, Conger noted, the German mountain troops seemed technically amateurish in terms of mountain skills, at least in comparison with Swiss troops he had seen. There had obviously been no real attempt to acclimatize men and animals to mountain conditions. The Swiss did that first, before any tactical training. The German maneuvers had featured two rest days (Wednesday and Saturday) during the first week, something that would have been unnecessary under the Swiss system. The Germans never actually made bivouac in the mountains, but stayed in houses in Oberammergau and adjacent villages.[55]

Conger also noted the difference of the men themselves: mostly Bavarians and Saxons, they were easygoing and informal, quite different from the Prussians whom Conger had observed. The atmosphere and discipline were "more representative of conditions in our own army . . . than is the case with the north German divisions." This was not necessarily a bad thing, but he found a regrettable lack of efficiency on the part of both officers and men. The maneuver lacked that *planmässig* (systematic) quality so typical of other *Reichswehr* maneuvers at which he had been present. Things seemed haphazard, left to chance. Furthermore, neither the regimental commander, Adam, nor most of his officers had any personal experience in the mountains. Conger's verdict was that "tactically the troops would defend well a mountain position for a day or two. After that, . . . , they would have a large sick-report list of both men and animals."[56]

The 1930 Fall Maneuvers

The fall maneuvers of 1930 were the largest held in Germany since World War I, involving to some extent every division in the army.[57] In attendance were President Hindenburg, Defense Minister Groener, Chief of the Army Command Heye, and—as Heye's personal guests—former officers of the wartime and postwar army, representatives of the *Reichstag*, cabinet ministers, members of the state governments, officials from the German diplomatic corps and industry, and officers of foreign armies. Every accredited military attaché except those from France, the Soviet Union, and Poland were present. Those three were representatives of countries that had systematically excluded German officers from their maneuvers.

Taking place in Franconia in northwestern Bavaria, these were the first large maneuvers since the Silesian exercises of 1928. The *Reichstag* had refused to appropriate funds for large fall maneuvers in 1929, and economy was obviously still on the minds of the military high command. It would no longer be possible to have all the personnel and field equipment of a given unit present, as had been done in the past, at such exercises because it was simply too expensive to assemble the whole army. An obvious way to save money was to have the units present in skeleton form only (e.g., with a partial staff, a platoon, or company representing an entire regiment). Seeckt had experimented with this technique in the Silesian maneuvers of 1926, using only staffs and signal services.[58] But, based on past experience, most German officers felt that such "skeleton exercises" (*Rahmenübungen*) had problems. Specifically, movement and combat took place much faster than they would in real life. Moreover, operations were carried out that were in fact impossible. To eliminate the first problem, the 1930 maneuvers tested two remedies. First, a small portion of the units on both sides were present at full strength and with full field equipment: in this case each side, red and blue, had a complete division with full supply train that was to serve as a guide to the directors and umpires in slowing down the movement of the skeleton units. Second, each day of the maneuver featured two "neutral periods" (from 7:00 to 9:00 A.M. and from 6:00 to 9:00 P.M.), during which no tactical movement was allowed. Preventing the second problem (impossible operations), was as always in the hands of the umpires, and the staff this year was even larger than in the past, with some 700 officers and a large number of enlisted men.

There were also questions in the army about the degree of "skeletonization" possible, while still retaining any instructional advantage. There were three types of units in the 1930 maneuvers: (1) complete units (*Vollverbände*), already discussed; (2) flag units (*Flaggverbände*), whose commander and staffs were actually present down to and including battalions, but whose front line positions were outlined by men with flags; and (3) skeleton divisions (*Rahmendivisionen*), of which only the division commander and staff were present. The units' front lines were outlined, upon contact with the enemy, by small, mobile bodies of "umpire troops" under the command of the directors and the umpires.[59]

Each of the ten divisions in the army was thus represented in some form. The blue forces, led by 1st Group Commander General von Hasse, with General Adam as his "corps chief of staff," consisted of the following units: 1st Infantry Division (flag division), 2nd Infantry Division (skeleton),

3rd Infantry Division (flag), 4th Infantry Division (flag), 2nd Cavalry Division (skeleton), and 3rd Cavalry Division (full). The red, forces commanded by 2nd Group Commander General von Kayser, with General von Liebmann as his chief of staff, included the 5th Infantry Division (full), 6th and 7th Infantry Divisions (flag), and 1st Cavalry Division (skeleton).[60] Both sides were equipped with all the paraphernalia of modern war forbidden to Germany: tanks, heavy artillery, aircraft. There were also provisional corps troops on both sides, subordinated directly to the commanders on both asides. Nonstandard divisional organizations were also used.

In virtually all ways, then, the 1930 maneuvers were, in the words of the Berlin newspaper *Tempo*, "a grand experiment."[61] It began with the reading of the initial situation to both asides. It postulated an invasion of Germany (blue) by a superior red force advancing from the Rhine into central Germany. The red side's orders were to continue its drive along the valleys of the Lahn and the Main rivers; Blue forces were to counterattack the red army that was advancing along the Main with its weight south of the river. At the start of the maneuver, a red and a blue army were assumed to have stabilized a line southeast of Bamberg, with the northwest flanks at Bamberg. The Blue army decided to launch an attack by one infantry and one cavalry division on the red left (i.e., northern) flank. But the red army, after advancing cautiously, had taken up a defensive position in response to this threat. The blue flanking attack, led by the complete 3rd Cavalry Division, managed to gain ground and appeared capable of separating the left-wing division (the complete 5th Infantry) from the main body of the red army. The blue commander, however, declaring that the "operation has succeeded in bringing about the desired result" (i.e., hindering the red advance), now called off the attack and began a slow retreat.[62]

No startling doctrinal developments were in evidence here. The maneuver once again featured a flanking attempt by a cavalry division against an infantry division (when all the skeleton and flag units were stripped away). And once again, the results were mixed. *Tempo* wrote that the one-year layoff had obviously not been beneficial. The officers had seemed tentative at times, and the attempted flanking movement of the 3rd Cavalry, for example, had taken so long that it had failed to achieve a decisive victory. The paper might have added that the blue commander's decision to retreat in the middle of an apparently successful operation did not reflect well upon him, either. The troops, however, were truly impressive: three days in the field, in a situation of almost continuous maneuver warfare, they were called upon to attack and defend alternately. Yet the verve and enthusiasm on the last day was just as great as on the first. The demands on the men, wrote *Tempo*, "were far greater than those to which the troops were put in prewar times, and are hardly required as a matter of course in any other European army."[63]

The Mobilization Exercise of 1930

Despite the command problems and the trite infantry-cavalry focus, the 1930 fall maneuvers had gone far beyond a mere battlefield maneuver. Virtually the entire command structure of the army had been involved, making the maneuvers nothing less than a mobilization exercise.[64] In August, Col. Walther von Brauchitsch of the Army Training Office (T-4) had sent out a manuals and instructions for the upcoming exercise. These went to General Heye as overall exercise commander (*Leitender*) and, directly under him the exercise directors (*Übungsleitung*), General Hammerstein and General Brauchitsch, each with his own staff. For Heye, it included Col. Ritter von Schobert, Majors Fumetti and Vierow, Capt. Graf von Hülsen and Lt. Adolf Heusinger (who would go on to fame as the first commander of the post-World War II *Bundeswehr*). For the *Übungsleitung* there was a much larger staff of 59 officers, including men such as Major Reinhardt, Colonel Heinrici, Colonel Halder, Major Keitel, Lieutenant Helm Speidel, Major Kumpf, Lieutenant Jodl, and Colonel von Bredow. Four more officers were detailed to conduct the guests and press representatives about the maneuver field (including Major Marcks), while Colonel Kühlenthal, along with seven assistants, was in charge of the foreign attachés and officers. There was also a team of six officers in charge of the *Übungsleitung* own signal troops (not the ones handling signal operations for the maneuvering troops, but only for the directors). Finally, other officers "at the service of the Chief of the Army Command" included the chiefs of the various *Truppenamt* departments: von Vollard-Bockelberg for the *Heereswaffenamt* (Army Weapons Office); Hammerstein and Bussche for the *Wehramt* (Defense Office); and the inspectors of the infantry, cavalry, artillery, and the weapons schools.[65]

The first of the materials sent to all participants was *Assignments for the Umpires and Directors at the Great Skeleton Maneuver 1930.*[66] It was simply a formal list of all the personnel mentioned above, and many more besides. All told, the Training Office (*Ausbuildingsamt*) produced some 855 of these. Subtracting fifty copies for foreign guests, we arrive at a rough figure of 800 officers taking part in the maneuver, or 20 percent of Germany's total officer corps of 4,000 men.

According to the *Assignments,* the umpire service was to consist of two "chief umpires" (*Oberschiedsrichter*), one for the west, roughly corresponding to the red attacking side of the battlefield, and one for the east, corresponding to the blue sector. The *Oberschiedsrichter* West was General Ritter von Prager, the inspector of infantry. He had his own chief of dtaff, Colonel Oswald, a section commander in the Defense Ministry; two assistants (Major Thomas of the *Waffenamt* and Captain Chevallerie of the *Wehramt*); a staff officer from the director's signal troops (Colonel Salzmann of the *Waffenamt*); three mounted assistants, all majors from the Cavalry School at Hanover; a sanitation officer, three ordnance officers,

and a staff commandant. The high umpire in the east was General Sehns-
dorf, the inspector for the pioneers and fortresses. His organization mir-
rored Prager's, from his chief of staff (Colonel Keitel) down to his staff
commandant (Colonel Puttkamer).[67] Under these two high umpires were a
total of seven "umpire staffs" (*Schiedsrichterstäbe*), each composed of
three "umpire groups" (*Schiedsrichtergruppen*). Each group consisted of
a leader, two assistants for infantry, two assistants for artillery, and two
ordnance officers. There was also a separate staff for the skeleton divisions, commanded by Colonel List with a staff of eight subordinates.[68]

The *Assignments* also provided for a staff devoted solely to liaison between the directors and the combat troops. The *Leitungsverbindungskom-
mando* for 1st Group Command (blue) was commanded by General En-
ders, chief of staff of the *Heereswaffenamt*. He had two general assistants,
three officers responsible for air intelligence, two for liaison with the signal troops, two for artillery, one for motorized units, and two ordnance officers. Again, the depth of detail is worth mentioning. These officers were
not directing the maneuver; the *Leitung* and *Übungsleitung* did that. Nor
were they umpires. This was simply a staff intended for one purpose: to
transmit appropriate messages from the director to the troops and vice
versa. Now, going well beyond that general purpose were special director
commands for liaison with the corps troops and individual divisions taking
part in the maneuver. The blue side had eight such officers: one for the
skeleton flak battalion; two for the reconnaissance battalion, another skeleton unit; three for the skeleton air squadron (*Flieger-Rahmenstaffel* 101);
and two for the skeleton Panzer battalion (*Kpfw. Rahmenbataillon* 101).
There was also a separate direction liaison command (*Leitungsverbind-
ungskommando*) for each of the blue divisions: the 1st, 2nd, 3rd, and 4th
Infantry Divisions and the 2nd and 3rd Cavalry Divisions.[69] As detailed as
this structure was, it is necessary to remember that it was reproduced exactly for the red side as well: a direction liaison command for 2nd Group
Command (red), led by Colonel Boetticher, the commander of the Artillery
School; direction officers for the red corps troops (again consisting of a
flak detachment, a reconnaissance detachment, a flying squadron, and a
tank battalion, all represented by skeleton units), plus direction liaison
commands for each red division (the 5th, 6th, and 7th Infantry, along with
the 1st Cavalry).[70]

The second booklet sent to the maneuver participants was entitled
Rules for the Great Skeleton Exercise 1930, drawn up by Chief of Staff
Hammerstein.[71] Sent to the *Leitung*, the umpires, and the officers fighting
on both the red and blue sides, it was made into some 2,600 copies. Again,
subtracting 100 for guests and others, over 2,500 German officers were involved (62 percent of the German officer corps).

Again, befitting the depth of detail, the *Rules* themselves were a hefty
47 pages, and were accompanied by no less than 16 appendixes. The in-
troductory remarks stressed that these rules were to be used in connection

with the regulations already in force for maneuvers, the *Rules for Large Troop Exercises* (*Bestimmungen für die grösseren Truppenübungen*), the *Rules for the Umpire Service at Troop Exercises* (*Bestimmungen für die Schiedsrichterdienst bei Truppenübungen*), and the "Compilation of Rules for Troop Exercises in Open Country" (*Zusammenstellung der Bestimmungen für Truppenübungen im freien Gelände*). All staff members and troops were to study all four documents thoroughly before the maneuvers began. Three areas in particular received specific mention:

1. Due to the thinly populated nature of the region, the quartering of troops presented a serious burden to the local population. Since so many officers were to be present (for the flag and skeleton units), they would be unable to demand "officer's quarters." In parts of the Thuringian Wood, and in the small villages, the simplest kind of accommodations for men and horses were to be expected.
2. The severe financial situation demanded avoidance of all unnecessary expense. All the participants had to work together to keep the costs of the great maneuvers down to the lowest possible level. This was especially true in terms of damage to crops and the use of motorized vehicles. It was necessary, for example, to find the shortest possible routes, to "car pool" as many individuals as possible and to avoid duplication of routes.
3. All participants in the exercise had to do their best to see that secrecy was maintained.[72]

The first few chapters of the *Rules for the Great Skeleton Exercise 1930* dealt with the Direction of the maneuvers (General Heye), the location of its headquarters, and the makeup of its staff; the presence of the Reich President (and details of his honor guard from the 7th Infantry Division), defense minister and guests; and the mundane issues of scheduling and timing. The maneuver ran from 12 September (with the arrival of the *Leitung*) to 19 September. The troops would arrive on three days: the 11th, 12th, and 13th. After several days of preparation, the first actual exercise day was the 15th. Troops would actually be in the field for four days, until 18 September. This was the period designated in the *Rules* as *kriegsmässig* (under war conditions). The "state of war" (*Kriegszustand*) ended at noon on 18 September, and was to be followed by a final critique on 19 September at 10:30 A.M. and a parade in the president's honor at noon.[73] The regulations for transport away from the battlefield were included in the appendixes.

Next, there were detailed instructions for the three kinds of units used: full, flag, and skeleton. For a flag division, for example, each infantry company was represented by five flags, three for rifle and two for machine gun companies; each cavalry squadron by two special "mounted cavalry pennants"; antitank companies by three trench mortar flags. Artillery received no flags: its commanders were expected to report in with their own firing position and targets. Commanders of all these units were enjoined to maintain *Kriegsmässigkeit* (state of war conditions) at all times: only in this way would the instructional value of the maneuver be maintained. In battle, only the front line of such a division would be represented, and then only infantry and antitank positions. Once enemy troops made contact with the line, it was up to the directors and the umpires to establish the situation. Probing attempts by full division would cease, and the umpires would then tell the troops what had happened, what losses had been sustained, and what the situation was regarding a further advance in this sector.

There were also instructions for the various markings troops were likely to encounter. White squares on the windshields indicated a neutral vehicle belonging to the umpires or guests; a white mark with a black cross, a member of the direction. Green cloths on the ground indicated a region that had been gassed; red smoke the presence of enemy aircraft.[74]

Other sections of the *Rules* dealt with the umpire service, the war situation, and the issuing of orders; the necessity of keeping war diaries (*Kriegstagebücher*) and issuing daily reports (*Tagesmeldungen*), the use of maps, uniforms (a red helmet band for red, none for blue). Munitions, too, received a special section. Since the war situation being gamed exceeded existing ammunition stocks by 400 percent, each shot in the maneuvers was deemed to represent four. For the flag divisions the situation was even more extreme: each rifle shot represented 120 shots; each shot from a light machine gun represented 2,000 real ones.[75] The *Rules* ended with sections on the signal services (telegraph, telephone, field post); the sanitation service (one officer for every 500 men); the veterinary service, including the horse hospital (*Pferdelazarette*) for each side; the use of motor vehicles (e.g., responsibility for their maintenance, marking of unusable or destroyed bridges, location of tank parks); shelter and food for the troops; compensation for damage to property and crops; and conduct of the press and other observers. Security against enemy espionage was also a concern. These large maneuvers would understandably be the target of hostile (especially French) spies. Cases of suspected security breaches were to be reported at once to the appropriate direction liaison command. Troops of the *Landespolizei*, a police force with a great deal of military training, were on hand during the maneuver to both help out on this point and to help regulate civilian traffic in the maneuver area.

The depth of detail in this simulated war is best viewed in the enclosures accompanying the *Rules*. The enclosures included a schematic diagram of the umpire and direction services, an inventory of specific documents required from each of the units and services (e.g., division requests for ammunition), as well as a roster of appendixes.[76] Sent to the participants for the blue party, the participants for the red party, and the neutrals, they included the following: Summary of the Composition and Organization of the Exercise Direction (Appendix 1); Summary of Transport, March, and Quarters from the Start to 15 September (for blue, Appendix 2a, for red, 2b).[77] It included the unit's designation, whether it was arriving by rail or on foot, the day and probable time of its arrival, the station where it would detrain, the location of its quarters, and the government district in which the quarters were located, plus any special comments (usually cavalry or tank subunits in an infantry unit that might require special accommodations). It might be mentioned that the vast majority of units (with the exception of the 5th Artillery Regiment from Fulda, Ulm, and Ludwigsburg) came by train. This, then, was as close as the *Reichswehr* would come to a full-blown mobilization exercise.

Nothing was to be left to chance. A model for the daily report (Appendix 3a) was issued to the commanders, staffs of the cavalry brigades and infantry regiments, and the staffs of the independent battalions and detachments. There was a separate model for daily reports from the troops (3b). It all appears curiously businesslike today, and almost stereotypically German (if such a quality exists). Appendix 7, for example, actually constructed an entire field post system for both the blue and red sides: there were post box numbers and arrangements for mail distribution in the field, extending as far down as individual platoons, but the emphasis was on the field post in a mobile war, with provisions for shifting the mail distribution systems on the third day of the maneuver.[78] Shifting the postal *Schwerpunkt*, it might have been called (and probably was—by someone). A second shift was planned for the fifth day, though it does not appear to have been carried out.

Conclusion

So ended the *Rules* for the maneuvers of 1930. They had dealt with every possible situation that might arise, from French spies to General Heye's upset stomach. Clearly the tactical situation was a secondary concern. In line with the old saw that "an army travels on its stomach," the *Reichswehr* had concocted a fantastically detailed exercise taxing the supply, personnel, and sanitary services to their utmost.

German historians have recently tended to view defense planning in the late Weimar era as going well beyond mere battlefield activity. They see a revival of militarism in this period, a tendency to fuse civil and military institutions into a sort of quasi-totalitarian "defense state" (*Wehrstaat*)[79] That may be so, and it is clearly impossible to absolve the army of its sorry role in the downfall of the republic—a weak system, to be sure, but worth saving when one considers what came after. But the *Reichswehr*, for all its new thinking and more accommodating posture toward the civilian government, had not suddenly transformed itself into a purely political institution. As the 1930 maneuvers showed, the army could still plan for war with the best of them. See, for example, the "Room Chart" for the exercise directors,[80] in which every officer is assigned his specific place, or the schematic diagram of the umpire's telephone net.[81] This was planning of a type that peacetime (and perhaps peaceloving) armies seldom do. The actual course of the maneuvers—this or that unit failing to take another in the flank—is much less important than its sheer size and scope.[82] Scholars need to discard the notion of "German rearmament" in 1935. Rearmament, at least in spirit, was a Weimar phenomenon.

What is perhaps most amazing is the secrecy with which the entire exercise—involving, it should be noted, every unit in the army—is still shrouded today. Newspaper accounts, quoted above, discussed the fairly standard infantry-cavalry encounter, along with a great parade in honor of Hindenburg. Foreign military attachés also saw little of note. But had they only seen copies of a few of the documents discussed above, the 1930 maneuver would have led to serious international tension. The maneuvers were a violation of the anti-mobilization decrees in the Treaty of Versailles, and although the maneuvers did not involve civilian industry, they involved everything else: command structure, railroad schedules; and the creation of a wartime supply and service network. It is no wonder that the Germans did not invite a French observer. The danger was simply too great of a discovery that this was much more than annual fall maneuvers. Held at the very time that the army was becoming deeply enmeshed in the political struggles of the Weimar Republic's death throes, the 1930 maneuvers stand as proof that war planning was entering a new, more serious phase. That is not necessarily to say to say that "aggressive war planning" was beginning: the 1930 maneuvers, after all, postulated a French attack into central Germany. But virtually all of the maneuvers' contents had application to a war of attack as well as defense, and at any rate, German doctrine never really differentiated between the two.

Notes

1. The term "neue Sachlichkeit" may also be translated as "the new matter-of-factness" or the "new sobriety." See John Willett, *Art and Politics in the Weimar Period: The New Sobriety, 1917–1933* (New York: Pantheon Books, 1978). Peter Gay, *Weimar Culture: The Outsider as Insider* (New York: Harper & Row, 1968), is the pathbreaking work that gave us the term "the revolt of the sons against the fathers."

2. Col. Werner Blomberg, chief of the *Truppenamt*, to State Secretary Karl von Schubert, Berlin, 27 January 1928, found in *Akten des Auswärtigen Amtes* (Records of the German Foreign Office). A microfilmed copy of these documents is deposited in the National Archives, Washington, DC), reel 3613, serial K6, frames K000 354–355. For microfilmed records from this collection, the following

sequence will be used hereafter: AA (standing for *Auswärtiges Amt*), to be followed
by reel, serial, and frame numbers. Under this system of abbreviation, the above
document would be cited as AA, 3613, K6, K000 354–355. A schedule for the
wargame, headed "Zeiteinteilung," is appended to Blomberg's note. For Schubert's
response, see State Secretary Karl von Schubert to Colonel Werner Blomberg, chief
of the *Truppenamt*, Berlin, 4 February 1928, AA, 3613, K6, K000 356.

3. Dirk Forster, Foreign Office, *Aufzeichnung über die Truppenamtsreise in
Schlesien vom Ende April 1928,* Berlin, 2 May 1928, AA, 3613, K6, K000
383–383, especially Section I: "Verlauf der Reise."

4. Ibid., especially section II: "Persönliche Eindrücke."

5. Ibid., epecially the untitled section III (AA, 3613, K6, K000 383).

6. See the memorandum entitled "Landesschutz," AA, 3613, K6, K000
384–387.

7. Ibid., AA, 3613, K6, K000 386.

8. For Foreign Office commentary on "Landesschutz," see Dirk Forster,
Aufzeichnung, Berlin, 12 May 1928, AA, 3613, K6, K000 388–389.

9. Forster, *Aufzeichnung,* AA, 3613, K6, K000 388.

10. Defense Minister Gen. Wilhelm Groener to State Secretary Karl von Schubert, Berlin, 14 June 1928, AA, 3613, K6, K000 393–394.

11. Colonel Kühlenthal (T-3) to Dirk Forster, Foreign Office, Berlin, 18 September 1928 (AA, 3613, K6, K000 396–397), and Forster, *Aufzeichnung über die
Teilnahme von Vertretern des Auswärtigen Amts an den grossen schlesichen Herbst-
manövern,* Berlin, 2 October 1928 (AA, 3613, K6, K000 399–403).

12. The best work on the Russo-Polish war is Norman Davies, *White Eagle—
Red Star* (London: Macdonald & Co., 1972). For the impact of the war on Germany's eastern provinces, especially East Prussia, see Robert Citino, *The Evolution
of Blitzkrieg Tactics: Germany Defends Itself Against Poland, 1918–1933* (Westport, CT: Greenwood Press, 1987), pp. 15–33.

13. *Organisationskriegsspiel: Beitrag zur Gdingenfrage,* part 1, "Polen: Mil-
itär-ische Küstenbeschreibung, Streitkräfte, Strategische Lage," p. 7, in German
Naval Archives (hereafter GNA), University of Michigan Microfilming Project No.
2, reel 30, serial PG 34066, frame 239. In shorthand notation, the citation for this
document would be GNA, 30, PG 34066, 239.

14. Ibid., p. 8, GNA, 30, PG 34066, 240.

15. *Vorarbeiten zur Studie Gdingen,* GNA, 31, PG 34101, 973–981, especially
part D., "Ziel und Zweck eines Überfalls auf Gdingen," p. 5, frame 978.

16. Ibid., part A, "Die polnische gegen Landangriffe voraussichtlich sogleich
verfügbaren Kräfte: Aktive Truppen," pp. 1–2, GNA 31, PG 34101, 974–975.

17. Ibid., part A, "Die polnische gegen Landangriffe voraussichtlich sogleich
verfügbaren Kräfte: Grenzschutzformationen," pp. 2–3, GNA, 31, PG 34101,
975–976.

18. "Vorarbeiten zur Studie Gdingen," part B, "Wege und Gelände," pp. 3–4,
GNA 31, PG 34101, 976–977.

19. "Handstreich auf Gdingen," Truppenamt to *Wehrkreiskommando II* (Stettin), Berlin, 30 June 1928, GNA, 31, PG 34101, 971–972.

20. *Vorarbeiten zur Studie Gdingen,* part E, "Überlegungen zur Durchführung
des Handstreiches zu Lande," pp. 6–8, GNA, 31, PG 34101, 979–981.

21. Ibid., p. 8,. GNA, 31, PG 34101, 981.

22. Truppenamt to Marinekommandoamt, Berlin, 23 January 1930, GNA, 31,
PG 34101, 996–1003.

23. The most detailed account of the intended operation is found in "Denkschrift des Flottenkommandos über die Durchführung der Studie 'O'," GNA, 32,
PG 34102, 43–74.

24. Erich Raeder, *Mein Leben*, vol 1, pp. 256–257.

25. Adm. Erich Raeder, "Entwurf, Studie Polen," Part A., "Einleitung," Berlin, 22 April 1929, GNA, 30, PG 34066, 157.

26. Ibid., Part B., "Abhandlung," GNA, 30, PG 34066, 158–159.

27. Among many documents, see especially *Organisations-Kriegsspiel: Studie Gdingen,* 3 June 1929, GNA, 30, PG 34066, 161–163, and the extended version of "Organisationskriegsspiel: Beitrag zur Gdingenfrage," part 1, "Polen: Militärische Küstenbeschreibung, Streitkräfte, Strategische Lage," p. 28, GNA, 30, PG 34066, 260.

28. Fleet Commander Admiral Oldekop to Raeder, 29 September 1929, Berlin, GNA, 30, PG 34066, 231.

29. For discussion of the role of air power in *Studie Ost*, see "Stellungnahme zu den Fragen der Luftwaffe im Kriegsspiel der Flotte 1931," GNA, 32, PG 34102, 75–84, and Adm. Erich Raeder to Flottenkommando, Berlin, 10 May 1932, "Planstudie," GNA, 32, PG 34102, 92–96, especially section 4, "Luftwaffe."

30. For this account of *Studie Ost*, see "Denkschrift des Flottenkommandos über die Durchführung der Studie 'O,'" section 3, "Durchführung der Studie 'O'," pp. 16–23, GNA, 32, PG 34102, 61–68.

31. *Fall Maneuvers 1927, German Army,* H.H. Zornig, acting military attaché, to War Department, Berlin, 4 November 1927, found in *United States Military Intelligence Reports: Germany, 1919–1941* (Frederick, MD: University Publications of America, 1983), microfilm reel XV, frames 1–38. In shorthand notation, the above document would be labeled USMI, XV, 1–38. See especially Zornig's narrative and analysis in "Maneuvers of 2nd Group Command," USMI, XV, 2–7.

32. "Orders and Problems," in Zornig, *Maneuvers of 2nd Group Command,* USMI, XV, 2.

33. See "Grand Maneuver, 1927: War Situation for September 26–28 (Blue)," USMI, XV, 8; and Grand Maneuver, 1927: War Situation for September 26–28 (Red)," USMI, XV, 25.

34. "Critique," in Zornig, *Maneuvers of 2nd Group Command,* USMI, XV, 2–3.

35. "Attaché's Comments," in Zornig, *Maneuvers of 2nd Group Command,* USMI, XV, 3.

36. "Events of September 28," in Zornig, *Maneuvers of 2nd Group Command,* USMI, XV, 3–4.

37. "Critique," in Zornig, *Maneuvers of 2nd Group Command,* USMI, XV, 4–5.

38. "General Comments: Mechanization," in Zornig, *Maneuvers of 2nd Group Command,* USMI, XV, 5.

39. "General Comments: Infantry," in Zornig, *Maneuvers of 2nd Group Command,* USMI, XV, 6.

40. "General Comments: Motor Transportation," in Zornig, *Maneuvers of 2nd Group Command,* USMI, XV, 6–7.

41. An English translation of the *Militär Wochenblatt* article, which appeared in the 4 November 1928 issue, is found in "The Great Silesian Maneuvers of September 24 and 25, 1928," Col. Edward Carpenter, military attaché, to War Department, Berlin, 24 December 1928, USMI, XVII, 0833–0838.

42. *1928 Maneuvers, 1st Division, German Army,* Col. Edward Carpenter, military attaché, to War Department, Berlin, 17 December 1928, USMI, XVII, 758–819.

43. "Events of September 3 and 4," in Carpenter, *1928 Maneuvers,* USMI, XVII, 763–764.

44. "Attaché's Comments," in Carpenter, *1928 Maneuvers,* USMI, XVII, 764–765.

45. "Maneuvers of September 6–8: Problems," and "Events of September 6–8," in Carpenter, *1928 Maneuvers,* USMI, XVII, 765–767.

46. "Comments on the Maneuver: General," in Carpenter, *1928 Maneuvers*, USMI, XVII, 769.

47. "Comments on the Maneuver: Umpires," in Carpenter, *1928 Maneuvers*, USMI, XVII, 771–772.

48. "Comments on the Maneuver: Cavalry," in Carpenter, *1928 Maneuvers*, USMI, XVII, 769.

49. See the "Comments on the Maneuver" regarding "Lack of Aircraft," "Machine Guns," and "Tanks," in Carpenter, *1928 Maneuvers*, USMI, XVII, 769–770.

50. *Mountain Troops in the German Army*, Maj. H. H. Zornig, Acting Military Attaché, to War Department, Berlin, 26 January 1928, USMI, XVII, 754–757. The report includes an English translation of a *Militär Wochenblatt* article that appeared in the 4 January 1928 edition.

51. Zornig, *Mountain Troops*, USMI, XVII, 756.

52. *Mountain Infantry Maneuvers*, Col. A. L. Conger, military attaché, to War Department, Berlin, 1 June 1928, USMI, XVII, 820–828.

53. "First Day: 21 May," in Conger, *Mountain Infantry*, USMI, XVII, 820–821.

54. "Second Day: 22 May," in Conger, *Mountain Infantry*, USMI, XVII, 822–823.

55. "Impressions," in Conger, *Mountain Infantry*, USMI, XVII, 826.

56. "The Troops," in Conger, *Mountain Infantry*, USMI, XVII, 826–827.

57. *The 1930 Fall Maneuver for the German Army*, Major H. H. Zornig, Assistant military attaché," to War Department, Berlin, 19 December 1930, USMI, XIX, 376–419.

58. See the facsimile of Seeckt's orders for the 1926 maneuver in Friedrich von Rabenau, *Seeckt: Aus seinem Leben, 1918–1936* (Leipzig: von Hase und Koehler Verlag, 1940), p. 526.

59. Zornig, *1930 Fall Maneuver*, USMI, XIX, 377–378.

60. "Troops Engaged," in *1930 Fall Maneuver*, USMI, XIX, 380–381.

61. "Newspaper Comment," in *1930 Fall Maneuver*, USMI, XIX, 406–407.

62. See "The Blue Situation" and "The Red Situation," in 1930 Fall Maneuver, USMI, XIX, 384–388.

63. "Newspaper Comment," in *1930 Fall Maneuver*, USMI, XIX, 407–408.

64. "Grosse Rahmenübung 1930," found in *Records of the German Army High Command* (*Oberkommando des Heeres*, or OKH, the post 1935–designation of the *Heeresleitung*). A microfilmed copy of these records is on file in the U.S. National Archives in Washington, DC, Microcopy T-78, serial H24/14, reels 281–282, frames 6229704–6230033. In shorthand notation, these documents would be identified as OKH, H24/14, 281–282, 6229704–6230033.

65. See the circular letter from Col. Walther Brauchitsch, T-4, Berlin, 9 August 1930 (OKH, H24/14, 281, 6229705–6229706), as well as the appendix, "Übersicht über die Offiziere und Beamten der Übungsleitung" (OKH, H24/14, 281, 6229707–6229712).

66. *Stellenbesetzung für den Schiedsrichter- und Leitungsdienst bei der Gr. Rahmenübung 1930*, hereafter *S.S.L.* (Berlin: E. Mittler und Sohn, 1930), found in OKH, H24/14, 281, 6229715–6229734.

67. See *S.S.L.*, p. 9, for the "Oberschiedsrichter West" and "Oberschiedsrichter Ost," OKH, H24/14, 281, 6229719.

68. *S.S.L.*, pp. 10–17 (OKH, H24/14, 281, 6229720–6229724).

69. *S.S.L.*, appendix 1, "Stellenbesetzung der Leitungsverbindungskommandos und der Leitungsoffiziere der Korpstruppen: Blau," pp. 21–27 (OKH, H24/14, 281, 6229725–6229728).

70. *S.S.L.*, appendix 2, "Stellenbesetzung der Leitungsverbindungskommandos und der Leitungsoffiziere der Korpstruppen: Rot," pp. 29–34 (OKH, H24/14, 281, 6229729–6229732).

71. "Bestimmungen für die Grosse Rahmenübung 1930," hereafter *B.G.R.* (Berlin: E. Mittler und Sohn, 1930), in OKH, H24/14, 281, 6229736–6229784.

72. "Vorbemerkungen," in *B.G.R.*, p. 6 (OKH, H24/14, 281, 6229739).

73. See chapter I ("Leitung"), chapter II ("Reichspräsident, Reichswehrminister, Gäste"), and chapter III ("Zeiteneinteilung"), in *B.G.R.*, pp. 79 (OKH, H24/14, 281, 6229740–6229741.

74. See chapter V ("Truppendarstellung, Flaggen, und Abzeichen"), in *B.G.R.*, OKH, H24/14, 281, 6229742–6229745.

75. See, for example, chapter VI ("Schiedsrichter und Leitungsdienst"), pp. 12–16 (OKH, H24/14, 281, 6229745–6229749(and chapter XI ("Munition"), pp. 19–22 (OKH, H24/14, 281, 6229752–6229755), both in *B.G.R.*

76. See "Schematische Darstellung des Schiedsrichter u. Leitungsdienstes," "Verzeichnis der Eingaben," and "Verzeichnis der Anlagen zu der Bestimmungen für die Gr. Rahmenübung 1930," all in *B.G.R.*, pp. 47–52 (OKH, H24/14, 281, 6229780–6229784).

77. See "Übersicht über Zusammensetzung und Geschäftseinteilung der Übungsleitung" (appendix 1), "Übersicht über Antransporte, Anmärsche, und Unterbringung vom Eintreffetag bis 15.9: Blaue Partei" (appendix 2a), and the same for red (appendix 2b), all in *B.G.R.*, OKH, H24/14, 281, 6229789–6229815.

78. See "Postnummern und Abholpostanstalten der blauen Partei" (appendix 7a) and the same for Red (appendix 7b), in OKH, H24/14, 281, 6229856–6229866.

79. This is the heart of Michael Geyer's argument in *Aufrüstung oder Sicherheit: Die Reichswehr in der Krise der Machtpolitik, 1924–1936* (Wiesbaden: Franz Steiner Verlag, 1980). See also the discussion of the *Wehrstaat* in Eberhard Kolb, *The Weimar Republic* (London: Unwin Hyman, 1988), pp. 155–156.

80. See "Geschäftsräume der Übungsleitung," OKH, H24/14, 282, 6229917.

81. "Skizze des neutralen Fernsprechnetzes für die Grosse Rahmenübung 1930," OKH, H24/14, 282, 6229939.

82. For further documentation of this crucial event, see "Anordnugnen für die Übungsleitung der Grossen Rahmenübung 1930" (Berlin: E. Mittler und Sohn, 1930), in OKH, H24/14, 282, 6229894–6229900; "Anordnungen für den Rücktransport und Rückmarsch von der Gr. Rahmenübung 1930" (Berlin: E. Mittler und Sohn, 1930), in OKH, H24/14, 282, 6229919–6229937; and "Schiedsrichter- und Leitungsdienst bei der Grossen Rahmenübung 1930" (Berlin: E. Mittler und Sohn, 1930), in OKH, H24/14, 282, 6229938–6229954. For correspondence relating to the exercise, see OKH, H24/14, 282, 6229955–6230029. Finally, for a map of the maneuver area, see OKH, H24/14, 282, 6230030–6230033.

CHAPTER 8

Toward the New Era

The last three years of the Weimar Republic—years of dissolution in political and cultural life—were the most fertile yet for the *Reichswehr*. There was a whole series of tactical exercises that highlighted the new role of tanks, antitank, and mechanized formations. Operational maneuvers took place that trained German commanders in the handling of corps-sized formations. Auxiliary services such as the radio net, the air raid warning service, and the pioneers underwent intensive training. Preparations in the sphere of national defense (*Landesverteidigung*) became an all-encompassing system for the military training of German youth. The German army command was readying the nation for total war long before Hitler's declaration of rearmament in 1935.

German Experiments with Armor

Although the name Heinz Guderian is the one most people associate with the rise of German armor, historians are beginning to question his actual prominence in the years before 1933. The evidence for his preeminence comes mainly from his own writings, especially his self-aggrandizing autobiography *Panzer Leader,* and is based on a handful of perhaps apocryphal anecdotes. But during the period 1922–1928, when the *Reichswehr* began to experiment seriously with new armored tactics, Guderian wrote just five signed articles for the semiofficial military journal *Militär Wochenblatt*. His book *Achtung—Panzer!* was a very sound work, brilliant in the eyes of some. But it was written in 1936–1937, by which time armored forces were well established in the German army. This is not to belittle Guderian's role in the 1930s as an armored division commander, or his combat record in World War II, but perhaps a revision of the historical record is in order.[1]

First of all, there is the legacy of General von Seeckt to consider. He had not only directed German tactical doctrine toward a higher stress on mobility. On a practical level, his policy of promoting cooperation with the Soviet Union led to the opening of a tank school in Kazan, deep inside that country where German officers could receive hands-on training in tank tactics.[2] Design work began as well, resulting in a "new model vehicle" (*Neubaufahrzeuge,* or Nb.Fz.), a medium tank of 23 tons, armed with a 75mm gun, as well as a coaxially mounted 37mm gun in the turret.[3] Krupp and Rheinmetall built five all told, but it was clear that developing a medium tank would be a time-consuming process. The result was increased attention to light tanks, similar to the British Carden Lloyd. The Pzkw. I (for *Panzerkampfwagen,* or armored fighting vehicle) was the result. Armed with a pair of machine guns, this Krupp design was cheap and easy to produce. It would be the foundation stone of German rearmament.

Other figures, Ernst Volckheim, for example, seem much more important than Guderian. His 1923 work, *German Tanks in the World War (Die deutsche Kampfwagen in Weltkriege),* was followed by *Tanks in Modern Warfare (Der Kampfwagen in der heutigen Kriegführung)* (1924) and over two dozen articles in the *Militär Wochenblatt.*[4] Guderian's commander, inspector of Motor Transport Troops Col. Oswald Lutz, also played a key role.[5] As inspector, he oversaw seven battalions of motor transport troops, one assigned to each division of the army. Guderian commanded one of them, the 3rd Battalion, stationed in Berlin. After 1927, all seven carried out similar experiments, which became particularly intense after 1930, and all seven were basically identical, comprising trucks, dummy tanks, and wooden artillery and antitank guns. The idea that we most often associate with Guderian, his call for concentrating the armor rather than dispersing it along the front (which he summed up in the phrase *"Klotzen nicht kleckern"*) was shared by virtually all German armored theorists of the interwar period.

In 1931–1932, for example, Lutz directed a key series of exercises involving dummy tank battalions at the Jüterbog and Grafenwöhr training grounds. In September 1932, he summed up the lessons learned in a report intended to help with the intended revision of *Leadership and Battle.* Sending it on to Col. Walther von Brauchitsch, head of the *Truppenamt's* Army Training Office, Lutz asked that it be used as a point of departure for further training.[6]

Lutz began with the basic principles. First, tank units should receive independent battle missions, taking into account their special attributes. Tying them down to support the infantry was a mistake, since it would rob the armor of its principal advantages: speed and range. There could be exceptions, an attack with limited objectives, for instance. However, even this type of use contradicted the basic point made above: tanks were for the *Schwerpunkt* only, too valuable to waste on a sideshow.

If independence was the first principle, mass was the second. Using tanks in anything under battalion strength was a blunder. Even given the then, rather primitive, state of antitank weapons and training, an attack by a tank company would not achieve a decisive result. The use of such small units represented a dispersion of the new queen of battle, thus violating the principle of concentration of force.

Lutz's third principle was surprise. An attack at dawn was best, he felt. The assault should be "surprising, sudden, and on a broad front" to splinter the defense. It was also necessary to echelon that attack in enough depth to make it possible to switch the *Schwerpunkt* itself during the pursuit, as well as to crush any newly arriving targets or obstructions.[8]

Lutz also dealt extensively with antitank tactics. The forward infantry should simply allow the tanks to pass through their positions, he argued, and then take up the battle against enemy infantry advancing behind their own tanks. Active antitank defense was the task of all weapons—light trench mortars, antitank guns, and artillery, but especially the divisional antitank company, envisioned as a motorized formation. He cautioned against deploying antitank guns too far forward. Here they were vulnerable to enemy fire and perhaps even to capture by a surprise attack. Instead, they should be deployed deep inside the defensive position, based on the company commander's independent assessment of the ground and the possibilities for attack—his mission was to build a cohesive antitank front, in cooperation with the artillery, across possible lines of enemy advance. Liaison with the artillery was crucial. But while trying to ensure that every line of attack was covered, the company commander must rigorously avoid dispersing the antitank weapons. Even in regimental exercises, Lutz insisted that the guns of the entire divisional antitank company be kept together and used en masse. A concentration some 3 kilometers behind the front seemed sensible, giving a deployment time of some six to eight minutes.[9]

Modern battle was more than a mere tank-antitank struggle, however. Lutz dealt at great length with cooperation of the arms. As was borne out not only in the exercises but repeatedly during the war, attacking infantry had to move up closely behind (*dicht auf*) the tanks. Only in that way would it be in a position to fall on the defenders while they were "crippled morally" by the sudden onrush of tanks and seeking to take cover. In the attack the infantry had to forget about relying on its own heavy weapons. Waiting for the latter weakened the momentum of the attack and loosened the all-important contact with the armor. Tanks replaced heavy weapons in such a situation, as long as the infantry was following immediately behind.[10]

Lutz concluded by looking to the future. The exercises had proven themselves an effective means of training mobile troops. It was now necessary to hold even larger exercises, perhaps involving two battalions. Exercises on a smaller scale (involving a company, for instance) gave a "false picture of both weapons and troops."[11] Clearly, the panzer division was on its way.

It is no exaggeration to say that the exercises of 1931–1932, carried out by a disarmed power with dummy tanks, marked the true birth of

Blitzkrieg. The unchaining of tanks from the speed of the infantry, the reliance on mass and surprise to tear a hole in the bewildered defense, the exploitation by mobile reserves of all arms—it was this vision that would revolutionize the face of warfare from 1939 to 1941.

The question was much more profound than simply, "What is the proper employment of the tank?" The exercises had not used armor alone—true to the traditional German emphasis on combined arms, they had included infantry, artillery, and antitank units. A large part of the report dealt with cooperation of all the arms, which the German clearly regarded as the fundamental question of armor, unlike the British stress on the tanks alone.[12] Tanks were crucial, of course. Due to their mobility, firepower, and shock value, whenever they went into action, they temporarily became the principal arm. The main battlefield problem, as Lutz saw it, was how to get the other arms—infantry, artillery, pioneers, air—to recognize that fact and lend better support to the armor. Lutz omitted the cavalry, which apparently had no place in his vision of the modern battlefield.

Motorized Reconnaissance

The reconnaissance units were the first to be motorized in the German army. In June 1932, Gen. Wilhelm Adam, the chief of the *Truppenamt*, drew up a short report, based on the recently concluded trials, of the capabilities of a "motorized reconnaissance detachment" (MRD). Its worth depended on many things, he wrote: the quality of the vehicles, the condition of the terrain, the weather, but most of all on the means of communication available to the detachment.[13]

Adam felt that operational reconnaissance was, in the first instance the responsibility of the flier. But there were limits to what air reconnaissance could achieve: it was never certain that an area in which air reconnaissance had found no foes was truly enemy free. Aircraft could not maintain contact with the enemy on the ground, one of the principal tasks of operational reconnaissance. Using intelligence provided by aircraft, the MRD was capable of scouting great distances, due to its high speed and radius of action.[14] Furthermore, the line between operational and tactical reconnaissance was not always easy to draw. Although tactical reconnaissance was primarily the task of the cavalry, motorized units were also quite capable in this sphere.

It was crucial to remember that the *Schwerpunkt* of the MRD's activity lay in the field of reconnaissance. Other tasks were only to be undertaken in exceptional cases—keeping open distant bridges or routes through enemy obstructions, for example. For manning or blocking other, nearer important points, there were other troops available, also possibly motorized.[15] The MRD was trained to scout, not fight. It was to be drawn from the front whenever possible in a battle situation and deployed where its unique abilities offered a real chance for success: on the flanks, in gaps in the front, and where great distances needed to be covered.[16] It was best employed when attached to a cavalry division or directly to a corps, rather than to an infantry division where it had a tendency to become embroiled in battle.

The composition of an MRD depended more than anything on the mission it had to fulfill. At least two armored companies were necessary, Adam felt. So were various means of security, since this could not be a task of the reconnaissance organs themselves. Security from enemy infantry would be offered by guns mounted on motorcycles and antitank defenses (and tanks were the units most likely to be encountered by the MRD) composed of antitank guns, obstructions, and mines. Pioneer detachments would also be appropriate for this last task, as well as for demolitions work. Since the MRD had to carry through its reconnaissance even in the event of strong enemy preparations, motorized artillery and other heavy weapons were also necessary. Keeping in mind the need for mobility and manageability, the ideal MRD would consist of two tank and two motorcycle companies. There was also the possibility of subdividing the tank companies, depending on the mission. If there was an insufficient number of tanks, light armored cars could take over many of their duties. In fact, they were not a second-line resource at all, but were well suited to a number of tasks. In most situations, Adam felt, the tank company should be subdivided into heavy and light platoons, which would in turn be subdivided into patrols.[17]

The mobility of one of these units was staggering. Adam considered that each MRD could patrol a zone of 50 kilometers wide and 200–250 kilometers deep, depending on the availability of fuel.[18] In the advance the MRD was to proceed by bounds, echeloned in depth. As far as possible it should use the main road network. Great crossroads were of particular importance.

The orders for an MRD should include—along with the mission—a specific time to break off from the main force; the march route and objectives of the main force; the tasks of neighboring MRDs, the attitude to be taken in case of encounter with the enemy; communication with friendly aircraft; regulations for reporting back; and the disposition of the population in the reconnaissance area. Above all, though, the order should simply state what the MRD was to find out and what the higher commander wanted to know. Such an emphasis would remove the danger of doing a great deal of unnecessary work.

Whether the commander wanted to assign a specific "recon sector" for an MRD, or simply give it a direction and objective, could change from case to case. The latter course offered the advantage of freedom of action to the highly mobile unit. But if too many MRDs were in action side by side, a line of separation was required between them. The outside flank, however, should always remain open for purposes of maneuver. A road assigned to either of the MRDs was usually the last line of separation. What was crucial, though, was that the higher commanders not load so many restrictions with regard to routes, sectors, and objectives that the orders became a hindrance to the MRD.[19]

The task of the MRD commander was especially taxing. While the MRD was still deployed with the main body, he had to decide whether to send out patrols immediately at the point of departure, or whether he had enough of an enemy-free zone in front of him that he could set out "at speed," as it were. In any event, deploying at least one patrol of tanks to the front was recommended, Adam wrote, if only to increase the fluidity of the march.

When companies were to be split into patrols, the MRD commander was to meet with each of the patrol commanders, give them their missions, discuss alternative routes in case the roads were blocked, and generally share his thoughts with them. In general, the heaviest patrols were to be sent against the most important roads and tactical objectives. Officers were to lead the patrols personally. Regulations for reporting back to the MRD commander were crucial because reconnaissance was only valuable if it were reported. Of course, the single most important report was first contact with the enemy; it required no special orders, but should be ingrained in the soldier by training. Items also worthy of reporting were the attainment of important sectors, lines, or objectives. Once contact was made with the enemy, it was the patrol commander's responsibility to see that it was not lost. Enemy patrols were to be avoided if at all possible. Once again, the purpose of a patrol was reconnaissance, not battle. The same was true for the MRD itself.

The detachment commander also had to ensure a "reconnaissance reserve." It was not appropriate simply to divide up the entire recon area and deploy both tank patrols side by side. It was much better to deploy one company forward, covering the whole area with patrols, while keeping the other company concentrated to the rear as a reserve. Only in this way would the battalion commander have the necessary strength to shift reconnaissance in a new direction, or to thicken or break off the reconnaissance already in motion.[20]

With regard to reporting results, Adam was emphatic in the need for more and better radios. Other means were also to be used when appropriate. In friendly territory (when in the absence of the enemy) the telegraph service might be useful, for example. Although radio communications were hindered by the short range of the current equipment, this was not so much a problem during peacetime maneuvers, due to the small size of the field. In fact, the result was a blizzard of radio messages in the exercises, filling the air waves with babble and resulting in a great many messages arriving late or not at all.[21]

In closing, Adam returned to his main point. The principal advantages of the MRD over other forms of reconnaissance were its great speed and maneuverability. This was the fact that every man in the MRD had to keep in mind. These advantages must never become lost in the confusion and heat of battle. It was the responsibility of the detachment's personnel to use them to the utmost to provide the higher staff with timely and accurate information.[22]

Auxiliary Services:
The Air Raid Exercise in East Prussia, 1932, the Pioneer Exercise on the Oder, and the Great Radio Exercise

It might seem that the *Reichswehr* high command was solely concerned with the development of new tactical forms for ground warfare in the early 1930s, but that was not at all the case. The summer of 1932 saw an operational exercise testing air raid precautions (*Flugmeldeübung*) in East Prussia. Carried on by the *Heeresleitung*, in cooperation with the 1st Infantry Division headquarters in Königsberg, and kept completely secret from the press, its goal was "the tactical and technical evaluation of the air raid network and the air raid personnel trained by the civilian authorities in early 1932 in all of East Prussia, save for the small sector north of the Gumbinnen-Insterburg-Libau line."[23] The Prussian government would also use the exercise to test the local warning service in Königsberg and Allenstein, as well as the organization of civil air defense and the use of civilian auxiliary forces (e.g., firefighters, bomb disposal squads) Finally, the *Heeresleitung* wanted to test cooperation with the naval authorities in the province, as well as officials of the national rail system (*Reichsbahn*). Army officials were also interested in working with some of the larger industrial installations, such as the power plant in Friedland, in order to test camouflage preparations. The same went for other strategically important buildings such as the Königsberg arsenal. The direction of the maneuver was in the hands of the Defense Ministry's office, specifically General Mittelberger, the inspector of the weapons schools (the *Waffenschulen*).

Because of the impossibility of testing the entire provincial air raid net, the exercise proceeded sector by sector. Day one tested the districts of Insterburg, Lötzen, Gerdauen, and Königsberg (each designated *Flukos* in this exercise, an abbreviation for *Flugmeldekommando*); day two evaluated the previous day; and day three looked at the Allenstein, Wormditt, and Bartenstein *Flukos*, as well as retesting Königsberg (as the largest city in the state). The entire *Übung* lasted five days.

Each *Fluko* was staffed by numbers of "air watches" (*Flugwachen*) consisting of at least one commander and three men; they reported to the *Fluko* itself, which was made up of at least one commander, two "evaluators" who tried to make sense of the incoming reports, and a staff. The exercise proceeded on the assumption of large-scale air assaults from the south (i.e., Poland). While it involved relatively small numbers of men—just the *Flugwachen* and *Fluko* headquarters—it required a significant number of directors. All of these officers were from the 1st Infantry Division, participating on a voluntary basis. The goal was rapid and complete evaluation of incoming reports to establish the direction and probable targets of a given enemy flight. Thus both *Leitung* and personnel required a large commitment of armored cars and motorcycles for transmission of messages.[24]

There was also a large-scale pioneer exercise in early September 1932, along the banks of the Oder between Glogau and Beuthen, overseen by Colonel Haff, the inspector of pioneers and fortifications. Designed to test various methods of crossing the river, the maneuver showed how far concepts of motorization had seeped into the *Reichswehr*. Each of the three pioneer battalions taking part were, in fact, completely motorized, down to their pontoon sections.[25]

Also during 1932, there was a list published of all the various kinds of *Übungsreisen* (staff tours for commanders and General Staff officers, camouflaged under the term *Führergehilfen*). Designed to give experience in terms of large-unit command, cooperation of the various arms, and supply, the tours encompassed a bewildering array of different types. There were, for instance, tactical district exercises (*Taktische Wehrkreisübungsreisen*) for training officers in the principles of combat in the context of a grand operation. There were supply exercises (*Nachschub-Wehrkreisübungsreisen*) for training staff, sanitation, and veterinary officers in the principles of logistics. There were divisional exercises (*Divisionsübungsreisen*) and artillery exercises for the division (*Artillerie-Übungsreisen für Divisionen*) and officer terrain discussions (*Offizier-Geländebesprechungen*). There were even exercises for the Defense Ministry and the *Heeresleitung*—accustoming them to problems of supply and communication in the event of war, and many, many more. It is a comprehensive, and impressive, list.[26]

In June 1932 the *Heeresleitung* carried out another exercise, designed to test the ability of Germany's radio network in the event of a war.[27] This *Funkübung* differed from earlier, purely technical, exercises among the signal troops by reason of its size, scope, and tactical character. Radio exercises had taken place in the *Reichswehr* before, but they had never placed the men involved in a realistic wartime situation, with all the special problems that entailed. Typically, the exercises had taught the trainee how to solve problems arising from technical difficulties (e.g., insufficient range, malfunctions), but this exercise intended to pose problems arising from the tactical and operational situation. It placed modern tactical concepts (conduct of battle by border protection units, leadership in the mobile battle, delaying defense) in the foreground, in order to investigate the technical problems they posed for the signal service. In part, the exercise intended to point out the important role of radio and radio telegraphy in a war of movement.[28]

The postmaneuver report listed two formal goals for the exercise: (1) to test, under wartime conditions, operation and equipment on a large scale and (2) to educate the signal commanders of all grades in giving orders and overcoming technical difficulties. These aims required a situation in which radio equipment could be used as in an actual war. Since there was no situation in which radios would function alone as the signal corps' only means of communication, the *Heeresleitung* assumed that both the telephone and postal net were also in use, at least in a simulated (*kriegsspielmässig*) way. This required a large number of men and equipment, some 300 officers, 2,000 men, 450 vehicles, 88 complete radio sets, and 300 horses, as well as a large neutral radio and telephone net for the directors and umpires.[29]

The situation postulated a war between a red side (Czechoslovakia) and a blue side (Germany), breaking out on May 20. Under the protection of its border defense, the red army had by June assembled Army Group A on both sides of the Elbe near Leitmeritz (Litoměřice), as well as an independent 1st Army in the Karlsbad (Karlovy Vary) region. The latter included eight divisions, two cavalry divisions, one "armored unit" (*Panzerverband*), and one mountain brigade. The red army command planned a drive by the army group along the Elbe toward Berlin. At the same time, the red 1st Army would strike a rapid blow in the direction of Erfurt to prevent unified action by forces in northern and southern Germany and to seize armaments factories in the central part of the country. The blue side had deployed a border defense force between the Danube and Elbe by the beginning of June, with border defense commands in Nürnberg and Chemnitz. The border defenses were to fight a delaying defense and retire sector by sector.

On June 1 red forces crossed the border, and by June 5 Army Group A was approaching Dresden. The 1st Army, meanwhile, had broken through the blue border defense cordon, and its cavalry corps (1st and 2nd Cavalry Divisions) was already northwest of Zwickau, while infantry units had achieved the line Hof-Plauen. The red armored unit had already driven into Bayreuth and advanced units were as far west as Kulmbach. But the red force also had to deploy an entire army corps (the III) in the rear to deal with an uprising by the blue civilian population that had broken out almost immediately and had already developed into a series of guerrilla operations. Thus, even as the red force advanced, its rearward communications were already endangered.

To oppose the red advance, the blue army command assembled Field Command (*Feldkommando*) II, with its headquarters at Münster, made up of the 6th and 7th Infantry Division, arriving by rail from Hanover and Munich, respectively; the 3rd Cavalry Division, coming up from Wittenberg; and new units like the 9th Cavalry Brigade and the 42nd Infantry Regiment (motorized), neither of which actually existed on the rolls of the

Reichswehr. Field Command II had orders to protect the Leipzig-Halle-Jena industrial region and maintain communication between northern and southern Germany. Unfortunately, by the time most of the command had assembled, red armor had already reached Bamberg and was wheeling north, threatening to envelop the newly arrived 7th Infantry Division at Saalfeld. The rest of the blue command also found itself threatened by forward red units as the latter drove quickly to the north. The first task of the exercise (and this one was much more tightly controlled than previous ones in terms of specific assignments that had to be fulfilled) was for each blue unit to radio its position and readiness for combat, as quickly as possible, to Field Command II in Münster.

Thus, the red and blue signal services each had unique situations and problems. The red situation was that of a systematic and well-planned advance and attack, directed from the beginning by a definite and strict operational conception. Its signal services, therefore, bore the same stamp, "prepared calmly and systematically from the beginning." The blue situation was characterized by a necessity to improvise, both technically and tactically. Its rapidly and haphazardly inserted active units found themselves intermingled with border defense units and forced to cooperate in a common strategy of delaying defense. The difference in organization and equipment between their signal units did not promise to make this an easy task. Moreover, the blue side had to maintain telegraph communications in the face of overwhelming red superiority in the air and far-ranging red armored units. The red side, too, faced problems, notably the civilian uprising in its rear areas that threatened to close telegraph communications altogether.[30]

To deal most effectively with these problems both sides were operating with a completely motorized signal net. The blue net included a telegraph company, a transmitter company, and a receiver company, all motorized. The red net commanded a telephone company, a telegraph repair company, a transmitter repair company, a receiver company, and a light signal equipment company (with 500 kilometers of heavy field cable), again totally motorized.[31]

In evaluating the course of the *Funkübung*, inspector of the Signal Troops General von Bonin began by remarking that the problems it posed, especially those on the blue side, were seldom seen in peacetime training. But "a future war will require us to master them," he said.[32] Signal troop training had up until then concentrated on operations up to division size, and the exercise had confirmed that communications within the division were generally good. But signal troops had much less practice in operational-level communications. This, too, had been evident. It had taken almost one full day of the exercises to make the operational net (i.e., between the component divisions and the corps headquarters) fully operational. In a real war, however, the smooth flow of radio traffic within the first twenty-four hours might be crucial. A stricter adherence to training regulations was necessary.

Bonin saw another danger, as well: what he called the "bureaucratization" of the radio service. Certainly, only trained personnel should operate the radios, but that did mean that the "spirit of the filing cabinet" should prevail. A radioman was not simply a factotum who encrypted, sent, received, and decoded other people's messages. He had to be completely and totally immersed in the tactical situation and its requirements, and it was up to him in many cases what to send and what not to send; not all messages were equally important. For example, the arrival of an eagerly awaited message from a reconnaissance battalion required breaking in on a less important transmission. The entire "soul" of the radio unit, he said, from commander down to operator, must be permeated with the idea of rapid transmission. In keeping to the *Reichswehr's* general trend since the days of Seeckt, Bonin wanted radio messages kept short. There was no time in a rapidly changing situation for longwinded reports or detailed orders. All should be kept as brief as possible.[33]

In general, Bonin felt that the *Funkübung* had been worthwhile, providing a great deal of valuable experience to troops and a good testing ground for equipment (especially the radio-equipped vehicles). As he saw it, these were the principal points of the exercise:

1. The radio training manuals had not sufficed for the demands of a modern signal service for large units, and required revision.
2. Signal troops had demonstrated skill in small unit (i.e., tactical) maneuvers, but required a great deal of training in activities above the divisional level.
3. The handling of radio traffic in no way demonstrated the flexibility higher commanders had a right to demand. At the same time, commanders had to be aware that a radio net was not a telegraph. It required different handling and orders.
4. Since each radio broadcast was potentially available to the enemy, radio should be used sparingly and in a manner that it helped achieve the overall mission without betraying it to the enemy. Disguising and encoding messages required a great deal of cleverness. The point each commander had to keep in mind was that each radio message was a tactical act for which he bore responsibility.[34]

The German concept of mobile war required entirely new forms of technology, training, and doctrine. The discussion among historians about motorization generally confines itself to tactical fighting units, but the importance of air defense, motorized support units, and improvement of the area of command, control and communication, have not received the attention they deserve. By 1932, the *Reichswehr* was already well on its way to solving some of these thorny problems, creating a truly comprehensive doctrine of mechanized warfare.

National Defense Preparations, 1928–1933

As mentioned, the concept of national defense after 1927 far exceeded mere battlefield training. By 1931, it included thorough plans for military training for German youth. The plans arose out of conversations between General Adam, chief of the *Truppenamt*, Col. Wilhelm Keitel of the *Heeresorganisationsabteilung* (T-2), and "a number of nonpartisan organizations positively disposed to defense questions" such as the German Pathfinder League (*Deutscher Pfadfinderbund*) and a number of student organizations. The *Truppenamt* had also opened discussions with the People's Sports Schools (*Volkssportschulen*) and the Small Caliber Shooting Association (*Kleinkaliberschützenverband*).[35]

All of these groups, felt the *Truppenamt*, were dedicated to the spiritual and physical education of their members, with the ultimate aim of increasing their military capabilities (*Wehrfähigkeit*). Along with the army, the groups wished to develop new and more useful methods of training. Thus, they had requested that General Vogt (*Truppenamt* officer in charge of liaison between the *Truppenamt* and the civilian groups involved) take direction of this work. Nonetheless, General Adam insisted that this cooperative effort refrain from actual military training. An emphasis on physical education would be enough. Military training was the province of the *Reichswehr* alone.

This was not to say that this training lacked military implications. As Adam envisioned it, training would include, for example, shooting lessons, both indoor and outdoor; instruction in trajectory and line of sight; handling and care of weapons; and loading, sighting, and firing. He also placed a large emphasis on outdoor experiences: hiking, mountain climbing, exploring. Outdoor life could help to teach map reading, the use of the compass, knowledge of the stars as directional guides at night, and a great deal more. Even the technique of reporting back to higher headquarters, he felt, was appropriate to this sort of activity. So too were riding and flying lessons. Adam—and virtually the entire Defense Ministry and *Truppenamt*—had visions of the German people in arms. It is interesting to speculate how far this program might have gone if Hitler had not come to power in 1933.

Fall Maneuvers, 1932

Aside from such plans for training German youth, the defense of Germany still rested on the shoulders of the *Reichswehr* itself. The last great exercise of the Weimar era, the fall maneuvers of 1932, were clearly intended to represent a Polish invasion of Germany. The exercise took place near Frankfurt on the Oder, and consisted of a rapid passage by a Polish (red) cavalry corps through the German (blue) lines, as well as the seizure of an Oder bridgehead by an MRD. There was no attempt to copy Polish military organization.[36]

The maneuver analyzed two basic problems: (1) the employment of experimental organizations of the infantry and cavalry that were being tried out for the first time in larger operations, in which the main point of departure was the use of the highly mobile MRD as an integral part of the divisions; and (2) the technique of getting large bodies of troops over a wide, rapidly flowing river.[37]

The actual troops involved were the 3rd Infantry Division for blue and the 1st and 2nd Cavalry Divisions for red (the latter two being organized into a motorized cavalry corps, the largest motorized formation yet tested in any country's military maneuvers). Commanding the forces on both sides, and thus cutting their teeth on the battlefield operation of motorized formations, were many names later to become famous: Lt. Gen. Gerd von Rundstedt for the blue side, Lt. Gen. Fedor von Bock for the red, and Maj. Gen. Werner von Fritsch and Ewald von Kleist for the red 1st and 2nd Cavalry Divisions, respectively.[38]

The MRD had its first field testing under operational conditions. It consisted of an interesting mix of units. The battalion headquarters, for instance, included a signal platoon (mounted); an armored car platoon of four cars; an antitank platoon (two 37mm guns); a bicycle company (of three platoons); a machine gun troop (four heavy machine guns), and one cavalry troop. In accordance with the Versailles Treaty restrictions (and the large number of foreign observers present made it necessary to follow those restrictions), the antitank platoon was equipped with wooden dummies mounted on actual gun platforms. The organization of this headquarters unit shows a *Reichswehr* in the transitional stage of motorization, with horses, cars, and motorcycles all present. The unit itself was also a mixed bag of types, liberally equipped with radios: two armored car companies (armed with light cannon and machine guns), two motorcycle companies, a so-called heavy company (a motorized gun platoon, an antitank platoon, and a pioneer platoon), and a signal platoon.[39]

The red motorized cavalry corps, too, combined horse, dummy tanks, and motorized units into a rather complicated mix. The two component divisions, for example, had besides their regular regiments a full and bewildering array of auxiliary units. The 1st Cavalry Division included a bicycle battalion (of three companies) and a motorized reconnaissance battalion, as well as a fully motorized division headquarters. The 3rd Cavalry Division had a motorcycle battalion attached, along with its two brigades of cavalry (not regiments, as was the case with the 1st). Corps headquarters included a motorized antiaircraft battalion, as well as a motorized heavy artillery battalion and an observation squadron of six planes.[40] The 1932 maneuver, then, may justly be called the German cavalry's last stand. The inspector of cavalry, General von Hirschberg, still thought in terms of "heavy cavalry," that is, cavalry trained and equipped to fight on its own, rather than merely to carry out reconnaissance for the other arms. In fact, he felt that operational reconnaissance could be left to the motorized units, freeing the cavalry to fight.

He must have been disappointed by the maneuver. The red motorized Cavalry Corps was so jampacked with units of diverse types that simply giving it a march order was next to impossible. Trying to get it across the Oder was a nightmare. It is hard to debate the pithy comment of President von Hindenburg, who observed, "In war, only what is simple can succeed. I visited the staff of the Cavalry Corps. What I saw there was not simple."[41] Chief of the *Heeresleitung* Hammerstein agreed, citing "the intense confusion" that had arisen in the river-crossing attempt.[42] Not only had it delayed the operation, but caused unnecessary and fatiguing movement by large bodies of troops assembled along the river bank. Given the complete summer that had just been devoted to river-crossing exercises along the Oder, Hammerstein felt that the maneuver had not at all lived up to his expectations.

The employment of the MRDs, however, received much more praise. Hammerstein was impressed with "the dash of the newly formed motorized units." Even when they had been used unwisely in various tactical situations, their speed had enabled them to achieve results. Even though both motorized and cavalry units had carried out reconnaissance assignments, Hammerstein admitted in his after-action report that the former were much more flexible, capable of both operational (long-range) and tactical (short-range) assignments. The implication was that there was little left for horse cavalry to do in terms of reconnaissance, though it is hard to say whether Hammerstein fully realized it.

Nonetheless, it had been an interesting exercise, with much "hard fighting," interesting maneuver, and above all, speed. Foreign attachés and representatives, including General Mikhail Tukhachevsky from the Soviet Union and General Monti, chief of staff of the Italian army, often had to cover 300 kilometers or more in a single day to catch even a glimpse of the action.[43] The U.S. military attaché, Lt. Col. Jacob Wuest, felt that the maneuver was as close to real war as possible. Operations were continuous through twenty-four-hour days; troops and animals were subjected to the actual hardships of field duty. The motorized units had advanced 300 kilometers in three days; other units' marches seemed limited only by their mission, not by any artificial constraint. Troops bivouacked when and where they could.

Still, Wuest noted no undue signs of stress in the men. His overall impression was of "an army of young men," carefully selected and rigorously trained. It was also a well-disciplined army, though given the requirements of an all-volunteer force, the character of the discipline had changed. There were no more tales of "brow-beaten recruits and rough handling in the squadrooms." It was an army of "thinking individuals with a sense of freedom of action arising from good team training." The German soldier was "no longer machine-made, but . . . a hand-worked product of carefully selected stock."

As to the officers, few of those Wuest had seen were over fifty years old, and all seemed physically fit. They were "serious minded and keen," he observed, "quiet, with a natural sense of dignity." They were good at their work, "which they regard as a duty highly ordained and therefore scrupulously to be performed." He also noted that the tough economic conditions in Depression-era Germany forced them into simple living: "The gaieties of social life no longer make demands upon their time." In fact, he wrote, they had become "a class of careful students" of the profession of arms, "which they follow with a seriousness not known in our army."[44]

Those certainly had been modern maneuvers. Every participating unit was motorized to some degree. The Blue infantry division included a fully functioning motorized reconnaissance detachment. The red cavalry corps had it all: motorcycles, dummy tanks, trucks, and armored cars. Germany's new cipher machine, code-named "Enigma," had made its first appearance. Even more important, the *Reichswehr* High Command, though still tentative in its approach and wedded to an essentially unworkable combination of motor and horse, was beginning to devise operational doctrine and methods to employ its new mobile forces. The red cavalry corps's initial plan on 19 September to "attack the Blue forces fighting on the Oder deep in the flank and rear" was the essence of would later come to be known as *Blitzkrieg.*[45]

Moreover, it was clear by 1933 that the *Heeresleitung* was ready to move even further and faster in the direction of mechanization. Colonel Guderian was already testing models of two types of medium and three types of light tanks. The tank that would come to be known as the Pzkw. I, armed with two turret-mounted machine guns, was already beginning production and would be ready for action by 1934. Colonel Lutz had already approved plans for the Pzkw. II, with its 20mm gun. Planning had been begun for the *Heeresleitung's* 1933 fall maneuvers, the first to be held under the Hitler regime. It would pit a cavalry division and a reinforced infantry regiment against an infantry division. This time, an entire *Kraftfahr* battalion, with two companies of tanks and two companies of motorcycles, would be an integral part of the cavalry division, along with a motorized pioneer battalion and a fully motorized supply train. The reinforced infantry regiment had a motorized antitank company attached, as well as a company of medium tanks. The infantry division was to be a new, much heavier organization, including tanks, antitank guns, and an entire "foot artillery brigade" (four artillery regiments), and, once again, a fully motorized supply service. Another complete tank battalion would also be available to it, although it was not an organic component of the division.[46]

Conclusion: The German Army in 1933

Looking forward to 1933, chief of the Army Command Kurt von Hammerstein saw a number of important tasks yet to be accomplished, particularly in the areas of motorization, speed, and a more efficient conduct of battle.[47] He detailed his concerns in a document entitled *Points for Training in 1932–1933 (Hinweise)*. Orders, he warned, "were still not simple enough," but packed with "too many details." They should concentrate on stating a clear mission; carrying it out should be left to subordinates. Even worse, he had seen longwinded written orders being handed out during battle at the maneuvers. He stressed that orders given during battle were to be oral and based exclusively on the terrain.[48] Often, troops at rest had received long written orders that forced them to march at once. These orders could, in shortened form, have been delivered hours earlier, thus allowing the men longer preparation time. There had been repeated complaints from the troops and commanders participating in these maneuvers about the length of the rules (*Bestimmungen*). For 1933, Hammerstein wanted greater simplicity in this area, as well.

He also discussed the directives for the umpire service at maneuvers. Three areas required more concentration. First, troops on the move all too often ignored indicated roadblocks and obstructions. Umpires had to be physically present at these to slow the advance to a realistic wartime level. Second, the increasing use of MRDs was leading to problems for the umpires: these far-flung patrols had often driven "out of bounds." It was crucial that they be accompanied by umpires. It was not correct simply to declare such units out of action, force them to pause for a time, and then allow them to take up the reconnaissance again under better conditions. Instead, umpires had to lead such motorized units, under neutral colors, back to their departure point, from which the units would be free for use at a later time. The third directive to the umpires dealt with the dummy tank. Setting them outside the battle was proving difficult because their crews often failed to hear the signals; so, signs and flags had been introduced as a result (usually raised and lowered arms on a white flag). But the only way to allow the umpires to control armored vehicles was to give them their own vehicles. Umpires had to move quickly in giving their decision and assessing casualties on both sides, especially after an armored attack. Vehicles put out of action, as already observed for the MRD, were not to be left where they were, but driven back under an umpire's guidance to a designated assembly point, where they would later be granted freedom of movement. Remaining armored vehicles were to press forward vigorously in the attack after reassembling, just as in real combat. The tank commander was to report his action at once to the umpire. The only concession that might be made to the umpire was to specify a top speed for the armored vehicles—established as 20 kph.[49] Lessons of battle would still be learned, while umpires would be better able to keep matters in hand.

Hammerstein then turned to directives for the individual arms. The single most important task before the army, he emphasized, was defense against enemy tanks. Hammerstein took what we may call the "conservative" position—that tanks had to be fired upon before they hit the main battle line (as opposed to the "radical" notion, argued by Colonel Lutz, that infantry should simply go to ground, allow enemy tanks to pass and be dealt with by friendly tanks and antitank guns, and then deal with the follow-up infantry). Infantry therefore required a large number of antitank guns. The smaller the number available, the greater the reliance there needed to be on antitank obstructions—mines, barbed wire (showing the lightness of the envisioned armored vehicle that wire could be considered an obstacle), and the careful use of terrain unsuited for tanks. In constructing an infantry position, a great deal of thought needed to go into the placement of resistance nests in difficult terrain (clumps of trees, for example).

Hammerstein also disagreed with Lutz on the importance of the motorized divisional antitank company, as we have seen. It was an important unit, he felt, and indeed he included much of Lutz's own analysis of the unit verbatim in this report. But it was not the primary tank defense of the division, and its presence certainly did not preclude the infantry antitank guns he found so essential.

As for the employment of motorized units, Hammerstein was fully in agreement with Lutz's point of view. Armored units had to attack in concentrated fashion to succeed, and never under battalion strength. Surprise was the fundamental basis for their success. Attacks had to go in on a broad front (between 800 and 1,500 meters per battalion). Again, most of this section is a verbatim rewrite of Lutz's "Taktik der Kampfwagen."[50]

Regarding cavalry, there seemed to be continued confusion in the German command about its role on the modern battlefield. Hammerstein had to chastise the infantry for using complete cavalry regiments as reconnaissance units; the infantry division had its own cavalry platoon for that purpose. Coming at a time when the cavalry inspectorate was still talking in terms of battleworthy, independent heavy cavalry, and had even experimented with a corps-sized organization for that purpose, Hammerstein's scolding of the infantry betrays the same deep-seated confusion over the role of cavalry that had existed since the earliest days of the *Reichswehr*.[51] For battle or reconnaissance? The cavalry never really give an answer to that question; the reason it never gave an answer was that it did not have one.

Using the *Hinweise* as a basis, Hammerstein then drew up a schedule of *Reichswehr* exercises for 1933, a detailed description of what the army would be doing during Hitler's first year in office. Once again, it was a comprehensive if not incredible list of activities, and showed just how accelerated the German military program had become. Although constantly bemoaning the lack of available funds, the *Reichswehr* managed to scrounge up sufficient cash to plan enough exercises in the 1933 training year to take care of each and every unit—all twenty-one infantry regiments, seven artillery regiments, and eighteen cavalry regiments, as well as all the motorized, transport, and pioneer battalions. By 1933 the *Reichswehr* had to be the best drilled army in the history of the world. The seven-day exercises of each of the motorized battalions deserve special mention. So, too, do the fall maneuvers scheduled for the four infantry and two cavalry divisions of 1st Group Command, by far the most comprehensive since the end of the World War I.[52]

U.S. Military Attaché Wuest, a man with close connections to the German high command, put it best in December 1932: "Germany was already deeply engrossed with the question of increasing and readjusting her armaments and it was generally understood that the decision had been reached to proceed with this readjustment with or without the consent of the rest of the world."[53]

Notes

1. See Michael Geyer's complaint about the "adulation of Guderian in the English literature," in "German Strategy in the Age of Machine Warfare, 1914–1945," Peter Paret, ed., *Makers of Modern Strategy: From Machiavelli to the Nuclear Age* (Princeton, NJ: Princeton University Press, 1986), p. 558n. For a complete analysis of the question, see Robert M. Citino, *Armored Forces: History and Sourcebook* (Westport, CT: Greenwood Press, 1994), pp. 31–65.

2. For the impact of the Soviet connection on the rise of German armor, see W. Heinemann, "The Development of German Armoured Forces 1918–1940," in J. P. Harris and F. H. Toase, eds., *Armoured Warfare* (London: B. T. Batsford Ltd., 1990), pp. 51–69. For a detailed look at the links between the *Reichswehr* and the Red (Soviet) Army throughout the Weimar period, based on extensive research in recently opened archives in the former Soviet Union, see Manfred Zeidler, *Reichswehr und Rote Armee: Wage und Stationen einer ungewöhnlichen Zusammenarbeit 1930–1933* (Munich: R. Odlenbourg Verlag, 1993).

3. Richard M. Ogorkiewicz, *Armoured Forces: A History of Armoured Forces and Their Vehicles* (New York: Arco, 1970), pp. 209–210.

4. For a biographical sketch of Volckheim, see Citino, *Armored Forces*, pp. 277–278. Volckheim's own works include *Betrachtungen über Kampfwagen-Organisation und-Verwendung* (Berlin: E. Mittler und Sohn, 1924); *Der Kampfwagen in der heutigen Kriegführung* (Berlin: E. Mittler und Sohn, 1924); *Deutsche Kampfwagen Greifen An! Erlebnisse eines Kampfwagenführers an der Westfront 1918* (Berlin: E. Mittler und Sohn, 1937); *Die deutschen Kampfwagen im Weltkriege* (Berlin: E. Mittler und Sohn, 1923); and *Kampfwagen und Abwehr dagegen* (Berlin: E. Mittler und Sohn, 1925).

5. For a biographical sketch of Lutz, see Citino, *Armored Forces*, pp. 251–252.

6. *Anregungen und Lehren aus dem unter Leitung der Inspektion der Kraftfahrtruppen abgehaltenen Übungen der Kampfwagen-Nachbildungs-Bataillone zusammen mit Infanterie und Artillerie auf den Truppenübungsplätzen Grafenwöhr und Jüterbog,* found in "Records of the German Army High Command" (*Oberkommando des Heeres,* or OKH, the post 1935–designation of the *Heeresleitung*). A microfilmed copy of these records is on file in the U.S. National Archives in

Washington, DC, Microcopy T-78, serial H25/24, reel 300, frames 6250579–6250595. In shorthand notation, these documents would be identified as OKH, H25/24, 300, 6250579–6250595.

8. "Taktik der Kampfwagen," in Lutz, *Anregungen und Lehren,* OKH, H25/24, 300, 6250581–6250586. Lutz specified a breadth of 800–1,500 meters for the attack of a tank battalion.

9. "Übungen und Erfahrungen in der Abwehr von Kampfwafgen," in Lutz, *Anregungen und Lehren,* OKH, H25/24, 300, 6250587–6250591. Not everyone in the *Reichswehr* was sold on Lutz's ideas, however. General Hammerstein, then inspector of infantry, maintained that antitank weapons had to be parceled out among the infantry and deployed as far forward as possible to forestall an enemy tank attack before it reached the main defensive position. The division antitank company could never be the primary defensive weapon against tanks. It was best deployed deep in the defensive zone, as a last means when the infantry had failed to halt the enemy's advance. Although Hammerstein was willing to admit that antitank strength required an increase at all levels, he was against the formation of another divisional antitank company. Rather, he preferred an increase in the number of antitank guns deployed directly with the infantry battalions and cavalry regiments. See, for example, "Erfahrungen der Kpf. w. Nachb. Batle. in Grafenwöhr und Jüterbog," Gen. Kurt Freiherr von Hammerstein-Equord, inspector of the infantry, to Col. Walther von Brauchitsch (T-4), Berlin, 30 September 1932, OKH, H25/24, 300, 6250617–6250618.

10. "Übungen und Erfahrungen im Zusammenwirken von Kampfwagen mit anderen Waffen," in Lutz, *Anregungen und Lehren,* OKH, H25/24, 300, 6250592–6250593.

11. "Erfahrungen in der Leitung derart beweglichen Übungen," in Lutz, *Anregungen und Lehren,* OKH, H25/24, 300, 6250593–6250595.

12. "Zweck der Übungen," in Lutz, *Anregungen und Lehren,* OKH, H25/24, 300, 6250580.

13. Gen. Wilhelm Adam, chief of the *Truppenamt, Einige gesichtspunkte für die Verwendung motorisierter Aufklärungsabteilungen,* Berlin, 6 June 1932, OKH, H25/24, 299, 6250470–6250479.

14. "Eingliederung der mot. Aufklärungsabteilungen in das Gebiet der gesamter Aufklärung," in Adam, *Verwendung motorisierter Aufklärungsabteilungen,* OKH, H25/24, 299, 6250470–6250479.

15. "Aufgaben mot. Aufklärungsabteilungen," in Adam, *Verwendung motorisierter Aufklärungsabteilungen,* OKH, H25/24, 299, 6250471.

16. "Unterstellung mot. Aufklärungsabteilungen," in Adam, *Verwendung motorisierter Aufklärungsabteilungen,* OKH, H25/24, 299, 6250471–6250472.

17. "Zusammensetzung mot. Aufklärungsabteilungen," in Adam, *Verwendung motorisierter Aufklärungsabteilungen,* OKH, H25/24, 299, 6250472–6250473.

18. "Ansatz und Vorgehen von mot. Aufklärungsabteilungen," in Adam, *Verwendung motorisierter Aufklärungsabteilungen,* OKH, H25/24, 299, 6250473.

19. "Der Befehl der höheren Führung für den Einsatz einer mot. Aufklärungsabteilung," in Adam, *Verwendung motorisierter Aufklärungsabteilungen,* OKH, H25/24, 299, 6250473, 6250475. Pages 5 and 6 of this document have been microfilmed out of sequence.

20. "Der Befehl des Kommandeurs der mot. Aufklärungsabteilung und Verhalten der Patrouillen," in Adam, *Verwendung motorisierter Aufklärungsabteilungen,* OKH, H25/24, 299, 6250474, 6250476–6250477.

21. "Meldewesen," in Adam, *Verwendung motorisierter Aufklärungsabteilungen,* OKH, H25/24, 299, 6250477–6250478.

22. "Worauf es kommt," in Adam, *Verwendung motorisierter Aufklärungs-abteilungen,* OKH, H25/24, 299, 6250474, 6250478.

23. General Wilhelm Adam, Chief of the *Truppenamt, Flugmeldeübung Ostpreussens 1932,* Berlin, 4 April 1932, OKH, K 25/24, 299, 6250399–6250402.

24. "Dem Leitungsstab muss ferner eine zureichende Zahl von Pkw. und Krädern zur Verfügung stehen . . . ," in Adam, *Flugmeldeübung,* p. 4, OKH, H25/24, 299, 6250402.

25. *Bestimmungen für die Pioneerübung an der Oder 1932* (Berlin: E. Mittler und Sohn, 1932), in OKH, H25/24, 300, 6250523–6250570.

26. *Bestimmungen der Übungsreisen* (Berlin: Reichswehrministerium, 1932), in OKH, H24/78, 295, 6245075–6245095.

27. *Erfahrungsbericht über die Funkübung 1932,* Berlin, 31 January 1933, OKH, H25/24, 300, 6250780–6250796.

28. "Zweck der Übung," in *Funkübung 1932,* p. 5, OKH, H25/24, 300, 6250782).

29. "Vorbereitung der Übung," in *Funkübung 1932,* p. 6, OKH, H25/24, 300, 6250783.

30. "Kriegslage bis zum 6.6 6,00 Uhr," in *Funkübung 1932,* pp. 7–9, OKH, H25/24, 300, 6250784–6250786.

31. See the organizational charts "Einsatz Armee-Nachr. Abt.1 am 6.6 06,00 Uhr," OKH, H25/24, 300, 6250776, and "Nachrichtenlage F.K. II am 5.6. abends," OKH, H25/24, 300, 6250777.

32. "Auswertung und Beurteilung des technischen Verlaufes," in *Funkübung 1932,* p. 13, OKH, H25/24, 300, 6250790.

33. "Bürokratisierung," in *Funkübung 1932,* pp. 14–15, OKH, H25/24, 300, 6250791–6250792.

34. "Schlussbemerkung," in *Funkübung 1932,* p. 19, OKH, H25/24, 300, 6250796.

35. See the documents in the serial H24/64, "Förderung des Wehrgedankens und Wehrertüchtigung," OKH, reel 295, 6244563–6244575, especially the memorandum from General Adam, Berlin, 20 March 1931, OKH, H24/64, 295, 6244571–6244573.

36. See *Bericht über die Herbstübungen 1932* (Berlin: Reichsdrückerei, 1932), OKH, H24/70, 295, 6244654–6244692; also, *The German Maneuvers, September 19–22, 1932,* Lieutenant Colonel Jacob Wuest, U.S. military attaché, to War Department, Berlin, 25 November 1932, in *United States Military Intelligence Reports: Germany, 1919–1941* (Frederick, MD: University Publications of America, 1983), microfilm reel XIX, frames 847–874. In shorthand notation, the above document would be labeled USMI, XIX, 847–874.

37. Robert M. Citino, *The Evolution of Blitzkrieg Tactics: Germany Defends Itself Against Poland, 1918–1933* (Westport, CT: Grenwood Press, 1987), pp. 184–190, contains a detailed account of the 1932 maneuvers. For the organization of the participating units, see the charts in OKH, 300, H25/24, 6250650–6250655.

38. "The Exercise," in Wuest, *German Maneuvers 1932,* p. 4, USMI, XIX, 850.

39. Oswald Lutz, "Beispiel für die Gliederung einer Aufklärungsabteilung," Berlin, 1 December 1932, OKH, H25/24, 300, 6250656–6250654.

40. See "Appendix B: Organization of the Major Tactical Units which took part in the Fall Maneuver," in Wuest, *German Maneuvers 1932,* USMI, XIX, 866–870.

41. Heinz Guderian, *Panzer Leader* (New York: Ballantine Books, 1957), p. 18.

42. "Development of the Exercise," in Wuest, *German Maneuvers 1932*, p. 10, USMI, XIX, 856.

43. Wuest, *German Maneuvers 1932*, pp. 1–4, USMI, XIX, 847–850.

44. "Comments: Conduct of the Exercise," in Wuest, *German Maneuvers 1932*, pp. 12–13, USMI, XIX, 858–859.

45. "September 19th," in Wuest, *German Maneuvers 1932*, p. 8, XIX, 854.

46. See the organization charts drawn up by the *Truppenamt* in November 1932: "Truppengliederung der 3. K.D."; "Truppengliederung der verst. I.R. 72"; and "Truppengliederung der 6. Division," in OKH, H25/24, 300, 6250650–6250654.

47. Kurt von Hammerstein, "Hinweise für die Ausbildung im Jahre 1932/33 auf Grund von Heeresleitung bei Truppen-und Herbstübungen in vergangenen Ausbildungsjahre," in OKH, H25/24, 300, 6250682–6250697.

48. "Es muss wieder Regel werden dass im Gefecht die Führer der unteren Verbände mündlich und nach dem Gelände befehlen." In Hammerstein, *Hinweise*, No. 1, "Befehlgebung" (OKH, H25/24, 300, 6250683).

49. Ibid., No. 3, "Erfahrungen im Schiedsrichterdienst bei Beurteilung neuzeitlicher Kampfmittel" (OKH, H25/24, 300, 6250684–6250685).

50. Ibid., No. 4, "Hinweise für die Ausbildung bei allen Waffen" (OKH, H25/24, 300, 6250685–6250686).

51. Ibid., No. 2, "Anlage und Leitung von Übungen" (OKH, H25/24, 300, 6250683).

52. Gen. Kurt Freiherr von Hammerstein-Equord, chief of the Army Command, Berlin, 8 July 1932, *Übungsübersichten 1933* (OKH, H25/24, 299, 6250485–6250507).

53. In Wuest, *German Maneuvers 1932*, pp. 3–4, XIX, 849–850.

CHAPTER 9

From Reichswehr to Wehrmacht

It is no longer possible to argue, as many have in the past, that the Panzer forces were a particularly National Socialist phenomenon, designed to fight a peculiarly National Socialist type of war.[1] By the time Hitler came to power in 1933, the German army had already laid down the entire theoretical groundwork for *Blitzkrieg*. It is true that Hitler's declaration of rearmament in 1935 allowed tanks to be produced in the open and Panzer divisions to be formed for the first time, but it is equally true that he had absolutely nothing to do with the origin of *Blitzkrieg* as a military doctrine. To be fair, however, this footsoldier of the Great War did seem to embrace the concept of mechanized warfare more readily than many of his senior officers. To put it in broader terms, there is almost complete continuity between the two German armies of the interwar era.

Truppenführung

The smooth transition from *Reichswehr* to *Wehrmacht* is evident in the new field service regulations issued in 1933 and carried over into the era of rearmament. Entitled *Truppenführung*, the new regulations bore the stamp of the recently appointed chief of the *Truppenamt* (and chief of the General Staff after 1935), General Ludwig Beck. But even more than that, they bear the stamp of the previous regulations, *Führung und Gefecht der verbundenen Waffen (F.u.G.)* Many of the older regulations, in fact, turned up verbatim in the new ones. There is the same stress on simplicity of orders, the necessity for combined arms warfare in both attack and defense, the importance of the leader. Above all, it eschewed simplistic definitions of war. "The conduct of war," it stated, "is an art, a free, creative activity that rests on scientific principles."[2] Wartime situations displayed "an unlimited diversity that changes often and suddenly," and that is seldom predicted beforehand.[3] So much rested on the person of the leader. "The officer is a leader and a teacher,"[4] who had to have a knowledge of people, and who also had to be "cold-blooded, decisive, and courageous."[5] He must not merely rely on harsh discipline. "Mutual trust is the surest basis of discipline in necessity and danger."[6] Both officers and men had to realize that "the first demand in war is decisive action."[7] They had to be aware that "omissions and neglect incriminate [the officer] more severely than a mistake in the choice of means."[8] Once again, "great successes presume boldness and daring, preceded by good judgment."[9]

Truppenführung reiterated much of what *F.u.G.* had said in terms of leadership. Battle could never be a matter of prescribed and preordained action. Rather, flexibility had to be the key: "Out of the mission and the situation comes the decision."[10]

> The mission designates the objective to be attained. The leader must never lose sight of it. A mission that specifies several objectives easily diverts attention from the main objective.
> Obscurity of the situation is the rule. Seldom will one have exact information on the enemy. Clarification of the hostile situation is a self-evident demand. However, to wait in tense situations for information is seldom a token of strong leadership, more often a serious weakness.[11]

Decisions, once taken, were not to be abandoned easily. However, "in the changing conditions of war an inflexible maintenance of the original decision leads to mistakes."[12] Recognizing the necessity to change one's decisions—that was the "art of leadership."

Truppenführung's conception of modern battle ranged far beyond the battlefield itself. Communications between the commander and his units was a priority. The enemy's strength and dispositions had to be ascertained rapidly by air and ground reconnaissance and then relayed equally rapidly to the commander. Even "apparently unimportant details" might, in conjunction with other reports, have considerable worth.[13] Such reports must not cease even during battle: "Battle itself provides the most reliable means of estimating the enemy."[14] The flow of information between commanders and men was the key to success—the visible manifestation of which was the situation map, which was to be kept and updated in every higher headquarters.[15]

Once the commander was armed with the necessary information, he had to make his decision, in the context of his mission, and then formulate his orders. They should be simple, direct, free from ambiguity and excess verbiage: "An order shall contain all that is necessary for the lower commander to know in order for him to execute independently his task. It should contain no more." In fact, for lower commanders, a verbal order should suffice more than often than not.[16]

Reconnaissance received high priority—consonant with the regulations' metaphor of "war as information flow." If carried out by ground forces, it had to be aggressive, to aim not only to find the enemy's reconnaissance screen, but to defeat it. Both cavalry and motorized reconnaissance battalions were suited to the work. Aerial reconnaissance, whether visual or photographic, could also be very useful in securing a picture deep into the hostile area, a view usually denied ground reconnaissance. The portrait of the terrain, enemy strength and dispositions, and possible intentions could be greatly augmented by friendly intelligence services and even by counterespionage activity. This was another reason to limit the use of written orders: "Reconnaissance and security forces, and the advanced elements in combat, shall have no kind of order that may be of value to the enemy."[17]

Like *F.u.G.*, *Truppenführung* provides a detailed look at the various types of modern battle: attack (and pursuit), defense (and withdrawal), delaying action, and special types of battle (darkness or fog, engagements in cities, towns, or villages, fighting in woods, river defense and crossing, mountains, combat in and around defiles, border defense, and even guerrilla warfare).

In the section on attack, the thrust against the flanks and rear of the enemy received the most emphasis. Against any foe approaching equal strength, the frontal attack was "a long, obstinate struggle for superiority." The flank attack, however, was more effective: "A deep envelopment of one or more hostile flanks can lead to the annihilation of the enemy." Such a flanking maneuver was best carried out from a distance, since it was difficult to begin such a maneuver when in contact with the enemy.

Enveloping the enemy's flank was not without dangers of its own. It involved dispersal of one's own forces and opened the door to enemy maneuver as well. "He who envelops is in danger of being enveloped," something the commander had to keep in mind when planning his maneuver.[18] But if the enemy was first fixed frontally, and then surprised by the flanking maneuver, he would have no time to take counter measures. The principal prerequisite for the envelopment was superior speed and mobility.[19]

Truppenführung also shared *F.u.G.*'s stress on the necessity for each battle to have a *Schwerpunkt*, where the main force and the mass of the equipment had to be employed. This would be the flanking force in the event of an envelopment. The *Schwerpunkt* would be characterized by the following:

1. A narrow zone of attack. An infantry division making a decisive frontal assault, for example, should not exceed 3,000 meters in breadth.
2. Provision for the unified fire of all arms. This would include the fire of neighboring elements as well as the ones making the assault.
3. Reinforcement of the attacking elements by heavy weapons and artillery.[20]

An emphasis on combined arms in the attack was another characteristic shared by *Truppenführung* and its predecessor. Only through the coordinated use of all arms could infantry carry out "the decisive action against the enemy with sufficient firepower and shock action" to "drive through deeply and break down the final hostile resistance." The first stage would be complete when the hostile artillery was taken or forced to retire. There had to be full cooperation with the artillery, and the gunners had to be kept aware of the infantry's needs. The divisional artillery officer was to be in close proximity to the division commander. Likewise the infantry had to know how the artillery was organized and deployed; which units were supporting it; the location of the artillery's observation posts; and what terrain the artillery could command with its observation and fire.[21]

Truppenführung made the same point about tanks in the attack—still not seen as decisive, independent weapons, but as important support for the infantry. Tanks and infantry that worked together would normally have the same objective (the hostile artillery), though tanks should only be employed where the decisive action is sought. The direction of their attack might be the same or different from the attacking infantry, according to the terrain. But care had to be taken:

> Closely tied to the infantry, the tanks lose the advantage of their speed and they may become a victim of the opposing defense. They are to be used so that they put out of action the hostile arms that are holding up the infantry (above all the hostile artillery), or they are employed together with the infantry to break through the enemy.[22]

The tank was no panacea, no wonder weapon. Like all weapons it had strengths and weaknesses. It was simply another piece—an important piece, to be sure—of the German army's combined arms puzzle. In fact, *Truppenführung* speaks at length of the necessity for the tank attacks to be supported by the other arms, not just infantry, but motorized and/or armored artillery and antitank guns, motorized engineers, smoke, and tactical air support: "Attack aviation supports the tanks by attacking hostile defense weapons, artillery, and reserves. Planes flying deep into hostile territory can maintain communications between the troop commander and the tanks and can warn of hostile tank attacks."[23]

It was combined arms, then, not tanks alone, that would rupture the enemy line. As a rule, the advance would consist of numerous, small attack groups (*Angriffsgruppen*), composed of infantry, artillery, and, according to the situation, tanks. And once that had occurred, it was mixed-arms battlegroups that would conduct the pursuit. It was to be ruthless, aimed at nothing less than the total destruction of the defeated enemy: "Fatigue on the part of the troops may never be the basis for lack of pursuit. The leader is justified in demanding what appears to be impossible. Boldness and daring must guide him. Each must give to the utmost."[24]

The victor was to pursue on a broad front, always striving to outflank the enemy, to outdistance him, to strike his retreat in the flank, or to force him away from his lines of communication. Such a task was especially the province of highly mobile forces like army cavalry and strong motorized forces, as well as fighter and bomber aircraft: "Aviation increases the dissolution of the hostile force and disrupts the traffic on the main roads to the rear, at critical points, and at railheads."[25] Pursuit had to start from the bottom up; as soon as the enemy yielded, the lower commanders were to follow up. "They must act boldly and independently," carrying on the pursuit day and night.[26]

Along with its analysis of attack and pursuit, *Truppenführung* contained a companion look at defense and withdrawal. Again, the tone is that of *F.u.G.*, though augmented by the previous ten years of intensive exercises and maneuvers. Basically a matter of fire superiority, defense required a thorough knowledge of the terrain, the possibility of strengthening it through defensive works, which at the same time provided better cover and heightened the effect of fire against a moving attacker. As in the section on attack, *Truppenführung* also stressed the importance of conducting reconnaissance, protecting friendly flanks, surprising and deceiving the enemy, and of placing of strong reserves to protect open flanks.[27]

Likewise, even purely defensive battles had to have a *Schwerpunkt*. The principal part of the defensive position (*Stellung*) was the *Hauptkampffeld* (main battle zone), which was to be held to the last. It was to be organized in depth, with an emphasis on combined arms, a "series of mutually supporting defensive areas with obstacles, trenches, and nests of individual arms." Adjacent sectors had to able to support each other. The entire position was to be constructed in such a way that it was difficult to recognize, either from the land or from the air.[28] Advanced positions (*vorgeschobene Stellungen*) were crucial, both to delay and bloody the attacker. They were to contain heavy machine guns, antitank weapons, and light batteries, with special provision made for their withdrawal to the main position.[29]

If the enemy succeeded in breaking into the position, the primary task was to destroy him by fire. Infantry and supporting weapons in the vicinity must launch an immediate counterblow (*Gegenstoss*) "to hurl back the enemy before he has the opportunity to establish himself." If the local counterattack failed it was the decision of the higher commander to order either a general counterattack (*Gegenangriff*), or a withdrawal. If he opted for the former, *Truppenführung* stipulated that "the counterattack, where possible, must be launched against the hostile flank." It had to be thoroughly prepared, and consist again of all arms: infantry, artillery, tanks, and aircraft. Tanks, in particular, were "a decisive reserve in the hands of the commander, suited especially for a general counterattack or for action against hostile tanks."[30]

Truppenführung also spends considerable time discussing both the delaying engagement (*hinhaltendes Gefecht*) and the delaying resistance (*hinhaltender Widerstand*).[31] The former was the conception of the higher commander; the latter the execution of the commander's intention by the troops themselves.[32] This was a style of battle, dealt with in some detail in *F.u.G.*, in which the intention was not to hold the battle position but to delay and injure the advance of a superior force. The main object was "to conserve our forces and to inflict the greatest possible loss on the enemy. It was, of course, still an appropriate operational posture for the German army of 1933, which faced the same problem it had faced since 1918— how to defend the borders against enemies enjoying gross numerical superiority. It required the establishment of numerous lines of resistance, one behind the other. Retreating troops, after they had mauled an enemy advance with heavy fire, would then make a "well-regulated retirement" to the next position and take up the struggle again.[33] But it was not merely to be a passive defense; a purely defensive posture could only be temporary. The delaying engagement was also to consist of attacks with limited objectives, directed against the wings, flanks, or rear of the advancing force, as well as against weak spots in his front.[34] And here too we see the flexible hand of *Auftragstaktik*: "In order to be ready to exploit favorable opportunities, the lower commanders must be given considerable freedom as to aggressive conduct."

Part I of *Truppenführung* (the published half, available to the outside world) ended with a look at army cavalry (*Heereskavallerie*), defined as "the mounted, horse-drawn, and motorized units of the army" distinct from the cavalry assigned directly to divisional reconnaissance.[35] It was evidently still regarded by Beck as an important strategic weapon, but it is interesting to note how closely the language used here would later apply to the panzer forces and their commanders.

Because of its great mobility cavalry was of the utmost importance to the army. It was best employed on an open flank or in a broad gap between two elements of a friendly force. If sent on a distant mission, it could seldom be closely directed from the rear. Therefore, the cavalry commander had to have considerable freedom of decision and execution. The requirements of such a leader were high. He had to have a "high degree of elasticity, cold-blooded daring, physical agility, operational understanding, and the ability to make snap decisions and issue short, crisp orders."[36]

Cavalry's missions included attack versus the flank and rear of an enemy force, reconnaissance and screening, and the pursuit of a defeated enemy. Once again, combined arms was the key. Motorized units (especially truck-borne and motorcycle infantry) should be attached, and "special instructions should be issued [to the cavalry] concerning its communication with the other troops employed in the pursuit, with the air force, and especially with reconnaissance aircraft."[37] Where possible, the pursuit was to aim against the flank or rear of the enemy, and every effort had to be made to encircle him. Taking advantage of their speed and mobility, cavalry units "must push past the disorganized enemy," breaking any attempt at new resistance through rapid, surprise attack.

To complete the picture of army cavalry, its mobility also made it especially effective in the role of a "delaying resistance." It would screen friendly concentrations and secure maneuvers; it would block off broad sectors to the enemy advance; and it would hold up superior forces from approaching the battlefield and pin the enemy where he did not want to be. Finally, it would protect friendly lines of retreat (and *hinhaltender Widerstand* was, above all, to be a series of friendly retreats).

When the German army went to war in 1939, it did in fact have a force that was capable of all these tasks—and many, many more—and that was led by officers of "cold-blooded daring" and "mental elasticity." That force, however, would not be army cavalry.

Rearmament

Although *Blitzkrieg* may not have been Hitler's idea, his declaration of rearmament in 1935 was the *sine qua non* of the rebirth of the German army. What had been done in secret could now be done in the open, what had previously been constrained to the realm of the theoretical could now undergo the kind of examination that only maneuvers and proving ground tests could provide.

Hitler's original edict rearming Germany (March 1935) created an army of thirty-six infantry divisions grouped into twelve corps, a more than fivefold increase in the size of the army.[38] The best way to fill these new formations, as well as to create a trained reserve in the shortest possible time, was to stipulate a one-year term of enlistment. Soon found to be unacceptably short, the single year gave way to a two-year term in August 1936. According to U.S. military attaché, Maj. Truman Smith, the new edict came as no surprise:

> As has been repeatedly stated in reports describing visits to German units in recent months, the almost unanimous opinion of German officers of every branch of the service has been that a twelve months training period was too short to produce a well-trained soldier. The wear and tear on the officer and non-commissioned officer corps of trying deliberately to cram two years training into one had been producing, for some time, a state of nervous tension in units of every type, which could not possibly be left to continue indefinitely.[39]

It was as if every day in German army barracks was as tense as a general inspection day. As one observer put it to Major Smith, "If the Germans don't drop this high pressure method pretty soon, they will have to commence converting their new barracks into insane asylums for officers."[40]

Although the one-year term did have certain advantages, it had one crucial weakness. Each year, from November 1 to March 1, the German army basically ceased to exist. During this four-month period, it was a force consisting completely of officers, NCOs, and a huge mass of untrained recruits. According to Major Smith, it was "scarcely fit to take the field and cross swords with any of the armies of Germany's neighbors." The result was "an obligatory foreign political respite" for one-third of the year. With the outbreak of fighting in Spain in the summer of 1936, the new two-year period of enlistment guaranteed a German force in being through what promised to be dangerous times ahead.[41]

The year 1935 also saw the birth of the German panzer division.[42] As we have seen, experimentation with tank and motorized formations dated back into the 1920s, and had reached a crescendo in 1931 and 1932. In early 1933 Guderian had taken part in a demonstration of recently developed weapons for the new chancellor. For thirty minutes, Hitler sat and watched a number of units go through their paces: a motorcycle platoon, an anti-tank platoon of 37mm guns (the German standard at the time); one platoon of light and one of heavy armored cars; and a platoon of experimental light tanks. This model would eventually become the aforementioned Pzkw. I, originally intended as a trainer only, but which remained in the German arsenal through the early years of the war. It was no King Tiger. Its armament consisted of two machine guns in a small turret on the right-hand side of the vehicle, and its armor (between 8 and 15 millimeters) was enough to stop small-arms fire only. But Hitler, a veteran of the trenches himself, seemed enthralled by its possibilities, repeatedly exclaiming "That's what I need! That's what I want to have," as the tiny machines drove back and forth in front of him.[43]

Matters proceeded rapidly after that. In July 1934 a Tank Forces Command (*Kommando der Panzertruppen*) was established, under Lt. Gen. Oswald Lutz, with Guderian as his chief of staff.[44] The new command had orders to continue organizational and tactical experiments with armored forces. Design work proceeded apace, resulting in another light tank, the Pzkw. II. It was a much improved model, with a 20mm gun. In 1935 the design for the Pzkw. IV was completed, a medium tank of some twenty tons, armed with a 75mm short-barrel gun. Finally, in 1936, the government placed orders for the Pzkw. III, a medium tank with a 37mm gun. This rounded out the quartet of tanks with which Germany would go to war in 1939.

In the fall of 1935 Tank Forces Command staged large armored maneuvers at Münsterlager. With the findings obtained there, Lutz and Guderian recommended the formation of three panzer divisions. It cannot be said that there was fierce resistance from the High Command. The chief of the Army Command, Gen. Werner von Fritsch, was certainly no armor enthusiast, but he was likely to answer Guderian's arguments with a twist of his monocle and a laconic, "You may be right."[45] The chief of the Gen. Staff, Gen. Ludwig Beck, was more open in his opposition. He saw tanks as infantry support weapons above all, and had no use for the concept of a panzer division. "You move too fast for me," he once hissed at Guderian, referring not just to his enthusiastic subordinate but to tank supporters in general. Command would inevitably break down on a mobile battlefield, he felt. "But you can't command without maps and telephones. Haven't you ever read Schlieffen?"[46] Still, Guderian's claim to have fought a "long, drawn-out fight" with Beck is sheer exaggeration. Beck became chief of the *Truppenamt* in 1933; panzer divisions were in the field within two years. This hardly qualifies as last-ditch resistance to tanks. In fact, compared with what had happened in Britain or France, it seems the model of dispatch.

The first three German panzer divisions came into existence in October 1935: 1st Panzer Division under Gen. Maximilian Freiherr von Weichs (stationed at Weimar); 2nd Panzer Division under Guderian (Würzburg); and 3rd Panzer Division, under General Fessmann (at Berlin). Each consisted of a tank brigade backed by a motorized infantry brigade. This was the same organization as the Light Mechanized Division formed in France the previous year, and also very reflective of contemporary British thinking. What was different was the German emphasis on combined arms. The panzer division had enough tanks to satisfy even the purist: two tank regiments of two battalions each, with a strength of 128 Pzkw. Is per battalion. Counting command tanks, the division contained some 561 in all. But there was also a very strong infantry component, consisting of a two-battalion motorized infantry regiment, plus a motorcycle battalion. In addition, in what was the true mark of the panzer division, there was a complete cast of supporting arms: a motorized artillery regiment, a motorized antitank battalion, and a motorized pioneer company, later expanded into a battalion. There was also a motorized reconnaissance battalion, such as the Germans had been experimenting with since the 1932 maneuvers, made up of armored cars and motorcycles. The panzer division, then, was not just tanks. It was, in the well-chosen words of armor historian Richard Ogorkiewicz, "a self-contained combined arms team in which tanks were backed by other arms brought up, as far as possible, to the tanks' standards of mobility."[47]

Exercises and Wargames

Although 1935 did create a new army, it did not break any radically new ground in training, doctrine, or military education. The schedule of maneuvers, exercises, and wargames was just as grueling as it had been during the Weimar period, but no more so, and the content of these exercises was virtually indistinguishable from what had gone before. The education of *Wehrmacht* staff officers, for example, displays almost complete continuity with that of the *Reichswehr*.[48]

The old divisional school of the 3rd Infantry Division in Berlin now ran the *Offizierlehrgänge* (officer training courses), a three-year command and General Staff training course. It would become the *Kriegsakademie* once again after the declaration of rearmament. Restricted to officers in the ranks of 1st lieutenant or captain with at least eight years of service, it was a highly selective course of study. Candidates were chosen on the basis of character, leadership, education, psychological aptitude, and social background—in that order. They arrived in Berlin in September to begin their studies. The school was run by Maj. Gen. Kurt Liebmann, an adjutant, and twenty *Truppenamt* officers.

The assistant U.S. military attaché, Capt. James C. Crockett, visited the school, and his report shows how little had changed since the 1920s. The curriculum still emphasized command, tactics, troop movements, military history (battles and campaigns), and riding. The first year (*Lehrgang I*) dealt with units up to and including the reinforced brigade; *Lehrgang II* covered the division (infantry, cavalry, motorized, and mechanized), either acting alone or in conjunction with a larger unit; *Lehrgang* III dealt with the operations of the corps, the army, and even the army group. In 1935 each had about 100 officers.

According to documents Crockett had seen, there were five essential components to the training of these future staff officers, points that were emphasized over and over again in maneuvers, exercises, and wargames:

1. Prompt decisionmaking. "Slowness in arriving at a tactical decision within the division, brigade, or regiment," wrote one observer, "is regarded as a serious fault."[49] The ability to make quick decisions outweighed any commitment to orthodoxy.
2. The ability to present a clear, brief verbal order.
3. The appropriate tactical use of terrain. In both terrain exercises and sandtable wargames, the student was constantly asked his assessment of the terrain.
4. The ability to assess the situation and issue orders in the absence of precise information about the enemy. It was a common refrain of the instructors: the officer who waited until he had clear information always acts too late.
5. Independent initiative. The officer was receiving training for mobile war, and therefore had to feel free to act as he saw fit. Staff officers who disagreed with their superior's orders were not only free, but encouraged, to give a short statement of their own views and recommendations.

In battle, the General Staff officer always spoke in the name of the commander, remaining "faceless," as it were. Nevertheless, each of his orders was legal and binding on any recipients, even if they outranked him. If the commander were wounded or killed in battle, the senior staff officer temporarily commanded the unit, again regardless of his rank or that of his subordinate unit commanders. This situation remained until the appointment of a new commander by the next highest authority. For example, the chief of staff of a division would probably be a captain or a major. If the commander became a casualty, the chief of staff would take over, regardless of the rank of the regimental commanders. Only in this way, the instructors at the school argued, could continuity of operations be maintained on the highly mobile battlefield of the future.

In November 1934 Captain Crockett attended two exercises carried out by *Lehrgang II*, one on the ground, the other played out on the map.[50] In the terrain exercise, the instructor divided the group into three sections. The red and blue sides were identical seven-man teams: a division commander; three regiment commanders, artillery regiment commander, reconnaissance battalion commander, and commander of an engineer battalion. A third group, designated the *Leitung* (direction staff), served as assistants to the instructor—keeping the situation maps, computing time and space factors for every movement ordered, making notes for the postgame critique, and so on. Crockett stressed the paucity of information given to each side, usually in verbal form.

> In the problems, although there are two sides and Red and Blue are confronting each other, only the most meager enemy information is given. . . . It is never definite and commanders must weigh and interpret the meaning themselves. Students are continually cautioned that this uncertainty as to the enemy is in keeping with the realities of war.

Thus informed, the commander now had to issue orders to his subordinates, almost always in verbal form, or take such action as he decided was appropriate. The instructor (and *Leitung*) was there to judge him, not to advise him.

It was this freedom that was most noteworthy to the U.S. observer. The instructor interrupted with orders only when it was necessary to keep the game within the realm of possibility. The training potential of such an exercise, he wrote, was limited only by the "imagination and skill of the commanding instructor," who was typically an officer chosen for his extensive wartime experience. It was his job to guard against artificiality, technically correct but practically impossible solutions, and overly involved maneuvers or orders: "Every order given by the student officers is tested for its time and space possibilities, for its simplicity, clearness, and directness. Every effort is made to crush out formalism, or 'type' solutions. There are no approved solutions, but due to the two-sided play, faulty decisions and dispositions are obvious."[51]

After October 1935 the *Lehrgäng* would become known once again by its prewar name, the *Kriegsakademie*. Its curriculum, its comprehensive schedule of wargames and terrain exercises, and even its faculty remained identical to what they had been during the Weimar period. The school had provided an excellent training for the *Reichswehr's* staff officers, and it would continue to do the same thing for the *Wehrmacht*.[52]

The Maneuvers of 1936

The first great *Wehrmacht* maneuvers were those of 1936, held in Hesse from 21 to 25 of September. These were the largest held since 1913: close to 50,000 men were in the field, elements of five divisions and three air squadrons. Playing blue was the IX Army Corps (6, 9th, and 19th Divisions, commanded by Gen. Friedrich Dollmann); red commanded the V Army Corps (10th and 15th Divisions, Gen. Hermann Geyer). The maneuver area was bounded by Eisenach, Marburg, Frankfurt and Schweinfurt, although only a fraction of the 80-mile-wide sector came into play.[53]

The maneuver situation was hardly a complex one. Both red and blue sides were flanked on both sides by phantom forces, leaving little for both sides to do beyond advancing and retiring. The extreme simplicity of the fighting, however, was appropriate to an army that was, in effect, a little over one year old. The red forces concentrated first. Its two divisions launched an attack on the blue 9th Division. The arrival of a second blue division (the 19th) stabilized the line. The third blue division (the 6th) arrived late in the maneuver after 30–40-mile march over several days. The maneuver ended with a full-scale blue attack by all three divisions, followed by a red retreat into an entrenched position.

According to a British observer, there was much to praise here. Despite an obvious shortage of officers and NCOs, both the commanders and the men seemed to be "of an excellent stamp, professionally most competent." The discipline of the men was "above reproach," and it was clear that "the German army of 1936 promises to be in no way inferior to that of 1914."

> In billets and on the march, everything pointed to complete control of the men by their officers and NCO's. There were manifest all the symptoms of a thoroughly good spirit among the troops, as well as familiarity with life in the field. The *Reichswehr* has certainly done its work well, in that it has successfully passed on to those young soldiers all the knowledge and methods of the old pre-war army. . . . The traditions, titles, and trophies of the old army, which were preserved in the *Reichswehr*, have now

been passed on to the new creation. There can be little doubt that the new regiments will be inspired by the quality and history of their predecessors.[54]

The tactics employed in the maneuver were also impressive. Infantry was flexible in the approach and used ground wisely. Artillery fired from concealed positions and was consistently difficult to locate. All the troops were well camouflaged, using branches or bits of foliage, and the men were studious in using the numerous woods and copses as cover from hostile aircraft.

The motorized reconnaissance battalion was also in evidence, "a mechanized creation of the most modern type." Armored cars, two companies of truck-borne infantry, light mobile artillery (including an antitank gun detachment and a section of light infantry mortars), and a machine gun company all went to make up what "at first sight, appeared to be somewhat of a menagerie of weapons." During the action, however, "the unit proved to be perfectly well-knit."

> It would seem that the whole unit would be pushed forward to reconnoiter; then, as soon as contact was imminent, the infantry and the machine gun company would form a screen, while the antitank guns and mortars might be employed as circumstances should dictate. The armoured cars, for their part, moved by "bounds" from one tactical feature to another. Such at any rate seemed to be the procedure on the initial day of the manoeuvers, when the opposing detachments established touch with each other.[55]

Tanks had also made an appearance, a regiment of Pzkw. Is. They launched a successful attack against a hill strongly held by blue forces on day one of the exercise, although the tanks suffered such heavy losses that the regiment was ruled out of play on the second day. On the final day, they transferred to the blue side, and the whole regiment—all 140 machines—carried out a spectacular attack on the red entrenchments. Over all, the British observer found his German hosts reticent on the subject of armor. He had heard reports that heavier machines were soon to be introduced, and that the number of tank divisions would soon rise from three to five. But "what the role assigned to these divisions might be in war it would be difficult to say." He had also heard a number of officers discuss the likelihood of an eastern theater of war:

> On the muddy plains of Poland and western Russia the motor, it is urged, may be of doubtful utility. Consequently, with a view to a possible campaign in these parts, the horse must be retained. Such, at any rate, is the plea put forward by competent German officers when the subject of mechanization is pressed.

"The whole question of mechanization," he concluded, "is in fact very much in the air."[56] German officers seemed uncertain about the future course of development, and he saw no reason to doubt their sincerity.

The Great Fall Maneuvers of 1937

The event that really made the panzer division's reputation in the higher counsels of the *Wehrmacht* was the great fall maneuvers of 1937 that took place in Mecklenburg.[57] By far the largest maneuvers held in Germany since the war, they involved 160,000 men, 25,000 horses, over 21,000 vehicles, 830 tanks, and 54 aircraft. Units taking part were eight infantry divisions (two of them masquerading as border defense units, or *Grenzschutz* divisions); one Panzer division, one Panzer brigade, six reconnaissance squadrons of aircraft, and seven antiaircraft (*Flak*) battalions. Red forces formed an army, Blue forces an entire army group. Even the length was exceptional. Instead of the two-to-three day maneuvers of the old *Reichswehr*, the *Wehrmacht* went through its paces for a full seven days on continuous action (18–24 September), although not every unit took part for the full period. The strain on the commanders of both sides, however, was probably as close to real war as any maneuvers have ever gotten.

The region chosen for the maneuvers exhibited a number of different terrain characteristics that strongly influenced the course of operations. The southern half of the maneuver area featured a transition from the hilly region of the Baltic coast to the flatness of the Mecklenburg lakes. Overall, the land had the topical features of a moraine, a rolling landscape of rolling hills and knolls that offered good cover to both attacker and defender—not at all the "North German Plain" of legend. Another important attribute was the tremendous number of rivers and streams winding their way through the lakes and to the Baltic, forming innumerable confluences. At times of high water (as, for example, during the period of the maneuvers), they formed a considerable hindrance to the smooth movement of all forces. The thinly settled area possessed only a few good roads, and movement apart from them could be quite difficult.[58]

As always, the maneuver began with both sides receiving an initial situation report (*Ausgangslage*). Increased tension between a western nation ("Redland") and an eastern one ("Blueland") had led to the declaration of mobilization in both countries on 15 September. The first mobilization day for both nations would be 16 September. The red 5th Army deployed on the northern (left) flank of the red forces, facing to the east. Its mission was to defend the Red heights between the Elbe river and the Baltic from attack by land. For the blue forces, the 1st Army deployed on the northern wing of Army Group North, in the district of Greifswald-Neusterlitz-Stettiner Haff; 2nd Army deployed to the south, adjacent to 1st Army.

The red 5th Army (headquarters at Schwerin) was divided into two sectors: (1) Southern Sector (*Abschnitt Sud*), held by V Corps (headquarters at Ludwigslust; and (2) Northern Sector (*Abschnitt Nord*), held by X Corps (headquarters at Güstrow). This was the actual corps involved in the exercises, consisting of the 10th *Grenzschutz* Division, the 30th Division, and various corps troops (e.g., artillery, pioneers, aerial reconnaissance, motorized flak units).[59]

The blue 1st Army consisted of the II Corps, already in place on the frontier (12th Division, 32nd Division, 1st *Grenzschutz* Division, and corps troops). A second corps was expected as a reinforcement, but not before 21 September.[60]

The situation featured the classic hallmark of German maneuvers in the period: extremely limited information about the enemy. According to the red *Ausgangslage*

> It is known that Blue will achieve readiness about two days later than Red, but there is no reliable information about the intentions of the Blue command. In case of a Blue attack between the Elbe and the Baltic, an early commitment of their tanks forces is possible. There can scarcely be a unified attack by all Blue forces before September 22. If Blue attacks our Northern Sector, the expected *Schwerpunkt* will be out of the bridge-head west of Malchin and Demmin. In peacetime, Blue's 12th Division is deployed in the area east of our Northern Sector.[61]

The blue *Ausgangslage* saw things differently:

> It is known that the Red army had a two day lead in achieving a state of readiness. An attack by Red's main force is expected south of the Elbe. In the area between the Elbe and the Baltic, Blue may reckon with weak Red forces. In peacetime, Red's 30th Division is stationed in the northern sector of the border area.[62]

The red X Corps commander, proceeding on directives drawn up in peacetime, now ordered his 10th *Grenzschutz* Division into action. Its mission was border defense, needless to say, but interpreted in the very broadest context. It included establishing the mission, deployment, and intentions of any hostile border defense forces in the vicinity; early recognition of intentions to attack on the part of the enemy main force; and the repulse of any hostile reconnaissance or scout forces. It was also to strengthen its own positions as soon as possible, consolidating numerous disconnected positions into a continuous defensive line.[63] The red 30th Division, upon achieving a state of readiness, was to be used as its divisional commander saw fit; he had already drawn up orders and expected his division to be at the border by 8:00 A.M. on 19 September. Having considered the terrain, he expected an attack by blue forces in the flat, open terrain in front of the Malchin-Demmin bridgehead (the blue advanced position over the winding Peene River). Consequently, he intended to concentrate against this spot.[64]

The blue deployment proceeded in a similar fashion, with the 1st *Grenzschutz* Division being thrown forward to secure the frontier. The rest of the 1st Army received orders to deploy in such a fashion that the possession of the high ground west of the line Demmin-Lake Malchin ("the bridgehead") was secure against a sudden enemy attack. The *Grenzschutz* division was in the bridgehead itself, 12th Division was in reserve behind it; and the 32nd Division was coming up from the southeast to guard the flank of the position.[65]

The first actual day of the maneuver, 18 September, found both sides arriving in the theater of war, and featured a number of border violations and skirmishes rather than actual combat. But even though hostilities had not yet formally opened between blue and red sides, the red 30th Division commander had already decided upon a bold stratagem. Seeing the *Grenzschutz* units to his immediate front, he suggested to X Corps headquarters a rapid surprise strike by his entire division with the intention of seizing the Demmin-Malchin bridgehead.[66] Realizing that his two-day head start in deployment offered an advantage that would soon vanish, the X Corps commander agreed. Expecting an opening of hostilities on 20 September, he now requested armored support from 5th Army.[67] His intention was to hit the bridgehead frontally (with 30th Division) and from the south (with the panzers). The commander of 5th Army approved this plan. Although his initial mission spoke of defending the red heights between the Elbe and the Baltic from a land attack, he reasoned that possession of the Demmin-Malchin bridgehead would give him a shorter, better defensive line to hold, as well as crippling any blue attacks from that direction. And now he made the decision that would make the 1937 maneuvers the interwar era's most important: to ensure the success of the attack, an entire panzer division was placed at its disposal, along with a complete infantry division (the 22nd) and powerful army-level units (a heavy artillery regiment, a pioneer regiment, and a motorized reconnaissance battalion).[68]

The moment was indeed a fateful one. Given the incredible success of the German panzer forces in the opening battles of World War II (the Polish campaign was less than two years away, and in less than three years many of these same soldiers would be marching through Paris), it is easy to overlook the uncertainty of the tank's future as things stood in 1937. They had their supporters—even their fanatics—and their equally fervent detractors. No one questioned the presence of tanks in a modern army. The dispute centered on what role they might play. Were tank divisions simply another support weapon for the infantry? Or were they fit for long-range, independent operations? Writing on the eve of the war, a General Staff officer, Col. Walter Spannenkrebs, described the debate this way: "Two extreme views stand out sharply here: the one side is distrustful and assigns only a subordinate role to the tanks; the other sees in them the decisive main weapon and tends to underestimate all nonarmored forces."[69]

Since the formation of the panzer divisions in late 1935, very little had changed. Enthusiasts (head of Tank Forces Command General Lutz, his bright, young chief of staff Guderian, later the commander of the 2nd Panzer Division) stood on one side, exalting the virtues of their miracle weapon.

Detractors stood on the other side (General Beck, the cautious chief of the General Staff, defense-minded officers like General Ritter von Leeb) stood on the other, not so much denigrating the tank as urging those on the other side to move more slowly.[70]

The panzer maneuvers at Münsterlager in 1935 had taken place before the advent of the actual divisions. As we have seen, the 1936 maneuvers had been designed more to test the quality of noncommissioned officers and men in the new mass army than to evaluate the ability of tank units as such. The 1937 Mecklenburg maneuvers, therefore, were the first occasion on which the panzer division got to perform in front of the entire *Wehrmacht*. The lessons would never be forgotten by the vast majority of those assembled, from elements of the High Command to the lowliest *Landser*.

Both sides were assembling their forces on the border and preparing for battle on September 19. The 3rd Panzer Division had been part of the army reserve, stationed west of Schwerin and Wismar. It was ready to move by 8:00 A.M., under the air umbrella of the 3/113 aerial squadron (part of the 3rd Reconnaissance *Lehrgruppe*, stationed at Jüterbog). The division received its orders and was on the road by 3:00 P.M., approaching its jumpoff point, the town of Krakow, by two march routes. It arrived there by 9:00 P.M., and received the result of air reconnaissance carried out by 3rd Reconnaissance Squadron that allowed it to draw an accurate picture of the terrain. The division's attack plan for 20 September was to send forward its infantry brigade to engage the troops defending the bridgehead, while the division's panzer brigade struck the extreme left flank of the defense. The tanks would effect a breakthrough and drive on Stavenhagen (that is, a position actually *behind* the defenders' position), thereby cutting the principal supply road into the bridgehead (the road from Malchin to Neubrandenburg).[71]

The blue side was not sitting by passively. Its plans called for an advance and "an occupation of the land bridge between Wismar and Lake Schwerin." From here, the blue Army Group would simultaneously advance along the Baltic coast and carry out a drive on Hamburg. Additional forces were on the way, a III Corps (consisting of the 3rd and 23rd Infantry Divisions), as well as the 1st Infantry Division, currently being transported by sea to the port of Stettin. The blue command recognized the possibility of a red attack toward Demmin and Malchin, but felt it could best be forestalled by a blue advance on Güstrow.[72]

Each side, therefore, had an attack planned on the other. As the maneuver director, General Beck, viewed matters, red command had chosen the boldest possible solution, a rapid attack by an entire corps and a panzer division, on a broad, 40-kilometer front. The corps was not echeloned in depth, however, and the flank attack by the panzers was risky at best. A less dangerous path—a frontal assault by the Panzer division, for example—might also lead to success.[73]

As matters unfolded on 20 September, General Beck's caution proved unfounded. The attack of the 3rd Panzer Division—although held up a bit by the 6th Panzer Regiment's having to top off its fuel tanks and by the numerous waterways crisscrossing the division's path of advance—did everything that the most rabid of armored fanatics could have hoped.[74] After an approach march of 100 kilometers, the division's attack on the bridgehead succeeded that first day in forcing blue forces to commit their defensive reserves, although the dug-in blue infantry did manage to hold a cohesive line.[75] By the next day, however, the blue situation had become critical. The red side had managed to unite all three divisions into a concentric attack on Malchin. Aided again by useful and accurate air reconnaissance, it was able to paint an accurate picture of enemy dispositions and plan its attack accordingly. On the red right flank, the 3rd Panzer Division played the key role. Despite heavy losses, it broke into and through the enemy defensive position, driving on Stavenhagen, and from there on to Malchin. By early afternoon, the blue position was untenable, and the bridgehead was in red hands by early afternoon on 21 September.[76]

The situation was unprecedented in interwar German maneuvers. In what was supposed to be a seven-day exercise, the bold red armored thrust had essentially decided the issue halfway through day four. General Beck did not seem to be amused. In an equally unprecedented development—absolutely unheard of in the maneuver records since the days of the Kaiser— General Beck now took the occasion to disagree with the umpire's decision regarding the 3rd Panzer Division's drive on Malchin, generally, accusing the umpires of underestimating the power of defensive fire against the tanks.

> The difficult decision of the commander of the [blue] 12th Division and the commander of the [blue] 48th Infantry Regiment to give up the Malchin bridgehead was a result of the rapid collapse of the defense. It must be noted that it was not heavy fire, but the umpire's decisions that led to this result.
> Whether 3rd Panzer Division could really have reached Malchin, given a more accurate umpire's decision about the actual strength of 32nd Division, is open to question. Given the number of antitank weapons at the disposal of 32nd Division, the panzer unit should have been able to count on higher losses.[77]

It is difficult to establish this point fully from the documentation, but it appears that Beck now ordered 3rd Panzer Division out of the maneuver. It had suffered heavy losses in its attack, but whether those losses were crippling or not is open to question. At any rate, 3rd Panzer Division played no further role in the fighting, marching back whence it had come and disappearing from the maneuver record.[78]

The rest of the exercise consisted of a concentrated blue counterattack: I Corps along the coast; II Corps in the center; a newly arriving III

Corps arriving from the vicinity of Berlin; plus 1st Division that had landed at Stettin on 22 September. These forces succeeded in pushing back the numerically inferior red forces in the south, although no startling new tactical or operational departures were in evidence. Of course, the blue success owed a great deal to the absence of the red 3rd Panzer Division. The blue side had tanks as well, a panzer brigade supporting II Corps, but significantly this unit failed to distinguish itself. Having no real infantry component of its own, the brigade had a great deal of difficulty effecting cooperation with the neighboring infantry and artillery.[79]

It is clear from the historical record in general, as well as from the records of the 1937 maneuvers, that Beck was no enthusiast of the panzer division. Its achievements had nearly wrecked the maneuver, however, and that might have had something to do with his bad humor. But even he had to admit what he had seen, which was that "Red solved the problems allotted to it, through a well-planned, swift, and energetic use of its means. It destroyed a considerable part of the Blue force in the successful battle of Malchin, and quickly established a new defensive line in the Malchin bend. Here it held off strong Blue attacking forces."[80] Others agreed. No less a personage than Gen. Franz Halder, Beck's successor in 1938 as chief of the General Staff, was stunned at the "fluid mobility" he saw in the panzer division.[81]

The 1937 maneuvers were an impressive affair that showed the maturation of German military doctrine. Not only did it include tanks, but aircraft as well, which were extremely effective in cooperation with the panzer units. There were also motorized reconnaissance units and pioneers, modern antitank weapons, even a *Fallschirmjäger* (paratroop) company (that did not carry out a jump, but did distinguish itself by a vicious and highly successful night attack on elements of the blue 32nd Division). But the panzer division had clearly been the star, establishing once and for all its suitability for independent operations.

Several months later, German panzers were in action again, this time for real, as Hitler ordered his military forces into Austria as part of the *Anschluss* of March 1938. General Guderian, by now commander of the XVI Corps, rejoined his old division, the 2nd Panzer, to lead it across the border. Alerted to the action late on 10 March, Guderian took the division from its garrison at Würzburg to Passau on the Austrian border by the morning of 12 March, a distance of about 250 miles. The march into Austria, during which the division was reinforced by Colonel Sepp Dietrich and the *SS-Leibstandarte Adolf Hitler* motorized infantry battalion, went well enough, despite the reports one still reads about the massive number of breakdowns suffered by German tanks. The action did reveal problems in staff work and tank maintenance, but as Guderian pointed out, the "improvised march to Vienna" meant that 2nd Panzer Division had to cover about 420 miles, the *Leibstandarte* about 600, all in the space of a

mere forty-eight hours. "In general these tasks were performed satisfactorily," he felt.[82] It was the first great panzer drive in history; it would not be
the last.

Employment of the Panzer Division

If one distinction may be made between the pre- and post-1935 German
army, it is the presence of the panzer division. But what is equally obvious
is how smoothly the presence of the new formation was factored into the
staff training at the *Kriegsakademie*. In 1938 students at the academy received a list of general principles regulating the use of the panzer division.[83] This document described the division as a flexible instrument in the
hands of its commander, relying not just on tanks, but on combined-arms
warfare. For example, if the situation were unclear, and time or circum-
stance had not permitted a thorough reconnaissance, then the division's infantry brigade would lead the attack, followed by the panzer brigade. The
attack of the infantry brigade would clarify hostile deployment and seize
favorable terrain, following which the panzer brigade would attack
through its own infantry. If the ground had been reconnoitered and the situation clarified, then the panzer brigade would lead the attack, "followed
by bounds by the infantry brigade, which will defend ground neutralized
or captured by the tanks, or will exploit success enjoyed by the tanks."[84]
Artillery would support every attack, antitank units would be well forward; the motorcycle battalion would screen the deployment of the attack,
then protect the exposed flank of the attack after it had begun. The motorized reconnaissance battalion would fill gaps and cover exposed flanks;
the engineer battalion would perform its specialized tasks (e.g., clearing
roads, repairing bridges), and the division air observation squadron would
conduct deep reconnaissance—all with an eye to facilitating the rapid advance of the division. Before the attack, the squadron would have reconnoitered at least a day's march (calculated here at 120 to 150 kilometers)
in advance of the division, paying special attention to potential obstacles
upon which it might call down artillery fire once the advance had begun.
     The attack had to combine surprise and overwhelming power. Marches
were to take place by night, since it was difficult to conceal masses of
motor vehicles. The assault should take place at dawn whenever possible.
Enemy observation would be hindered and the element of surprise greatly
enhanced. When attacking, the tanks should be employed "in mass and in
great depth,"[85] and the Panzer brigade deployed with its regiments abreast
(in column of battalions). Only in this way could the division display its
truly awesome combination of firepower, shock action, and mobility. "It is
false," the students learned, "to restrict the mobility of the unit to that of
the infantry." Shock action meant using the tanks *en masse* at a decisive

point in the line. Detaching small groups of tanks to assist the infantry was invariably a mistake. The mission of the panzer division, instead, was "penetration or breakthrough, enveloping the flank or encircling deep to attack from the rear."[86]

A tactical problem given to students at the *Kriegsakademie* in April 1938 provides a portrait of the panzer division's potential.[87] A blue force was defending west of the Oder in the Göerlitz-Breslau-Oppeln sector. Reinforcing its III Corps was the 1st Panzer Division; their combined mission was to defend against red forces advancing on both sides of the Oder. As the red forces have temporarily paused in its advance to await reinforcements, the blue side has decided to counterattack all along the front. Deployed on the right of III Corps, the 1st Panzer played a crucial role in the operation, thrusting into the open left flank of the enemy advance, moving on into the rear, scattering the reserves it met there, and overrunning the enemy's artillery. It then turned to present a defensive front against red reinforcements coming up from the southeast. The defense was the task of the reconnaissance battalion and the infantry brigade (reinforced by the motorized machine gun battalion), which seized a line of high ground in the path of the advancing enemy. The tank brigade came up, and the entire division then launched a concentrated attack on the red forces. Once again, the attack broke into the red rear, overran its artillery, and generally shattered the attempt to intervene against the blue advance.

Conclusion

By the start of World War II, the German army possessed a mature doctrine for armored warfare. Its best known expression is General Guderian's 1937 book, *Achtung—Panzer!*, although a great many other officers in the *Wehrmacht* held his ideas. The book applied the principle of concentration of force to the tanks, arguing for massing all mechanized forces at the decisive point (*Schwerpunkt*) to achieve a breakthrough. He summed up this idea in the colloquial *Klotzen nicht kleckern,* an untranslatable phrase usually rendered in English as "boot 'em, don't spatter 'em," but which really means "strike concentrated, not dispersed." A decisive tank attack, he wrote, required "suitable terrain, surprise, and mass attack in the necessary breadth and depth." And again, "concentration of the available armored forces will always be more effective than dispersing them, irrespective of whether we are talking about a defensive or an offensive posture, a breakthrough or an envelopment, a pursuit or a counterattack." Unlike many of the "tank prophets" abroad—J. F. C. Fuller, for example—Guderian kept his armored doctrine grounded firmly in the context of combined arms warfare. His panzer division was "a formation of all arms." Tanks would "play the primary role," with all the other weapons "brought up to their

standard of speed and cross country performance." The cooperation between tanks and air power was especially important. In a passage that
presages the U.S. Army's development of the AirLand Battle concept of
the 1980s, he wrote that success was possible "only when the entire defensive system can be brought under attack at more or less the same time."
It was the job of the air forces to prevent or at least delay the flow of reserves to the area of the breakthrough.[88]

The transition from *Reichswehr* to *Wehrmacht* was about as smooth as
such a complex undertaking could have been. Although there were some
organization problems in the switch from a tiny force of long-term volunteers to a mass army based on conscription, they were minor ones that
shrank in importance after the introduction of the two-year term of service
in August 1936. In terms of doctrine, the principal concern of this study,
there were virtually no problems at all. The doctrine of the post-1935
army, emphasizing the close cooperation of mechanized, motorized, and
air forces, did not require invention out of whole cloth after Hitler's declaration of rearmament. It was not an innovation of the Nazi period, as it
was often characterized at the time. No one man—and certainly not
Hitler—"invented" *Blitzkrieg*. Rather, the birth of this new style of war
was an evolutionary development, the result of 15 years of doctrinal experimentation that began during the Seeckt era, was further developed by
Groener, and culminated in the 1930s under Beck. In its training, wargames, and maneuvers, the *Wehrmacht* continued and refined the new military doctrine that had first arisen in the *Reichswehr* era—during a period
when Germany was officially "disarmed."

Notes

1. For an effective refutation of the notion that *Blitzkrieg* is a Nazi phenomenon, see the essay by W. Heinemann, "The Development of German Armoured
Forces 1918–1940," in J. P. Harris and F. H. Toase, eds., *Armoured Warfare* (London: B. T. Batsford Ltd, 1990), pp. 51–69, and especially pp. 55–56.

2. *Truppenführung* (Berlin: E.S. Mittler und Sohn, 1936), paragraph 1. There
is an English translation of the regulations in the records of the U.S. military attaché in Berlin. See Maj. Truman Smith, U.S. military attaché, Berlin, to War Department, 3 February 1936, *The German Field Service Regulations, "Truppenführung,"* in *United States Military Intelligence Reports: Germany, 1919–1941*
(Frederick, MD: University Publications of America, 1983), microfilm reel XIII,
frames 482–624. In shorthand notation, the document would be labeled USMI,
XIII, 482–624.

3. *Truppenführung*, 3

4. Ibid., 7.

5. Ibid., 8. "Der Offizier, der vor dem Feinde Kaltblütigkeit, Entschlossenheit
und Wagemut zeigt, reisst die Truppe mit sich fort."

6. Ibid., "Das gegenseitige Vertrauen ist die sicherste Grundlage der Manns-
zucht in Not und Gefahr."

7. *Truppenführung*, 15, " . . . entschlossenes Handeln."

8. Ibid.

9. Ibid., 27. The English translation fails to convey the play on words in the original German of *Wagen* (reflection) and *Wägen* (daring), as in *Erst wägen dann wagen,* loosely rendered as "Look before you leap." See also General Beck's speech at the reopening of the *Kriegsakademie* in October 1935, in Heinz-Ludger Borgert, "Grundzüge der Landkriegführung von Schlieffen bis Guderian," *Handbuch zur deutschen Militärgeschichte 1648–1939*, IX: *Grundzüge der militärischen Kriegführung* (Munich: Bernard & Graefe Verlag, 1979), p. 557.

10. *Truppenführung*, 37, "Aus Auftrag und Lage ensteht der Entschluss."

11. Ibid., 36.

12. Ibid., 37.

13. Ibid., 48.

14. Ibid., 54. "Das Gefecht gibt den zuverlässigsten Anhalt für due Beurteilung des Feindes."

15. Ibid., 58.

16. Ibid., 73.

17. See Chapter IV, "Aufklärung," in *Truppenführung*, especially 124 and 131. For the comments on counterespionage and the necessity of keeping written orders out of the hands of the troops, see 184 (in "Nachrichtengewinnung durch besondere Mittel" and 191 (in "Spionageabwehr").

18. See Chapter VI, "Angriff," in *Truppenführung*, especially 315–316, "Wer umfasst, setzt sich der Gefahr aus, umfasst zu machen."

19. *Truppenführung*, 317–318.

20. Ibid., 323, 326.

21. Ibid., 329, 331, 337.

22. Ibid., 339.

23. Ibid., 340.

24. See Chapter VII, "Verfolgung," in *Truppenführung*, especially 410.

25. *Truppenführung*, 412–414.

26. Ibid., 415–16, 426.

27. See Chapter VIII, "Abwehr," in *Truppenführung*, especially 427, 429, 431, 433.

28. *Truppenführung*, 438, 442, 444.

29. Ibid., 456.

30. Ibid., 467.

31. See the section on "Hinhaltender Widerstand," *Truppenführung*, 475–485.

32. *Truppenführung*, 532, "Hinhaltender Widerstand ist die hauptsächlichste Kampfart beim hinhaltenden Gefecht."

33. Ibid., 481.

34. Ibid., 534.

35. See Chapter XIII, "Heereskavallerie," in *Truppenführung*, especially 699.

36. *Truppenführung*, 704, " . . . Spannkraft, kaltblütigen Wagemut, körperliche Beweglichkeit, operatives Verständnis, raschen Entschluss, und knappe Befehlssprache."

37. Ibid., 708.

38. For an English translation of Hitler's rearmament decree, see Capt. James C. Crockett, Assistant U.S. military attaché, to War Department, Berlin, 25 May 1935, *National Defense Policy Pertaining to Army, Navy, Air,* in USMI, XIII, 315–325.

39. Maj. Truman Smith, U.S. military attaché, Berlin, to War Department, 26 August 1936, *Two Year Term of Service for the German Army,* in USMI, XIII, 326–329.

40. "Comment by Attaché," in Smith, *Two Year Term of Service,* USMI, XIII, 327.

41. Ibid., USMI, XIII, 328.

42. For an overview of armored developments in all the European armies during the interwar period, see Robert M. Citino, *Armored Forces: History and Sourcebook* (Westport, CT: Greenwood Press, 1994), pp. 31–65.

43. Guderian, *panzer Leader* (New York: Ballantine Books, 1957), p. 19.

44. Heinemann, "German Armoured Forces 1918–1940," pp. 56–57 argues that it was "this Lutz-Guderian partnership that brought the panzer forces into existence."

45. Guderian, *Panzer Leader*, pp. 20–21. According to Guderian, after the balloon went up ending the October 1935 maneuvers, Gen. Werner von Fritsch, the chief of the Army Command, turned to him and laughed, "There's only one thing missing. The balloon should have *Guderian's Panzers are Best* marked on it." (pp. 24–25).

46. Both of the Beck quotes are in Ibid., p. 21.

47. Richard Ogorkiewicz, *Armoured Forces* (New York: Arco Publishing, 1970), p. 73.

48. Capt. James C. Crockett, Assistant U.S. military attaché, Berlin, to War Department, 3 January 1935, *The Selection and Training of the German General Staff,* in USMI, XIV, 421–423.

49. Ibid., USMI, XIV, 422.

50. Capt. James C. Crockett, Assistant U.S. military attaché, Berlin, to War Department, 15 November 1934, *Terrain Exercises in the German Army,* in USMI, XIV, 418–421.

51. Ibid., USMI, XIV, 420.

52. For further examples of the *Kriegsakademie's* instructional exercises and wargames, see Capt. James C. Crockett, Assistant U.S. military attaché, Berlin, to War Department, 27 January 1936, *Tactical Training of Commands and Staffs of Larger Units,* in USMI, XIV, 500–501 and Maj. Truman Smith, U.S. military attaché, Berlin, to War Department, 15 May 1936, *German Staff School Problems,* in USMI, XIV, 502–522. See also Capt. James C. Crockett, Assistant U.S. military attaché, Berlin, to War Department, 16 October 1935, *The German Kriegsakademie,* in USMI, XIV, 523–524.

53. Lieutenant-Colonel H. de Watteville, "The German Army Maneuvers, 1936," in *Journal of the Royal United Service Institution* 81, November 1936, pp. 780–786.

54. Ibid., p. 781.

55. Ibid., p. 783.

56. Ibid., p. 784.

57. See *Bericht über die Wehrmachtmanöver (Heer) 1937* (Berlin: Reichsdruckerei, 1938). There is a copy on file in the Crerar German Military Library, Department of National Defence, Ottawa, Canada. For the appendixes to the report, see *Anlagen zum Bericht über die Wehrmachtmanöver (Heer) 1937* (Berlin: Reichsdruckerei, 1938), a copy of which is also on file at the Crerar Library.

58. "Vorbermerkungen," in *Wehrmachtmanöver*, pp. 13–14.

59. "Die Rote Partei: die Ausgangslage," in *Wehrmachtmanöver*, p. 15. For organizational charts of all the Red forces involved in the maneuver, see *Anlagen zum Bericht*, paras. 1–4.

60. "Die Blaue Partei: die Ausgangslage," in *Wehrmachtmanöver*, pp. 17–18. For organizational charts of all the blue forces involved in the maneuver, see *Anlagen zum Bericht*, paras. 5–9.

61. "Rote Partei: Ausgangslage," in *Wehrmachtmanöver*, p. 15.

62. "Blaue Partei: Ausgangslage," in *Wehrmachtmanöver*, p. 17.

63. "Rote Partei: Ausgangslage," in *Wehrmachtmanöver*, p. 15.

64. "Massnahmen des Kdr. der 30. Division für den Schutz der Grenze," in *Wehrmachtmanöver*, pp. 15–16.

65. "Blaue Partei: Ausgangslage," in *Wehrmachtmanöver*, p. 17.

66. "Der 18. und 19. Sepotember bei Rot: Der Verlauf des 18.9. im Abschnitt Nord," in *Wehrmachtmanöver*, p. 21.

67. "Das Kps. Kdo. X übernimmt den Befehl," in *Wehrmachtmanöver*, pp. 21–22.

68. "Der Armeebefehl für den Angriff am 20.9.," in *Wehrmachtmanöver*, p. 22. For the organization charts of 3rd Panzer Division, 22nd Infantry Division, and army troops involved in the attack, see *Anlagen zum Bericht*, paras. 11–13.

69. Walter Spannenkrebs, *Angriff mit Kampfwagen* (Berlin: Gerhard Stalling, 1939), p. 45.

70. For a short biography of Leeb, see Citino, *Armored Forces*, pp. 249–250.

71. "Die Bewegungen der 3. Pz. Div. am 19.9. und ihre Bereitstellung zum Angriff," in *Wehrmachtmanöver*, pp. 28–29.

72. "Das A.O.K. übernimmt den Befehl: Der Befehl der Heeresgruppe Nord," in *Wehrmachtmanöver*, p. 35. For the units attached to the blue 1st Army, see *Anlagen zum Bericht*, paras. 28–29.

73. "Rot: Betrachtungen zum 18. und 19.9.," in *Wehrmachtmanöver*, pp. 38–39.

74. "Der 20. September: Die Ereignisse bei der 3. Pz. Division," in *Wehrmachtmanöver*, p. 42.

75. "Rot: Betrachtungen zum 20.9." and "Blau: Betrachtungen zum 20.9.," in *Wehrmachtmanöver*, pp. 56–57.

76. "Der 21. September: Die Ereignisse bei der 3. Pz. Div.," in *Wehrmachtmanöver*, pp. 58–59.

77. "Rot: Betrachtungen zum 21.9.," and "Blau: Betrachtungen zum 21.9.," in *Wehrmachtmanöver*, p. 69.

78. "Der Rückmarsch der 3. Pz. Div.," in *Wehrmachtmanöver*, p. 73.

79. "Der Angriff der 1. Pz. Brigade," in *Wehrmachtmanöver*, pp. 98–99.

80. "Schlussbetrachtung," in *Wehrmachtmanöver*, p. 119.

81. Herbert Schottelius und Gustav-Adolf Caspar, "Die Organisation des Heeres 1933–1939," *Handbuch zur deutschen Militärgeschichte 1648–1939*, VII: *Wehrmacht und Nationalsozialismus 1933–1939* (Munich: Bernard & Graefe Verlag, 1979), p. 341.

82. Guderian, *Panzer Leader*, p. 35.

83. Capt. Albert C. Wedemeyer, Berlin, to War Department, 7 April 1938, *The German Armored Division,* in USMI XIV, 424–499. Part I of this lengthy report deals with the organizations, speed, and formations (both march and battle) of the panzer division. Part II is a copy of a tactical problem from the *Kriegsakademie*.

84. Ibid., USMI, XIV, 465.

85. Ibid., USMI, XIV, 466.

86. Ibid., USMI, XIV, 470.

87. Ibid., "Problem Given to Students in the German General Staff School Involving the Employment of an Armored Division," in Ibid., USMI, XIV, 471–498.

88. Heinz Guderian, *Achtung—Panzer!* (London: Arms and Armour, 1992), pp. 180–181.

CHAPTER 10

Conclusion: Ten Days that Shook the World

Although historians rightly look to the Polish campaign in September 1939 as the debut of *Blitzkrieg*, it was the events of the following spring that proved the full worth of the new German military doctrine. The German offensive in the West, code-named Case Yellow, was the brainchild of staff officer Gen. Erich von Manstein.[1] When unleashed on 10 May 1940, it played out almost exactly as Manstein had drawn it on the board, a rare, perhaps unique, occurrence in the annals of military history. Case Yellow was the exception to Helmuth von Moltke's dictum that plans "seldom survive contact with the enemy's main body." It brought the German army as complete and improbable a victory as the world will ever see.

It was a daring plan. A strong force would invade Holland and Belgium, to draw Allied attention and forces to the north. In reality, however, the point of main effort would be in the south. Here, the vast majority of the German armor would pass through the Ardennes Forest. With its tangled undergrowth and winding trails, it was not at all "tank country"—so it would probably be lightly defended. The panzers would break through here and drive for the English Channel, cutting across the rear of the Allied forces and trapping them in a huge cauldron. There were above-average risks: getting tanks through the Ardennes might not be easy; a major river crossing was involved (the Meuse); and as the tank columns drove for the Channel they would be isolated, strung out along the roads, and vulnerable to an Allied counterstroke from north or south.[2] All in all, Plan Yellow engendered a great deal of controversy in the German high command, overcome only by Hitler himself.

Some of the controversy was justified. The Allies not only outnumbered the *Wehrmacht*, their equipment was superior in many ways. The French medium tank, the SOMUA S-35, along with the heavy Char B1, were superior to their German adversaries in speed, armament, and armor.[3] It was not French tanks, but French tank doctrine, that was the problem. Seeing tanks as infantry support weapons, the French parceled them out among the infantry; thus they were not used in independent, concentrated masses. Strategically, things were little better. The French commander, Gen. Maurice Gamelin, assumed that the *Wehrmacht* would repeat the Schlieffen Plan of 1914, a passage through Belgium in the north. He planned to counter it by moving into Belgium to take up strong defensive positions on the Dyle River ("Plan D"). He did not know that he would be walking directly into a carefully laid trap.

Plan Yellow began with a strong thrust on the northern sector of the front (carried out by Army Group B under General Fedor von Bock). Bock's assault was planned to generate maximum "noise": there were three panzer divisions, strong air attacks, paratroopers, and even a spectacular glider assault on the Belgian fortress Eben Emael, the modern and supposedly impregnable fortress guarding the left bank of the Albert Canal.[4] Convinced that this was the main German attack, the British and French reacted by putting Plan D into action. At dawn on 10 May, the Allied armies rolled into Belgium, moving without incident up to the Dyle line as the Belgian army withdrew from its advanced positions to join them.

The principal German thrust was actually taking place in the south. Here a massive force, Gen. Gerd von Rundstedt's Army Group A, including seven of Germany's ten panzer divisions, had entered the Ardennes. A tremendous column of mechanized and motorized vehicles some 50 miles long began to wind its way through the dark forest. The problem of traffic control alone was a prodigious one, and there was a great deal of concern on the part of the Germans about what might happen if the Allied air forces suddenly showed up. But the passage through the Ardennes went without incident. Brushing aside small units of Belgian and French motorized cavalry, the head of the snake emerged into the open on the third day of the offensive, 12 May, between Sedan and Dinant.

At this point, the Germans had won the campaign. With the mass of German armor about to pounce on a neglected, weakly defended point in the French lines, and with the vast majority of the Allied armies engaged in a strategically pointless defensive battle far to the north, Manstein's plan had worked perfectly. German relief that the gamble had indeed paid off was palpable. "I could have wept for joy," Hitler later recalled, "they had fallen into the trap."[5]

On 13 May, German armor, spearheaded by General Guderian's XIX Panzer Corps, supported by hundreds of Stukas, launched a massive assault against the over-age French reservists stationed at Sedan.[6] There was a second crossing at Monthermé to the north, and a third at Dinant led by dynamic young Gen. Erwin Rommel and his 7th Panzer Division.[7] Cracking the French line, the panzers crossed the river and broke into open country, racing for the Channel. On 20 May, they reached Abbeville at the mouth of the Somme; that same evening a battalion of the 2nd Panzer Division reached the Atlantic coast. During their historic ride to the Channel,

the panzers were almost unmolested. The French did manage a small counterattack at Crécy on 17 May, the British at Arras on 21 May, but neither
halted German momentum. The Allies were trapped in a gigantic pocket,
hemmed in on all sides. Although the British managed to retreat to
Dunkirk and evacuate the Continent by June, the French army was essentially destroyed.

It was the greatest victory in the history of modern war. In an incredibly short time, the *Wehrmacht* had crushed the French, Dutch, and Belgian armies, driven the British from Europe altogether, and inflicted some
1,200,000 casualties. German losses were only about 65,000 men. What
the well-drilled infantry and the powerful artillery of the Kaiser's army
had been unable to achieve in four full years of combat—the subjugation
of France—the panzer divisions had now done in ten days.

It was the speed that was most shocking. "The whole rhythm of modern warfare had changed its tempo," wrote the great French historian (and
participant in the campaign) Marc Bloch. Monitoring what he called, iron-
ically, a "semi-permanent fuel park" at Landrecies, Bloch observed the following incredible encounter:

> One fine morning in May, the officer in charge ran into a column of tanks
> in the main street. They were, he thought, painted a very odd color, but
> that did not worry him overmuch, because he could not possibly know all
> the various types in use in the French Army. But what did upset him con-
> siderably was the very curious route that they seemed to be taking! They
> were moving in the direction of Cambrai; in other words, away from the
> front. But that, too, could be explained without much difficulty, since it
> was only natural that in the winding streets of a little town the guides
> might go wrong. He was just about to run after the commander of the
> convoy in order to put him right, when a casual passer-by, better in-
> formed than he was, shouted—"Look out! They're Germans!"[8]

Case Yellow was proof of the brilliance of German military doctrine.
Blitzkrieg meant not merely the use of tanks, but the application of machine power, especially the internal combustion engine, to increase the
tempo of warfare. By 1918, virtually every soldier in the world had known
that tanks were an important part of the contemporary arsenal. How best to
use them was the troubling question. The world's armies followed a number of false leads in attempting to answer it. For the British, there was the
disastrous distinction between the cruiser and the infantry tank, and the
creation of tank-heavy "armoured divisions" with almost no infantry component; for the Americans, there was the fiasco of the "tank destroyer"
concept.[9] The Red Army under Marshal Tukahchevksy envisioned something called "deep battle" with huge mechanized corps and shock armies;
his execution in 1937 meant a return to smaller tank brigades and a policy
of chaining the tanks to close support of the infantry. The events of 1940
caused Soviet planners to change their minds, and the German invasion of

1941 caught the Red Army in the midst of yet another reorganization, this time back to mechanized corps.[10]

What proved to be the correct application of armor—employing tanks as part of an all-mechanized combined-arms force—was something that the Germans had figured out by 1932. For the most part it was done on the maneuver grounds of Grafenwöhr and Jüterbog, with dummy tanks, at a time when the country was officially disarmed. Perhaps a final word about the Treaty of Versailles is in order. The disarmament provisions of the treaty did cut down the size of the German army and navy, rendering Germany impotent in any near-term war scenario. If, however, the treaty actually aimed at the destruction of the Prussian-German military tradition, then it was a total and abject failure.

The military history of the past fifty years, from Case Yellow to the almost bloodless Coalition triumph in Operation Desert Storm,[11] bears the deep mark of the German doctrinal revolution between 1920 and 1939.

Notes

1. The controversy over the German operational plan has been well chronicled, but never more passionately than by Erich von Manstein, *Lost Victories* (Novato, CA: Presidio Press, 1982), pp. 94–126. See also Matthew Cooper, *The German Army, 1933–1945* (Chelsea, MI: Scarborough House, 1991), pp. 198–216.

2. See, for example, the negative opinion of the plan voiced by General Bock in Alistair Horne, *To Lose a Battle, France 1940* (New York: Penguin Books, 1979), p. 197.

3. See the article by Russel H. S. Stolfi, "Equipment for Victory in France 1940," *History* 52, February 1970, pp. 1–20.

4. For the glider assault on Eben Emael, see James E. Mrazek, *The Fall of Eben Emael* (Novato, CA: Presidio Press, 1991).

5. Horne, *To Lose a Battle*, p. 267.

6. Guderian's exploits in Case Yellow form the basis for Florian K. Rothbrust, *Guderian's XIXth Panzer Corps and the Battle of France: Breakthrough in the Ardennes, May 1940* (New York: Praeger, 1990).

7. A fine account of the 7th Panzer Division in action is Russel H. S. Stolfi, *A Bias For Action: The German 7th Panzer Division in France and Russia 1940–1941* (Quantico, VA: Marine Corps Association, 1991).

8. Marc Bloch, *Strange Defeat: A Statement of Evidence Written in 1940* (New Yori: W. W. Norton, 1968), pp. 42, 47–48.

9. On the split of the British armored force into cruiser and infantry tanks, see Ogorkiewicz, *Armoured Forces*, pp. 155–157 and H. C. B. Rogers, *Tanks in Battle* (London: Seeley Service & Co., 1965), pp. 96–100. The best treatment of the troubled development of U.S. armor doctrine in World War II is Charles M. Baily, *Faint Praise: American Tanks and Tank Destroyers During World War II* (Hamden, CT: Archon Books, 1983).

10. For "deep battle," see Richard E. Simpkin, *Deep Battle: The Brainchild of Marshal Tukhachevskii* (New York: Pergamon, 1987). See also Paddy Griffith, *Forward Into Battle: Fighting Tactics from Waterloo to the Near Future* (Novato, CA: Presidio Press, 1990), p. 131. Describing the 1936 Soviet field regulations,

Griffith writes that "deep battle with an all-mechanized, all-arms force was envisaged, including 'maneuver tanks,' 'mechanized cavalry,' and mechanized airborne forces simultaneously to disrupt the enemy's rear and exploit breakthroughs in his forward positions." For Soviet formations in the interwar period, see Ogorkiewicz, *Armoured Forces*, pp. 97–99. See also C. J. Dick, "The Operational Employment of Soviet Armour in the Great Patriotic War," in J. P. Harris and F. H. Toase, eds., *Armoured Warfare* (London: B. T. Batsford, 1990), pp. 90–91.

11. The 1940 campaign has been the subject of intense study by the U.S. Army during the 1980s, when U.S. military doctrine was being reformed from one based on attrition and firepower to one based on maneuver, surprise, and "operational art." See, for example, Maj. John F. Antal, "Maneuver versus Attrition: A Historical Perspective," *Military Review* 72, October 1992, pp. 21–33.

Bibliography

Unpublished Sources

Two indispensable research guides for any work with unpublished German sources are George O. Kent, editor. *A Catalog of Files and Microfilms of the German Foreign Ministry Archives, 1920–1945*, 4 vols. (Stanford, CA: Hoover Institution Publications, 1962), and Christopher M. Kimmich, editor. *German Foreign Policy, 1918–1945: A Guide to Research and Research Materials* (Wilmington, DE: Scholarly Resources Inc., 1981).

1. *Records of the German Army High Command* (OKH) (National Archives, Washington, DC, Microcopy T-78):

Reel 281
Folder H 24/8. Gesellschaftlicher Verkehr des Chefs der Heeresleitung Gen. d. I. Frhr. von Hammerstein.
Folder H24/9. Dienstwohnung des Chefs der Heeresleitung, 1921–1937.
Folder H24/14. Akten betreffend Grosse Rahmenübung 1930. Heft Nr. 1.

Reel 282
Folder H24/14 (continued). Akten betreffend Grosse Rahmenübung 1930. Heft Nr. 1.
Folder H24/53. Chef der Heeresleitung. Akten betreffend Dienstreisen 1926–1927.
Folder H24/15. Akten betreffend Dienstreisen 1928.
Folder H24/16. Akten betreffend Dienstreisen 1929.

Reel 283
Folder H24/16 (continued). Akten betreffend Dienstreisen 1929.
Folder H24/17. Akten betreffend Dienstreisen 1929.
Folder H24/18. Akten betreffend Dienstreisen Winter 1929/1930.
Folder H24/19. Akten betreffend Dienstreisen des Heern Chefs der Heeresleitung Summer 1930.
Folder H24/20. Dienstreisen pp. Chef der Heeresleitung ab 15.4.1932—31.12.1935.

Reel 295
Folder H24/64. Förderung des Wehrgedankens und Wehrertüchtigung.
Folder H24/70. Bericht über die Herbstübungen der Heeresleitung 1932.
Folder H24/78. Bestimmungen für Übungsreisen. Neudruck 1932.

Folder H24/87. Merkblatt über französiche Truppenführung und Taktik.

Reels 299–300.
Folder H25/24. Truppenamt (T-2). Akten betreffend militärische Ausbildung und Truppenübungen. Lehrgänge. G24/36. Heft 1. Dezember 1931–Dezember 1933.

2. *United States Military Intelligence Reports: Germany, 1919–1941. A Microfilm Project of University Publications of America, Inc.* Frederick, MD: 1983. 28 reels.

3. *German Naval Archives* (University of Michigan Microfilming Project No. 2, reels 27–39). For listings, see Hinsley, F.H. and H.M. Ehrmann, *A Catalog of Selected Files of the German Naval Archives Microfilmed at the Admiralty, London for the University of Cambridge and the University of Michigan,* vols. 1 and 2 (London: The Admiralty, 1959 and 1964).

Reel 30
Serial PG 34065. Kriegsaufgaben.
Serial PG 34066. Kriegsaufgaben.
Serial PG 34068. Schiffbauersatzplan, 1926–1930.
Serial PG 34069. Schiffbauersatzplan, 1932–1935.
Serial PG 34070. Minen- und Sperrwesen, 1923–1931.
Serial PG 34071. Minen- und Sperrwesen, 1932–1934.
Serial PG 34072. Verwendung der Marine im Kriegsfall.
Serial 7896. AIa-XIV Hoheitsgewässer.
Serial PG 34073. Kriegsspiele, 1922, 1923.

Reel 31
Serial PG 34073/1. Kriegsspiele, 1923.
Serial PG 34076. Kommandoamtskriegsspiel April 1933 und Schlussbesprechung.
Serial PG 34083. Verwaltungsangelegenheiten: A-Vorarbeiten.
Serial PG 34086. Bauvorhaben, 1928–1930.
Serial PG 34087. Bauvorhaben, 1929–1936.
Serial PG 30489. Ostseeverteidigung Pillau.
Serial 7895. AIa-XXV. Heeresangelegenheiten, 1927–1930.
Serial PG 34095. Heeresangelegenheiten, 1929–1934.
Serial PG 34096. Marineangelegenheiten.
Serial PG 34096/1. Innere Unruhen.
Serial PG 34097. Innere Unruhen.
Serial PG 34101. Studie "Gdingen," 1929–1930.

Reel 32
Serial PG 34102. Studie "Gdingen," Landunternehmungen, 1931–1933.
Serial PG 34106. Luft- und Luftschutzangelegenheiten.
Serial PG 34107. Truppentransport über See.
Serial PG 34108. Umbau.
Serial PG 34112. Polizei.
Serial PG 34117. Studie "Fall Danzig."
Serial PG 34118. Studie Ost: Läufender Scriftwechsel betr. Änderungen, Stand, usw.
Serial 7895. AIa-44. Ostpreussen.
Serial PG 34120. Innere Unruhen, Handmappe.
Serial PG 34122. Studienmaterial.
Serial PG 34125. Sammelakte.

Reel 33

Serial PG 34005. Führerkriegsspiel Dezember 1927: Entwurf der Vorschrift "Führerkriegsspiel."

Serial PG 34009. Führerreise 1928: Vorarbeiten einzelner Marineteilnehmer.

Serial PG 34010. Führerreise 1928, Sammelheft.

Serial PG 34016. Führerreise 1933 des Truppenamts.

Reel 34

Serial 7896. AIIa-43. Zusammenarbeit mit Heer, Heft 1.

Serial 7896. AIIa-43. Zusammenarbeit mit Heer, Heft 2.

Reel 39

Serial PG 31775. Material Admiral Raeder: Schiffbauersatzplan

Serial PG 31039. Material Admiral Raeder: Die marinepolitische Entwicklung, die operativen und taktischen Grundüberlegungen der Kriegsmarine und ihr daraus folgernder Aufbau in der Zeit von 1919 bis Kriegsausbruch 1939.

4. *Records of the German Foreign Office* (National Archives, Washington, DC, Microcopy T-120):

Serial 2945. Büro des Reichsministers: Polen. Reels 1424–1431.

Serial 3170. Büro des Reichsministers: Entwaffnung, Interallierte Kommissionen, und Ostfestungen. Reels 1605–1612.

Serial 3177. Büro des Reichsministers: Militärwesen. Reels 1567–1574.

Serial 4556. Büro des Staatssekretärs: Russland, Polen, Randstaaten. Reel 2302.

Serial 5982. Frankreich—Militärs. Reel 2805.

Serial 5986. Frankreich—Militärangelegenheiten. Reel 2806.

Serial 5989. Frankreich—Wirtschaftliche Verteidigungsbereitschaft. Reel 2808.

Serial 9182H. Geheimakten 1920–1936: Polen, Deutscher Militärattaché in Polen. Reel 3527.

Serial 9285. Abteilung II F Militär und Marine: Auflösung der Selbstschutzorganisation, Einwohnerwehren. Reels 3496–3497.

Serial 9476. Abteilung II F Militär und Marine: Garantie für das Landheer. Reel 3664.

Serial 9537. Abteilung II F Militär und Marine: Schlussbericht der I. M. K. K. Reels 3685–3688.

Serial 9622. Abteilung II F Militär und Marine: Frage des Kontrollrechts der durch die Genfer Beschlüsse von 12–12–1926 bei Zerstörung von Unterständen der Ostfestungen. Reel 3596.

Serial 9854. Abteilung II F Militär und Marine: Bildung von Schutz- und Ortswehren in Ostpreussen. Sicherheitspolizei und Reichswehr in Ostpreussen. Reel 3623.

Serial K6. Geheimakten 1920–1936: Militärpolitik. Reel 3613.

Serial K7. Geheimakten 1920–1936: Besprechung mit der Marineleitung über Danzig (Studie Ost). Reel 3613.

Serial K190. Geheimakten 1920–1936: Polen, Militärangelegenheiten. Reels 3758–3760.

Serial K191. Geheimakten 1920–1936: Polen, Marineangelegenheiten. Reel 3761.

Serial K336. Militärangelegenheiten. Reel 3956.

Serial K936. Frankreich—Politische Beziehungen Frankreich-Deutschland. Reels 4505–4507.

Serial K950. Alte Reichskanzlei: Auswärtige Angelegenheiten; Entwaffnung. Reels 4517–4518.

Serial K951. Alte Reichskanzlei: Volkswehr und Wehrpflicht; Reichswehr. Reels 4519–4520.

Serial K952. Alte Reichskanzlei: Heeresorganisation. Reel 4521.
Serial K953. Alte Reichskanzlei: Landesverteidigung. Reel 4521.
Serial K1706. Amerika—Militärs. Reel 5149.
Serial K1796. Amerika—Militärangelegenheiten. Reel 5168.
Serial K1798. Amerika—Militärische Erfindungen. Reel 5170.
Serial K1799. Amerika—Marine. Reel 5170.
Serial K1997. England—Militärangelegenheiten. Reel 5388.
Serial K1998. England—Marineangelegenheiten. Reel 5388.
Serial K2075. Frankreich—Marineangelegenheiten. Reel 5170.
Serial L129. Abteilung II F Militär und Marine: Anfragen der I.M.K.K. wegen des Systems der Ostbefestigungen. Reel 4041.
Serial L330. Einladungen zu den Heeres- und Flottenmanövern. Reel 4259.
Serial L380. Panzerkreuzer Neubau. Reel 4398.
Serial L1518. Rheinland, Militärische Angelegenheiten im Besetzten Rheinland. Reels 5608–5609.
Serial L1659 Frankreich—Militärangelegenheiten. Reel 5684.
Serial M342. Geheimakten 1920–1936: Militärische Nachrichten. Reel 5487.

5. Personal Papers (National Archives, Washington, DC).

Papers of General Hans von Seeckt. Microcopy M132, 28 reels.

Papers of General Wilhelm Groener. Microcopy M137, 27 reels.

Published Sources

For an historical analysis, as well as comprehensive bibliographical essays and listings on the rise of *Blitzkrieg* in the interwar period, the reader is directed to Robert M. Citino, *Armored Forces: History and Sourcebook* (Westport, CT: Greenwood Press, 1994), pp. 31–65 and pp. 163–177. The book also contains biographical profiles of the most important military figures of the day.

Addington, Larry H. Jr. *The Blitzkrieg Era and the German General Staff, 1865–1941.* New Brunswick, NJ: Rutgers University Press, 1971.
———. *The Patterns of War Since the Eighteenth Century.* Second edition. Bloomington, IN: Indiana University Press, 1994.
Barnett, Correlli. *The Swordbearers: Supreme Command in the First World War.* (New York: Morrow, 1963).
Beck, Ludwig. *Studien.* Stuttgart: K.F. Koehler, 1955.
Bennett, Edward W. *German Rearmament and the West, 1932–1933.* Princeton, NJ: Princeton University Press, 1979.
Benoist-Méchin, Jacques. *Histoire de l'Armée Allemande.* 3 vols. Paris: Editions Albin Michel, 1938.
Bond, Brian. *British Military Policy Between Two World Wars.* Oxord: Oxford University Press, 1980.
———. *Liddell Hart: A Study of His Military Thought.* New Bruswick, NJ: Rutgers University Press, 1977.
———. *The Pursuit of Victory: From Napoleon to Saddam Hussein.* Oxford: Oxford University Press, 1996.
Borgert, Heinz-Ludger. "Grundzüge der Landkriegführung von Schlieffen bis Guderian," *Handbuch zur deutschen Militärgeschichte 1648–1939,* IX: *Grundzüge der militärischen Kriegführung.* Munich: Bernard & Graefe Verlag, 1979.

Bucholz, Arden. *Hans Delbrück and the German Military Establishment: War Images in Conflict.* Iowa City: University of Iowa Press, 1985.

———. *Moltke, Schlieffen, and Prussian War Planning.* Providence, RI: Berg, 1991.

Carsten, F. L. *The Reichswehr and Politics 1918–1933.* London: Oxford University Press, 1966.

Carver, R.M.P. Lord. *The Apostles of Mobility: The Theory and Practice of Armored Warfare.* London: Weidenfeld and Nicolson. 1979.

Cary, James. *Tanks and Armor in Modern Warfare.* New York: Franklin Watts, 1996.

Castellan, Georges. *Le Réarmement Clandestin du Reich, 1230–1935.* Paris: Librairie Plon, 1954.

Citino, Robert, M. *The Evolution of Blitzkrieg Tactics: Germany Defends Itself Against Poland, 1918–1933.* Westport, CT: Greenwood Press, 1987.

———. *Armored Forces: History and Sourcebook.* Westport, CT: Greenwood Press, 1994.

Cooper, Bryan. *The Battle of Cambrai.* New York: Stein and Day, 1968.

Cooper, Matthew. *The German Army, 1933–1945.* Chelsea, MI: Scarborough House, 1991.

Corum, James. S. *The Roots of Blitzkrieg: Hans von Seeckt and German Military Reform.*Lawrence, KS: University Press of Kansas, 1992.

Craig, Gordon A. *The Politics of the Prussian Army, 1640–1945.* London: Oxford University Press, 1955.

Crow, Duncan, ed. *Armored Fighting Vehicles of the World.* Windsor: Profile Publications Limited, 1970.

Crutwell, C. R. M. F. *A History of the Great War, 1914–1918.* Chicago: Academy Chicago, 1991.

Czernin, Ferdinand. *Versailles, 1919: The Forces, Events, and Personalities that Shaped the Treaty,* New York: G. P. Putnam's Sons, 1964.

Davies, W.J.K. *German Army Handbook, 1939–1945.* New York: Arco Publishing, 1984.

Deist, Wilhelm, ed. *The German Military in the Age of Total War.* Leamington Spa: Berk, 1985.

———, et al., ed. *Germany and the Second World War.* Vol 1: *The Build-up of German Aggression.* London: Oxford University Press, 1990.

———. "The Rearmament of the Werhmacht." In Wilhelm Deist, et al., ed. *Germany and the Second World War.* Vol 1: *The Build-up of German Aggression.* London: Oxford University Press, 1990.

———. "The Road to Ideological War: Germany, 1918–1945." In Williamson Murray, MacGregor Knox, and Alvin Bernstein, editors. *The Making of Strategy: Rulers, States, and War,* 352–392. New York: Cambridge University Press, 1994.

———. *The Wehrmacht and German Rearmament.* Toronto: University of Toronto Press, 1981.

Deutschen Gesellschaft für Wehrpolitik und Wehrwissenschaften. *Generaloberst von Seeckt: Ein Erinnerungsbuch.* Berlin: Verlag von E. S. Mittler und Sohn, 1937.

Dick, C. J. "The Operational Employment of Soviet Armour in the Great Patriotic War," in J. P. Harris and F. H. Toase, eds., *Armoured Warfare.* London: B. T. Batsford, 1990.

Diehl, James M. *Paramilitary Politics in Weimar Germany.* Bloomington: Indiana University Press, 1977.

Dirksen, Herbert. *Moscow, Tokyo, London: Twenty Years of German Foreign Policy.* Norman, OK: University of Oklahoma Press, 1952.

Dorpalen, Andreas. *German History in Marxist Perpspective: The East German Approach.* Detroit: Wayne State University Press, 1988

———. *Hindenburg and the Weimar Republic.* Princeton, NJ: Princeton University Press, 1964.

Doughty, Robert A. *The Seeds of Disaster: The Development of French Army Doctrine 1919–1939.* Hamden, CT: Archon Books, 1985.

Dülffer, Jost. *Weimar, Hitler und die Marine: Reichspolitik und Flottenbau 1920–1939.* Düsseldorf: Droste Verlag, 1973.

Dupuy, Trevor N. *The Evolution of Weapons and Warfare.* Indianapolis: Bobbs-Merrill, 1980.

———. *A Genius for War: The German Army and the General Staff, 1807–1945.* Englewood Cliffs, NJ: Prentice-Hall, 1977.

Earle, Edward Meade, ed. *Makers of Modern Strategy: Military Thought from Machiavelli to Hitler.* Princeton: Princeton University Press, 1941.

Edwards, Roger. *Panzer: A Revolution in Warfare, 1939–1945.* London: Arms and Armour, 1989.

Eimannsberger, Ludwig Ritter von. *Der Kampfwagenkrieg.* München: J.F. Lehmann, 1938.

Erfurth, Waldemar. *Die Geschichte des deutschen Generalstables von 1918 bis 1945*, 2nd edition. Göttingen: Musterschmidt Verlag, 1960.

Eyck, Erich. *A History of the Weimar Republic*, 2 vols. Cambridge, MA: Harvard University Press, 1962.

Feuchtwanger, E. J. *From Weimar to Hitler: Germany, 1918–33.* New York: St. Martin's Press, 1993.

Fleischer, Wolfgang. *Military Vehicles of the Reichswehr.* Altglen, PA: Schiffer Publishing, 1996.

Fletcher, David. "The Origins of Armour." In J.P. Harris and F.H. Toase, eds. *Armoured Warfare.* London: B.T. Batsford, 1990.

Foertsch, Hermann. *Kriegskunst heute und morgen.* Berlin: Zeitgeschichte-Verlag Wilhelm Andermann, 1939.

Führung und Gefecht der verbundenen Waffen. Berlin: Offene Worte, 1921.

Fuller, J.F.C. *Memoirs of an Unconventional Soldier.* London: Iver Nicholson and Watson, 1936.

———. *The Reformation of War.* London: Hutchinson, 1923.

Gatzke, Hans W. *Stresemann and the Rearmament of Germany.* Baltimore: Johns Hopkins University Press, 1954.

Gay, Peter. *Weimar Culture: The Outsider as Insider.* New York: Harper & Row, 1968.

Gemzell, Carl-Axel. *Organization, Conflict, and Innovation: A Study of German Naval Strategic Planning, 1888–1940.* Stockholm: Esselte Studium, 1973.

Gessler, Otto. *Reichswehrpolitik in der Weimarer Zeit.* Stuttgart: Deutsche Verlags-Anstalt, 1958.

Geyer, Michael. *Aufrüstung oder Sicherheit: Die Reichswehr in der Krise der Machtpolitik, 1924–1936* (Wiesbaden: Franz Steiner Verlag, 1980).

———. "German Strategy in the Age of Machine Warfare, 1914–1945." In Peter Paret, ed. *Makers of Modern Strategy*, 527–597. Princeton, NJ: Princeton University Press, 1986.

Goerlitz, Walter. *History of the German General Staff, 1657–1945.* New York: Praeger, 1953.

Gordon, Harold J., Jr. *Hitler and the Beer Hall Putsch.* Princeton, NJ: Princeton University Press, 1972.

———. *The Reichswehr and the German Republic 1919–1926.* Princeton, NJ: Princeton University Press, 1957.

————. "The Character of Hans von Seeckt." *Military Affairs* 20 (1956): 94–101.

Griffith, Paddy. *Forward Into Battle: Fighting Tactics from Waterloo to the Near Future.* Novato, CA: Presidio Press, 1990.

Groener, Wilhelm. *Das Testament des Grafen Schlieffens.* Berlin: E. S. Mittler und Sohn, 1927.

————. *Der Feldherr wider Willen: Operative Studien über den Weltkrieg.* Berlin: E. S. Mittler und Sohn, 1931.

Groener-Geyer, Dorothea. *General Groener: Soldat und Staatsmann.* Frankfurt am Main: Societäts-Verlag, 1954.

Guderian, Heinz. *Achtung—Panzer!* London: Arms and Armour, 1992.

————. *Panzer Leader.* New York: Ballantine Books, 1957.

Gudmundsson, Bruce I. *Stormtroop Tactics: Innovation in the German Army, 1914–1918.* Westport, CT: Praeger, 1989.

Guske, Claus. *Das Politische Denken des Generals von Seeckt. Historische Studien,* Heft 422. Lübeck and Hamburg: Matthiesen Verlag, 1971.

Halperin, S. W. *Germany Tried Democracy: A Political History of the Reich from 1918 to 1933.* New York: Norton, 1946.

Harris, J.P. "British Armour 1918–1940: Doctrine and Development." In J.P. Harris and F.H. Toase, eds. *Armoured Warfare.* London: B.T. Batsford, 1990.

————. "British Armour and Rearmament in the 1930's." *Journal of Strategic Studies* 11, June 1988, 220–244.

Harris, J. P. and F. H. Toase, editors, *Armoured Warfare.* London: B. T. Batsford Ltd., 1990.

Heinemann, W. "The Development of German Armoured Forces 1918–1940." In J. P. Harris and F.H. Toase, eds., *Armoured Warfare.* London: B.T. Batsford Ltd., 1990.

Herwig, Holger. *Hammer or Anvil: Modern Germany, 1648–Present.* Lexington, MA: D. C. Heath, 1994.

Hillgruber, Andreas. *Grossmachtpolitik und Militarismus im 20. Jahrhundert: Drei Beiträge zum Kontinuitäts-problem* (Düsseldorf: Droste, 1974),

Holborn, Hajo. "The Prusso-German School: Moltke and the Rise of the General Staff." In Peter Paret, ed. *Makers of Modern Strategy,* 281–295. Princeton, NJ: Princeton University Press, 1986.

Howard, Michael, ed. *The Theory and Practice of War: A Festschrift for Liddell Hart on his Seventieth Birthday.* Bloomington: Indiana University Press, 1965.

Hughes, Daniel J., ed. *Moltke on the Art of War: Selected Writings.* Novato, CA: Presidio Press, 1993.

Hürten, Heinz, editor. *Die Anfänge der Ära Seeckt: Militär und Innenpolitik, 1920–1922: Quellen zur Geschichte des Parlamentarismus und der politischen Parteien,* series 2, vol. III. Düsseldorf: Droste, 1979.

Hürter, Johannes. *Wilhelm Groener: Reichswehrminister am Ende der Weimarer Republik, 1928–1932.* Munich: R. Oldenbourg Verlag, 1993.

Icks, Robert J. *Tanks and Armored Vehicles, 1900–1985.* Old Greenwich, CT: W.E., 1970.

Keegan, John. "Blitzkrieg in the Mountains: The Battle of Caporetto," *Military Review* 50: January 1996, 78–92.

Kitchen, Martin. *A Military History of Germany: From the Eighteenth Century to the Present Day.* Bloomington: Indiana University Press, 1975.

Kolb, Eberhard. *The Weimar Republic.* London: Unwin Hyman, 1988.

Laqueur, Walter. *Weimar: A Cultural History.* New York: G. P. Putnam's Sons, 1974.

Larson, Robert H. *The British Army and the Theory of Armored Warfare.* Newark, NJ: University of Delaware Press, 1984.

Leeb, Wilhelm, Ritter von. *Defense*. Harrisburg, PA: Military Service Publishing Company, 1944.

Lewis, S. J. *Forgotten Legions: German Army Infantry Policy, 1918–1941*. New York: Praeger, 1985.

Liddell Hart, B. H. *The Real War, 1914–1918*. Boston: Little, Brown, 1930.

———. *The Tanks: The History of the Royal Tank Regiment*. Vol. 1, 1914–1939. London: Cassell, 1959.

Loos, Werner, ed. *Oberkommando des Heeres/Generalstab des Heeres: Bestand RH 2*. Koblenz: Bundesarchiv, 1988.

Lubs, Gerhard. *Aus der Geschichte eines Pommerschen Regiments 1920–1945*. Bochum: Berg-Verlag, 1965.

Luckau, Alma. "Kapp Putsch: Success or Failure?" *Journal of Central European Affairs* 7: 398 ff.

Lupfer, Timothy. *The Dynamics of Doctrine: The Changes in German Tactical Doctrine During the First World War*. Fort Leavenworth, KS: U.S. Army Command and General Staff College, 1981.

MacDonald, Lyn. *They Call It Passchendaele: The Story of the Third Battle of Ypres and the Men Who Fought in It*. London: Michael Joseph, 1978.

Macksey, Kenneth. *Armoured Crusader: A Biography of Major-General Sir Percy Hobart*. London: Hutchinson, 1967.

———. *Guderian: Panzer General*. London: Macdonald and Jane's, 1975.

———. *The Tank Pioneers*. London: Jane's, 1981.

———. *Tank Warfare: A History of Tanks in Battle*. New York: Stein and Day, 1972.

Macksey, Kenneth, and John H. Batchelor. *Tank: A History of the Armoured Fighting Vehicle*. New York: Charles Scribner's Sons, 1970.

Matuschka, Edgar Graf von. "Organisation des Reichsheeres," *Handbuch zur deutschen Militärgeschichte* 1648–1939, VI: *Reichswehr und Republik*. Frankfurt am Main: Bernard & Graefe Verlag für Wehrwesen, 1964.

McNeil, William H. *The Pursuit of Power: Technology, Armed Force, and Society Since A.D. 1000*. Chicago: University of Chicago Press, 1982.

Meier-Welcker, Hans. *Seeckt*. Frankfurt am Main: Bernard & Graefe Verlag für Wehrwesen, 1967.

Messerschmidt, Manfred. "Foreign Policy and Preparation for War." In Wilhelm Deist, et al., ed. *Germany and the Second World War*. Vol 1: *The Build-up of German Aggression*. London: Oxford University Press, 1990.

———. "German Military Effectiveness Between 1919 and 1939." In Allan R. Millett and Williamson Murray, *Military Effectiveness, Vol II: The Interwar Period*. Boston: Allen and Unwin, 1988.

Middlebrook, Martin. *The First Day on the Somme*. New York; Norton, 1971.

Miles, Wilfrid. *The Battle of Cambrai*. London: HMSO, 1948.

Moore, William. *A Wood called Bourlon: The Cover Up After Camrai*, 1988.

Morgan, J. H. *Assize of Arms: The Disarmament of Germany and her Rearmament, 1919–1939*. New York: Oxford University Press, 1946.

Mueller, Klaus-Jürgen. *Ludwig Beck—Studien und Dokumente zu seinem politischen und militärischen Denken*. Boppard am Rhein: Harald Boldt Verlag.

———. *General Ludwig Beck*. Boppard am Rhein: Harald Boldt Verlag, 1980.

Mueller-Hillebrand, Burkhart. *Das Heer 1933–1945*, vol. 1. *Das Heer bis zum Kriegsbeginn*. Darmstadt: E. Mittler und Sohn, 1954.

Nehring, Walther. *Die Geschichte der deutschen Panzerwaffe 1916 bis 1945*. Berlin: Propylaen Verlag, 1969.

Nolan, Mary. *Visions of Modernity: American Business and the Modernization of*

Germany. New York: Oxford University Press, 1994.

Nowarra, Heinz J. *German Tanks, 1914–1968*. New York: Arco Publishing, 1968.

Nuss, Karl. *Militär und Wiederaufrüstung in der Weimarer Republik*. Berlin (Ost): Militärverlag der deutschen Demokratischen Republik, 1977.

Ogorkiewicz, Richard M. *Armour: A History of Mechanized Forces*. New York: Praeger, 1960.

———. *Armoured Forces: A History of Armoured Forces and Their Vehicles*. New York: Arco, 1970.

———. *Design and Development of Fighting Vehicles*. Garden City, NY: Doubleday, 1968.

O'Neill, Robert. "Doctrine and Training in the German Army, 1919–1939." In Michael Howard, ed. *The Theory and Practice of War: A Festschrift for Liddell Hart on his Seventieth Birthday*. Bloomington: Indiana University Press, 1965.

Oswald, Werner. *Kraftfahrzeuge und Panzer der Reichswehr, Wehrmacht, und Bundeswehr*. Stuttgart: Motorbuch Verlag, 1982.

Papen, Franz von. *Memoirs*. New York: E. P. Dutton and Company, 1953.

Paret, Peter, editor. *Makers of Modern Strategy: From Machiavelli to the Nuclear Age*. Princeton: Princeton University Press, 1986.

Paschall, Rod. *The Defeat of Imperial Germany, 1917–1918*. Chapel Hill, NC: Algonquin Books of Chapel Hill, 1989.

Paul, Wolfgang. *Das Potsdamer Infanterie-Regiment 9, 1918–1945*. Osnabrück: Biblio Verlag, 1985.

Perrett, Bryan. *Knights of the Black Cross: Hitler's Panzerwaffe and its Leaders*. New York: Dorset Press, 1986.

Peukert, Detlev J. K. *The Weimar Republic: The Crisis of Classical Modernity*. New York: Hill and Wang, 1992.

Phelps, Reginald. "Aus den Groener Dokumenten." *Deutsche Rundschau* 76: 616–625, 830–840.

Posen, Barry. *The Sources of Military Doctrine*. Ithaca, NY: Cornell University Press, 1984.

Post, Gaines, Jr. *The Civil-Military Fabric of Weimar Foreign Policy*. Princeton, NJ: Princeton University Press, 1973.

Praun, A. *Soldat in der Telegraphen und Nachrichtentruppe*. Würzburg: Selbstverlag, 1965.

Rabenau, Friedrich, von. *Seeckt*. Leipzig: Gesellschaft der Freunde der deutschen Bücherei, 1942.

———. *Seeckt: Aus seinem Leben, 1918–1936*. Leipzig: Von Hase und Koehler Verlag, 1940.

Raeder, Erich. *Mein Leben*, vols. 1 and 2. Tübingen: Verlag Fritz Schlichtenmayer, 1956.

Rangliste der deutschen Reichsheeres. Berlin: E.S. Mittler und Sohn, 1923–1930.

Reinicke, Adolf. *Das Reichsheer 1921–1934: Ziele, Methoden der Ausbildung und Erziehung sowie der Dienstgestaltung*. Osnabrück: Biblio Verlag, 1986.

Remarque, Enrich Maria. *All Quiet on the Western Front*. New York: Fawcett Crest, 1991.

Riekhoff, Harald von. *German-Polish Relations, 1918–1933*. Baltimore: Johns Hopkins Press, 1971.

Ritter, Gerhard. *Der Schlieffenplan: Kritik eines Mythos*. München: Verlag R. Oldenbourg, 1956.

———. *The Sword and the Scepter*, 4 volumes. Miami: University of Miami Press, 1969–1973.

Rommel, Erwin. Erwin. *Attacks*. Vienna, VA: Athens Press, 1979.

Rosinski, Herbert. *The German Army*. Washington: The Infantry Journal, 1944.

Rothenberg, Gunther. "Molkte, Schlieffen, and the Doctrine of Strategic Envelopment." In Peter Paret, ed. *Makers of Modern Strategy*, 296–325. Princeton, NJ: Princeton University Press, 1986.

Salewski, Michael. *Entwaffnung und Militärkontrolle in Deutschland, 1919–1927*. München: Oldenbourg, 1966.

Schmädeke, Jürgen. *Militärische Kommandogewalt und parlamentarische Demokratie: Zum Problem der Verantwortlichkeit des Reichswehrministers in der Weimarer Republik. Historische Studien*, Heft 398. Lübeck und Hamburg: Matthiesen Verlag, 1966.

Schottelius, Herbert und Gustav-Adolf Caspar. "Die Organisation des Heeres 1933–1939," *Handbuch zur deutschen Militärgeschichte 1648–1939*, VII: *Wehrmacht und Nationalsozialismus 1933–1939*. München: Bernard & Graefe Verlag, 1979.

Schüddekopf, Otto Ernst. *Heer und Republik: Quellen zur Politik der Reichswehrführung, 1918 bis 1933*. Hannover und Frankfurt am Main: Norddeutsche Verlagsanstalt O. Goedel, 1955.

Schützle, Kurt. *Reichswehr wider die Nation: Zur Rolle der Reichswehr bei der Vorbereitung und Errichtung der faschistischen Diktatur in Deutschland, 1929–1933*. Berlin (Ost): Deutscher Militärverlag, 1963.

Seaton, Albert. *The German Army, 1933–1945*. London: Weidenfeld and Nicolson, 1982.

Seeckt, Hans von. *Aus meinem leben, 1866–1917*. Friedrich von Rabenau, editor. Leipzig: von Hase und Koehler, 1938.

———. *Gedanken eines Soldaten*. Leipzig: K. F. Koehler, 1935.

———. "Grundsätze moderner Landesverteidigung." In *Gedanken eines Soldaten*. Leipzig: von Hase und Koehler, 1935.

———. "Moderne Heere." In *Gedanken eines Soldaten*. Leipzig: von Hase und Koehler, 1935.

———. *Moltke: Ein Vorbild*. Berlin: Verlag für Kulturpolitik, 1930.

———. "Neuzeitliche Kavallerie." In *Gedanken eines Soldaten*. Leipzig: von Hase und Koehler, 1935.

———. *Die Reichswehr*. Leipzig: R. Kittler Verlag, 1933.

———. "Schlagworte." In *Gedanken eines Soldaten*. Leipzig: von Hase und Koehler, 1935.

Senger und Etterlin, F.M. von. *Die Kampfpanzer von 1916–1966*. München: J. F. Lehmann, 1966.

Smithers, A.J. *A New Excalibur: The Development of the Tank, 1909–1939*. London: Leo Cooper, 1986.

Spannenkrebs, Walter. *Angriff mit Kampfwagen*. Berlin: Gerhard Stalling, 1939.

Speidel, Helm. "Reichswehr und Rote Armee." *Vierteljahrshefte für Zeitgeschichte* 1, 1 (Jan. 1953).

Spielberger, Walter J. *Die Panzerkampfwagen I und II und ihre Abarten*. Stuttgart: Motorbuch Verlag, 1974.

———. *Die Panzerkampfwagen 35(t) und 38(t)*. Stuttgart: Motorbuch Verlag, 11980.

Spires, David N. *Image and Reality? The Making of the German Officer, 1921–1933*. Westport, CT: Greenwood Press, 1984.

Tessin, Georg. *Deutsche Verbände und Truppen, 1918–1939*. Osnabrück: Biblio Verlag, 1974.

Thomas, Charles S. *The German Navy in the Nazi Era*. Annapolis: Naval Institute Press, 1990.

Trial of the Major War Criminals Before the International Military Tribunal, vol.

34. Nuremberg, 1949.

Trials of War Criminals Before the Nuremberg Military Tribunals, vol. 10. Washington, 1951.

Truppenführung (Berlin: E. Mittler und Sohn, 1936).,

United States Military Intelligence Reports: Germany, 1919–1941. Fredrich, MD: University Publications of America, 1983.

Ursachen und Folgen vom deutschen Zusammenbruch 1918 und 1945 bis zur staatlichen Neuordnung Deutschlands in der Gegenwart, vol. 7, *Die Weimarer Republik vom Kellogg-Pakt zur Weltwirtschaftskrise 1928–1930.* Berlin: Dokumenten-Verlag Dr. Herbert Wendler & Co., 1962.

Velten, Wilhelm. *Das deutsche Reichsheer und die Grundlagen seiner Truppenführung.* Munster: Ullstein, 1982.

Volckheim, Ernst. *Betrachtungen über Kampfwagen-Organisation und-Verwendung.* Berlin: E. S. Mittler und Sohn, 1924.

———. *Der Kampfwagen in der heutigen Kriegführung.* Berlin: E. S. Mittler und Sohn, 1924.

———. *Deutsche Kampfwagen Greifen An! Erlebnisse eines Kampfwagenführers an der Westfront 1918.* Berlin: E. S. Mittler und Sohn, 1937.

———. *Die deutschen Kampfwagen im Weltkriege.* Berlin: E. S. Mittler und Sohn, 1923.

———. *Kampfwagen und Abwehr dagegen.* Berlin: E. S. Mittler und Sohn, 1925.

Wacker, Wolfgang. "Der Bau des Panzerschiffes 'A' und die Reichstag," *Tübinger Studien zur Geschichte und Politik,* vol. 11. Tübingen: J.C.R. Mohr, 1959.

Waite, R. G. L. *Vanguard of Nazism: The Free Corps Movement in Postwar Germany, 1918–1923.* Cambridge: Harvard University Press, 1952.

Walde, Karl J. *Guderian.* Frankfurt am Main: Verlag Ullstein, 1976.

Wallach, Jehuda. *The Dogma of the Battle of Annihilation: The Theories of Clausewitz and Schlieffen and their Impact on the German Conduct of Two World Wars.* Westport, CT: Greenwood Press, 1986.

de Watteville, H. "The German Army Maneuvers, 1936." In *Journal of the Royal United Service Institution* 81, November 1936, 780–786.

Wette, Wolfram, "Ideology, Propaganda, and Internal Policitics as Preconditions of the War Policy of the Third Reich." In Wilhelm Deist, et al., ed. *Germany and the Second World War.* Vol 1: *The Build-up of German Aggression.* London: Oxford University Press, 1990.

Wheeler-Bennett, J. W. *The Nemesis of Power: The German Army in Politics, 1918–1945.* London: Macmillan & Co., 1964.

Willett, John. *Art and Politics in the Weimar Period: The New Sobriety, 1917–1933.* New York: Pantheon Books, 1978.

Winter, Denis. *Death's Men: Soldiers of the Great War.* New York: Penguin, 1978.

Wohlfeil, Rainer. "Heer und Republik," *Handbuch zur deutschen Militärgeschichte 1648–1939,* VI: *Reichswehr und Republik.* Munich: Bernard & Graefe Verlag, 1979.

Woolcombe, Robert. *The First Tank Battle: Cambrai 1917.* London: Barker, 1967.

Wünsche, Wolfgang. *Strategie der Niederlage: Zur imperialistischen deutschen Militärwissenschaft zwischen den beiden Weltkriegen.* Berlin (Ost): Deutscher Militärverlag, 1961.

Zabecki, David T. *Steel Wind: Colonel Georg Bruchmüller and the Birth of Modern Artillery.* Westport, CT: Praeger, 1994.

Zeidler, Manfred. *Reichswehr und Rote Armee 1920–1933: Wege und Stationen einer ungewöhnlichen Zusammenarbeit.* Munich: R. Oldenbourg Verlag, 1993.

Index

Abbeville, 250

Adam, Wilhelm, 186, 188, 204–207; and the motorized reconnaissance detachment, 211–212

Airborne Forces, 241

Air Defense, 59, 136, 153; Air Raid Exercise in East Prussia (*Flugmeldeübung*, 1932), 207

Airpower, 45, 51, 73, 178–181; in 1924 maneuvers, 120–121, 122; in 1925 maneuvers, 129–130; in 1926 Group Command Maneuvers, 135; in 1930 Mobilization Exercise, 191; balloons representing aircraft in maneuvers, 178; "Guiding Principles for Judging the Effect of Weapons," 115–116; "Observations of the Chief of the Army Command Based on his Inspections in 1924," 54; in *Truppenführung*, 226

Albert Canal, 250

Allenstein, 207

Amiens, 2, 3

Angriffsgruppen (attack groups), 226. *See also Kampfgruppen*

Anschluss, 241–242

Antiaircraft: *Kampfschule für die Infanterie*, 77–78

Antitank Guns: in *Ausbildungsvorschrift für die Infanterie*, 26; 1924 maneuvers, 120

Ardennes Forest, 249–250

Armor, 45, 51; in 1924 maneuvers, 122; in 1925 maneuvers, 124, 126–127, 129; in 1926 Group Command Maneuvers, 135; in 1926

maneuvers at Arys, 60–61; in 1926 troop exercises, 131–132; in 1930 Mobilization Exercise, 191; in 1931/32 exercises, 202–204; in 1936 maneuvers, 235; in 1937 maneuvers, 236–241; in Operation Barbarossa, 2; in Case Yellow (France and the West), 2; dummy tanks, description, 121, 126, 129, 136; "Guiding Principles for Judging the Effect of Weapons," 115–116; Hammerstein's view, 216–217; *Heereskavallerie*, 228–229; in maneuvers, 73; "Observations of the Chief of the Army Command Based on his Inspections in 1925," 58; in Polish Campaign, 1; Seeckt's views, 11, 22; in *Truppenführung*, 226

Armored Cars, 124, 181–182

"Armoured Divisions," British 251

Army Command. *See Heeresleitung*

Army Group A, in 1940, 250–251

Army Group B, in 1940, 250

Arras, 251

Artillery, 15; in 1924 Fall Maneuvers, 122; "Guiding Principles for Judging the Effect of Weapons," 114–115; "Observations of the Chief of the Army Command Based on his Inspections in 1921," 47–48; "Observations of the Chief of the Army Command Based on his Inspections in 1922," 50; "Observations of the Chief of the Army Command Based on his Inspections in 1923," 53;

About the Book

In 1939, the German army shocked and terrorized the world with Blitzkrieg, its form of mobile warfare. How the Germans rebuilt their army after defeat in World War I—circumventing the prohibitions of the treaty at Versailles—is one of the major questions in military history.

Citino shows that German officers of the army of the Weimar Republic (the Reichswehr), men like General Hans von Seeckt, General Wilhelm Groener, and Colonel Oswald Lutz, initiated and carried out a thorough reform of the army's warfighting doctrine and capability that laid the groundwork for Hitler's seemingly effortless rearmament of Germany. Using largely unpublished materials from U.S. and German archives, he grounds his book in a study of key autumn maneuvers of the German army in the thirties. His analysis traces the smooth and inexorable development of the Reichswehr into the Wehrmacht, quite likely the finest military machine in history.

Robert M. Citino is professor of history at Eastern Michigan University. His numerous publications include *The Evolution of Blitzkrieg Tactics* and *Armored Forces: History and Sourcebook*.